"This vital book challenges us to think about hope in a new way—as a response to life in which we are partners in the ongoing work of imagining and creating a better world. Through its nuanced readings of biblical, classical, and mystical texts, *Choosing Hope* offers a deep and refreshing understanding of the centrality of hope not only in Jewish theology, prayer, and ritual; Jewish values; and even contemporary Israel but also in our own lives. So dive in—and choose hope."

—RABBI LAURA GELLER, Rabbi Emerita of
    Temple Emanuel of Beverly Hills

"This careful, thorough examination of hope in Jewish sources and thought will lift the spirits of all who read it."

—RABBI STEVEN BOB, author of *Jonah and the Meaning of Our Lives*

"*Choosing Hope* is not only a profound exploration of the meaning and claim of hope but a wonderfully inspiring interpretation of the Jewish tradition. Drawing on meticulous reading of vast sources and teachings, this extraordinary book bears witness to the core idea of Jewish faith itself: as an awakening to confront our sorrows and despair with the personal and communal ongoing task of *tikkun*."

—MOSHE HALBERTAL, John and Golda Cohen Professor of
    Jewish Thought and Philosophy at the Hebrew University

"Serious, well-reasoned, literate, and uplifting, *Choosing Hope* should be in a great many hands and hearts."

—RABBI LAWRENCE KUSHNER, scholar-in-residence,
    Congregation Emanu-El in San Francisco

"This book is a blessing, a sublime meditation on hope, an erudite feast of Jewish wisdom, and a wellspring of surprising, subversive, deeply satisfying epiphanies about the relationship between hope and all the emotions and experiences that comprise a life of meaning. Doubt, despair, anger, activism, memory, humor, love, prayer, repentance, forgiveness, the Holocaust, and the State of Israel are among the topics explored by David Arnow in his masterful illumination of the purpose and power of hope."

—Letty Cottin Pogrebin, author of *Deborah, Golda,
    and Me: Being Female and Jewish in America*

Choosing Hope

University of Nebraska Press
Lincoln

Choosing Hope

The Heritage of Judaism

DAVID ARNOW

The Jewish Publication Society
Philadelphia

Portions of chapter 1 first appeared as "Reflections on
Jonah and Yom Kippur," *Conservative Judaism* 54, no. 4
(Summer 2002): 33–48.

Library of Congress Cataloging-in-Publication Data
Names: Arnow, David, author.
Title: Choosing hope: the heritage of Judaism / David
Arnow.
Description: Philadelphia: Jewish Publication Society;
Lincoln: University of Nebraska Press, [2022] | Series: JPS
essential Judaism series | Includes bibliographical refer-
ences and index.
Identifiers: LCCN 2021042973
ISBN 9780827615205 (paperback)
ISBN 9780827618893 (epub)
ISBN 9780827618909 (pdf)
Subjects: LCSH: Hope—Religious aspects—Judaism. |
Hope in the Bible. | Bible. Old Testament—Criticism
and interpretation. | Rabbinical literature—History and
criticism.
Classification: LCC BM645.H64 A76 2022 |
DDC 234/.25—dc23
LC record available at https://lccn.loc.gov/2021042973

Set in Merope by Laura Buis.

To Madeleine,

My partner in hope and everything else,

לִבַּבְתִּנִי

You have captured my heart.

—Song of Songs 4:9

Contents

Acknowledgments xi

Introduction. xiii

   What Hope Is and Why It Matters. xiv

   Judaism as a Reservoir of Hope. xvii

   Difficulty Tapping Jewish Sources of Hope xviii

   A Way toward Hope xx

   About This Book xxii

   Making the Most of This Book. xxiii

   Notes on Translation and Gendered Language xxiv

1. Repentance: The Gateway to Hope. 1

   Introduction 1

   A Theology for Looking in the Mirror. 2

   Prayer and Hope 6

   The Season of *Teshuvah* 8

   Seasonal Rituals 9

   Conclusion. 19

2. *Tikkun Olam*: Turning Hope into Action 21

   Introduction 21

   Biblical Roots in Ecclesiastes. 22

   Rabbinic Origins in the Mishnah. 24

   An Intertextual Reading of the Sages and Ecclesiastes. . . . 26

   Aleinu's Hope of Repairing the World. 29

   Tikkun Olam in the Mysticism of Isaac Luria 34

Tikkun Olam Today 39

Conclusion. 45

3. Abraham and Sarah: Living in Hope 47

Introduction 47

Hope in God and Abraham's Relationship 47

Hope amid Abraham and Sarah's Trials 49

The Binding of Isaac as a Story of Hope 53

Conclusion. 60

4. The Exodus: Hope at the Heart .61

Introduction 61

Brueggemann's Archetypical Tale of Hope. 61

Exodus as the Jewish Master Story 64

Despair versus Hope in Midrash and Commentary 70

Putting Exodus Memories into Practice 78

Conclusion. 81

5. The Covenant: Hope in Israel's Relationship with God. 82

Introduction 82

Covenantal Hope in the Morning Liturgy 83

Covenantal Hope and the Ancient Trials of History 90

The Post-Holocaust Conversation. 95

Conclusion. 101

6. The Book of Job: Hope for Vindication 103

Introduction 103

Reframing Job 104

Verses of Despair, Verses of Hope. 106

Hope for Vindication 121

Conclusion. 125

7. Jewish Eschatology: Hopes for the World to Come....... 128

    Introduction 128

    The Road to Resurrection in the Bible. 129

    The Rise of the Rabbis and the Triumph of Resurrection . . .136

    The Messiah of the Rabbis 140

    Maimonides on the Messiah and the Afterlife. 144

    Reform Judaism's Hopes for the Afterlife. 148

    Humans Fulfilling Hopes for Immortality? 152

    Conclusion. 154

8. Israel: Hope in the Homeland. 156

    Introduction 156

    Zionist Hope 157

    Fulfilling the Hopes of Statehood .165

    Reuven Rivlin's Israeli Hope. 171

    Snapshots of Israeli Hope: Israeli Activists Speak. 173

    Conclusion. 194

9. Jewish Humor: The Currency of Hope 195

    Introduction 195

    Humor and Hope 196

    The Beginning of Jewish Laughter 200

    Waiting for the Messiah. 202

    The Schlemiel 205

    Laughing and Hoping in Hell. 208

    God Laughs Too. 210

    Conclusion. 211

  Final Thoughts. 212

    A Succinct Jewish Theology of Hope 212

Finding Hope in Our Ancient Texts. .213

Hope Means Work 215

Transmitting Our Heritage of Hope 220

Notes. 223

Bibliography. 275

Subject Index 299

Index of Texts. 313

Acknowledgments

Writing a book about hope has certainly heightened my awareness of the social matrixes that sustain it. My wife of forty-six short years, Madeleine, has been the greatest imaginable support, listening with unending patience to virtually every idea and piece of minutiae associated with this project. Her patience and advice have been great gifts to me. My parents, Joan and Robert Arnow (z"l), did not live to see the publication of *Choosing Hope*, but they encouraged me to write it. More than that, they taught me what hope looks like: about the work and the persistence it takes to transform dreams into reality.

I owe special thanks to Jeffrey Hoffman and Matthew Goldstone, with whom I've studied, discussed many of the ideas in this book, and worked on translations of Hebrew texts about hope. A number of individuals were kind enough to read parts of the manuscript and provide me with important suggestions. I am extremely grateful to Noah Arnow and Andrew Weiner for reviewing the entire manuscript and to Joshua Arnow, Madeleine Arnow, Peter Arnow, David Ellenson, Elliott Malki, Steve Shaw (z"l), and Moshe Sokol for reading parts of it.

Many people helped me by answering particular questions that arose in the course of my research or sharing insights or texts about hope: Lina Alatawna, Amran Armani, Adam Arnow, Ruth Arnow, Tamara Arnow, Mordechai Bar-On, Menachem Bombach, Miles B. Cohen, Steven M. Lev Cohen, Kher Elbaz, Michael Ben-Eli, Tamar Eldad-Appelbaum, Robert Friedland, Sheila Friedland, Marc Gellman, Alexander Gordin, Sally Gottesman, Moshe Halbertal, Eran Halperin, Robert Harris, Judith Hauptman, Shai Held, Aron Hirt-Manheimer, Itzak Galnoor, Gloria Jackel, Jill Jacobs, Alon Lee Green, Yoaz Hendel, Lawrence A. Hoffman, Jonathan Jacoby, Sigal Kanotopsky, Michael Kaplan, Rachel Libeskind, Alon Liel, Rachel Liel, Barbara Lowenfels, Ruth Messinger, Robert Norris, Shir Nosatzki, Ilay Ofran, Paul Ohana, Jonah Pesner, Yehuda Rapaport, Gilbert

Rosenthal, Mindy Rubin, John Ruskay, Chaim Seidler-Feller, Nahid Abu Shareb, Nachum Shargel, Shmuel Shatach, Eilon Schwartz, Alice Shalvi, Abigail Dauber Sterne, Alon Tal, Annie Tucker, Gordon Tucker, Burton L. Visotzky, Peter Weintraub, Eleanor Yadin, Adina Yoffie, Adir Yolkut, Brenda Zlatin, and the members of the daily minyan at Temple Israel Center of White Plains, New York.

Finally, I am extremely grateful to Barry L. Schwartz, director of The Jewish Publication Society, for encouraging me through the process that led to the book's acceptance for publication; and to Joy Weinberg, managing director of JPS and editor extraordinaire. Her sharp eye, good sense, and deft pen improved the manuscript immeasurably and resulted in what we both hope is a more reader-friendly volume. I give thanks as well to Elizabeth Zaleski and the wonderful editorial and production staff at the University of Nebraska Press for co-publishing this volume.

Introduction

Rabbi Yitzchak said, "Everything depends on hoping . . ."
—Genesis Rabbah 98:14 (fifth- or sixth-century midrash)

When I was seven, my mother survived what were thought to be fatal complications when giving birth to her third child. Doctors told my father to prepare himself to tell his two sons that their mother had died. My father prayed. Later, I remember him saying, "I prayed to my God and He answered me." He responded with a lifelong devotion to God and Judaism, which changed his life and ours as well.

Attributing my mother's survival to God's munificence never sat well with me. What about all the other wives and mothers who didn't pull through? Still, the incident left me with an indelible sense that Judaism and hope were connected in the deepest possible ways.

Many years later, when reading "Sketch of a Phenomenology and a Metaphysic of Hope," one of the twentieth century's most influential works on hope, by the French philosopher and theologian Gabriel Marcel (1889–1973), I would often think about my father's reaction to what he faced. My father was not optimistic about the prospects of his wife's survival, but his degree of optimism or pessimism would have been irrelevant to Marcel's understanding of hope. Since there was seemingly nothing my father could do to save his wife, he did the only thing he could. His prayer, poured out with all his heart and with all his might, embodied Marcel's understanding of hope. "Hope," Marcel wrote, "is situated within the framework of the trial, not only corresponding to it, but constituting our being's veritable *response*."[1]

What Hope Is and Why It Matters

Here is how I understand hope:

Hope reflects our embrace of the possibility of a particular, deeply desired future, and hope fuels our actions to help bring it about.

Let's unpack the key words:

Reflects: We can perceive the presence of hope (and its absence, despair) in ourselves and others.

Embrace: Hope draws us toward it, beyond the present.

Possibility: Hope expresses "a passion for what is possible."[2] Where certainty reigns there's neither need nor room for hope.

Particular: Developing strategies to fulfill our hope requires a clear and focused sense of what we are trying to achieve.

Future: Hope aims at bringing a better reality into being.

Desired: Hope sees a lack and its fulfillment. The gap between the two infuses hope with tension, if not pain. Hope knows the "not yet." (Despair knows only the "not.")

Fuels: Hope unleashes energy and motivation to persist toward our goal in times of trial.

Action: Hope embodies our ongoing determination and effort to shape the future, regardless of circumstance. For example, if we have a terminal illness we may give up hope for a cure but continue to live in hope that we will be able to conduct ourselves with an element of dignity to the end.

Help: Hope is humble. It requires allies. Marcel put it this way: "There can be no hope that does not constitute itself through a we and for a we. I would be tempted to say that all hope is at the bottom choral."[3]

Thus, hope is not the same as faith. We might think of faith as an unshakable belief—in God or the goodness of humanity, for example—that supports a particular hope. For me, my faith in the fundamental goodness of human beings as bearers of the divine image serves as foundation for my hope (desired goal) to see a world that ever increasingly reflects this. My hope (response to trial) finds expression in my efforts to build that world despite all the obstacles and setbacks along the way. Similarly, I myself have faith that when I'm engaged in dialogic prayer, the inner voice I "hear" answering me is not mine alone. My hope (desired goal) is to clearly understand the guidance I receive during prayer. My hope (response to trial) becomes manifest in my struggle to accept and implement that guidance even though it may require difficult changes in my behavior.[4]

In essence, then, hope is *not* the same as faith in God or how likely we consider a particular outcome to be. Hope is about *the energy and determination we are willing to invest in making that outcome happen whether it is likely or not.* Hope is active. As writer Rebecca Solnit put it, "Hope is an ax you break down doors with in an emergency . . . hope should shove you out the door."[5] In this light hope can be distinguished from optimism, which does not require action and solely expresses one's estimation that a desired outcome is likely; and from wishes and dreams, perhaps best understood as hopes shorn of action. Hope, alternatively, rests on two underlying beliefs: *reality can change*, and *our actions can help change it.*

REAL VERSUS FALSE HOPES

Complicating the matter is the question, Which hopes are "real" and which are "false"? Do people who have faith in medical cures disputed by science — and report improvement (perhaps from a placebo effect) — have false hopes? Philosophers try to distinguish between realistic and false hope by arguing that "people with false hope base their hope on an assessment of the probability of fulfillment that does not correspond to . . . the standard assessment of competent judges."[6] But even a standard like this has its limits. How many competent judges would agree that an eight-year-old's hope to compete in the Olympics has a reasonable probability of fulfillment? If the hopes of all youngsters were dashed by such considerations, the world of sports would be the poorer.

Charles R. Snyder (1944–2006), an American psychologist who spent much of his life studying hope, warned against handing out labels of false hope too quickly. People who scored high on Snyder's measures of hope were sometimes able to solve so-called impossible laboratory tasks that had not been puzzled out in fifteen years of research. "These 'heroic' efforts are dependent on hopeful thinking to succeed," Snyder wrote. "Given that society as a whole tends to advance in leaps when 'impossible' goals are reached by individuals who dared to try, it seems counterproductive to adopt a policy of automatically dissuading everyone from pursuing seemingly impossible goals. Hence, care should be taken in concluding that an individual's goals are 'pipe dreams.'"[7]

WHY HOPE MATTERS

When we consider the extraordinary trials we face as a species, as individuals, and that Jews face as a people, the ability to overcome them may well depend on the willingness to choose hope. Recognizing this, near the beginning of the global COVID pandemic, the editors of *Time* magazine published a special double issue (April 27/May 4, 2020), "Finding Hope," featuring statements from its selection of the world's most influential people on hope and resilience in the search for a better, healthier world.

Scientists understand that hope plays a role in influencing positive outcomes in everything from climate activism to human health. Thus, climate scientists are writing about hope because they know it matters—that without it, we won't muster the energy to save the planet. Indeed, research shows that higher levels of hope are associated with making greater efforts to conserve energy and being more concerned about environmental sustainability.[8] Studies of climate scientists who continue with their work even as much of the world fails to appreciate the grimness of their findings demonstrate that they share a deep commitment to "hope as action."[9]

On an individual level, longitudinal studies are finding that "higher-hope" older adults live longer than their "lower-hope" peers, possibly because higher levels of hope are linked to so many other health-enhancing behaviors. Higher levels of hope are additionally associated with enhanced athletic and academic performance, more successful work performance, higher measures of well-being, and coping more successfully with old age.[10]

And even without the science to prove it, Jews know in their *kishkas* that if their ancestors had responded to their circumstances with despair instead of hope, the Jewish people would have vanished from the earth long ago.

"The death of hope is the death of all generous impulses in me," wrote author and Holocaust survivor Elie Wiesel (1928–2016, Romania, France, United States). "It is the end of all possibilities, options, inquiries, renewals of redemption.... Where, under which sky, would we be if we were deserted by hope?"[11]

Judaism as a Reservoir of Hope

Judaism can be understood as an enormous reservoir of hope, one that can ennoble the desires we pursue and fortify our response to the trials we face.

A GOD OF HOPE

The metaphorical likening of hope to a reservoir is not accidental. In a time of drought the prophet Jeremiah (14:8) refers to God as *Mikveh Yisrael*, "Hope of Israel," which can also mean that God is Israel's reservoir, or pool of water. In Hebrew the root letters of "hope" and "reservoir" are identical: *kof-vav-hey*.[12] Jeremiah seems to be saying that God is hope and that in sustaining life, God recognizes our vital need for both water and hope. A midrashic reading of this might conclude that water sustains the body, hope the soul. In times of challenge, hope requires us to pool our inner spiritual resources.

We can think of God as hope in another sense as well. At the burning bush when Moses wants to know God's name, God says, *Ehyeh-Asher-Ehyeh*, "I will be what I will be" (Exod. 3:14). This means that God is not static but rather dynamic, changing, evolving. Like God, in whose image we are created, we are not defined by the past or present. I take this to mean that together with God, we inhabit an open future, the place where hope resides.

BIBLICAL MODELS OF HOPE

Jeremiah's invocation of God as the Hope of Israel during a drought is not far from Marcel's notion that hope is a response to a trial, a motif present in many biblical narratives — explicitly so as we see in some stories, implicitly in others. Rabbinic literature counts ten trials that God posed for Abraham, culminating in God's final test — the order to sacrifice Isaac, Abraham and Sarah's long-awaited son. Examining how Abraham — and often Sarah as well — responds to these trials reveals profiles in hope. Likewise, the story of Job unfolds against the background of a wager between God and *HaSatan*, "the Adversary," that if pious, blameless Job is subjected to a stiff enough test, he'll curse God. The result is a book in which words associated with hope appear with greater frequency than in most books in the Bible, and the story can well be read as charting the passage from despair to hope. In other biblical stories the trial is implicit, but the decision to respond with hope is just as plain. The women of the Exodus—the midwives Shifra and Puah, Yocheved (Moses' mother), Miriam (Moses' sister), and Pharaoh's daughter—all act in hope as they defy Pharaoh's brutal regime.

Immersing ourselves in the stories of biblical characters with high hope can also influence our own capacity to hope. Shayne Lopez (1970–2016), a prominent researcher in the psychology of hope, wrote this about the human tendency to emulate hope:

> We draw on our memories of the most hopeful people we know, of our own hopeful pursuits, and of our successes at getting out of tight spots in the past. These thoughts and feelings may help us see pathways where others see brick walls. We persevere when others give up; we work harder when it would be easier to quit. And the whole time, we are carried along on a current of energy to a better place in the future. . . . Hopeful narratives steeped with meaning provide survival tools for the storyteller and for the audience. . . . The most hopeful stories trigger positive emotions in others, making them feel lifted up, joyful, or curious, and ultimately drawing them closer to us.[13]

Lopez and other psychologists stress that levels of hope are malleable and can be raised by systematic exposure to stories of high-hope individuals.[14] The Jewish people's sacred texts, history, and homeland, Israel, are filled with stories about the kinds of people who act against all odds and change the world. Keeping their stories before us can strengthen our hope.

Difficulty Tapping Jewish Sources of Hope

And yet, with all this going for them, many Jews find it difficult to tap into Judaism as a font of hope—particularly, I believe, for two reasons.

HOPE IN THE CLOSET

First, hope largely remains stuck in the closet. Perhaps Jews have taken hope for granted and have felt comfortable leaving it on the back burner. Maybe Jews have felt a little uneasy focusing on hope because it is one of the Christian theological virtues (along with faith and love); thus they may see hope as "theirs" and not "ours." It could also be that although Jews know that hope is important, they don't understand it very well. Additionally Jews might shy away from focusing on hope because it seems too ephemeral or Pollyannaish.

As a result, at least in my experience as a regular synagogue attendee, I can only recall a single sermon devoted to hope in the past decade. While I've been reminded in sermons not to lose hope or give in to despair, to me those reminders are light-years away from thoroughly exploring the nature of hope: what strengthens it, what Jewish law, liturgy, ritual, the Talmud, the Midrash, medieval Jewish philosophy and poetry have to say about it, and so forth.

Hope has rarely been a topic of Jewish study. Historian Yosef Hayim Yerushalmi (1932–2009, United States) puts it this way:

> Now if the history of hope may be important for the history of mankind, it must surely be pivotal for an understanding of Jewish history. And yet, for all its diverse lines of investigation and its genuine triumphs in recovering unknown aspects of the Jewish past, contemporary Jewish scholarship has betrayed little interest in such matters.[15]

Yerushalmi notes that all the sources for writing a history of Jewish hope are already available:

> No new texts need be discovered. Those we have will suffice, if we learn to read them afresh, closely and between the lines.[16]

This insight supplies the key to reinterpreting the texts, concepts, and practices that constitute Judaism's reservoir of hope.

The second difficulty lies in how the classical sources most Jews encounter—the Bible and the prayer book—talk about hope: as awaiting the redeeming hand of God. Exodus provides the biblical archetype. After the Israelites were enslaved for centuries in Egypt, God remembered the covenant with Abraham, Isaac, and Jacob and vowed to "come down to rescue . . . [the Israelites] from the Egyptians and to bring them out of that land to a good and spacious land, a land flowing with milk and honey . . ." (Exod. 3:8). The covenant promises Israel a bright future if the people follow

God's commandments, and assures suffering if Israel strays. Individual or collective suffering signifies divine punishment for a covenantal breach but also serves as a down payment for rewards in the world to come.

The prayer book similarly expresses hope for God to redeem us and bring our suffering to an end. Consider these two blessings from the *Amidah* (literally, the "standing" prayer), Judaism's central prayer, recited thrice every weekday:

> See our affliction, and fight our fight; redeem us quickly for the sake of your name, for You are a mighty redeemer. Blessed are You, [YHWH], who redeems Israel.[17]

> Speedily cause the offspring of Your servant David to flourish, and let his glory be exalted by Your help, for we hope for Your salvation all day. Blessed are You, [YHWH], who causes salvation to flourish.[18]

Because so many of these prayers and biblical narratives seem to reflect a theology based on the expectation of direct divine intervention, it can be difficult for those who may not share those beliefs to take hope seriously.

A Way toward Hope

Fortunately, Jewish theology has come a long way from what we encounter in the Bible and the prayer book. And these developments have important implications for how we think about hope, shifting the responsibility for filling our hopes from God to humanity. Consider the words of Joseph B. Soloveitchik (1903–93, Belarus and United States), the twentieth century's leading light of Modern Orthodoxy:

> Man acts as a divine agent and redeems himself.[19]

Soloveitchik taught that God intentionally left the world in a state of incompletion so that humanity, created in the divine image, could exercise its full creative capacity to perfect creation:

The creature is commanded to become a partner with the Creator in the renewal of the cosmos; complete and ultimate creation—this is the deepest desire of the Jewish people . . . the realization of all its hopes.[20]

Soloveitchik's student Irving Greenberg (1933–, United States) took the human onus of responsibility for the world even further. According to Greenberg, God has turned *complete* responsibility for the world over to humanity. Now, the Divine is fully hidden, and only to be found in each of us, images of God. What becomes of our hopes now lies completely in human hands.

Surprising as it may sound, some ancient Jewish sources reflect a similar view. A midrash on the book of Ecclesiastes imagines God telling Adam about the responsibility he bears:

Pay heed that you do not corrupt and destroy My world; for if you corrupt it there is no one to repair it after you.[21]

The transnatural theology of Mordecai Kaplan (1881–1983, Lithuania and United States), predicate theology of Harold M. Schulweis (1925–2014, United States), and process theology of Bradley Shavit Artson (1959–, United States) likewise stress that God doesn't act directly but only through us when we act in godly ways. Or, as author and theologian Lawrence Kushner (1943–, United States) explains, "For, while God does not have hands, we do. Our hands are God's. And when people behave as if their hands were the hands of God, then God 'acts' in history."[22]

These understandings provide fundamental sources of hope. First, in emphasizing that humanity is created in God's image, they affirm the essential trustworthiness of human beings—that we *can* build relationships and work with others to fix what's broken in the world. Second, as images of God, we have virtually unlimited creativity and power. We occupy the stage of history, with God as our audience. We have the capacity to fulfill our hopes. God may offer us inspiration, may cheer us on, may hope in us even when we despair. But God will not bail us out—or prevent despair from triumphing over hope. Only we can do that. In the Bible and the prayer book human beings hope for God's strong hand and outstretched arm to redeem Israel and the world. From a modern Jewish theological stance, God hopes to see us do the same thing.

About This Book

Choosing Hope explores key narratives, concepts, texts, prayers, and practices in Judaism that have sustained hope for the Jewish people over the ages and, when viewed through an appropriate lens, can do so for us. It is not a history of Jewish hope. Rather, in keeping with the historian Yerushalmi's observation that the texts we have on hope "will suffice, if we learn to read them afresh, closely and between the lines," I have tried to offer fresh readings of both less known as well as familiar texts. By providing readers with freer access to Judaism's reservoir of hope, I hope to support readers in choosing hope over despair—in their personal lives, and in regard to the broader issues facing society, the Jewish community, Israel, and the world.

In brief, the nine chapters that follow (indicated by numbers 1–9) expand upon the following core teachings: (1) *Teshuvah*, repentance as understood in Judaism, provides a "gateway to hope." The notion that human beings are created in God's image is a powerful source of hope, as is the idea that when we fall short we have the possibility of doing *teshuvah*, a process that makes tangible and strengthens our hope that we truly can change for the better. (2) Just as *teshuvah* creates hope that we can improve *ourselves*, *tikkun olam* embodies the hope that through action with others, we can slowly repair our *world*. Emerging in early Rabbinic times, the *tikkun olam* concept stands against Ecclesiastes' dreary cynicism that what is crooked can never be made straight. Our stories—(3) Abraham and Sarah, (4) the Exodus from Egypt, (5) the covenant between God and Israel, and (6) the book of Job—remind us, each in its own way, how to hold onto hope in the face of trials that might well induce despair. (7) Job's inability to square the notion of an all-powerful God with the suffering of innocents spawned bold new ideas long after his story had been written. In the second-century BCE Maccabean revolt, the torture and killing of pious Jews led to a full-fledged expression of a hope that had only been hinted at in earlier biblical sources—resurrection of the dead and an afterlife where the righteous would receive the rewards denied them in this life. The Rabbis would build these ideas into elaborate portraits of the world to come, implanting promises of resurrection in Judaism's most central prayers. For some of us today, these sustainers of hope for our ancestors retain their appeal, even in communities where these ideas had once fallen out of favor. (8) The Zionist movement achieved the Jewish people's long-hoped-for return to their ancient homeland, led by an unusual succession of high-hope individuals. Keeping Israel's founding promises of assuring complete political and social equality for all its citizens remains a work in progress, but efforts by Israel's former president Reuven Rivlin and NGO activists are slowly building new foundations for Israeli hope. (9) Where would Jews be without humor? It's "hope's last weapon," as theologian Harvey Cox once called it.[23] In the Bible, laughter makes its debut when a superannuated childless couple, Abraham and Sarah, learn from God they will be parents to a son. They laugh, but they do what it takes to make this hope come true. And they name their covenantally promised son Yitzchak, "He will laugh." Like hope, humor reflects our ability to envision a different reality, and laughter enhances our ability to persevere until such time as we can build it.

Making the Most of This Book

I encourage all individuals wishing to explore the Jewish reservoir of hope more deeply; educators, study groups, and youth group leaders looking for curricula on Jewish hope; rabbis seeking material for teaching or preaching; and book groups interested in structuring conversations about hope to utilize the variety of free resources located at this book's companion website, choosinghope.net. Readers will find an anthology of Jewish texts on hope from ancient to contemporary times and a thematically organized study guide with texts and discussion questions pertaining to each chapter in the book. Units in the study guide, also available at https://jps .org/study-guides/, include "What Is Hope?," "Finding Hope in Prayer," "Turning Hope into Action: *Tikkun Olam*," "The *Akedah* as a Story of Hope," "Despair and Hope: Hagar and Ishmael in the Desert versus the *Akedah*," "The Book of Job: A Journey from Despair to Hope," and "Immortality: An Undying Hope."

Notes on Translation and Gendered Language

ON TRANSLATION

The two principal three-letter roots for the word "hope" in the Bible are *kof-vav-hey* (as in the familiar *tikvah*) and *yud-chet-lamed* (as in the less familiar *tochelet*), both of which are often, and inconsistently, translated as "waiting" or "hoping." Scholarly biblical research can't offer definitive guidance on which translation is necessarily "correct."

For example, compare the Koren and Alter translations of the opening phrase in Psalm 40:2, *kavo kiviti* YHWH, which doubles the verb *kof-vav-hey* for intensity:

> I waited patiently for the Lord; and He inclined to me, and heard my cry (Koren).

> I urgently hoped for the Lord, He bent down toward me and heard my voice (Alter).

"Waiting patiently" conveys passivity, composure, and certainty that the awaited object will arrive in due time. "Urgently hoping" expresses activity, agitation, and an element of uncertainty about how the object of hope will respond. Some scholars believe that the root *kof-vav-hey* derives from a word that means "thread" or "chord" (see Josh. 2:18, 21) and includes an element of being taut or tense.[24] Hope always includes that element of tension; waiting may not. Therefore, throughout this book, I've chosen Bible translations that render "hope" (or "expectation," "yearning," etc.) over those that prefer "wait" (or "look," "trust," and the like). In this era of history, I believe our emphasis needs to be on active hoping more than passive waiting.

Translations involving hope or other issues in which I've departed from The New Jewish Publication Society (NJPS) translation or its gender-sensitive adaption, *The Contemporary Torah*, are noted throughout.

ON GENDER AND GOD LANGUAGE

It's my preference not to refer to God with masculine or feminine pronouns, or other forms of gendered language, and I avoid doing so in my own writing throughout *Choosing Hope*. But Hebrew is a gendered language, and many sources from the Bible, Rabbinic literature, and later commentators refer to God with masculine pronouns, as do many contemporary writers whom I quote. Remedying this is not a simple matter. Gender-sensitive translations of the Bible are a work in progress. As of this writing, The Jewish Publication Society has published a gender-sensitive translation of the Five Books of Moses, *The Contemporary Torah*, which I've generally followed. Where *The Contemporary Torah* leaves the four-letter name of God, traditionally translated as "Lord," in Hebrew, I've rendered it as YHWH. For biblical passages not found in the Five Books, I've tried to create gender-sensitive renderings, replacing "Lord" with YHWH. When encountering masculine pronouns that refer to the Divine, I've often substituted God or YHWH in brackets, though in other cases I've maintained translations of biblical passages or prayers that do include gendered language. When midrashic or other Rabbinic texts depend on a gendered reading of the text, I've also chosen to preserve a gendered biblical translation.

When quoting authors who do use gendered language I've sometimes adjusted these passages with bracketed text to create greater gender sensitivity. In cases that are not amenable to this remedy, gendered language has been retained.

The net result leads to a bit of inconsistency, which I hope the reader will overlook in light of the overall effort to address the issues of gender sensitivity and language in a more forward-looking way.

Philosopher and theologian Jonathan Sacks (1948–2020, United Kingdom) once wrote:

> The whole of Judaism—though it would take a book to show it—is a set of laws and narratives designed to create in people, families, communities and a nation, habits that defeat despair. Judaism is the voice of hope in the conversation of mankind.[25]

This is the book I have tried to write. May your journey through the Jewish heritage of hope be fruitful.

Choosing Hope

Repentance

THE GATEWAY TO HOPE

> Repentance encompasses the major part of the Torah and life; upon it are based all the hopes of the individual . . . as well as the community. . . . This is the entire basis of repentance: ascent of will and its transformation to virtuousness, emergence from darkness to light, from the "valley of disturbance" to the "gateway of hope."
> —Rav Abraham Isaac Kook, *The Lights of Repentance*

Introduction

For many years my wife and I have hosted a large family gathering in our home on the eve of Rosh Hashanah. You might call it a Rosh Hashanah seder with readings and songs. We begin with something I wrote in the mid-1990s:

> The leaves begin to turn, summer fades, and we return—to school, to a heavier work schedule, to "reality," as some would have it, and to a season full of Jewish holy days. These begin with Rosh Hashanah, the first day of the seventh month of Tishrei, the birthday of the whole world! During this time we return—to ponder how to improve our selves, our relationships, and our troubled world. . . . Our songs unveil the vision of the hidden world we seek. From the power of our joined voices, let us draw strength to rebuild it.[1]

The season from the late-summer Hebrew month of Elul through the High Holy Days provides the opportunity and the tools to fulfill what may be our greatest personal hope in life: to become the person we wish to be. Engaging in the process of *teshuvah* (repentance, or returning) may help each of us to become better versions of ourselves.

My own efforts to do *teshuvah* encompass three components. The first is contemplation of the key elements in what I call "A Theology for Looking in the Mirror." This theology frequently dips into the thought of Rav Kook (1865–1935), the first Ashkenazi chief rabbi of Palestine under the British Mandate. The second is prayer, a key tool for laying conflicting hopes on the table for an honest assessment of their virtues. The third is the practice of rituals associated with the season of *teshuvah*: blowing the shofar, reciting Psalms 27 and 130, and reading the book of Jonah on the afternoon of Yom Kippur.

As we see in this chapter, each of these approaches bears a special relationship to hope.

A Theology for Looking in the Mirror

When we take an honest look at ourselves, there's almost always a divergence between our conduct and our ideals, a sense of falling short, of failing to be our best selves. *Teshuvah* involves the struggle to narrow that gap. Becoming aware of that disparity gives rise to a range of reactions—including shame, guilt, and despair, but also hope—hope that with sufficient effort we can change for the better.

Because *teshuvah* is so tightly bound to images of divine judgment, mercy, pardon, and so on, I've set this discussion in the theological framework that has worked for me. The essential point is that *teshuvah* aims to allow the divine image we all possess to exert greater influence on our behavior.

How we carry out *teshuvah* depends on what we are trying to improve.

If we've wronged someone, Judaism calls on us to acknowledge it and ask for that individual's forgiveness. Maimonides clarifies that if we've asked for forgiveness three times and it has not been granted, "then the sin rests upon [the one] who refuses forgiveness." Maimonides additionally explains what to do if someone dies before you've had an opportunity to ask for forgiveness: a graveside confession in the presence of ten adults and the repaying of any debts to the heirs of the deceased or to the community if there are no known heirs.[2]

But often the sense of failing to measure up doesn't involve something specific we've done to harm someone. Striving to be our best self may have more to do with examining our relationships, priorities, and how we spend our time. For example, we may allow ourselves to become so busy with work that we don't have time for community affairs. Or we become so devoted to community affairs that we don't have enough time for family and friendships. Perhaps we have a sick relative or friend whom we visit, but not frequently enough. Or maybe we tend to get angry too easily, feel envious of the success of others, or find ourselves compulsively chasing the limelight. This dimension of *teshuvah* is difficult because it involves more than an isolated action. It touches on ingrained traits of character.[3]

We can at least take comfort from the fact that we deserve credit for working on these issues. As Maimonides says, one who has done *teshuvah* is on a higher level than one who has not sinned.[4]

Teshuvah also involves assessment of where we are on our spiritual journey, even if we don't necessarily think of ourselves as "spiritual." Where do we stand in relation to the values and principles to which we assign ultimate importance?

Hope is inseparable from *teshuvah*. Hope is the gateway to *teshuvah* because hope says we can change. Despair says we can't.[5] *Teshuvah* then furnishes the means to fulfill the hope that we *can* change, that the self we see in the mirror can grow or be repaired. The primary meaning of *teshuvah*, "return," reminds us that once, maybe long ago, we were closer to our best selves, and that a kernel of that best self still resides within us. Getting back to it may be difficult, but knowing that we've already been there sustains a measure of hope that return is possible. Rav Kook puts it this way:

> The principal repentance, which immediately illuminates the dark places, is the return of [one to one's] self, to the source of [one's] soul . . . and immediately [one] will return to God, the Soul of all souls and [one] will progress higher and higher in holiness and purity.[6]

For Rav Kook, *teshuvah* begins with a return to the core of goodness that resides within each of us, a spark we must and *can* recover.

I think about that return to self and God as connecting with the image of God within me that I want to guide my actions, but that I too often ignore or can't seem to find. It reminds me of a story. When God decided to create humanity in the divine image, the angels feared the consequences of entrusting something so pure to a creature so susceptible to corruption. They resolved to steal the divine image. But where to hide it? On the top of a mountain? No. Men and women would eventually scale the summit and discover it. In the depths of the sea? No. Men and women would eventually plumb the depths and find it. So they hid it where no one would ever look: in the hearts of human beings. And that's where it remains to this day.[7] *Teshuvah* creates an opportunity to rediscover the spark of that divine image that lies hidden in our hearts.

I think about my very awareness of the gap between my actual and ideal selves as that inner divine image pressing for greater expression in my character, more influence in my decision making. The internal image of God speaks in a "still, small voice." That is what the prophet Elijah learned: when God passed by him, he discovered God was not in the mighty wind, the splitting of mountains, the earthquake, or the fire, but in the "still, small voice" (1 Kings 19:11–13).[8]

God's voice calls me to be better, to do better. The God within shares my hopes to make my life a better reflection of the divine image I bear.[9] When I disregard God's call, something feels wrong. I need to do *teshuvah*.

In Jewish thought, God shares our hopes to better reflect God's vision, both individually and collectively. We see this in Rashi's comment on "Hope deferred sickens the heart, but desire realized is a tree of life" (Prov. 13:12). In its context, the verse is clearly speaking about the individual, but Rashi reads it as applying also to the people Israel: "The hope that the Holy One had hoped for Israel, the hope that they would repent, ultimately brought Israel to heartsickness when they did not repent. When they fulfilled God's desire, that hope was a tree of life to them." Abraham Joshua Heschel (1907–72, Poland and United States) put it this way: "God is in search of man, waiting, hoping for man to do His will."[10]

Initiating the process of *teshuvah* simply involves acknowledging our shortcomings. Rav Kook likens that gnawing sense of discontent within us to a condensed inner "seed-like point" that achieves ever-greater radiance, reflecting the divine image within that is always seeking greater expression.[11]

Knowing that God shares our best hopes and yearns for us to fulfill them sets a positive cycle in motion. We may not love what we see when we take that first look in the mirror, but doing so puts us in touch with something deeply positive—our own divine image. That experience, in turn, strengthens our capacity to look inward, ever more deeply and honestly.

Teshuvah requires overcoming a natural sense of shame that arises from confronting our shortcomings. Since excessive shame can short-circuit the entire process, Rav Kook offers two observations to guard against this. First, the experience of shame may be an inevitable part of the process, but the ultimate goal of *teshuvah* is not to make us miserable. Suffering is not the means toward renewal. The aim of *teshuvah*, Kook says, "is not meant to embitter life but to make it pleasant." Second, even though there may be times when looking inward seems to yield such an unmitigated negative self-assessment that you "can find no vestige of virtue . . . this fact in itself possesses great virtue." Thus "it is impossible that one should not discover in oneself some share of virtue." And so Rav Kook describes *teshuvah* as a process that leads to the "emergence from darkness to light, from the 'valley of disturbance' to the 'gateway of hope.'"[12]

Rebbe Nachman of Breslov (1772–1810), a Hasidic master known to have suffered from depression, offers a different approach toward judging oneself less harshly. Commenting on the passage, "Be in the habit of judging people favorably" (*Pirkei Avot* 1:6), he says:

> After honing this on others, we must then use it on ourselves as well, so that each of us can focus on the good within us, and thus make it less marginal and more central to who we are. . . . And by means of this, because we find in ourselves even a little goodness, we can truly move from being guilty to being meritorious and we will be enabled to engage in true *teshuvah*.[13]

As the door to *teshuvah* begins to open, we can begin to hear that divine inner voice of forgiveness—which may be a lot less harsh on us than we are on ourselves. When we look inside ourselves, we can choose, in some sense, to see the worst, which leads to despair, or to see the good, that inner point of good, God's image, at our core.

What if we are deeply stuck in our ways and have been unable to change? Can it ever be too late to do *teshuvah*? As long you are alive, Jewish tradition maintains that *teshuvah* remains an option. Rabbeinu Yona of Gerona (d. 1263) made this point very clearly, and he knew of what he spoke. Author of *The Gates of Repentance*, a famous treatise on *teshuvah*, Rabbeinu Yona had been a zealous opponent of Maimonides, to the point of advocating the burning of his philosophical works—which the Inquisition carried out in 1232. According to tradition, some years later, when the Inquisition burned the Talmud, Rabbeinu Yona realized the error of his ways.[14] This is what he said about Ecclesiastes 9:4: "One who is attached to all the living has hope (*bitachon*). . . . It means that one has hope that one can improve oneself. It is known and certain that living human beings are given a choice to choose the correct path. Therefore, as long as one is alive, there is hope that one can improve."[15]

The Talmud recounts a tale of a rabbi said to have hired every prostitute in the world. He crossed seven rivers to visit one woman reputed to be especially beautiful. When he was with her she whispered that his *teshuvah* would never be accepted. This upset him so, he put his head between his knees and wept until his soul departed—whereupon a heavenly voice proclaimed that he was destined for eternal life in the world to come (his repentance had been accepted). Upon hearing this, Rabbi Judah ha-Nasi (leader of the Jewish community around 200 CE and compiler of the Mishnah) declared, "One may acquire eternal life after many years, another in one hour!"[16]

Prayer and Hope

The scope of prayer encompasses the range of human emotion and experience, including expressions of gratitude, regret, awe, wonder, anger, and hope concerning ourselves, others, and the world at large. In the context of *teshuvah*, prayer provides first an opportunity for observing, and then a means of narrowing, the gap between the way we are and the way we could be. Although the High Holy Day liturgy focuses on this particularly, so does the regular weekday liturgy.

The fifth blessing of the weekday *Amidah* (recited three times daily) makes that perfectly clear: "Turn us back, in perfect *teshuvah* before You. Blessed are You, YHWH, who takes pleasure in *teshuvah*." God wants and hopes for our *teshuvah*—and this is in fact one of God's central qualities. God is a God who wants us to succeed in improving!

Of course, reciting a fixed liturgy is not essential for *teshuvah*. Any moment of heightened self-awareness can create an opening for *teshuvah*.

A midrash from the fifth or sixth century describes God as Israel's pool of hope (*Mikveh Yisrael*), always accessible. God says: "You are to pray in the synagogue in your city; when you cannot pray in the synagogue, pray in your open field; when you cannot pray in your open field, pray in your house; when you cannot pray in your house, pray upon your bed; when you cannot pray upon your bed, commune with your heart."[17]

That said, I have found that prayer provides a special opportunity for looking inward to reflect upon and express a range of feelings—gratitude, confusion, regret, and, of course, hope—in the encounter with my deepest hopes about how I can be a better human being tomorrow than I am today.

I've begun to understand and experience prayer in this way since 2010, when I began attending a daily minyan (a quorum of ten Jews required for public prayer—who may be counted varies across denominations) after my mother died. Like any serious undertaking, prayer requires practice and discipline, both of which the morning minyan has provided in great abundance! Heschel put it this way: "Prayer is not a stratagem for occasional use, a refuge to resort to now and then. It is rather like an established residence for the innermost self."[18]

The daily liturgy often refers to God as *ha-Makom*, literally, "the place." For me, *teshuvah*-oriented prayer is the place for a dialogue with God on my deepest hopes about how to be my best self amid whatever challenges I'm facing. Sometimes I experience "the place" as outside, beyond me, but more often it feels like an internal place, the image of God within. Either way, prayer can be a daily exercise in *teshuvah*.

Heschel's view of prayer similarly combines the themes of hope and *teshuvah*:

Prayer clarifies our hope and intentions. It helps us discover our true aspirations, the pangs we ignore, the longings we forget. . . . Prayer makes visible the right, and reveals what is hampering and false. In its radiance, we behold the worth of our efforts, the range of our hopes, and the meaning of our deeds. . . . The idea of prayer is based upon the assumption of [one's] . . . ability to accost God, to lay our hopes, sorrows, and wishes before [God]. . . . Prayer is an answer to God: "Here am I. And this is the record of my days. Look into my heart, into my hopes and my regrets." . . . "The highest form of worship is that of silence and hope."[19]

In prayer I meet God not as a being that fulfills yearnings or grants forgiveness, but as a partner in sorting out my hopes and facing my regrets. In prayer I ask God's help in assessing the worthiness of my deepest hopes. And I ask whether those hopes truly reflect my values, because not all hopes are equally justified, and not all hopes reflect our better angels. In the wise words of Proverbs, "The hope (*tochelet*) of the righteous shall be gladness; but the expectation (*tikvah*) of the wicked shall perish" (10:28).[20] Improving the nature of our hopes may itself be a critical element of *teshuvah*.

Focusing our hopes on the kind of person we wish to be—thus excluding a raft of more trivial hopes—still does not eliminate the question of whether our hopes are worthy. As I see it, prayer should always leave room for a dialogue with God about the moral considerations surrounding Immanuel Kant's famous question: "What may I hope?"[21] I hear God's answer to my prayer through that inner voice that tells me what's worthy and what needs fixing. To immerse myself in prayer is to discover the hopes I share with God.

Even if our hopes are worthy, they still depend, as psychologist C. R. Snyder notes, on willpower, determination to reach a goal.[22] Prayer thus becomes a place to ask God to help renew my resolve when it flags. That's how I understand a verse from Isaiah: "But they who hope to YHWH shall renew their strength" (40:31).[23] God doesn't dispense perseverance pills. But I have found that recognizing my need for help and making it part of my prayer-dialogue with God is enormously strengthening to me. This may have been what the French philosopher and theologian Gabriel Marcel (1889–1973) had in mind when he wrote, "The zone of hope is also that of prayer."[24]

The Season of *Teshuvah*

The time of the year most closely associated with *teshuvah*, the forty-day period from the first day of the Hebrew month of Elul through Yom Kippur, corresponds to the period from when God called Moses to ascend Mount Sinai to receive the second set of tablets until he descended from the mountain forty days later.[25] On the fortieth day, an exchange took place between God and Moses that included the thirteen Divine Attributes, which figure so prominently in the High Holy Day liturgy. (Some interpreters ascribe the declaration of the Divine Attributes to God and others to Moses.)

The mending that occurs over the period from the creation of the Golden Calf and the smashing of the first set of tablets to the receiving of the new tablets is a narrative about *teshuvah*. In turning to the Golden Calf, the Israelites fall far and fast. God's angry disappointment nearly leads to their annihilation. With much persuasion by Moses, God and the Israelites *both* do *teshuvah* and return to a healthier place. God gives up the urge to destroy the Israelites, and the Israelites turn away from their idol-worshipping ways. The period from Elul to Yom Kippur stands as an archetype for the possibility of change. The second set of tablets represents the fulfillment of the hope for a second chance—back then and now too.

A medieval midrash takes this concept a step further, asserting that the second set of tablets was *superior* to the first. Moses tells God that he regrets having broken the tablets, and God tells him "not to worry"; the first included only the Ten Commandments, but the second also includes allusions that support the subsequent development of Jewish law and midrash.[26] The midrash implies that after rapprochement, the fractured relationship between God and the Israelites was stronger than it had been before the Golden Calf.

In other words, we are to give heed to that "still small voice" that calls us to seek out those situations where we yearn for a second chance to make things right. The results might exceed our hopes.

Seasonal Rituals

The blowing of the shofar, the recitation of Psalms 27 and 130, and the reading of the book of Jonah underscore additional important connections between *teshuvah* and hope.

BLOWING THE SHOFAR

In its depiction of the holy day as a day of judgment, *U'Netaneh Tokef*, one of the principal prayers in the Rosh Hashanah and Yom Kippur liturgy, connects listening to the divine inner voice and the process of *teshuvah* with the sound of the shofar: "The great shofar will be sounded, and the still small voice will be heard." The sound of the shofar can clear our heads so that we can actually hear that inner divine voice calling for greater influence in our lives.

This opportunity includes more than just the days of Rosh Hashanah and Yom Kippur. The shofar is customarily blown in synagogue every morning (except Shabbat) during Elul, the month that precedes Rosh Hashanah. Maimonides understood its purpose as containing an allusion:

> Although the sounding of the shofar on the New Year is a decree of the Written Law, still it has a deep meaning, as if saying, "Awake, awake, O sleeper, from your sleep; O slumberers, arouse yourselves from your slumbers; examine your deeds, return in repentance, and remember your Creator. Those of you who forget the truth in the follies of the times and go astray the whole year in vanity and emptiness which neither profit nor save, look to your souls; improve your ways and works. Abandon, every one of you, [your] evil course and the thought that is not good."
>
> It is necessary, therefore, that each person should regard [oneself] throughout the year as if [one] were half innocent and half guilty and should regard the whole of mankind as half innocent and half guilty. If then [one] commits one more sin, [one] presses down the scale of guilt against [oneself] and the whole world and causes [one's] destruction. If [one] fulfills one commandment, [one] turns the scale of merit in [one's] favor and in favor of the whole world, and brings salvation and deliverance to all [one's] fellow creatures and to [oneself].[27]

Maimonides sees the shofar as an alarm clock, first rousing us, then reminding us of the alarmingly profound choices we face. Our actions can change us and the world.

The message can be frightening—Maimonides puts awesome responsibility on our shoulders—but his message also encourages hope. He underscores the potential for change and that our actions have implications far beyond our awareness. Says the Talmud: "Great is *teshuvah* for it brings healing to the world."[28]

Earlier I mentioned how we begin our family Erev Rosh Hashanah celebration. After reading Maimonides' interpretation of the shofar, we conclude with the highlight of the evening, a ritual that may be unique to our family. We take turns giving reasons why we are blowing the shofar *this* year, and after every reason we blow our shofars as long and loudly as we can. "To give us strength to combat climate change!" "To open our ears to those crying for our help!" "To blow certain politicians out of office!" . . . It's a long list of hopes for ourselves and the world. Between us we must have eight or ten shofars, so the sound definitely penetrates!

PSALM 27

Another tradition that begins with Elul and extends through the High Holy Days (in some communities through the end of Sukkot) involves the morning and evening recitation of Psalm 27, a psalm that has a great deal to say about hope. The custom entered Jewish practice relatively late, in early eighteenth-century Eastern Europe,[29] but long before that, the sages were struck by its unusual last verse: "Hope to YHWH. Let your heart be firm and bold, and hope to YHWH." They saw the verse as an embodiment of the essential elements of prayer. The Talmud notes that prayer must be infused with strength and cites this verse, which literally revolves around hope, as its model for exemplary prayer. Rashi says this verse shows that in prayer one should not hold back, but hope and then hope again.[30]

The Talmud likewise uses the verse to teach that if our prayers are not answered, we should pray and pray again.[31] It implicitly bases its conclusion on the fact that this verse instructs us to hope twice. In so doing, the Talmud points to an inseparable relationship between prayer and hope. Perhaps this accounts for injunctions in two medieval sources that this verse should be recited every day![32]

Let's take a look at the psalm:

[1]YHWH is my light and my help; whom should I fear? YHWH is the stronghold of my life, whom should I dread? [2]When evil men assail me to devour my flesh—it is they, my foes and my enemies, who stumble and fall. [3]Should an army besiege me, my heart would have no fear; should war beset me, still would I be confident. [4]One thing I ask of YHWH, only that do I seek: to live in the house of YHWH all

the days of my life, to gaze upon the beauty of YHWH, to frequent [YHWH's] temple. [5][YHWH] will shelter me in [YHWH's] pavilion on an evil day, grant me the protection of [YHWH's] tent, raise me high upon a rock. [6]Now is my head high over my enemies roundabout; I sacrifice in [YHWH's] tent with shouts of joy, singing and chanting a hymn to YHWH. [7]Hear, YHWH, when I cry aloud; have mercy on me, answer me. [8]In Your behalf my heart says: "Seek My face!" O YHWH, I seek Your face. [9]Do not hide Your face from me; do not thrust aside Your servant in anger; You have ever been my help. Do not forsake me, do not abandon me, O God, my deliverer. [10]Though my father and mother abandon me, YHWH will take me in. [11]Show me Your way, YHWH, and lead me on a level path because of my watchful foes. [12]Do not subject me to the will of my foes, for false witnesses and unjust accusers have appeared against me. [13]Had I not the assurance that I would enjoy the goodness of YHWH in the land of the living . . . [14]Hope to YHWH. Let your heart be firm and bold, and hope to YHWH.[33]

Note the stark contrast between the psalm's initial faith in divine protection (v. 1–6) and its concluding plea for an answer from God and evidence of God's goodness (v. 7–13). The shift in tone has led some commentators to conclude that the psalm is a composite of what had once been two completely separate compositions, a psalm of assurance followed by one of desperation.[34] I share the view of others who argue that the psalm's discordance reflects the complexity of human experience, which often includes both of these feelings, sometimes in quick succession. The contrasting moods may also correspond to different stages of life.

Psalm 27 contrasts the nature of faith versus hope as well. In his beautifully sensitive analysis, Edward Feld, author of *Joy, Despair, and Hope: Reading Psalms*, writes:

Rather than the brazen, "whom [should] I fear," with its absolute faith, there is now the need to buck up courage, to hope. The poet of Psalm 27 has moved from pride to humility. Faith has been replaced by hope. Faith believes absolutely in its rightness. Hope understands that though the evidence is to the contrary, though there is much room for doubt, nevertheless, the faithful manage to live with expectation. Faith is brazen, hope is humble.[35]

My reading of the psalm imagines an individual searching for balance between the realm of worldly pursuits—with all its inevitable seductions and conflicts—and the inner quest for ultimate purpose. Initially the search involves the fantasy of finding a protector who can assure triumph whenever conflict arises. Next comes a dawning awareness that no one, not even God, can guarantee that outcome. This prompts a different, but equally unrealistic, solution: complete withdrawal from the trials of public endeavor, dwelling "in the house of the Lord *all* the days of my life."

Between these extremes lies God's way, the "level path," the balance between worldly and spiritual pursuits. Who in our productivity-driven era does not need help finding that point of equilibrium? The season of *teshuvah*, with all those hours of prayer, gives us an annual opportunity to lay our hopes before God—the God within—about where and how to strike that balance. "Hope to YHWH. Let your heart be firm and bold, and hope to YHWH." In prayer we can share our hopes with God, especially hope for the strength to make needed changes in our lives. It's a process, not easy or quick, and it starts with hope.

About six hundred years ago, the rabbi and philosopher Joseph Albo (1380–1444, Spain) described the relationship between prayer and hope in remarkably similar terms:

[One] should hope that God in . . . compassion and mercy will make [one's] way straight, will deliver [one] from harm, and will choose what is good and suitable for [one] by putting in [one's] . . . heart to choose the good and reject the evil. . . . [This kind of] hope is fulfilled through prayer. . . . The Psalmist alludes to this when [saying] . . . , "Hope to YHWH! Let your heart be firm and bold, and hope to YHWH" (Ps. 27:14). This shows that hope is the cause of strength, and that strength is a cause for more hope . . . the two mutually reacting upon each other.[36]

As I see it, prayer and the exploration of our hopes lead us to discover the choices God has put before us, but choosing between the right path and the wrong path lies in our hands. Prayer helps us discern one from the other and gives us strength to continue down the right road—or, if necessary, abandon our errant ways.

PSALM 130

[1]Out of the depths I call You, O YHWH. [2]O YHWH, listen to my cry; let Your ears be attentive to my plea for mercy. [3]If You keep account of sins, O YHWH, who will survive? [4]Yours is the power to forgive so that You may be held in awe. [5]I hope to YHWH, my being hopes, and I hope for [YHWH's] word. [6]I am more eager for YHWH than watchmen for the morning, watchmen for the morning. [7]O Israel, hope for YHWH; for with YHWH is steadfast love and great power to redeem. [8]It is [YHWH] who will redeem Israel from all their iniquities.[37]

Like Psalm 27, Psalm 130 holds a special place in the seasonal liturgy. Many communities recite this hope-laden psalm in daily morning services between Rosh Hashanah and Yom Kippur. The Mishnah notes that in ancient times this psalm of hope was recited during public fasts prescribed to alleviate drought.[38] Today, its frequent inclusion in the Rosh Hashanah afternoon ceremony (*Tashlikh*) of throwing bread crumbs into a body of water to symbolically rid ourselves of sin is yet another expression of the hope to start the new year with a clean slate.[39] The similarity between the central themes of the High Holy Days and Psalm 130 could not be more clear: Both emphasize the prayerful plea for God's forgiveness and the resounding hope for lenient judgment.

It's worth noting that Psalm 130 has spoken to not only Jewish worshippers. Known in Latin as *De Profundis* (From the Depths), this psalm has been counted by the Catholic Church among its seven penitential psalms since the sixth century. And from Bach and Boulanger to Dowland and Dupré, dozens of composers have set it to music.

Various medieval and modern commentators have also pointed to its many expressions of hope. In the Middle Ages, it served as a declaration of the Jewish people's unwillingness to relinquish their hope for redemption amid centuries of exile and persecution.

The horrors of his lifetime certainly colored Bible scholar and philosopher Rabbi David Kimchi's commentary on Psalm 130. Kimchi (1160–1235,

France) lived during a period of expulsions throughout France, Europe's first blood libel (in Blois, France, 1171), and the Third Crusade (1189–92), which unleashed massacres against the Jews of England that gave rise to the self-immolation of 150 Jews in York to avoid slaughter or forced baptism.

Beginning with the idea that "the depths" represent exile, Kimchi writes that "this psalm is said by all pious Jews in exile." The expression "I hope for YHWH" refers to "God's promise to redeem me from exile." Kimchi was also a grammarian: Thus he notes that "hope" (*yacheil*) in verse 7 is an imperative, as if to order "Israel to hope that God will redeem it from exile because of God's steadfast love." How do we know this is so? "Because," he says, "God already redeemed you many times, from Egypt and Babylonia and from many difficult straights. So God will redeem you from this exile too."[40]

We can sense in his words the palpable strain of invoking images of God's earlier acts of redemption to sustain the hope that God's hand has not lost its redemptive power. Invoking the redemption from Egypt and later from Babylonia continued to sustain Jewish hopes during the travails of life in medieval Europe.

The commentary by Bible scholar, preacher, and kabbalist Bachya ben Asher (1255–1340, Spain) makes a related point. Bachya writes that "all the nations of the world are saying that Israel has no hope." God, he explains, granted King David (traditionally viewed as author of the Psalms) a vision of Israel's future exile so that David could help keep his descendants from falling into hopelessness. Noting the psalmist's use of the Hebrew roots of two different words for hope (*tikvah*, twice in verse 5, and *tochelet*, in verses 5 and 7), Bachya avers that "David doubled the words for hope in this psalm to strengthen hope during the periods when Israel would otherwise despair of redemption."[41]

More recent commentators on Psalm 130 have tended to read it in terms of an individual's personal spiritual struggle. The psalmist cries to God from the depths "of despair, of self-doubt, and of existential perplexity," as the contemporary commentator Jeffrey M. Cohen has put it.[42] Avigdor Nebenzahl, a former chief rabbi of the Old City of Jerusalem, notes that one of the words for "hope" in this psalm (*kiviti*, "I hope") shares the root of the word for "line," *kav*. Nebenzahl explains that this double meaning signifies that we hope our connection to God will be direct, like a line, the shortest distance between two points.[43] Moreover, as kabbalists had argued, the relationship between hope and *kav*—in Kabbalah, the line or ray of light with which creation begins—signifies that hope constitutes the fundamental connection between God and humanity and that hope embodies the royal road to *teshuvah*.[44]

To talmudist, philosopher, and revered leader of Modern Orthodoxy Joseph B. Soloveitchik (1903–93, Belarus and United States), this psalm contains the answer to two of our most radical hopes about *teshuvah*: that it be fast and durable. First, though *teshuvah* generally involves an extended process, this may not necessarily be the case. Because God is "steadfast with kindness," Soloveitchik says, God "can use it to extricate us from the slow process of forgiveness to transform it all at once—like the swift transition from the darkness of the night to the light of the morning." Second, there is a reason the psalm's concluding verse, that God "will redeem Israel from all their iniquities," includes the word "all." The psalm refers to more than "pardon . . . or the cleansing of sins." "All" refers to "complete liberation of the soul" and the potential for genuine, permanent change.[45]

THE BOOK OF JONAH

As we've seen, hope rests precisely on that capacity to envision a future that improves on the present—for ourselves, for others, and for the world at large.

A close reading of the book of Jonah reveals a similar, and arresting, theme. Through a series of allusions to earlier biblical stories, the book points to changes in the character of God! Specifically, the book subtly charts God's evolving approach to dealing with disappointment.[46]

It is not unusual for the Bible to portray God in anthropomorphic ways. In *The Personhood of God*, Bible scholar and theologian Yochanan Muffs (1932–2009, United States) points to God's display of a range of human emotions, from anger and frustration to surprise and compassion. The Bible also shows God as a being who develops, Muffs writes: "In the first chapters of Genesis, God emerges as a moral personality who grows and learns through tragedy and experimentation to become a model" for humankind. "The crucial message is that even God makes mistakes and actually learns from them."[47] What better lesson could there be on Yom Kippur for teaching us how to do *teshuvah*!

Yonah, the prophet Jonah's Hebrew name, means "dove." Who can hear about a dove on a boat in the middle of a raging storm without thinking of the Flood, when the dove is first mentioned in the Bible? When the world turned out to be less than perfect, God simply wiped it out and started over again:

Va'yinachem YHWH ki assah et ha'adam ba'aretz va'yitatzev el libo. . . . And YHWH regretted having made humankind on earth. With a sorrowful heart, YHWH said, "I will blot out from the earth humankind whom I created—humans together with beasts, creeping things, and birds of the sky, for I regret that I made them."[48] (Gen. 6:6–7)

No prophets, no hope for repentance, not even pity on the innocent children and animals, just obliteration. God tells Noah of the divine plan, but Noah, the most righteous person of his age, says not a single word to God in response. Why not? Perhaps a God who announces plans to "destroy all flesh under the sky in which there is a breath of life" except for one family and a pair of every animal is not exactly a God who inspires dialogue.

God's plan to destroy the evil city of Nineveh also echoes the earlier destruction of Sodom and Gomorrah, the first cities in the Bible singled out for divine wrath. The Hebrew verb *la'hafokh*, "to overturn," is used in reference to Sodom and Gomorrah as well as Nineveh. Once again, the evil or sinfulness of a city has come up before God. But, in comparison with the worldwide flood, targeting two specific cities indicates the development of considerable divine restraint. And at least Abraham tries to intercede, even if it proves futile. Note too Abraham's argument: "Shall not the Judge of all the earth deal justly?" (Gen. 18:25). The argument rests purely on justice, with no appeal to mercy or to the possibility of *teshuvah*.

Now, when Jonah explains to God why he fled, adding, "for I knew that You are a gracious God and compassionate, long-suffering and abounding in mercy and repenting of evil" (4:2),[49] he is paraphrasing Exodus 34:6–7, where God's merciful attributes first find expression: following the Golden Calf incident. Those attributes form a key refrain in our Yom Kippur liturgy—*YHWH, YHWH el rachum v'chanun* . . . (YHWH, YHWH, God, merciful and compassionate). God (and some say Moses) spoke these words after Moses repaired the shattered relationship between God and the Children of Israel. God had threatened to destroy this stiff-necked, backsliding people and make a new covenant with Moses; turning down the offer, Moses shrewdly argued that God's credibility in Egyptian eyes would suffer if the Israelites disappeared. And so, God yields to human persuasion, spares the Israelites, and in the process moves beyond the paradigm in which disappointment spells annihilation. God develops the capacity for mercy.

But, again, still not a whisper from God or Moses about the potential for *teshuvah*.

Yet, by the conclusion of Jonah, when the people of Nineveh change their evil ways, God happily gives up the plan to overturn the city: "*Va'yinachem ha-Elohim al ha'ra'ah asher diber la'a'sot la'hem, v'lo assah.* And God repented of the evil, which [God] spoke of doing to them; and did not do it" (Jon. 3:10).[50]

Finally, God's actions spontaneously display the compassion that previously resulted from Moses' artful persuasion. Now, *God* knows that people deserve a chance for *teshuvah*. In a complete reversal of roles, now *God* must teach compassion to the stiff-necked prophet Jonah, who demands the obliteration of a sinful people.

The key word is *va'yinachem*, God "repented" or "regretted" the planned destruction.[51] In the story of the Flood, *va'yinachem* denotes God's regret for the creation of life and signals its impending annihilation. In Jonah, *va'yinachem* describes God's capacity for mercy based on the recognition that change, that *teshuvah*, is always possible.

To underscore that point, a ninth-century midrash makes an astounding comment: Who was the king of Nineveh? Pharaoh! God resurrected him from the Red Sea and gave him another chance to do *teshuvah*![52] This midrash contains one of Judaism's most profound statements of hope that human beings can change their ways.

So, what we likely have in the book of Jonah is either a short history of God's evolving response to disappointment in humanity or a succession of evolving reconstructions of how human beings have understood God's nature. In either case, if we are created in God's image, I believe the goal for us is to arrive at a point at which we too can learn to restrain our more primitive impulses toward those who disappoint us and give them a chance to change their ways. If God learns to hope that those who have disappointed us can change, so can we. Our enemies need not always remain enemies. To act in a godly way is to hope that others can do *teshuvah*, just as we hope to turn ourselves.

Conclusion

As we've seen in this chapter, the process of *teshuvah* embodies the hope that we can change and Judaism's methodology for personal transformation, for allowing the divine image we bear to exert greater influence on our behavior. Indeed, the name of God revealed to Moses at the burning bush, *Ehyeh-Asher-Ehyeh*, "I will be what I will be" (Exod. 3:14), epitomizes God's capacity for change: God will be what God will be implies that God is not static, but rather dynamic, changing, evolving.[53] Appropriately, this name of God makes its only liturgical appearances on Rosh Hashanah and Yom Kippur.[54]

Thus, as I see it, our ability to be what we will be derives from our creation in the divine image and God's ability to be what God will be. Created in the divine image, we share God's capacity to evolve. Past and present need not define who we will be. Hope inhabits an open future.

To help us return to our old/new better selves, to allow that divine image within to shine forth more brightly, Judaism prescribes a time of year for introspection, prayer, and special rituals corresponding to the period when Moses ascended Mount Sinai for the second time and returned with a new set of tablets to replace the ones he smashed following the Golden Calf incident. Each year, that season of Elul, Rosh Hashanah, and Yom Kippur reminds us that we too have a second chance, as did our ancestors who lost their spiritual way in the desert. What was that calf our ancestors worshipped if not a seriously misplaced, unworthy hope?

Prayer, a primary component of *teshuvah*, affords us an opportunity to share our deepest hopes with the One of Being, to determine if they are truly worthy and to embrace better hopes if ours prove wanting. The blasts of the different shofar calls are not the same—the calls change, and so can we. The God of the book of Jonah seems a lot more compassionate than the God of the Flood. God can change, and so can we.

Two years before he was killed in the Holocaust, the great Hasidic scholar and teacher Issakhar Solomon Teikhthal (1885–1945, Hungary and Czechoslovakia) composed a teaching for the period between Rosh Hashanah and Yom Kippur. He gave it this title: "God Only Forgives Those Who Hope for God's Forgiveness."[55] *Teshuvah* requires effort and honesty, but it starts with the hope that change is really possible.

2

Tikkun Olam

TURNING HOPE INTO ACTION

The Jewish religion is founded on the divine assurance and human belief
that the world *will* be perfected. Life will triumph over its enemies—
war, oppression, hunger, poverty, sickness, death. . . . In offering hope of
perfection, the Jewish tradition takes the countervailing evidence fully into
account. . . . The party of hope fully admits the possibility of defeat but does
not yield the dream. Rather it offers a method to make the dream come true.
—Irving Greenberg, *The Jewish Way*

Introduction

Among the many lessons my parents tried to teach me as a child—tell the
truth, show respect for your elders, and so forth—one felt very different:
"Try to leave the world a better place than you found it." Had it been the
1980s, they would doubtless have spoken of *tikkun olam*—to mend, repair,
fix, straighten out, or perfect the world—a term that has since become
something of a rallying cry to address everything from providing hands-on
services to individuals in need to pursuing world peace. But back in the 1950s
this term had yet to make its debut on the stage of American Jewish life.

That said, *tikkun olam* is hardly a newfangled concept. This chapter
explores *tikkun olam* from its linguistic roots in the book of Ecclesiastes
to its earliest appearances in rabbinic literature, its meaning in the *Aleinu*
prayer, the ways in which the kabbalist Isaac Luria expanded its reach, and
the rise of *tikkun olam* in contemporary Jewish life.

The ties between *tikkun olam* and hope are many and deep. Both involve
a commitment to seeing an alternative, improved reality, and both live
fully in the present even as they point to the future. Without hope, *tikkun
olam* would languish; without *tikkun olam*, hope would be selfish or lack
concrete expression. If hope is the picture of a better future, *tikkun olam* is
the commitment to build it. We might think of *tikkun olam* as the hands of

hope. As we work to repair the world, we join in shared hope with humanity and with God. That labor enables hope to burn brighter, which in turn enhances our strength to continue the work of repair—as long as it takes.

Biblical Roots in Ecclesiastes

The root of the word *tikkun, tav-kof-nun*, appears only three times in the Bible, and all in Ecclesiastes.[1] The first two instances deserve our attention because, while the meaning of the word is quite clear, the context comes as quite a surprise. Early in the book, Kohelet, described as the "king in Jerusalem," announces that he has

> observed all the happenings beneath the sun, and . . . found that all is futile and pursuit of wind: That which is crooked cannot be made straight [*l'tkon*],[2] a lack that cannot be made good. (Eccles. 1:12–15)[3]

Seven chapters later, the motif recurs:

> Consider God's doing! Who can make straight [*l'takein*] that which [God] has made crooked?[4] So in a time of good fortune enjoy the good fortune; and in a time of misfortune, reflect: The one no less than the other was God's doing; consequently, humankind may find no fault with [God]. (Eccles. 7:13–14)

C. L. Seow, among the great modern interpreters of Ecclesiastes, describes the theme of the book's opening chapters: "Everything is ephemeral and unreliable." About verse 1:15, above, he says, "The point is that people cannot hope to find order and meaning where none is discernable: what is not there cannot be counted."[5] Seow also suggests that Ecclesiastes might have been rebutting this ancient Egyptian proverb with a decidedly more optimistic view:

> The crooked stick left on the ground,
> With sun and shade attacking it,
> If the carpenter takes it, he straightens it,
> Makes of it a noble's staff.[6]

In the context of Ecclesiastes, the verb *tav-kof-nun* is twice associated with dismissing the possibility of straightening something that has been twisted—in the second case, twisted by God![7] For Kohelet the stoic king, trying to improve the world "is futile and pursuit of wind" (Eccles. 1:14). "Wrongs cannot be corrected or lacks supplied," explains Michael V. Fox in his contemporary commentary on Ecclesiastes. "Kohelet is resigned to the intractability of the world's fundamental wrongs. He does not call for 'fixing' of distortions or the filling out of lacks, but only for the resignation to the state of affairs that God has built into the world." This contributes to Kohelet's dark state of mind: "And so I loathed life. . . . And . . . came to view with despair all the gains I had made under the sun" (2:17, 20). Fox likewise observes that "Kohelet does not tell us to pursue justice, though he sees injustice. He does not tell us to comfort the oppressed, though he sees their discomfort."[8]

Is Kohelet's do-nothing stance toward social injustice antithetical to Judaism?[9] The chasm between the "wise" king's lack of engagement with his society's troubles and Isaiah's prophetic activism—clothe the naked, feed the hungry, free the oppressed (Isa. 58:6–7)—seems unbridgeable. In fact, modern commentators suggest that the greatest enigma about Ecclesiastes may be how the book found its way into the canon.[10] Indeed, before the canon had been officially established, the Mishnah (*Eduyot* 5:3) reports that the school of Shammai argued against including it. Disagreement persisted among the sages for several generations, with some maintaining that Ecclesiastes should be hidden away because it might undermine meaningful engagement with the Torah.[11]

So much for *tikkun*. What about *ha-olam*? This word as well has a unique relationship with the book of Ecclesiastes. The word *olam* appears more than four hundred times in the Bible, and, with one possible exception, it means "antiquity," "eternity," or "time without end." Where is that exception? In Ecclesiastes! "He has also placed the love of the world [*ha-olam*] in men's hearts, except that they may not discover the work God has done from beginning to end" (3:11).[12] As Fox explains, "God implanted in humans a desire to process or understand the world."[13] Here, too, a number of modern translators render *ha-olam* as "eternity"—the difference boiling down to whether God has implanted a love of the world or a love of eternity within us.

Some of the Bible's most important historical translations and interpretations have favored "world," among them the Septuagint (Greek, third through first centuries BCE); the Vulgate (Latin, late fourth century); and the King James Version. Rashi reads the verse this way as well.[14] To me, this reading expresses God's endorsement of the healthy human desire for the pleasures of this world rather than a divinely implanted fascination with eternity. This rendering resonates well with one of Ecclesiastes' recurrent themes—that life is short and should be enjoyed:

> Go, eat your bread in gladness, and drink your wine in joy; for your action was long ago approved by God. Let your clothes always be freshly washed, and your head never lack ointment. Enjoy happiness with a woman you love all the fleeting days of life that have been granted to you under the sun—all your fleeting days. For that alone is what you can get out of life and out of the means you acquire under the sun. Whatever it is in your power to do, do with all your might. For there is no action, no reasoning, no learning, no wisdom in Sheol, where you are going. (Eccles. 9: 7–10)

How strange that *tikkun olam*, an expression now synonymous with improving the world, should have its biblical roots in verses from a book that denies the possibility of change. To understand that evolution, we must turn to the Rabbis of the Mishnah, who coined the phrase.

Rabbinic Origins in the Mishnah

The first references to *tikkun olam* appear in Judaism's oldest rabbinic law code, the Mishnah (early third century CE). The expression "*tikkun ha-olam*" occurs fifteen times, all but once in the section on the laws of divorce, although many of these references deal with matters unrelated to divorce.

Truth be told, it's not completely clear what *tikkun ha-olam* means. Marcus Jastrow's classic dictionary of rabbinic literature suggests "for the sake of the social order." Common translations offer "for the public interest," "for the public welfare," "as a precaution for the general good," or "for the good order of the world."[15] These translations put the stress on maintaining the social order. By contrast, scholars writing about the concept of *tikkun ha-olam* often prefer something along the lines of "improving society," "repairing" or "perfecting the world."[16] The latter, of course, harmonizes with our current understanding of *tikkun olam*. But is that really what the Rabbis meant?

The difference is not trivial. When the Rabbis used this phrase, did they see themselves primarily as proponents of the status quo or advocates of change?

For now, let's consider the Mishnah's first use of the phrase:

[If one sent a bill of divorce to his wife with a messenger, once she received it the divorce was final.] In earlier times, a man would convene a court in another place and cancel it. Rabban Gamaliel enacted that they should not do so, for the sake of *tikkun ha-olam*. (*Mishnah Gittin* 4:1–2)

This Mishnah deals with a case in which a husband sends a bill of divorce to his wife with a messenger, but unbeknownst to her, he has convened a court to cancel it. Having received an authentic bill of divorce, the woman will think she is free to remarry. But if she does so and bears a child, the child will be a bastard, since the woman is still legally married to her first husband. Known in Jewish law as a *mamzer*, the illegitimate child can only marry another individual with the same status. Rabban Gamaliel, leader of the rabbinic community from 20 to 50 CE, sets down a ruling to prevent this. If the woman receives a properly executed bill of divorce, the marriage is dissolved, and she is free to remarry regardless of her former husband's effort to annul the divorce decree.

A similar case arises when a man doesn't list his name properly on a bill of divorce and thereby creates the erroneous impression that he has executed a binding bill. Again, the wife might mistakenly believe she is divorced, remarry, and beget a *mamzer*. The Rabbis close this loophole as well, for the sake of *tikkun ha-olam* (*Mishnah Gittin* 4:2). Both cases grant increased protection for women whose husbands attempt to abuse the laws of divorce.

Let's consider one more example, this one involving a man who had been a slave to two masters. One master frees him; the other does not. As a result, the man is half-slave and half-free. According to the laws of the time, this man would be unable to marry, because marriages could only involve two slaves or two free people. This troubles the sages. "Should he not marry?" the Mishnah asks. "Wasn't the world created to be fruitful and multiply?" The Rabbis compel the man who still retains a half ownership of the slave to make the half-slave a loan so he can buy his freedom and with it the ability to marry—for the sake of *tikkun ha-olam*.

How far do some of these innovations go? Talmud professor Judith Hauptman explains:

> These new rules make an extraordinarily powerful statement about the rabbis' ability to introduce legislation independent of, and even as . . . [the Talmud] will point out, contradictory to Scripture, when acting to restore a stance of social justice to the system.[17]

An Intertextual Reading of the Sages and Ecclesiastes

I believe that there is a relationship between these two terms unique to Ecclesiastes within the biblical canon—the root *tav-kof-nun*, as in "That which is crooked cannot be made straight [*l'tkon*]" and *olam* (in the sense of "world")—and the meaning of *tikkun ha-olam* as it appears in the Mishnah. Daniel Boyarin's intertextual approach to midrash provides a useful lens through which to consider this relationship.

According to Boyarin, in the midrashic process, readers of Scripture observe the linguistic resonance between two sources, and use each one to illuminate the other in light of "cultural codes which enable them to make and find meaning."[18] As one scholar who has applied Boyarin's approach to the Mishnah's use of biblical Scripture concluded: "The new Mishnaic co-text is often radically different from that of Scripture, and it always has its own thematic orientation."[19] In the context of the relationship between the terms we've considered in Ecclesiastes and the Mishnah's use of *tikkun ha-olam*, we not only witness a thematic reorientation, but a measure of irony as well. Where Kohelet argued for the futility of trying to make the crooked straight, the Rabbis set down a group of particular laws *mipnei* (for the sake of) *tikkun ha-olam*, straightening out particular domains of their world where crookedness lurked.

Aside from the linguistic connections between the mishnaic phrase *tikkun ha-olam* and key words in Ecclesiastes, another piece of textual evidence ties these sources together. We've seen that the Rabbis initially invoke *tikkun ha-olam* when enacting laws to prevent adulterous union and illegitimate offspring. In addition, elsewhere the Mishnah also uses Ecclesiastes' proverb explicitly in connection to illegitimate offspring. In a statement repeated a score of times in subsequent rabbinic literature, the Mishnah asks, "What is 'that which is crooked cannot be made straight?' He that has a connection with one of the forbidden degrees [i.e., one of the categories of illicit sexual relationships] and by her begets a bastard issue" (*Chagigah* 1:7). Here, the moral condemnation falls on the man who has sexual relations with a married woman, but the legal penalties fall on the woman (who is now forbidden to her husband and to her lover) and the child of the prohibited union.

Taken together, *Mishnah Chagigah* 1:7 (which applies Ecclesiastes' "that which cannot be straightened," *litkon*, to forbidden sexual relationships and illegitimate offspring) and the aforementioned *Gittin* 4:2 (that uses *tikkun* to justify changing divorce laws to reduce the likelihood of a woman's husband tricking her into an adulterous relationship) provide a solid bridge between Ecclesiastes and the rabbinic term *tikkun* used in divorce law. When the Rabbis of the Mishnah formulated divorce laws to diminish the likelihood of illegitimate offspring, they looked to the language of Ecclesiastes, straightening out the rules to mitigate an undesirable outcome. When it was too late, and a forbidden (i.e., "crooked") relationship produced an illegitimate child, they looked to the same source to acknowledge the limits of their ability to straighten things out.

The sages share Kohelet's fascination with the world, but reject his belief that

> Only that shall happen which has happened, only that occur which has occurred. There is nothing new beneath the sun! ... I further observed all the oppression that goes on under the sun: the tears of the oppressed with none to comfort them; and the power of their oppressors. (Eccles. 1:9, 4:1)

The sages of the Mishnah who introduced the phrase *tikkun ha-olam* say "No!" "In earlier times," recounts the Mishnah (*Gittin* 4:1–2), they used to do it this way, but Rabban Gamaliel determined that going forward, "they would not do it that way." Rabbinic law would stand against the oppressor's power and, contra Ecclesiastes, provide that measure of comfort when possible. Within the limits of its power, rabbinic law would try to improve the world. If Ecclesiastes seems to be saying that what God establishes as crooked cannot be made straight, the Mishnah argues that law is in human/rabbinic hands, and, when it appears crooked, it *can* be changed.

I think that the sages of the Mishnah who first employed the phrase *tikkun ha-olam* intended to offer a subtle, but pointed, critique of Kohelet's worldview and to take a stand, not only for justice against oppression, but for hope against despair. As Fox points out:

> [Kohelet] has no hope that human action can correct or even alleviate wrongs. He takes a deterministic, passive attitude toward injustice. It is not that specific injustices are fated, but that injustice itself is built into the world and nothing can be done to remedy it.[20]

Because Kohelet discounts both the efficacy of human agency and the possibility of change, his world remains devoid of hope.[21]

Thus, the rabbinic intent behind the expression *tikkun ha-olam* was not primarily to maintain the social order, but to change it for the better. By incrementally altering the law, the Rabbis subverted Kohelet's maxim—irreparability of the twisted—as they rejected his despair. If they couldn't prevent some marriages from dissolving, they could at least craft laws of divorce fairer to women. If they couldn't ban slavery, they could at least provide a way for an individual who was half-slave and half-free and therefore unable to get married to gain complete freedom in order to marry. These decisions provided hope to those who would have otherwise been trapped by unjust laws.

More broadly, the Rabbis strengthened an outlook on life that sustains hope. When the crooked can be straightened—even if only sometimes and to a certain degree—hope flourishes and humanity renews its strength to repair the world.

Aleinu's Hope of Repairing the World

A traditional and more familiar source that speaks of *tikkun olam* is the *Aleinu* prayer that traditionally concludes all Jewish prayer services:

> We must praise the master of all, and render greatness to the creator of the universe, Who did not make us like the nations of the lands, and did not place us like the families of the earth, Who did not make our lot like theirs, or our destiny like all of them. [For they bow to vanity and emptiness, and pray to a god who does not save.][22] We bow down low in grateful acknowledgment before the king over the king of kings, the Holy One, blessed be He. For He spreads out the sky and establishes the earth, and His majestic abode is in the sky above, and His mighty dwelling place is in the lofty heights.... None is like Him—as is written in His Torah: "Know this day and reflect on it, because Adonai is our God in the sky above and the earth below." There is none else.
>
> Therefore, we hope to You, Adonai our God, soon to see Your majestic glory; to remove idols from the earth, so that the false gods will be destroyed; to perfect the world under the Almighty's kingdom (*l'takken olam b'malkhut Shaddai*),[23] so that all will call on Your name; and to turn all the wicked of the earth toward You. May all the inhabitants of the world realize and know that to You every knee must bow down, every tongue swear allegiance. Adonai our God, before You they will bow down and fall, and honor Your glorious name, and will accept the yoke of Your kingdom, that You might rule over them soon and forever.[24]

Notice how the scope of *tikkun olam* has broadened from its comparatively narrow focus in the Mishnah. As the contemporary Orthodox scholar Benjamin Blech puts it:

> Here, the idea has moved beyond ... the rabbinic motive for curbing possible corruptions of the halakhic system and it has come to signify an all-embracing goal of Jewish life and law, one whose acceptance would make possible the fulfillment of prophetic visions of a glorious universal future.[25]

If *tikkun olam* embodies Judaism's central goal, *Aleinu* ties it to our deepest hope. We work against long odds to straighten out our mixed-up world. Hope in the ultimate possibility of making progress toward the goal keeps us from giving up and merely tending our own gardens instead.

ORIGINS OF *ALEINU*

The origins of *Aleinu* remain obscure.[26] Our earliest textual evidence of the prayer comes from a mystical source from the early Geonic Period (589–1038), which attributes it to Rabbi Akiva (first and second centuries CE). According to this text, Rabbi Akiva recited the prayer to keep himself safe during his mystical ascent to the "throne of Glory."[27] Before the Middle Ages, it was customary to recite *Aleinu* only once a year, during the additional service on Rosh Hashanah. In around 1300 it assumed its position as the standard concluding prayer for daily and festival services. About a century later, the bracketed sentence in the first paragraph provoked charges that the prayer was anti-Christian, an accusation that recurred over the centuries until 1703, when Prussian authorities officially censored it, and the sentence gradually disappeared from Ashkenazic liturgy. Since the 1980s, some Orthodox prayer books have printed the passage in parentheses.[28]

What explains *Aleinu*'s prominence? Some maintain that as the daily liturgy developed, it lacked a conclusion, and *Aleinu*'s powerful declaration of faith fit the bill. Others focus on aspects of the prayer that had taken on anti-Christian polemical overtones and connect its liturgical extension to an early European blood libel. In 1171, authorities accused Jews in Blois, France, of using the blood of a Christian child to make matzah, and thirty-one Jews, most of the Jewish population of the city, were burned at the stake. Several contemporary accounts claim that, as they died, the martyrs sang *Aleinu*.[29] The date of the massacre—May 26/20 Sivan, 1171—became a fast day for Ashkenazic Jewry, and by 1189 we find the first examples of the prayer being used to conclude the daily morning service.[30]

TODAY VERSUS TOMORROW

Whatever the precise historical circumstances that contributed to *Aleinu*'s growing liturgical presence, given the vicissitudes of Jewish life in medieval Europe, it's not hard to understand its popularity. *Aleinu* begins with Jews' apparent wholehearted acceptance of God's sovereignty and of their unique position in the divine scheme and ends with hopes of a world remade.

The first paragraph, describing the present as experienced by the composer of the prayer, acknowledges God as creator of the universe and of a destiny for Jews that sets them apart from the rest of humanity. Jews bend in worship to the one, true God while other nations pray to a god who does not save. God's kingship reigns supreme, yet only Jews submit to it, and to God, the somewhat distant sovereign of heaven and earth ensconced in the lofty heights above. This part of the prayer resonates with how Jews have seen themselves over the millennia.

Yet the second paragraph, envisioning the future, changes tone entirely. It contains what Conservative theologian Rabbi Elliot Dorff calls the "thrust of the prayer" and begins with the worshippers' hopes.[31] Whereas the first paragraph accepts God's distance in the heights, the second wants to actually witness God's majestic glory. In the first paragraph, Jews alone bow before God as King; in the future, the prayer imagines a time when *all* the inhabitants of the world will bend the knee in recognition of God's sovereignty. In the first paragraph, Jews embrace a boundary setting them apart as sole worshippers of the one true God; in the second, the prayer looks to the dissolution of this boundary, when all will accept the yoke of God's kingship. In the first paragraph, Jews praise what seems to have been an immutable status quo; in the future, we find an expression of hope that change will come, and *soon* (the word *m'heirah* appears twice in the second paragraph). Idols will be removed, false gods will be destroyed, the wicked turned to God, and an imperfect world perfected—*l'takken olam b'malkhut Shaddai*, "to perfect the world under the Almighty's kingdom."

Aleinu demonstrates an extraordinary willingness to acknowledge the tension between God's reputed sovereignty and a world filled with utter disregard of the divine will. Hope that the world can and will be repaired mediates that tension. Hope is the hinge between a world in which Jews saw themselves as sole witnesses to God's sovereignty and the vision of a world in which all people share that responsibility. More broadly, hope draws the arc from the present, with all its flaws, to an improved future. Whatever else Jewish worship entails, when we conclude with *Aleinu*, we pray neither for escape to a realm of unmitigated, but detached, spiritual splendor, nor for the power to accept the defects of our world today.

Instead, we affirm our hope that the crooked can be made straight—soon and forever.

WHO REPAIRS THE WORLD?

What does *Aleinu* suggest about who effectuates *tikkun olam*—who truly repairs the world? Translations, reflecting syntactical difficulties in this section of the prayer, suggest different answers to this question. For example, consider these two translations, both published by the Conservative movement:

> And so we hope in You, Adonai our God . . . that You will perfect the world by Your sovereignty.

> We hope for the day when the world will be perfected under the kingdom of the Almighty.[32]

The first translation expresses the common view that *Aleinu* ascribes the work of *tikkun olam* to God exclusively. As Dorff writes, "Here . . . we pray that God, not we, will perfect the world."[33] The second translation does not specify who will perfect the world and leaves room to read *Aleinu* as a call for human participation in the task.

Yeshiva University professor Benjamin Blech supports this second view, resting his argument on the significance of the particular name of God, *El Shaddai*, used in connection with *tikkun olam*. The name first appears in connection with God's covenantal promises to Abraham and the requirement of circumcision (Gen. 17:1–14). A midrash recounts that when God said to Abraham, "I am El Shaddai," God meant that "I am the God who said, 'Enough!' *Dai!*" As one commentary explains, God says "Enough!" because "the people of the world have gone on long enough acting like children. It is time to demand righteous behavior of them, to proclaim that certain things are permitted and others forbidden. God's covenant of circumcision marks Abraham as committed to teaching humanity what the God-ordained life can mean."[34] When *Aleinu* speaks of perfecting the world under the kingship of the Almighty, *b'malkhut Shaddai*, and uses the divine name associated with circumcision and covenant, it means that just as God placed the requirement of circumcision in Abraham's hand, so too God puts the responsibility to perfect the world in our hands.

But if God didn't want men to have a foreskin, why are they born with one? Indeed, rabbinic texts recount that Turnus Rufus, the Roman military governor of Judea in the second century, asked Rabbi Akiva the same question, to which Akiva replied that baked bread is more beautiful than spikes of wheat, garments of clothing more beautiful than bundles of flax.[35]

Akiva's response echoes many rabbinic texts arguing that God and humanity are partners. Take, for example, a passage from the blessing to welcome the Sabbath on the sixth day: "The heavens and the earth were finished (*va'yikhulu ha-shamayim v'ha-aretz*)" (Gen. 2:1). The Talmud states that anyone who recites this is counted as a partner with God in the Creation. Why? Because instead of *va'yikhulu*, "they were finished," you should read *va'yikhlu*, "they [God and humankind] finished."[36]

The commitment to *tikkun olam* permeated Maimonides' thinking and served as what the Israeli philosopher Menachem Lorberbaum called a central "organizing principle" in his *Mishneh Torah*, one of Judaism's most important law codes.[37] Here is a stunning example of how Maimonides invoked *tikkun olam*:

> But it is beyond the human mind to fathom the designs of the Creator; for our ways are not [God's] ways, neither are our thoughts [God's] thoughts. All these matters relating to Jesus of Nazareth and the Ishmaelite [Muhammad] who came after him, only served to clear the way for King Messiah and to repair the whole world so as to worship God together, as it is written, *For then I will make the peoples pure of speech, so that they all invoke YHWH by name and serve [YHWH] with one accord* [Zeph. 3:9].[38]

Despite the hardships Jews suffered under Islam and Christianity in his lifetime, Maimonides refused to relinquish his hope that members of all three faiths would take up the work of *tikkun olam* to help pave the way for the Messiah—in his view, an earthly ruler under whose leadership peace, justice, and devotion to God would flourish (see chapter 7 of this volume). Maimonides' vision dovetails with a reading of *Aleinu* in which humanity is called "to perfect the world under the Almighty's kingdom" (*l'takken olam b'malkhut Shaddai*).

The revered Modern Orthodox leader Joseph B. Soloveitchik took the concept of repairing the world in partnership with God even further, calling it the object of *all* of Judaism's hopes:

> When man, the crowning glory of the cosmos, approaches the world, he finds his task at hand—the task of creation. He must stand guard over the pure, clear existence, repair the defects in the cosmos, and replenish the "privation" in being. Man, the creature, is commanded to become a partner with the Creator in the renewal of the cosmos; complete and ultimate creation—this is the deepest desire of the Jewish people . . . the realization of all its hopes.[39]

When I recite *Aleinu*, I read it as an acknowledgment of how much needs fixing and pray that God will strengthen our hands to take up the work of *tikkun olam*. I take *Aleinu* especially seriously in those times—more common of late—when humanity seems bent on taking steps backward toward greater cruelty and less compassion, when despair threatens to obliterate hope. I think about those Jews from Blois believed to have died chanting words about hope and repairing the world and in so doing helped assure that their prayer would be with us whenever Jews pray—morning, noon, and night.

Tikkun Olam in the Mysticism of Isaac Luria

Despite his short life, Isaac Luria (1534–72, Jerusalem, Egypt, Safed) was one of the most influential Jewish mystics of all time. Known as Ha-Ari (the lion), an abbreviation of Ha-Elohi Rabbi Yitzak (the godly Rabbi Isaac), Luria would have agreed with Maimonides that the work of *tikkun* lies in human hands. But Luria's sense of what needed mending and how to bring it about differed radically. For Luria, it was not only the world that needed repair, but God as well.

The essentials of Lurianic Kabbalah can be outlined in a few simple sentences, although the details would take volumes to explain and at least a lifetime to fully absorb. On one foot, so to speak, Luria's model begins with the infinite God's contraction (*tzimtzum*) to allow space for Creation. Next, God poured divine light into the vessels of Creation, but the light was so powerful that it shattered the vessels. Shards of the broken vessels fell to earth, divine light trapped within their shells (*kelipot*). Fulfilling mitzvot (divine commandments) in the proper manner with the correct intention frees the trapped light and allows those trapped sparks to rise, returning to their point of origin. This achieves *tikkun*, repairing the structure of the divine worlds, restoring the unity of male and female aspects of God, and reinstating balance to the cosmos itself. Accomplishing these repairs ushers in messianic times.

Gershom Scholem (1897–1982, Berlin and Jerusalem), founder of the modern academic study of Jewish mysticism, explained the rise of Lurianic Kabbalah in light of the devastating expulsion of Jews from Spain in 1492. The experience of exile stimulated a profound messianic yearning: "It is easy to understand that the entire religious literature of the first generation after the expulsion from Spain is replete with this issue, being entirely an actual hope for a close redemption."[40] While contemporary scholars, including Moshe Idel (1947, Israel, student of Scholem), question many of Scholem's conclusions, including that the kabbalistic doctrines emerging after the expulsion from Spain were more messianic than their predecessors, the notion that Luria transmitted a message of hope to his followers in the wake of a catastrophic dislocation seems beyond argument. Luria not only supplied a general vision of a better future; he created a detailed blueprint for how to build it—in virtually every action of one's life. As important, he situated the enterprise in a redemptive narrative that highlighted the role of human agency, a critical element of hope.

The vast scope of human agency in Luria's thought derived from a fundamental principle of theurgy expressed in the Zohar, Judaism's classic mystical text: "The act below stimulates a corresponding activity above" (3:92b). This bestows awesome power on human beings. Our actions have a direct impact on the Divine: They can either increase or diminish the wholeness of God.

Luria's abstract theories permeated his life in very tangible ways. For all his otherworldliness, Luria established deep relationships with the people around him, whose well-being mattered greatly to him. Repair of the cosmos began on earth with caring human relationships, as in the Torah's injunction to "love your fellow as yourself" (Lev. 19:18).

Strange as it may seem, Luria's focus on this precept was an innovation. Before the kabbalists of Safed, this injunction hardly received the attention in rabbinic literature one might have expected. Aside from the midrashic debate between Rabbi Akiva and Ben Azzai about the Torah's central precept — love your neighbor versus creation in the divine image — rabbinic literature doesn't have much to say about it.[41] Likewise, in ten of the fourteen times the Talmud refers to the commandment, it provides the rationale for choosing the least painful method of implementing the death penalty. The Zohar, which had an enormous influence on Luria, doesn't cite Leviticus 19:18 at all.

Perhaps Moses Cordovero (1522–70, Safed), for a brief time Luria's teacher, planted the seed. Cordovero held that

> a person must desire the well-being of his friend and look out for his wellbeing and the honor of one's friend should be as important to oneself as one's own. For the other is really oneself. Because of this, the Torah commanded us to "love your fellow as yourself." (Lev. 19:18)[42]

Luria applied this commandment to seemingly distant domains — sex and prayer. But for Luria, these were two sides of a coin, as it were, both aiming to effect a *tikkun* in the world above between the male and female aspects of God.

In order for sexual union to have its optimal supernal effect, husband and wife needed to approach the act with the proper intention. A tension existed in kabbalistic circles between pleasurable and instrumental aspects of sex (i.e., bringing about the supernal union). Luria himself seems to have at least left room for love in the process. In the Lurianic scheme, the optimal time for sex was after midnight on Friday night, Sabbath eve. Two verses in Exodus (31:12, 17) describing the Sabbath as a sign between God and the People of Israel drew Luria's attention. "By taking the initial letters of several combinations of words in these two verses, Luria discovered encoded the words for wife, love, and marital intercourse, from which he inferred that a husband ought to 'love his wife as himself' (*ohev ishto ke'gufo*)."[43]

A similar view infused Luria's daily prayer life. Chaim Vital (1543–1620, Italy, Israel, and Syria), one of Luria's students and chief transmitter of his ideas, writes:

Before [beginning one's] prayers in the synagogue, [one] should accept upon [oneself] the commandment of "Love your fellow as yourself" [Lev. 19:18]. [A person] should intend to love one of the children of Israel like [oneself]. Through this, [one's] prayers will ascend together with all the prayers of Israel. They will be able to ascend to Heaven and be fruitful. In particular with regard to the love of [their] colleagues who study Torah together, each one should include [oneself] as if [one] were a limb of [one's] colleague. If one colleague is troubled, they all need to participate in [that colleague's] troubles, whether because of illness or children, heaven forbid, and should pray for [that colleague]. [One] should participate with . . . colleagues in all of [their] prayers, needs, and words. My teacher exhorted me greatly in the matter of loving our colleagues.[44]

As with so many of Luria's practices, this one too found a home in the prayer books of many Jewish communities. Toward the beginning of a prayer book, look for something like this: "I hereby accept the positive commandment to 'Love your fellow as yourself.'"[45]

If Luria's preparation for prayer was unique, so too was his approach to the act of prayer itself. Luria believed prayer required meditation on the intricacies of the supernal union that we are trying to achieve. Generally speaking, the words of a prayer symbolized aspects of the Divine that needed to be brought into unification. One was not only to recite the words but to do so while meditating on the particular union associated with that prayer.

Most of us may never practice the meditation required to pray with the specific intentions Luria prescribed. Still, as one who tries to pray on a daily basis as a member of a morning minyan, I've gleaned something important from Luria's approach: Although prayer can easily be a mechanical, rote process, occasionally it *does* become a transcendent experience. At those moments, the thought has occurred to me: The *Shekhinah* is present! I feel a little shiver and a deep sense of gladness. The experience brings to mind

Kabbalah scholar Simcha H. Benyosef's description of prayer according to the teachings of Rafael Moshe Luria (d. 2009), a Jerusalem kabbalist and a descendent of the Ari. "Although in our generation we have no conscious perception of the union [with God] in this dimension, we are nevertheless infused by the immediacy of an unknown Presence whose vital energy fills us with a total sense of fulfillment."[46] This can really happen! Luria was able to experience this—or something related to it—more often than most, and he was able to help others do the same.

Luria himself was such a powerful embodiment of hope that some of his followers believed him to be a messianic figure. Legend identifies him as the Messiah ben Joseph, a mysterious figure who would set the messianic process in motion but would die before the ultimate Davidic Messiah's arrival. Not long before Luria's death of the plague in 1572, it is said that he instructed his followers to pray that the Messiah ben Joseph would not die. Other traditions connect him with widespread calculations during that period that the Messiah would come in the year 1575. Some said that Luria himself predicted this. On his deathbed he quoted a verse from Genesis: "Once again she bore a son, and named him Shelah" (38:5). The numerical value, or *gematria*, for Shelah equates to the year 1575.[47]

For some years after his death, Luria's disciples tried to conceal their master's teachings, as Luria himself had been extremely particular in choosing his limited number of students. This began to change by 1630, when works inspired by Luria's system began to appear in print and quickly spread throughout Europe. These unleashed a feverish messianic hope, which only grew in reaction to the 1648 and 1649 Chmielnitski massacres. In 1665, Nathan of Gaza declared that the Messiah had come in the person of Shabbatai Tzvi and that "there are no more sparks of the *Shekhinah* left in the demonic realm.... Hence we must no longer perform actions of *tiqqun*."[48] According to Nathan, Luria's cosmic process of *tikkun* had been completed.

Though Shabbatai Tzvi's messiahship quickly proved false, the movement, and the support it generated, expressed the essence of Lurianic hope: "messianic reformation, the extinction of the world's blemish, the restitution of all things in God [all brought about by]... the [individual]... of spiritual action who through the *Tikkun* breaks the exile, the historical exile of the Community of Israel and that inner exile in which all creation groans."[49]

Luria spawned many interpreters, among them Moshe Chaim Luzzatto (1707–46, Italy, Holland, Israel), who, like the Ari, also died at a young age from an outbreak of the plague in Israel. Luzzatto deserves mention because of his unique emphasis on hope in bringing about the ultimate *tikkun*. Luzzatto drew a connection between the ray or line (*kav*, spelled *kof-vav*) of light God emanated after the Divine contraction and hope (*tikvah*, spelled *tav-kof-vav-hey*). God's very first act of creation, the *kav* or ray of light, signifies that hope constitutes the fundamental connection between God and the act of creation itself and between God and humanity. Luzzatto taught that kabbalistic prayer, which gives voice to our deepest hope for salvation—of both God and humanity—holds the key to the final *tikkun*. Toward that end, he composed 515 short prayers of hope, each ending with Jacob's last words to God—"For Your salvation I hope, YHWH" (Gen. 49:18). Aptly, the verse can be read to express hope for salvation both *by* God and *of* God.[50]

Tikkun Olam Today

If the sages who coined the term almost two millennia ago returned today, among other things, they'd surely be surprised by what one scholar called the *"tikkun olam-ization"* of American Judaism.[51] Yale president Peter Salovey's 2015 commencement address—"Repair the World!"— provides a good example:

> What I am going to suggest to you today, however, is that your purpose in life as a graduate from Yale is simply this: to improve the world. In the Jewish tradition this is called *tikkun olam*, literally to *repair the world*. . . . Tikkun Olam is a theme and a phrase that has permeated American popular and political culture . . . [so much so that] there is a joke about an American traveling to Israel to work in an orphanage. He is met by his cousin at the airport. After exchanging greetings, the American asks his Israeli cousin, "How do you say Tikkun Olam in Hebrew?"[52]

Salovey, a liberal Jew who traces his lineage back to the Soloveitchik rabbinic dynasty, is right: many beyond the Jewish community speak of *tikkun olam*. On a trip to Israel in 2013, then president Barack Obama described himself "as a man who's been inspired in my own life by that timeless calling within the Jewish experience—'tikkun olam.'"[53] In his 2015 Passover message, President Obama said:

> The Exodus reminds us that progress has always come slow and the future has always been uncertain, but it also reminds us there is always reason for hope. Like the Israelites who Moses led out of slavery long ago, it is up to us to never lose faith in the better day that lies ahead. . . . And together, we can continue the hard but awesome work of tikkun olam, and do our part to repair the world.[54]

The concept began to spread dramatically in the late 1980s.[55] Scholars point to a number of factors that account for its growing popularity. For one, *tikkun olam* provides a powerful way of reframing post-Holocaust concepts of covenant. In the post-Holocaust era, many theologians describe covenant as a divine-human partnership in which both members share responsibility for repairing the world. The focus on *tikkun olam* also supplies a response to appeals for relevance in Jewish education, and offers a prime, Jewishly rooted call for political action and the pursuit of social justice that dovetails with the overwhelmingly liberal inclinations of American Jews.[56] I would simply add that *tikkun olam* also draws strength from its intimate relationship with hope.

The relationship between *tikkun olam* and hope finds expression in the frequent co-occurrence of both terms in the language of synagogues and Jewish nonprofits. The motto of the Jewish Child Care Association reads: "Repair the world, child by child." It advertises its annual benefit as a "celebration of hope," and its honorees receive a *tikkun olam* award. In 2015, when UJA/Federation of New York launched its Haiti Relief Fund, then CEO John Ruskay stated: "Our core values—our belief in tzedakah, justice, and tikkun olam, repairing a broken world, demand that we come together to bring light and hope to a people who have endured enough."[57] American Jewish World Service (AJWS) identifies itself as "a community of Jewish global citizens committed to repairing the world." When its long-time executive director Ruth Messinger stepped down, the organization published a booklet with excerpts from her speeches titled "Messinger of Hope." Messinger often speaks about the relationship between hope and *tikkun olam* when she invokes a powerful statement attributed to Grace Paley, "The only recognizable feature of hope is action."[58] The title of one of Messinger's talks, which inspired the title of this chapter, makes this link even more explicit, "Tikkun Olam Today: Turning Hope into Action." Hope without action is stillborn.[59] When hope acts, it seeks to transform a piece of the world, however small, however slowly.

INCREMENTALISM

Tikkun olam embodies incremental progress toward its goal, a prescription for a long-term, if not unending, project. The pace of repair may be slow, but that doesn't make it any less possible. Salovey's baccalaureate address puts the issue in perspective: "Improving the world is a difficult project to take on because . . . there really is no beginning, middle, or end here. There is no 'bottom line.' What may be most challenging is that even after a lifetime of work, further repair may be necessary. Maybe even more than when you started." Nonetheless, he urged graduates to heed the two-thousand-year-old teaching of Rabbi Tarfon: "It is not your responsibility to complete the work, but neither are you free to desist from it" (*Pirkei Avot* 2:21).[60]

As an antiwar activist in the 1960s and a full-time activist in the Jewish communal world from about 1985–2000, I can testify to the impact of sustained involvement. Sometimes I've witnessed truly dramatic change; more often, it's a matter of plugging away year after year for small gains. But witnessing and helping to bring about change feeds hope, which in turn builds motivation to continue the work. As researchers on hope confirm, reaching the goal depends on two factors well known to any activist: the capacity to generate new strategies and perseverance.[61]

The thrust of these incremental approaches stands in sharp contrast to less patient methods of transforming the world. Dramatic acts that promise immediate, far-reaching change speak the language of radical messianic hope. Scholem's study of the *Messianic Idea in Judaism* points out the dangers associated with this view and the often catastrophic actions it can unleash, with Bar Kokhba's disastrous rebellion against Rome as the classic example from Jewish history.[62] Scholem also documents the anti-apocalyptic, gradualist view of messianism that envisions an improved rather than a utopian world.[63] *Tikkun olam* evinces this more practical, anti-apocalyptic hope that acknowledges the length of the road—and the dangers of speeding.

REALISTIC HOPE OR PIPE DREAM?

How are we to respond to those who claim that the world's problems are so complex that meaningful progress is impossible, that Kohelet is right in saying, "That which is crooked cannot be made straight," that *tikkun olam* is nothing but a Pollyannaish buzzword designed to help us deny reality?

In fact, while professing greater realism, the Kohelet camp manifests a less accurate picture of the world than do advocates of *tikkun olam*. Why? Because those on the side of Kohelet see only the problems and remain impervious to the reality of progress. Those that espouse *tikkun olam* see both the problems *and* the progress.

Researchers find that human beings reveal an optimism bias when it comes to assessing their own personal futures and that of their local communities, but a pessimism bias when appraising the future of their countries and the world. Part of this reflects a lack of awareness of progress. For example, when asked whether the share of the world population living in extreme poverty has decreased, remained the same, or increased over the last twenty years, only 15 percent of Americans correctly answer that it has decreased.[64] Polls likewise find that, despite a steady decrease in the U.S. violent crime rate since the mid-1990s, the majority of Americans continue to believe the nation's crime rate is increasing every year.[65] Harvard psychologist Steven Pinker's 832-page book, *The Better Angels of Our Nature: Why Violence Has Declined* (2011), concluded that, worldwide, we are "living in the most peaceable era in our species' existence." Pinker explained the book's length: "First I have to convince you that violence really has gone down over the course of history, knowing that the very idea invites skepticism, incredulity, and sometimes anger."[66]

Indeed, by many measures, the lives of most people worldwide have improved dramatically, especially over the past decades. In 1990 nearly 36 percent of the world population lived in extreme poverty, a figure that had been on track to fall to 7.5 percent by 2021, but might rise as high as 9.4 percent due to COVID-19.[67] From 1950 to 2020 global life expectancy rose from forty-seven to seventy-three years, and between 1960 and 2019 literacy rose from 42 percent to 87 percent.[68]

If we want to see improvements in the world, why do we have such a hard time recognizing them when they occur? The skepticism that greeted Pinker's research led him to formulate a psychology of pessimism, grounded in two premises.[69] The first is the documented the fact that "bad is stronger than good." Painful experiences have sufficiently more influence than positive ones, so they create a bias toward negative expectations. A single traumatic experience as a child can lead you to form a dark picture of the future, while a single extremely positive event has far less influence on your view of what lies ahead. The good news is that many positive experiences can outweigh the effect of a few bad ones. As one group of researchers concluded, "Good can overcome bad by force of numbers. To maximize the power of good, these numbers must be increased."[70]

Second, Pinker points to the illusion of "the good old days." Historians confirm that "virtually every culture past or present has believed that men and women are not up to the standards of their parents and forebears." Researchers call this tendency "declinism." An Egyptian delivered such a verdict more than four thousand years ago: "To whom can I speak today? The iniquity that strikes the land has no end. To whom can I speak today? There are no righteous [people]. . . . The earth is surrendered to criminals."[71]

According to one series of studies, changes in one's *own* situation often lead to changes in how a person views the world. When people become parents, for example, they are more likely to believe that "the world is becoming a more dangerous place."[72] With age and declining cognitive capacities people are more likely to see the world as a source of frustration. When we don't sufficiently take into account the changes that we as individuals have undergone, we all too easily imagine that the world, not ourselves, has changed.

Pinker underscores the interaction of these factors with two others—the "availability heuristic" and the news. The availability heuristic is a cognitive shortcut (discovered by two Israeli psychologists, Amos Twersky and Nobel Prize–winner Daniel Kahneman) our brains use to make predictions and estimates. In a series of studies, Twersky and Kahneman found that a large majority of people make estimates about the probability of events based on how readily similar events are brought to mind. This introduces an important bias in our outlook because the ease with which something can be brought to mind may have nothing to do with its frequency or probability. If you ask people whether more words start with the letter *K* or have *K* as their third letter, about two-thirds will say more words begin with *K*. The truth is the other way around, but most people are fooled because it's much easier to recall words (they are more available) that begin with a letter than those that contain it in a particular place.

Now, extend this to less benign contexts. Passing by a car crash, for example, enhances our subjective impression that we are more likely to have an accident. A terrorist attack increases our estimation of the likelihood of a subsequent attack.[73] The media amplify this effect. "If it bleeds, it leads," as they say. And because the media bombard us with violence, criminal wrongdoing, and the like, when we think of the future, these negative images become the most readily available. Combine this with the fact that "bad is stronger than good," and it's no wonder that we discount the reality of world progress. Where this outlook achieves ascendance, Kohelet's ancient words of despair acquire the ring of ultimate truth.

The good news is that there's a great deal of pushback against this view. Just a few of the many examples include Matt Ridley's *The Rational Optimist*, Andrew Wear's *Solved*, *Time* magazine's special issue titled "The Optimists" (edited by Bill Gates), and Zinta Zommers and Keith Alverson's *Resilience: The Science of Adaptation to Climate Change*. So, too, Christiana Figueres and Tom Rivett-Carnac, the UN negotiators of the Paris Climate Accord, write at length in *The Future We Choose: Surviving the Climate Crisis* about the importance of hope and "stubborn optimism."[74] These "optimists" do not use the term to imply that things will automatically work out for the best. Their optimism rests on evidence of our ability to solve problems and on our commitment to do so. For example, Gates writes, "If you want to improve the world, you need something to be mad about. But it has to be balanced by upsides. When you see good things happening, you can channel your energy into driving even more progress."[75]

Conclusion

Almost two thousand years ago, the Rabbis who coined the phrase *tikkun olam* borrowed the words from Ecclesiastes in order to subvert its cynicism. Rejecting Ecclesiastes' pessimism, the Judaism the Rabbis bequeathed us affirms the hope that the crooked *can* be made straight, and it's our job to make that happen. *Aleinu*, the prayer that now concludes all Jewish prayer services, reminds us of the responsibility *l'takken olam b'malkhut Shaddai*, "to perfect the world under the Almighty's kingdom." In the twelfth century, when *Aleinu* first began appearing in daily prayer services, Maimonides made *tikkun olam* a central principle in his understanding of Jewish law. Three centuries later, Isaac Luria extended the object of repair to its ultimate limit: reestablishing the wholeness of God. In our era, the hope to mend the world has become a prime animating force in many sectors of the American Jewish community and beyond—and will likely remain the rallying cry to realize our overarching hopes for a long time to come. As liturgist and poet Marcia Falk notes, "Dedication to tikkun olam begins with hope."[76]

More than a century ago, Shmuel Bornsztain (1855–1926, Poland), a Hasidic scholar known as the Sochatchover Rebbe, pointed out that if we look only at what's wrong with ourselves and the world, we will be too overwhelmed with despair to pray to God, thus making matters worse. His secret to overcoming this despair was to affirm our potential to repair the world.

> When Hillel said, "If I am not for myself who will be for me," he meant that before you pray you must elevate and strengthen yourself by saying, "The world was created for me" as the Talmud teaches. Which means it's my responsibility to repair the world and no one else can do it for me. There are things each and every person must fix and it is for that purpose that they were brought into this world. And there is no one aside from that person who can fix those particular things.[77]

The best way to learn that the world can be fixed is to start by fixing our small piece of it. Once we start, we find evidence of the changes we've wrought. When measured in small increments and over the long haul, that evidence strengthens and affirms the practical basis for the hope that inspired the work at the outset. Hope and *tikkun olam* create the elements of a positive feedback loop in which hope embodies efforts to repair the world, those efforts then strengthen hope, and so it goes, on and on.

3

Abraham and Sarah

LIVING IN HOPE

The memory of Abraham and Sarah . . . induces a turn of mind and opens a possibility for overcoming a dire crisis. To the Israelites in exile, the memory of Abraham gives new hope for a return to the Promised Land, with the exiles resuming Abraham's original journey from Babylon to the Promised Land.

—Ronald Hendel, *Remembering Abraham*

Introduction

Jürgen Moltmann (1926–), a German theologian who has written extensively on hope, once observed, "It is through faith that [one] finds the path of true life, but it is only hope that keeps [one] on that path."[1] In that light, Judaism rightly reveres Abraham and Sarah as models of faith but arguably could pay more attention to their roles as powerful exemplars of hope.

For Abraham, faith pointed to the reality of God; hope embodied the expectation that this reality would become manifest, that God's promises would be kept. Abraham's dawning faith may have led him to sense God's call to go forth, but hope sustained the couple throughout the trials of their subsequent journey.

This chapter explores the role of hope in three aspects of Abraham and Sarah's story: the emerging relationship between God and Abraham, the trials the couple endures, and, in particular, the *Akedah* (Binding of Isaac). A more nuanced reading of these narratives finds stubborn hope and elements of doubt where most have seen only unwavering faith and certainty.

Hope in God and Abraham's Relationship

The Abraham narrative follows God's earlier failed efforts to create a moral human society: first with Adam and Eve, which ended with the Flood; and then with Noah's family, which ended with the Tower of Babel and the dispersion of humankind. Ten generations separate Adam and Eve from Noah, and another ten generations separate Noah from Abraham. Having tried and failed twice, God is going to try with Abraham once more.

What underlies God's effort to keep trying? God's hope that this attempt will turn out better than the first two. God has been searching for the right human partners with whom to build a moral world and hopes that Abraham and his family will fit the bill. This time, part of the divine plan will involve a series of trials to determine whether God's hope is well founded (more on that to come).

Abraham has also been searching. The Bible says little about Abraham's life before God calls him to go forth, but midrashic sources fill in the blanks about his quest. The most familiar legends describe how Abraham uses logic to reveal the fallacy of idol worship. Terah, Abraham's father, manufactured idols, and one day Abraham smashed all but the largest. He put a stick in one of the idols' hands, and when his father saw the damage and asked who was responsible, Abraham said the idol with the stick had broken the others. When Terah told his son idols couldn't do such things, Abraham asked his father, "Then why do you worship them?"[2]

Many midrashim conclude that Abraham's discovery of the true God did not require much searching at all, that it was revealed to him as an infant. But another midrashic tradition tells a different story. After Abraham realized the foolishness of idol worship, he worshipped the sun. Yet when the sun set and the moon rose, he believed the moon had displaced the sun and was more powerful. And when the sun rose again, he realized that neither could be divine: The true God must have created the sun, the moon, and all of the cosmos.[3]

Maimonides likewise offers a more sober evaluation of Abraham's spiritual development. Abraham, says Maimonides, had theological questions early, but no teacher or guide, and "was submerged in Ur of the Chaldees among silly idolaters" until the age of forty. Only then did he attain "the way of truth" and know "that there is one God."[4]

God's search for a better way to create a moral human society parallels Abraham's search for the true God. Having struck out (as it were) twice, God singles out Abraham "that he may instruct his children . . . to keep the way of YHWH by doing what is just and right" (Gen. 18:19). For his part, Abraham has rejected worshipping idols, the sun, and the moon, and feels drawn to God. God and Abraham thereby appeal to one another as promising partners. Neither knows the other, but they share the same hope—that the relationship they are about to begin will endure, that each partner will turn out to be the one the other has been seeking. A series of trials reveal whether their hopes will be fulfilled.

Hope amid Abraham and Sarah's Trials

In *Pirkei Avot* (5:3), the Mishnah teaches, "With ten trials was Abraham our father tried, and he withstood them all." Nearly eighteen hundred years after the Mishnah, the French philosopher, theologian, and playwright Gabriel Marcel (1889–1973) would make the trial central to his definition of hope. "Hope," he wrote, "is situated within the framework of the trial, not only corresponding to it, but constituting our being's veritable *response*."[5] For Abraham as well as Marcel, hope is not just a yearning; it necessitates a series of *actions* to bring about a desired outcome.

GOING FORTH IN HOPE

Abraham's first trial manifests in Genesis 12:1: "Go forth from your native land and from your father's house to the land that I will show you."[6] Along with God's call come divine promises—that Abraham will become a great nation, that God will make his name great and will bless him, and that Abraham himself will be a blessing to the families of the earth. So Abraham packs up his wife, a nephew, and all the wealth they had amassed and "went forth as YHWH had commanded him" (Gen. 12:4). On the surface the trial would seem to involve Abraham's accepting God's commandment to abandon a familiar place, leave his aged father, and set off for an undefined destination.[7] Yet in my view God's command reached even deeper. It tested the strength of the two core qualities of hope itself—the willingness to embrace the possibility of a future fundamentally different than the present and the readiness to help bring it about.

This understanding of the trial hinges on imagining how Abraham may have felt about his life up to this point—in a word, dissatisfied. When we first meet Abram (as he is then called), we learn that he's the oldest of three sons, one of whom has died, and he's married to a barren woman.

Terah, Abram's father, takes his son, his son's wife, and his son's nephew from Ur of the Chaldeans (in southern Iraq) to settle in the land of Canaan. The Bible remains silent on why they left, but the book of Jubilees (12:12–15), a Hebrew text from the second century BCE that didn't make it into the biblical canon, fills in the blanks with a chilling legend. Terah shared Abraham's disbelief in idols, yet feared that if Abraham made his beliefs public, the family would be in mortal danger. One night, Abraham secretly set fire to the "house of idols"; when his brother Haran rushed in to save the idols, he died in the flames. So Terah and company set off, but settle short of their destination, in a town (in northern Syria) called Charan, meaning "crossroad."⁸ With one brother dead, the other left at home; Abraham's mother (Terah's wife) inexplicably missing from the ensemble; and Abraham's wife barren, it's a sad family, stuck at a crossroads—or maybe a dead end. At this juncture, Abraham has an encounter with God that enables him to envision a life of fulfillment.

Why does Abraham follow God's command to "go forth"—*lekh lekha* in Hebrew? And why *lekh lekha*? The word *lekha* seems superfluous; *lekh*, meaning "go forth" (in the imperative), would have sufficed. Explaining that *lekha* denotes "for your own benefit and for your own advantage," Rashi implies that God's command creates a remedy of sorts. From obscurity, Abraham's name will become great. From childlessness, he will become a great nation. From a dead end, he will have an eternal future.

Abraham's willingness to go forth confirms what the French philosopher Henri Bergson aptly observed: "Every human action has its starting point in a dissatisfaction, and thereby in a feeling of absence."⁹ Abraham knows plenty about dissatisfaction and absence. Meeting God finally enables him to go forth in hope, to take the first steps in creating a new future.

ABRAHAM'S HOPE FOR SODOM AND GOMORRAH

While rabbinic sources don't count Abraham's argument with God over the fate of Sodom and Gomorrah among his trials, it is a crucial test for the relationship between Abraham and God. As the tale begins, God says, "'Shall I hide from Abraham what I am about to do . . . ? For I have singled him out that he may instruct his children and his posterity to keep the way of YHWH by doing what is just and right.' . . . Then YHWH said, 'The outrage of Sodom and Gomorrah is so great, and their sin so grave!'" (Gen. 18:17–20). According to a fifth- or sixth-century midrash, God's quandary about revealing the plan to destroy these two evil cities and decision to inform Abraham is necessary, since God has already covenantally promised the land, which includes these cities, to Abraham's descendants, and thus owes it to Abraham to seek his counsel.[10] Having already entered into a covenantal relationship with Abraham, God has become bound, as it were, by norms of fairness and justice. What God intuits about Abraham's commitment to doing what is "just and right" now also applies to God.

God may resent this constraint. But maybe God also hopes that Abraham will show more temerity than Noah, who remained completely silent when he learned of God's plan to destroy the world. This understanding dovetails with the Zohar's condemnation of Noah for failing to have prayed for the world's salvation, "because the Almighty is well pleased when one speaks in favor of [God's] children."[11]

If God is hoping for pushback, Abraham delivers in spades. He famously challenges God, "Will You sweep away the innocent along with the guilty? What if there should be fifty innocent within the city? . . . Far be it from You! Shall not the Judge of all the earth deal justly?" (Gen. 18:23–25). In the ensuing negotiation, Abraham bargains God down to sparing the cities if they contain ten righteous people.

Two words recur in the negotiation: "perhaps," which Abraham says six times; and "if," which God says four times. For example: "And Abraham spoke up and said . . . 'Perhaps the fifty innocent will lack five. Would You destroy the whole city for five?' And [God] said, 'I will not destroy there if I find there forty-five'" (Gen. 18:27–28).[12] These words speak to the kind of indeterminate future that hope can easily inhabit. Of note, Sarah and Abraham, both models of hope, are the first and second biblical figures, respectively, to use the word "perhaps."[13]

But how can the all-knowing God seem uncertain about what the search for innocent souls in Sodom and Gomorrah will reveal? Apparently, this speaks to God's hope. Rabbinical scholar Chaim Yosef David Azulai (1724–1804, Jerusalem and Leghorn) explains that God says, "Perhaps there is hope that even a single innocent soul would issue from the residents of these places."[14] Only when that reckoning fails to find a single innocent soul does God destroy the cities.

Abraham's chutzpah to argue with God can also be seen as a testament to his hopes for God. A midrash explains that "when the Holy One desired to destroy the cities, Abraham stood and sought mercy for them. He thought that there might be hope for them. As it says . . . 'Will You sweep away the innocent along with the guilty?'"[15] Furthermore, the midrash identifies the content of Abraham's hope: that this God with whom Abraham has been in relationship for more than ten years shall act justly.

As a result of their negotiation, God and Abraham affirm their hope in one another's commitment to justice.

HOPE FOR THE PROMISED CHILD

The rabbinic enumerations of Abraham's trials also omit the painful issue of Sarah's barrenness. The couple has long hoped for a child in light of God's initial promise to make Abraham "a great nation." The first time Abraham talks with God, he raises the issue of childlessness. When God speaks to Abraham in a vision and tells of great rewards that lie ahead, Abraham responds, "'O . . . God, what can You give me seeing that I shall die childless and the one in charge of my household is Dammesek Eliezer!' [He] said further, 'Since You have granted me no offspring, my steward will be my heir'" (Gen. 15:2–3). Lest God not hear Abraham's despair regarding the divine promise, Abraham expresses it twice. God reassures Abraham that his offspring shall be as numerous as the stars in the heavens. "And he put his trust in YHWH, who reckoned it to his merit" (Gen. 15:6).

This encounter with God has given rise to what is doubtless the most widely known statement about Abraham's hope. In his letter to the Romans, Paul, who identifies himself as "an Israelite, a descendant of Abraham, a member of the tribe of Benjamin" (Rom. 11:1), writes:

> Hoping against hope . . . [Abraham] believed that he would become "the father of many nations," according to what was said, "So numerous shall be your descendants be." He did not weaken in faith when he considered his own body, which was already as good as dead (for he was about a hundred years old), or when he considered the barrenness of Sarah's womb. (Rom. 4:18–19)[16]

Paul's "midrash" argues that Abraham hoped against hope for children. A classic fifth- or sixth-century Jewish midrash relays something similar about Sarah's hope against hope for children: "'Am I to lose hope in my Creator! Heaven forbid! I will not lose hope.' . . . Said the Holy One, to her, 'Since you did not lose hope, I too will not cause you to lose hope.' And YHWH took note of Sarah . . . [and she] conceived and bore a son" (Gen. 21:1–2).[17] Small wonder that so many books (and websites) about infertility bear the title "Pregnant with Hope."[18]

The Binding of Isaac as a Story of Hope

The expression *lekh lekha*, "go forth," occurs twice in the Bible, first when God commands Abraham to leave his native land and then when God orders him to go to the land of Moriah and sacrifice Isaac. As Abraham went forth in hope in response to God's initial command, I believe he did so again with regard to the second order as well.

Admittedly, reading the Binding of Isaac (*Akedah*) as a story of hope is not the predominant approach to this text, generally understood to teach obedience. The image of Abraham zealously rushing out to fulfill God's commandment to sacrifice Isaac has gained prominence since the time of the Crusades, when many Jewish parents chose to slay their children rather than let them fall into the hands of murderous Crusaders. "The Akedah," a liturgical poem of that era by Ephraim ben Jacob of Bonn (1132–97), conveyed that Abraham not only "ran" to carry out the commandment but actually slaughtered Isaac, who was then revived by the "resurrecting dew." When Abraham saw this, he set to slaughtering Isaac a second time—which, according to the poem, is why the angel called Abraham's name a second time.[19] This depiction, and others like it, reduce Abraham to a zealot who never evinces the slightest hesitation in obeying God's command to slaughter his son.[20] In such an understanding of the *Akedah*, hope plays no discernable role.

A familiar story in the Talmud takes a very different view of Abraham. It imagines a dialogue that ensues after God orders Abraham to "Take your son, your only one, Isaac, whom you love . . ." (Gen. 22:2). Abraham answers God, "I have two sons." God replies, "Your only son," and Abraham counters, "One is the only son to his mother, and the other is the only son to his mother." God says, "The one you love," and Abraham retorts, "I love them both." Finally, God answers, "Isaac."[21] In this account, Abraham's lawyerly temporizing indicates anything but a motivational state characterized by blind obedience. Abraham is clearly distressed by God's order. As literary critic Erich Auerbach (1892–1957, Germany and United States) put it, Abraham's "soul is torn between desperate rebellion and hopeful expectation."[22]

HOPE FOR ISAAC'S SURVIVAL AND GOD'S JUSTNESS

I prefer an interpretation of the text that highlights Abraham's dual hopes: that Isaac will survive the ordeal and that God will prove to be truthful, just, and a worthy covenantal partner.

As the story unfolds, Abraham faces terrible choices. God has promised him that his family line will continue through Isaac. He has already argued with God on behalf of Sodom and Gomorrah, thereby demonstrating that he expects God to act justly. For Abraham to slaughter Isaac, he must either relinquish his commitment to the sanctity of human life—especially that of his beloved son, who is supposed to continue the family line—or his trust in God's commitment to justice. Confronted with this conundrum, hope for Isaac's survival appears to provide the only way out.

And not only this: Abraham's hope also expresses his yearning to affirm that heeding God's initial call to go forth from his native land had been a wise decision after all.[23] The divine order to sacrifice Isaac provides Abraham with an opportunity to learn something crucial about his covenantal partner. Does this God reject the bloody norm of human sacrifice common in his era? (Bible scholar Nahum Sarna notes that in ancient Canaan, human sacrifice "was more in vogue . . . than elsewhere" in the region.[24]) The *Akedah* gives Abraham a way to find out. He takes the knife to slay Isaac (note: taking the knife does not signify that Abraham was willing to use it), and, sure enough, an angel of YHWH intervenes, telling Abraham not to raise his "hand against the boy" (Gen. 22:12). God's rejection of human sacrifice fulfills Abraham's hope in his covenantal partner's commitment to justice and further cements their relationship.[25]

Abraham's willingness to put his hope in God's goodness likewise reaffirms the soundness of the divine choice to have entered into a covenant with him in the first place. From both God's and Abraham's perspectives, the *Akedah*'s dénouement illustrates Gabriel Marcel's belief that, at bottom, hope is relational. As Marcel puts it: "I hope in thee for us."[26]

HOPE BORN OF UNCERTAINTY

Here, Marcel's view that hope "cannot ever be taken to imply I am in [on] the secret, I know the purpose of God or of the gods,"[27] sheds additional light on the story. Abraham maintains hope, but *not* because deep down he *knows* that God will spare Isaac. Uncertainty is crucial, because it carves out space for hope—in this case Abraham's hope that God will relent or that he will discover that he has misunderstood God's true intent.

Numerous sources explore Abraham's doubts as the story of the *Akedah* unfolds. One cause of doubt comes from an ambiguity in the biblical text. God does not actually tell Abraham to slaughter (*lishchot*) or sacrifice (*lizboach*) Isaac as an offering. Instead, God tells Abraham to "offer him [Isaac] there as a burnt offering" (Gen. 22:2). The Hebrew (*v'ha'a'leihu sham l'olah*) can also be read as "raise (or bring) him up there as a burnt offering." For example, the thirteenth- or fourteenth-century Midrash Ha-Gadol imagines Abraham saying to himself, "I don't know whether this means to bring him as an actual burnt offering or to raise him up to the top of the altar in place of a burnt offering to the place where the burnt offering is performed."[28] This midrash gives voice to Abraham's hope that Isaac will leave Mount Moriah alive.[29]

Maimonides' understanding of the *Akedah* also acknowledges the presence of Abraham's doubts, at least according to the philosopher Omri Boehm. For Boehm, Maimonides' reading includes a surface level that stresses obedience and certainty as well as an esoteric level that raises deeper truths, including the question of doubt. On this deeper level, Maimonides asks: "Why did Abraham obey the angel's command not to harm Isaac if he were so sure of God's original intent?" Maimonides' answer hinges on his observation of the names of God used in the story and on his theory of prophecy. In Genesis 22:1, where God commands Abraham to sacrifice Isaac, the divine name is *Elohim*. In 22:11, where an angel of God tells Abraham not to harm the boy, the divine name is YHWH. Says Maimonides, "Every Hebrew knows the term *Elohim* is equivocal, designating the deity, the angels, and the rulers of governing cities" (*Guide of the Perplexed* 1:2). Hence, Boehm contends, the fact that the story begins with an order to Abraham from *Elohim* introduces an element of doubt from the outset.

Next Boehm argues that we must look into Maimonides' thinking about prophecy, because it recurs throughout his discussion of the *Akedah*. Elsewhere in the *Guide of the Perplexed*, Maimonides outlines eleven degrees of prophecy. The highest involves being addressed by an angel in a vision, as was "Abraham at the time of the binding," that is, when the sacrifice was called off (2:45). By contrast, *Elohim*'s directive to Abraham to sacrifice Isaac reflects a much lower level of prophecy. Again, to Boehm, Maimonides is implying that the comparatively low level of the earlier prophetic experience, together with the fact that the initial command came from the equivocal name *Elohim*, created sufficient doubt for Abraham to give greater credence to the angel of YHWH's call to stop the sacrifice than to *Elohim*'s instruction to carry it out. As Boehm concludes, "The story demonstrates that Abraham doubted what 'God' [*Elohim*] had commanded—for otherwise he would not have stopped the sacrifice."[30]

A fascinating Hasidic commentary on a passage in the Zohar (Judaism's classic thirteenth-century mystical text) raises the issue of Abraham's doubt from yet another perspective. As Abraham approaches Mount Moriah, the Bible tells us that he "saw the place from afar" (Gen. 22:4). The Zohar says he saw it "through a dim glass." What does that mean? The nineteenth-century Hasidic master Mordechai Joseph Leiner explains: "That is, an explicit word did not reach him, and he was perplexed in his heart, and so could have decided the doubt either way."[31] As Mount Moriah looms in the distance, Leiner holds, Abraham is not really sure if God's command is completely clear and has doubts about whether to carry it out or not. Where doubt finds a foothold, hope takes root. If Abraham knew God's ultimate plan, if the outcome was assured, there'd be no real trial, no need for him to hope.

HOPING TO REMAIN ONESELF

Another essential element of Abraham's hope is his staying true to his character regardless of the ordeal before him. Marcel speaks of hope as maintaining the "firm determination to remain what I am."[32] Notably, from the beginning of his relationship with God through this test, Abraham consistently evinces inner strength. He trusts that somehow a way to navigate his various trials will emerge and acts to find it.

The *Akedah* provides a striking example of Abraham's constancy. When called upon—first by God, then by Isaac, and finally by the angel who calls off the trial—Abraham gives precisely the same answer: *Hineini*, "Here I am." The expression connotes a readiness to attend to another, but also the complete presence of the self, as if to say *I* am here. Abraham's use of *Hineini* at the beginning, middle, and end of the ordeal communicates that he remains his essential self throughout.

Sometimes, hope as the struggle to hold fast to one's character and values is all that's left. Viewing hope through this lens of character consistency allows hope to take root in situations in which one's hope for survival is next to impossible. Jews on their way into crematoria in Europe during the Holocaust may have given up hope of survival. But many likely retained the hope that (even if it involved great personal struggle) they could remain true to their best selves to the last minute. For some that meant reciting the *Shema*. For others it meant trying to comfort others.

HOPE AS MOVEMENT

To hope means that you keep on going. Hope, says Marcel, requires the looseness of a skier who manages to take the bumps in stride and keep on course.[33]

During the three days of travel to the place where God leads him to sacrifice Isaac, Abraham remains patient. He hopes that the passage of time will reveal the way through his conundrum. He doesn't stiffen or freeze up. He keeps moving, and his movement creates the space in which the spark of hope burns.

Finding the way through involves movement, a motif that occupies a central element in the *Akedah*, as well as the entire Abraham narrative. As we've seen, both God's initial call to Abraham and God's command to offer up Isaac as a burnt offering begin with *Lekh lekha*, "Go forth." Explains Yehudah Leib Alter of Ger (1847–1905), one of the great Hasidic leaders of his era: "A person should always keep walking. . . . Whoever stands still is not renewed, for nature holds him fast. The angels are above nature; they can be said to stand (Isa. 6:2). But the person has to keep walking."[34]

Furthermore, the movement concurrent with hope involves acting as if one can see the outcome one desires. Marcel puts it this way: "One cannot say that hope sees what is going to happen; but it affirms *as if* it saw."[35]

Abraham exhibits this acting "as if" when he states that both he and Isaac will return from the mountain: "You stay here with the ass. The boy and I will go up there; we will worship and we will return to you" (Gen 22:5).[36]

Abraham's acting "as if" can also be seen in his response to Isaac's question, "Where is the sheep for the burnt offering?" He responds, "God will see to the sheep" (Gen. 22:7–8). Philosopher and Talmud scholar Levi ben Gershom (Gersonides; 1288–1344, southern France) explains that Abraham's words were "a prayer that God would show him a sheep to sacrifice instead of his son."[37]

The philosopher Joseph ibn Kaspi (1279–1340, Provence) comments: "Had [Abraham] been a fool and not foreseen that possibility [that 'God will see to the sheep'], he would have hurried to slaughter his son."[38] Abraham tells Isaac that "God will see to the sheep" because it expresses his preferred vision of the future.

In the final analysis, to hope means to take action. Hoping is thus different than optimism, which can be understood as a tendency to offer a positive forecast. Optimists, Marcel notes, point to a contradiction between the way a particular situation may turn out and the general outcome of such cases, often framing their arguments such that "if you consider this case or that, you'll see that this one will also turn out well." In sum, says Marcel, "The optimist is essentially a maker of speeches."[39]

Abraham says little throughout the *Akedah* story. He invests all his energy in the actions he hopes will lead to the dénouement he seeks. They do.

ABRAHAM'S HOPE VERSUS HAGAR'S DESPAIR

Abraham's unwavering hope becomes all the more evident when compared to the expulsion of Hagar, the episode that immediately precedes the Binding of Isaac and which contains many parallels to it. But there, the text depicts Abraham's second wife,[40] Hagar, as demonstrating little if any hope.

Unable to conceive, Sarai persuades Abram (their names have not yet been changed) to take her maid, Hagar the Egyptian, as a wife and sire a child with her. When Hagar becomes pregnant, Sarai grows jealous and treats her harshly. Hagar runs away, but an angel of YHWH urges her to return, assuring her that God has heeded her suffering and will bless her with progeny.

Years later, after giving birth to Isaac, Sarah orders Abraham (with God's assent) to send Hagar, and their son, Ishmael, out into the desert with a single container of water. Already we see an *Akedah* parallel: the near death of a child through whom God has assured a parent of descendants too numerous to count.

> And she wandered about in the wilderness of Beer-sheba. When the water was gone from the skin, she left the child under one of the bushes, and went and sat down at a distance, a bowshot away; for she thought, "Let me not look on as the child dies." And sitting thus afar, she burst into tears. (Gen. 21:14–16)

Abraham moves purposefully forward. Hagar wanders. Abraham keeps going. Hagar sits down. Abraham remains in relationship with Isaac throughout. Hagar abandons her son. Abraham envisions the resolution he desires. Hagar can only foresee Ishmael's death.

Yet, the story of Hagar also ends with God's life-saving intervention and a renewed promise that the family line will indeed continue through the child whose life has been spared.

> An angel of God called to Hagar from heaven and said to her, ". . . Fear not, for God has heeded the cry of the boy where he is. Come, lift up the boy and hold him by the hand, for I will make a great nation of him." Then God opened her eyes and she saw a well of water . . . and let the boy drink. (Gen. 21:17–20)

Whereas Abraham responds to his trial with hope, Hagar responds to hers with despair.

This is not to say that Abraham hasn't had moments of despair, as we've seen, regarding his childlessness. "There can . . . be no hope except when the temptation to despair exists," says Marcel. "Hope is the act by which this temptation is actively and victoriously overcome."[41]

The difference between how Abraham and Hagar respond to their trials highlights the importance of supportive relationships in the capacity to maintain hope. Hagar the Egyptian, whose name is related to *ger*, "stranger," is not only separated from her native land, but also harshly mistreated by her mistress Sarah (Gen. 16:6). The Bible uses the same verb (*l'anot*) to describe Sarah's affliction of Hagar and Pharaoh's affliction of the Israelites. Philosopher and Bible scholar Nachmanides (1194–1270, Spain and Israel) concludes that both Sarah and Abraham were complicit in the sinful treatment of Hagar and that God punished their descendants with affliction by the seed of Ishmael—traditionally identified as the Arab world.

We read this story of Hagar and Ishmael on the first day of Rosh Hashanah and the *Akedah* on the second, the pairing illuminating the difference between despair and hope. As we begin a new year—"the season of hope," as Herman Wouk once called it—the Torah readings set before us a choice: despair versus hope.[42] Judaism wants us to choose hope and to treat others in a manner that will enable them to do the same.

Conclusion

Generally portrayed as icons of faith, Abraham and Sarah can well be viewed as models of hope. From a dead end in Charan, they typically respond to God's trials with hope and perseverance. God and Abraham hope to affirm a shared commitment to justice, and pass each other's tests to discover if their hopes are well founded. Even the Binding of Isaac, usually taught as a lesson of unquestioning obedience, emerges as a testament to hope.

Hope not only carries Abraham through this greatest of trials; he essentially begins a new life after his beloved Sarah dies. It turns out he has thirty-eight more years of living to do. He remarries and fathers six more sons before he dies at age 175. A midrash compares Abraham's hope to that of a tree described in the book of Job (14:7): "Abraham had hope, like 'There is hope for a tree; if it is cut down it will renew itself; its shoots will not cease.'"[43]

A rabbinic axiom holds that whatever happened to the patriarchs and matriarchs will happen to their descendants. In every generation, life inevitably puts our hopes to the test.

The stories of Abraham and Sarah don't give us detailed blueprints for how to respond to every trial we face, but they do impart vital lessons. Don't give up. Keep going: Movement creates space to discover new solutions. Act "as if." Choose to hope even against hope. And stay true to yourself throughout.

4

The Exodus

HOPE AT THE HEART

Passover is preeminently the great historical festival of the Jewish People and the Haggadah is its book of remembrance and redemption. Here the memory of the nation is annually revived and replenished, and the collective hope sustained. The ancient redemption of Israel from Egypt is recounted and relived, not merely as an evocation from the past, but above all as prototype and surety for the ultimate redemption yet to come.
—Yosef Hayim Yerushalmi, *Haggadah and History*

Introduction

It's not by chance that a people with such a long and painful history has made the Exodus its central motif of hope. A tale about the events in one particular place and time, the Exodus from Egypt has become a beacon of hope for Jews wherever and whenever they have lived—and will live.

This chapter explores theologian Walter Brueggemann's reading of the Exodus as the Bible's archetypal tale of hope, the elevation of this narrative as Judaism's master story, the portrayal in midrash and commentary of the Exodus as a struggle between hope and despair, and how Judaism puts into practice memories of the saga.

Brueggemann's Archetypical Tale of Hope

To the American Protestant theologian Walter Brueggemann (1931–), one of the most influential contemporary scholars of Hebrew Scripture, the Exodus is "the governing example of biblical hope," a "liturgical paradigm" meant to shape personal identity and the perception of experience.[1]

Brueggemann focuses on three underlying themes, each arising at a different point in the story and illustrating an important aspect of hope:

critique of ideology, public processing of pain, and the release of new social imagination.

Critique of ideology involves the hope-borne conviction that the oppressive Kingdom of Egypt—or whatever overbearing empire holds sway in any particular time or place—does not embody an acceptable or final situation. This critique emerges from the text's depiction of Pharaoh's treatment of the Israelites. Terms such as "slavery," "oppression," "ruthless," "harsh," "hard," and "bitter" define Pharaoh's malevolent regime (and all others to which such terms apply) as guilty of violating the basic dignity that ought to be conferred upon every human being made in the image of God. Because these terms are leveled against Pharaoh as indictments, they imply a vision of society constituted by norms that promote dignity rather than degradation. Here, Brueggemann explains, hope functions "to provide standing ground *outside the system* from which the system can be evaluated, critiqued, and perhaps changed." He elucidates: "*Hope keeps the present arrangement open and provisional.* Hope reminds us that the way things are (and all the extrapolations we make from that), is precarious and in jeopardy. Hope reminds us not to absolutize the present . . . not to treat it too honorably, because it will not last."[2]

The public processing of pain—the transition from Israel's silent endurance of slavery to its collective cry of pain—testifies to a dawning hope for change. As the text relays, "The Israelites were groaning under the bondage and cried out; and their cry for help from the bondage rose up to God" (Exod. 2:23).[3] Brueggemann explains: "Suffering brought to speech concerns hope, because such protest in prayer and in public life is a refusal to let things be this way when they are in fact unbearable." Tyrants prohibit collective protest because they know that from this seed revolutions grow. Brueggemann elaborates: "That act of pain is Israel's remarkably subversive assertion. It is an act of defiance and protest. It is also an act of hope. . . . People become dangerous voices of hope when they assemble or have a chance for solidarity, but if they can be kept mute they can be held in servility."[4]

The release of new social imagination—and hope—prevails when the empire loses its grip on those it had oppressed. The Revelation at Sinai and the Israelites' acceptance of Torah mark the beginning of this point and bring forth the design of a radically new social, political, and religious order: "You shall not wrong or oppress a stranger, for you were strangers in the land of Egypt. You shall not ill-treat any widow or orphan. If you do mistreat them, I will heed their outcry as soon as they cry out to Me" (Exod. 22:20–22). "Juices are set free which enable those who have not hoped for a long time to hope, those who have not imagined for a long time to imagine," Brueggemann says. "When the cry comes to voice . . . there is a new ability, courage, and will to hope, imagine, design, and implement alternative scenarios for how it could be. . . . The practice of social imagination . . . is an act of dangerous subversion, but also an act of concrete hope."[5] Despite episodes of backsliding—worshipping the Golden Calf and yearning for the fleshpots of Egypt—liberation from Egypt puts Israel on a new path. In Egypt the people had built garrison cities for Pharaoh. At Sinai, Israel assumes responsibility for an entirely new mission: fulfilling God's hope that it will become "a kingdom of priests and a holy nation" (Exod. 19:6).

God plays a vital role in the fulfillment of Brueggemann's concept of Exodus-based biblical hope, the substance of which "is a new world of justice, equity, freedom, and well-being."[6] To Brueggemann, since ultimately God determines which current arrangements may endure and which shall be overturned, and because hope points to a vision of the future, it's fair to say that hope rests with God in terms of how and when this new, liberated world will evolve.

But there's room to understand the relationship between God and our hope for liberation in many different ways. Some readers of the Exodus see the story as a vindication of hope in God's exclusive redemptive powers expressed through divine intervention in nature and history. Others see the Exodus as the paradigmatic example of the divine-human partnership. According to Modern Orthodox theologian Irving Greenberg (1933–, United States), "The Exodus model implies that a partnership between God and humanity will carry out transformation of the world. Despite the glorification of God and divine power in the biblical accounts, God is, from the beginning, dependent, as it were, on human testimony for awareness of the Divine Presence."[7] In this view, the divine-human partnership sustains hope and effectuates change.

Still others read the Exodus through the lens of Mordecai Kaplan's non- or anti-supernaturalism. Here, God becomes the "creative life of the universe, the antithesis of irrevocable fate and absolute evil" and becomes manifest in "human life as the Power that makes for freedom."[8] God's ultimate creativity and identification with change rather than fate thereby make God very close to the embodiment of hope. Indeed, Kaplan might well have called God "the Power that makes for hope." This perspective asserts that what we do with freedom and hope lies entirely in our hands.

Exodus as the Jewish Master Story

As it evolved, Judaism positioned the Exodus, its primary tale of hope, at its very core. The Exodus became Judaism's master story.

The theologian Rabbi Michael Goldberg describes a master story this way:

> By providing us with a paradigm for making sense of our existence, master stories furnish us with a basis for answering some of the most fundamental questions that we human beings can have: Who are we? What is our world like? And given who we are and what our world is like, what then is the best way for us to respond to such a world as this? The answers to those questions often constitute our most deep-seated convictions about our identity, responsibility, and destiny over the course of our existence. Hence, our master stories not only *inform* us, but more crucially, they *form* us.[9]

Greenberg means essentially the same thing when he writes about "Judaism as an Exodus Religion."[10] Jews, he says, are forever bound to remember their enslavement in Egypt, to stand outside whatever oppressive "system" reigns, to struggle for human dignity despite slim odds, and, when despair looms, to draw hope from the Exodus. Michael Fishbane's treatment of the Exodus motif as Judaism's primary "paradigm of historical renewal" belongs to this school of thought as well.[11]

The idea of a master story is closely related to a founding myth. What the historian of religions Mircea Eliade (1907–86, Romania and United States) said of myth might well be said of a master story: "It falls to the primordial myth to preserve *true history*, the history of the human condition; it is in the myth that the principles and paradigms for all conduct must be sought and recovered."[12] This sense of myth speaks of an ultimate truth. But myth also conjures up the notion of something false—in this case casting doubt on the historicity of the Exodus. After all, though the story may contain kernels of historical truth, most (but not all) scholars conclude that an event on the vast scale of the biblical narrative—"six hundred thousand men on foot, aside from children" (Exod. 12:37)—lacks archaeological or extra-biblical evidence.[13]

However, myths need not be historically true to reveal truths about the human condition. Even if the Exodus didn't happen as the Bible portrays it, the master story retains its truth because it speaks to the human hope and struggle for freedom against injustice wherever it needs to be fought.

To call the Exodus the Jewish master story is to say that Jews wear Exodus-colored glasses. We see the abuses of human dignity today through the lens of Egypt: We strive to remediate them because God freed us from slavery in Egypt. We see a world in need of redemption and ourselves as redeemers—albeit sometimes reluctantly, as Moses was himself. And we see all this with a strong tint of hope: We know how the original story turned out so long ago, and we work to have it end the same way today and tomorrow, for ourselves and for others.

My father's life contains a good illustration of what it means to wear glasses colored by the Exodus master story. Raised in the Depression and trained to be a pharmacist like his father, my dad ended up going into his father-in-law's real estate business instead. He became quite successful and devoted more and more of his time to philanthropy. The philanthropic focus of the last twenty-five years of his life was improving the status of the Bedouin in Israel, by any measure that country's most disadvantaged population. Puzzled interviewers would ask him why a New York businessman was so passionate about this down-and-out sector of Israeli society, and his answer was always, "The book of Exodus says, 'Know the heart of the stranger, because you were strangers in Egypt.'" When he'd meet with Israeli politicians to address discrimination against the Bedouin, he'd tell them the same thing.

We can further appreciate the notion of Exodus as Israel's master story of hope by looking at its influence on three areas: law, time and the calendar, and liturgy and ritual.

LAW

When giving the Ten Commandments, which is the first time God communicates with the People of Israel as a whole, God begins with this: "I

YHWH am your God who brought you out of the land of Egypt, out of the house of bondage: You shall have no other gods besides Me" (Exod. 20:2–3). With this, and God's subsequent words, it is clear: The covenant established between God and Israel at Sinai bases the people's observance of divine precepts on God's redemptive role in the Exodus.

> You have seen what I did to the Egyptians, how I bore you on eagles' wings and brought you to Me. Now then, if you will obey Me faithfully and keep My covenant, you shall be My treasured possession among all the peoples. (Exod. 19:4–5)

In this light, scholar of Jewish liturgy Reuven Hammer (1933–2019, United States and Israel) concludes: "Thus it is the Exodus that entitles God to demand the observance of [God's] rules and regulations. Because God brought about the Exodus, God is entitled to ask for Israel's obedience. Thus all of halakhah is based on this premise."[14]

The profound relationship between the Exodus and Jewish law keeps halakhah anchored to Jews' deepest hopes to build a world that rejects oppression and treats each of us as an image of God. A world without law is a world without justice—which looks a lot like the Kingdom of Pharaoh. Liberation from that Egypt—and all other such regimes—demands replacing brute power with the just application of law that reflects the dignity of every human being. Leviticus 19:33–34 exhorts: "When strangers reside with you in your land, you shall not wrong them. The strangers who reside with you shall be to you as your citizens; you shall love each one as yourself, for you were strangers in the land of Egypt; I YHWH am your God."

Indeed, philosopher David Hartman (1931–2013, United States and Israel) coined the term "*halakhic* hope" to explain the gradual struggle to improve the world through following the precepts of Jewish law:

> The giving and acceptance of the Torah does not present a picture of God's single-handed redemption of powerless slaves, nor of unilateral divine fiat ordering primal chaos. Rather, the experience of Sinai is one in which God speaks and [humankind] responds. . . . Hope need not be fueled by romantic dreams; it can be nurtured by feelings of

adequacy to bear the responsibility of becoming a spiritual [person], and by the knowledge that, in spite of failures, I am given a task.[15]

Hartman explains that "a sense of hope emerges from the memory of the command to become holy. . . . Despite human limitations, weaknesses, perversities, and ugliness, we are charged with responsibility for bringing about our own redemption by living out the values of the Torah."[16]

TIME

The liberation from Egypt is so momentous that it redefines the reckoning of time. God tells Moses and Aaron that the month in which the Exodus occurs, *chodesh ha-aviv*, shall be counted as the first month of the year. Originally Aviv referred to the first stage of grain's ripening, when its "ears" are well formed but still soft and green, the stalks standing fresh and verdant in the field;[17] later it came to mean "spring." After the Babylonian exile, the names of the months changed, and Aviv became Nisan.

God further instructs us to celebrate Passover "at its set time from year to year" (Exod. 13:10), meaning at the full moon of the vernal equinox. The complex Jewish calendar we know today—which reckons months by the moon and years by the sun and adds an extra month to the calendar seven out of nineteen years—was created so that Passover would be celebrated "at its set time." Otherwise, Passover, the season of our liberation, would have wandered through the year (as does the Islamic month of Ramadan).

Moreover, the celebration of the Exodus must occur in the proper season because this aligns two profound sources of hope: one that flows from the rebirth of the natural world in the spring and another that draws its power from the yearning for liberation. Greenberg puts it this way:

Biblical language and symbol point to spring as the proper season for deliverance. The rebirth of earth after winter is nature's indication that life overcomes death: Spring is nature's analogue to redemption. Life blossoming, breaking winter's death grip, gives great credence to the human yearning for liberation. A correct reading of the spring season would hear its message of breaking out and life reborn at the biological level simultaneously with an Exodus message of good overcoming evil, of love overpowering death, of freedom and redemption. The Bible envisions a world in which moral and physical states coincide, when nature and history, in harmony, confirm the triumph of life. The Exodus paradigm suggests that the outcome of history will be an eternal spring. Read with a historical/theological hermeneutic, spring is Exodus.[18]

LITURGY AND RITUAL

In the book of Deuteronomy, generally ascribed to the period of King Josiah's reign (640–609 BCE), the liturgical and ritual components of the Exodus begin to grow in significance.[19] When Deuteronomy mandates that farmers bring offerings of their First Fruits to the Temple in Jerusalem, it also prescribes a succinct rendition of the Exodus story, which begins: "A wandering Aramean was my father, and he went down to Egypt . . ." (26:5–10).[20] (Centuries later, this passage would become central to the Passover Haggadah.) Josiah transformed the Passover celebration into a powerful, centralized national festival that he hoped would unify the Southern Kingdom (Judah) and the many immigrants from the Northern Kingdom (Israel) who fled to the South following the Assyrians' destruction of their country in 722 BCE—and it did.[21]

> The king commanded all the people, "Offer the passover sacrifice to YHWH your God as prescribed in this scroll of the covenant." Now the passover sacrifice had not been offered in that manner in the days of the chieftains who ruled Israel, or during the days of the kings of Israel and the kings of Judah. Only in the eighteenth year of King Josiah was such a passover sacrifice offered in that manner to YHWH in Jerusalem. (2 Kings 23:21–23)

The seder as we know it—with its emphasis on telling the Exodus story—emerged as a hope-laden response to the Romans' destruction of the Temple in 70 CE. Historian and Talmud scholar Baruch Bokser (1945–90, United States) writes, "Within the biblical period the memory of the Exodus gave people hope that their imperfect present situation would end and a new liberation would occur, a message that also fit the Jews under Roman domination."[22] Over time, that message would broaden to address the exigencies of exile wherever Jews lived. In words that began to appear in *Haggadot* by the ninth century: "This is the bread of affliction our ancestors ate in the Land of Egypt. . . . This year here, next year in the Land of Israel. Now enslaved, next year free."[23]

More than a millennium later, the movement to free Soviet Jewry introduced a supplement to the Seder:

> This is the "Matzah of Hope." This matzah, which we set aside as a symbol of hope for the Jews of the Soviet Union, reminds us of the indestructible links that exist between us. As we observe this festival of freedom, we know that Soviet Jews are not free to leave without harassment; to learn of their past; to pass on their religious traditions; to learn the languages of their [ancestors]; to train the teachers and rabbis of future generations.[24]

The prayer life of the observant Jew overflows with reminders of the Exodus. The third paragraph of the *Shema*, recited morning and evening, describes the requirement to wear a fringed garment (e.g., a prayer shawl, or tallit) and concludes: "I YHWH am your God, who brought you out of the land of Egypt to be your God: I, your God YHWH" (Num. 15:41).[25] The Torah mandates wearing phylacteries "as a sign upon your hand and as a symbol on your forehead that with a mighty hand YHWH freed us from Egypt" (Exod. 13:16). The daily morning service includes the complete Song at the Sea that Moses and the Israelites sang after safely crossing through the Sea of Reeds. The Grace after Meals also recalls the Exodus, thanking God "for having taken us out . . . from the land of Egypt and freed us from the house of slavery." On the Sabbath, the *Kiddush* (blessing over wine) makes a direct liturgical link between the seventh day and the Exodus: "The Sabbath is the first among the holy festivals that recall the Exodus from Egypt." Likewise, the *Kiddush* for festivals refers to each as a "holy assembly in remembrance of the Exodus from Egypt."[26]

Over the course of Jewish history, these and other repeated encounters with the Exodus helped sustain a beleaguered people's hope that the first liberation would not be the last. Saadia Gaon (882–942), leader of the Jewish community in Babylonia, where many of the liturgical evocations of Egypt evolved, wrote of "the humiliation and the misery" that had befallen the Jews. The many references to the Exodus in the Bible, he explained, are to "remind us of the things we experienced in Egypt," and that God will redeem us again as the prophet Micah promised: "'I will show [Israel] wondrous deeds as in the days when you sallied forth from the land of Egypt' (7:15). . . . We do not expire nor does our courage falter, but we grow in strength and firmness as it says, 'Be strong, and let your heart be firm, all who hope in YHWH'" (Ps. 31:25).[27] (Saadia had a personal connection to the Exodus story. Also known as Saadia ben Yosef al-Fayumi, he was born in a northern Egyptian town called Fayum, which he identified as Pithom, the city Hebrew slaves had built for Pharaoh.[28]) Just about one thousand years later, Irving Greenberg offered a related reason for the Exodus's ubiquity in Jewish tradition: "It is as if the hope would crumble if it were not reaffirmed every few hours."[29]

Despair versus Hope in Midrash and Commentary

Yosef Hayim Yerushalmi, one of the greatest historians of the last century, made an observation that applies to understanding Jewish history in general as well as the Exodus:

> We cannot explore the history of Jewish hope without at the same time exploring the history of Jewish despair. Only when we become painfully aware of the historical depths of Jewish despair, only when we take it seriously, will we begin to realize that Jewish hope is not an historical "given" to be taken for granted, but an historical problem that we have not yet begun to recognize, let alone comprehend.[30]

Likewise, I believe, the story of the Exodus requires that we consider it to be a struggle between despair and hope.[31] A midrash on a classic verse from Proverbs—"Hope deferred sickens the heart" (Prov. 13:12)—highlights the point and explains, "This refers to Pharaoh, upon whom Moses continued to bring plagues, and after each plague Israel thought that they were going to be set free."[32] If the plagues signaled hope that the process of redemption had begun, Pharaoh's refusal to let the Israelites go bred heartsick despair.

BREEDING DESPAIR

Just as hope enhances the prospects for life and survival, despair augments the probability of death and defeat. Any tyrant knows that it's easier to oppress a despairing populace. Indeed, many traditional Jewish sources have viewed Pharaoh's treatment of the Israelites not just as an exercise in cruelty but as a program to break the people's spirit and render them more easily subdued.

In Exodus 1:10, Pharaoh begins to lay out his plan to enslave the Israelites: "Let us deal shrewdly with them, so that they may not increase; otherwise in the event of war they may join our enemies in fighting against us and rise from the ground." The tenth-century midrash Tanḥuma explains what Pharaoh means when he says, "Let us deal shrewdly." Pharaoh had initially gathered the Israelites together, spoken gently to them, and requested that they work for him as a favor. He himself took a basket and trowel and set to making bricks. When the Israelites saw this, they "immediately went quickly, and vigorously applied their skill along with him all the day because they were strong and mighty." When night came, he put taskmasters over them and told them to count the bricks each had made. Then he told them, "This many bricks you shall produce for me each and every day."[33] In other words, for Pharaoh, to deal "shrewdly" with the Israelites meant using their good qualities—their trust and willingness to work hard—against them. This kind of betrayal feeds despair.

Issakhar Solomon Teikhthal (1885–1945), a great Hasidic scholar and teacher who perished in the Holocaust, notes that when someone repays good with evil, he causes a grave spiritual wound. Basic trust leads to the expectation that one good turn deserves another. When you ask someone you have helped to help you and "that person responds with ingratitude, those dashed hopes break one's soul and spirit. . . . And that's how it was in Egypt."[34] When that hope and trust crumble, a vital part of yourself shrivels inside and despair gains the upper hand.

Exodus 1:11 continues: "So they set taskmasters over them to oppress them with forced labor; and they built garrison cities for Pharaoh: Pithom and Rameses." Notably, the Hebrew says, "So they set taskmasters over *him* (*alav*)," not "over them." The Talmud explains: "They brought a brick-mold and hung it around Pharaoh's neck; and every Israelite who complained that he was weak was told, 'Are you weaker than Pharaoh?'"[35] The ostensibly humorous story contains a serious observation: When oppressive regimes systematically seek to undermine the legitimacy of complaint, they weaken opposition. A later midrashic source makes the point more strongly. Pharaoh himself did the work of slaves "to break the spirit of the Israelites. They said, 'If Pharaoh does this labor, how much more so should we?'"[36] The image of Pharaoh as just one of the common people seems absurd. But the strategy—keeping the oppressed off balance and compliant to stave off rebellion—appears in the dictators' playbook from any era.

Another midrash explains that Pithom and Rameses, the garrison cities the Israelites built for Pharaoh, continually collapsed or sank into the ground, requiring the Israelites to rebuild them over and over again. "Work that is in vain causes affliction and exhaustion to the spirit," observes M. A. Mirkin, one of the great modern interpreters of midrash. "Sisyphean labor is one of the most painful punishments."[37]

A few verses later we read: "The Egyptians ruthlessly imposed on the Israelites the various labors they made them perform. Ruthlessly they made life bitter for them with harsh labor at mortar and bricks and with all sorts of tasks in the field" (Exod. 1:13–14). Teikhthal interprets the verses to mean that the Israelites were constantly being given one new job after another and explains "ruthless" in a psychological sense. A new job can be difficult at the beginning, but it becomes much easier once you're used to it. Yet if you get a new job every time you acclimate to the old one, you're struggling all the time. Your mind never has a chance to roam, to experience even that modicum of freedom.

The Maharal of Prague (1525–1609) also reads the verse as describing a program designed to break the Israelites' spirit. The Egyptians created work conditions for the Israelites that were "not fit for human life." The Talmud's elaboration—"They changed men's work for the women and the women's work for the men"—means, according to the Maharal, the taskmasters created not just a state of exhaustion, but one of utter disorientation.[38] Then came "all sorts of tasks in the field"—which many commentators take to imply that the Egyptians consigned the men to work in the fields without ever returning to their homes and their wives. Says the Maharal, "If you reside in your home, even if you work very hard, there is comfort in being in your own home." Given the rabbinic proclivity to speak interchangeably of one's home and wife, the Maharal may be referring to separation from both.[39] All of this amounts to treating the Israelites "as if they are not quite living beings," and so, the Maharal concludes, the Egyptians made life itself loathsome. For him, the last straw in subduing the Israelites' spirit comes with Pharaoh's decrees to kill their sons, who are their "*koach*," their energy, strength, and future.

Rabbinic literature additionally fleshes out the physical and psychological elements of Pharaoh's program to embitter the people's lives. A medieval Yemenite midrash poignantly describes four sources of bitterness: "the inability to conceive children . . . bereavement over children . . . a broken heart . . . and terrible illness. And when the Egyptians enslaved Israel, they caused all of these."[40] Another legend recounts that during the Israelites' enslavement, Pharaoh allowed them one day of rest, Shabbat, when they would read a hidden scroll of Genesis and draw hope from God's promise to redeem Abraham's descendants in Egypt. Once Pharaoh learned of their secret scroll, he intervened: "Let them no longer delight in false words and let them no longer rest on the Sabbath." Books that promise the oppressed hope—and the opportunity to read them—never last long in totalitarian regimes.[41]

HOPE FIGHTS BACK

A few years before his surprising rise to the presidency of Czechoslovakia (1989–92), Vaclav Havel, then a leading Czech dissident, had a bizarre accident. Falling into a sewer, he nearly drowned—which drove him to write about hope:

> Hope is not a prognostication—it's an orientation of the spirit. Each of us must find real, fundamental hope within [ourselves]. You can't delegate that to anyone else. Hope in this deep and powerful sense is not the same as joy when things are going well, or willingness to invest in enterprises that are obviously headed for early success, but rather an ability to work for something to succeed. Hope is definitely not the same thing as optimism. It's not the conviction that something will turn out well, but the certainty that something makes sense, regardless of how it turns out. It is this hope, above all, that gives us

strength to live and to continually try new things, even in conditions that seem as hopeless as ours do, here and now.[42]

Havel's observations seem apt when applied to the battle between despair and hope in Egypt. While Pharaoh's concern that the Israelites will "rise from the ground (aretz)" (Exod. 1:10) is generally understood to mean that the Israelites will rise up and leave the Land of Egypt, a medieval midrash reads aretz literally, as "earth" or "ground," and concludes that "whenever Israel is at the lowest point it rises."[43] A seventeenth-century commentary explains that these words were not actually spoken by Pharaoh, but by the Holy Spirit, to provide comfort to Israel lest the people fall into despair amid the "bitter exile and harsh enslavement." The words "are a remedy for the blows that fall against Israel."[44]

Chaim Tirer (1740–1816), a Hasidic teacher from Chernovitz inspired by the hope embedded in this midrash, uses various metaphors to explain why a fall or difficulty actually helps a person reach greater heights. He compares Israel's situation in Egypt to a bird trapped by hunters that musters all its power to flap its wings and escape. When it breaks free, its wings are beating with such strength that the bird rockets upward to the heavens. Elsewhere, Tirer likens Israel to the righteous person who, according to Proverbs (24:16), falls seven times but always gets right back up. "It's like a person who wants to throw something very, very high into the air. One must bend and reach one's right hand back to make the throw with all one's might. That's how it is when people fall. They fall to the dust but by means of this they rise to the heavens."[45] For Tirer, the fact that the descent into slavery was followed by the ascent to Sinai constitutes the foundation of hope throughout Jewish history. The story of the Exodus teaches us how to hold onto that hope through the ups and downs of our own lives.

The Talmud tells a fascinating story about the battle between hope and despair in relation to Pharaoh's charge to the Egyptians to throw every newborn Israelite male into the Nile:

Upon hearing of Pharaoh's decree to drown newborn Israelite males, Amram, "the greatest man of his generation" [also father of Miriam and the future father of Moses] said, "We are laboring in vain." Why have children if Pharaoh will kill them? So he divorces Yocheved, his wife. And the rest of the Israelite husbands follow suit. Miriam confronts her father. "Pharaoh decreed against the males but you decree against the males and females. . . . In the case of the wicked Pharaoh perhaps his decree will be fulfilled, perhaps not, whereas in your case, because you are so pious, your decree will certainly be followed." Whereupon Amram remarries Yocheved and the rest of the men take their wives back.[46]

Miriam bases her argument on logic, on an appeal to her father's ego, but also on hope: While Pharaoh's decree might be carried out, perhaps it will not. For Amram, the future is determined; for Miriam, it remains open. Where Amram sees certainty and feels despair, Miriam sees possibility. Amram seems to have forgotten the two midwives who'd refused to carry out Pharaoh's earlier order to kill the male infants they delivered—which, in fact, incited Pharaoh to charge "all his people" to throw every newborn Israelite male into the Nile. Still, their example gives Miriam hope that in this case, too, Pharaoh's order will not be followed. She manages to restore her father's hope that regardless of the steep odds, siring children still makes sense.

The Talmud continues the tale:

As a child, Miriam prophesied that her mother would give birth to a son who would redeem Israel. When he was born, light filled the room. Amram kissed Miriam on the head saying, "Your prophecy has been fulfilled." When they threw him into the river [in the basket] he slapped her on the head and said, "Where is your prophecy?" And thus it is written, "And his sister stationed herself at a distance, to learn what would [become of] him" (Exod. 2:4)—to know what would become of her prophecy.

In a continuation of the drama of hope versus despair, Miriam has a vision that her family will contribute the leadership on which the people's redemption from Egypt depends. With Moses' birth, the bright light of hope fills the room—Amram soars. When Moses' mother floats him down the Nile, a devastated Amram crashes. Not Miriam, however. She follows her dream, standing by, ready to help keep it alive. Miriam, the youthful girl, embodies the hope her father seems to have lost.[47]

Modern commentators have likewise described the hope expressed by Moses' mother, Yocheved, in conceiving and bearing a child in such a perilous time. Samson Raphael Hirsch (1808–88, Germany), one of the intellectual forebears of Modern Orthodoxy, urges us to "perceive the anxiety wrapped in hope, the glimmer of hope shimmering through the fear" Yocheved would have had "in such a time of terror."[48] Writer and Jewish educator Erica Brown remarks on Yocheved's notable reaction to Moses' birth:

> The mother of this child sees what others cannot. She sees hope where others see only despair. She sees new life. She sees a future. She, too, makes a pronouncement about the birth: *ki tov*—it "is good'" (Exod. 2:2). That child is Moses, future savior of the Jewish people, who does create a new vision of Jewish life. Through his leadership, Jews move from being a tribal slave entity to being a free nation with their own homeland. That creation is presaged by two words of hope at a time of persecution: *ki tov*.[49]

As Brown notes, God repeatedly utters these same words, *ki tov*, throughout the Creation. Human beings and God share the role of creators; they also share the hopes attendant upon bringing new life into the world.

Many midrashim celebrate the implicit hopes of Miriam and Yocheved. Rabbi Akiva goes further, asserting that "Israel was only redeemed because of the righteous women of that generation." His tale celebrates the power of hope-in-action. To thwart Pharaoh's genocidal plan for the Israelites, the women fill their jugs with fish, pretty themselves up, go out to the fields where their husbands are working, feed them, seduce them (under apple trees), and nine months later return to give birth. Song of Songs 8:5 provides the proof text for this midrash: "Under the apple tree I roused you; it was there your mother conceived you, there she who bore you conceived you."[50] Although this midrash is well known, it should be even more so because it underlies perhaps the most popular item on the seder plate: *charoset*. According to the Talmud, that's why *charoset* should be tart, to remind us of the apple trees in this midrash, under which the righteous Israelite women of that generation conceived.[51] Redemption hinges on hope, on the capacity to envision an alternative reality and the willingness to bring it to fruition.

Jewish tradition sees Moses' mother and sister as exemplars of hope, and it views Moses in the same light. One story recounts a dream of Pharaoh's that his adviser interprets as foretelling the birth of an Israelite male—referred to as the "hope of Israel" (*tikvat Yisrael*)—who would destroy Egypt and liberate the Israelites. To thwart this, the adviser recommends drowning all the newborn Israelite males.[52] A tenth-century midrash describes God's initial appeal to Moses at the Burning Bush: "For you Israel has waited. For you Israel has hoped."[53] A third legend holds that Moses had ten names, one of which was Yekutiel. Rearranging the Hebrew letters, the midrash reads the name as *yikavu El*, "they will hope in God," and explains that "Moses gave the children [of Israel] hope in their father in Heaven. And at the Red Sea, when Moses told the people not to fear, they had hope in his words."[54]

Moses' effort to persuade God not to destroy the Israelites after the incident of the Golden Calf provides a powerful example of a high-hope leader in action. "But Moses implored (*va'yichal*) his God YHWH, saying, 'Let not Your anger, YHWH, blaze forth against Your people, whom You delivered from the land of Egypt with great power and with a mighty hand'" (Exod. 32:11). Translations of the word *va'yichal* have differed—"placated," "besought," or "prayed" among them. Rashi understood the word to convey a hope-filled prayer, connecting *va'yichal* to *tochelet* as in "Hope [*tochelet*] deferred sickens the heart" (Prov. 13:12).[55]

In arguing with God, Moses takes aim at God's ego, as it were, suggesting that God's reputation would suffer if the newly freed Israelites were to meet destruction in the desert. The argument offers a classic illustration of what philosopher Joseph Albo (1380–1444, Spain) deemed a central source of hope over the ages: "One hopes that God will help one because God has been in the habit of providing help before, and if God failed one now, God's glory would suffer."[56]

When Moses returns to the Israelites and explains his effort to restore them to God's favor, he says, "*perhaps* I may win forgiveness for your sin" (Exod. 32:30). Abraham's use of the word "perhaps" gave voice to his hope that God would spare the people of Sodom and Gomorrah; Moses' use of it here expresses his hope that now God will spare Abraham's sinful descendants.

"Hope and the ability to see a better future and create it," writes Erica Brown, "have been the underlying strength of Jewish leadership for millennia."[57] A Harvard Business School study on leadership similarly concluded: "The overall positive emotional tone crafted by resonant leaders is characterized by a sense of hope."[58]

Putting Exodus Memories into Practice

The linkage of the Exodus with hope does, however, require qualification. For one, what ultimate good does hope serve if the hope of the oppressed is not solely to be free but also to exact revenge on their oppressors? The book of Proverbs cautions, "The earth shudders ... [when] a slave ... becomes king" (30:21–22). In this vein, the French psychiatrist Frantz Fanon (1925–61) depicted France's occupation of Algeria.

> The town belonging to the colonized people ... is a hungry town, starved of bread, of meat, of shoes, of coal, of light. The native town is a crouching village, a town on its knees, a town wallowing in the mire. The colonized [person] is an envious [person]. And this the settler knows very well; when their glances meet, [the colonizer] ascertains bitterly, always on the defensive, "They want to take our place." It is true, for there is no native who does not dream at least once a day of [taking over] ... the settler's place. [The native] is in fact ready at a moment's notice to exchange the role of the quarry for that of the hunter. The native is an oppressed person whose permanent dream is to become the persecutor.[59]

This understanding underlies the Bible's repeated exhortation to show empathy to the stranger by remembering that you were enslaved in Egypt. Variations of this commandment recur some three dozen times, making it the Torah's most frequently repeated injunction. Among them are:

> And you shall not oppress a stranger, for you know the feelings of the stranger, having yourselves been strangers in the land of Egypt. (Exod. 23:9)

Six days you shall labor and do all your work, the seventh day is a sabbath of your God YHWH; you shall not do any work—you, your son or your daughter, your male or female slave, your ox or your ass, or any of your cattle, or the stranger in your settlements, so that your male and female slave may rest as you do. Remember that you were a slave in the land of Egypt and your God YHWH freed you from there with a mighty hand and an outstretched arm. (Deut. 5:13–15)

If a fellow Hebrew man—or woman—is sold to you, he shall serve you six years, and in the seventh year you shall set him free. When you set him free, do not let him go empty-handed: Furnish him out of the flock, threshing floor, and vat, with which your God YHWH has blessed you. Bear in mind that you were slaves in the land of Egypt and your God YHWH redeemed you; therefore I enjoin this commandment upon you today. (Deut. 15:12–15)

Even more remarkably, Deuteronomy forbids harboring hatred against Egyptians: "You shall not abhor an Egyptian, for you were a stranger in that land" (23:8).[60]

The Torah implicitly understands that when an individual or a people has suffered, the memory of that experience is liable to induce vengeance unless strenuous efforts are made to inculcate empathy. Hillel's response to a heathen who wants to learn the whole Torah while standing on one foot reinforces this point: "What is hateful to you, do not do to your neighbor. That is the whole Torah. The rest is commentary. Now go and learn it."[61] Hillel does not cite the "Golden Rule" from Leviticus 19:18, "Love your neighbor as yourself." He pointedly focuses on the dark side of human emotion, on that which we have experienced as hateful, and urges us to curb the reflexive desire to inflict that very wound on others.

A third-century midrash shines additional light on how we should best apply our memories of the Exodus. God's instructions concerning the final plague, the slaying of the Egyptian firstborn, contain a loophole: God tells the Israelites not to leave their homes (Exod. 12:22) but says nothing about whether or not to let others enter. The midrash poses a hypothetical scenario: What if an Egyptian and an Israelite were in the same bed throughout the last plague? According to the midrash, the Egyptian would die but not the Israelite, because Scripture says, "I will pass over *you*" (Exod. 12:13).[62] Exodus Rabbah, a medieval midrash, developed the same case to teach a more empathetic lesson. "When the Egyptians heard that God would strike down their firstborn, some were afraid and some not. Those who were afraid brought their firstborn to an Israelite and said: 'Please allow him to pass this night with you'" (Exod. Rabbah 18:2).

I've taught this midrash for well over a decade to audiences eager for texts to discuss at their Passover seders. I ask people to make arguments for and against giving the Egyptian children sanctuary, and to put the matter to a vote. Invariably the arguments in favor of saving the children come more easily, for example, "I'm a mother. These Egyptian women are mothers. We're the only hope they have for their children. I can't say 'No' to another mother pleading for her child's life." The vote virtually always goes in this direction. Then I ask people what they think the midrash says about this, and again, audiences regularly expect that the Israelites *do* take in the Egyptian children. They are correct:

When midnight struck, God smote all the firstborn. *As for those who took asylum in the houses of the Israelites*, God passed between the Israelites and the Egyptians, killing the Egyptians and leaving Israelites alive. When the Jews awoke at midnight, they found the Egyptians dead among their surviving firstborn.

The midrash teaches that sometimes God's plans may trump human intervention, but we are not free to desist from trying to intercede—in this case on the side of empathy. The midrash may seem radical, but it comports well with Jewish tradition. Many sources condemn Noah for failing to challenge God's plan to destroy the world, the innocent along with the guilty, and laud Abraham for arguing with God over the fate of Sodom and Gomorrah even though his intervention did not save the cities. Likewise, we celebrate Moses for trying—and in this case succeeding—to persuade God not to destroy the Israelites after the Golden Calf incident. Often we don't know if our actions will bear fruit—which is why we have to act in hope that they will.

The Exodus, therefore, speaks to more than any one people's hope for liberation. It nourishes hope of breaking the chain of vengeance forged by memories of victimization and of building societies that harness the remembrance of powerlessness to foster empathy and the celebration of human dignity. Read this way, the story of the Exodus exemplifies the kind of narrative that philosopher Richard Rorty believes helps strengthen what he calls "social hope": "that some day we shall be willing and able to treat the needs of all human beings with the respect and consideration with which we treat the needs of those closest to us, those whom we love."[63]

Conclusion

The story of the Exodus has evolved into Judaism's master story of hope, coloring practically every aspect of Judaism, from fundamental justifications of Jewish law to the Hebrew calendar to liturgy and ritual. The story has provided fertile ground for a rich literature wrestling with both hope and despair over the ages. More than that, the Exodus has supplied the interpretive lens the Jewish people has long used to understand the ups and downs of its history—"from slavery to freedom, from sorrow to happiness, from mourning to celebration, and from darkness to great light," as the Passover Haggadah puts it. Jews have learned to see their history as an Exodus-shaped pattern of alternating periods of exile and redemption that through hope and work will culminate in a positive ending.

And so Vanessa Ochs's *The Passover Haggadah: A Biography* enjoins us to imagine holding in our hands

> an object claiming to be a Haggadah of the future. However curious it may be, you know that it is a Haggadah. How so? Because it celebrates an old story of miraculous liberation. Even though the hope that divine, human, or combined efforts will bring about a more complete liberation has gone unfulfilled for so very long, it keeps on hoping.[64]

5

The Covenant

HOPE IN ISRAEL'S RELATIONSHIP WITH GOD

God's covenantal consciousness has transformed history from a divine drama into a story of human achievement. Rather than hold God responsible for the world we live in, a covenantal perception of history understands that divine self-limitation has presented us with a world waiting to be shaped by human action. . . . Covenantal consciousness means we admit that the darkness is present—but it is present as episodes in human history; it can never be allowed to wipe out our hope for a covenantal future.

—David Hartman, *From Defender to Critic*

Introduction

Covenant describes a relationship between two parties, with obligations binding both.[1] In the ancient Near East, kings and vassals entered into covenants. Israelite culture was the first to give rise to the notion of *God* entering—and being bound by—a covenantal relationship.

In the covenant between God and the People of Israel, God promises a bright future for Israel, the people pledge loyalty to divine law, and both parties vow to stay in relationship with one another. God and Israel both live in what can be called covenantal hope, the aspiration that each will honor its promises and that their relationship will prove enduring. For Israel, covenantal hope implies that, regardless of whatever suffering the people endure, redemption lies ahead.

In rabbinic thought, Israel's suffering reflects punishment for straying from covenantal obligations, and redemption arises through repentance and return to God's commandments. Scholar of Hebrew literature Alan Mintz (1947–2017, United States) asserts that such a covenantal reading of Jewish history provides a powerful source of hope:

It was not just that national suffering became intelligible; in the depths of suffering there was a further basis of hope: God in . . . wrath would punish, but not destroy utterly. The relationship was at bottom unconditional and contained an element of *ḥesed*, "covenant love," which insured that there would always be a remnant and always a restoration.[2]

Yet the concept of covenant in Jewish thought has evolved far beyond the early notion of God's election of Israel for special reward in exchange for fealty to divine commandments. Some Jewish thinkers now understand covenant as a partnership with God. Others go further, defining covenant as the human assumption of responsibility for actualizing the kind of world the Bible tells us God had intended to create in the first place. And some Jewish thinkers now argue that the single, exclusive, obligatory covenant between God and Israel has been superseded by multiple voluntary covenants.

This chapter explores the expression of covenantal hope from two perspectives: the daily Jewish morning prayer service and the travails of Jewish history—ancient and modern.

Covenantal Hope in the Morning Liturgy

There was never a question in my mind about saying *Kaddish* for my mother when she died in 2010. I was just as sure of something else—that after eleven months I'd stop attending the morning minyan. Much to my surprise, when the time was up, I kept going every weekday morning. The minyan proved extremely supportive, and I realized my ongoing participation would help me create this important experience for others.

Over the years, I came to see the morning liturgy as a tapestry of metaphors that strengthen covenantal hope against capitulation to aloneness and despair. Below I focus on two such metaphors: covenant as memory (in the *Birkhot ha-Shachar* and *Pesukei de-Zimra*, or Morning Blessings and Verses of Song) and covenant as petition (in the *Amidah*, or Standing Prayer).[3] These metaphors, so deeply embedded in Jewish prayer, have sustained covenantal hope for our ancestors, and they can for us as well.

COVENANT AS MEMORY: MORNING
BLESSINGS AND VERSES OF SONG

Gabriel Marcel describes hope as "a memory of the future."[4] The Morning Blessings and Verses of Song within the morning liturgy contain an array of biblical passages and prayers that recall key moments in the covenantal relationship between God and Israel in order to help us look forward to the future with hope. Here we'll sample a few of these passages.

The Akedah: The theme of memory appears near the beginning of the traditional morning service with a reading of the Binding of Isaac (Gen. 22:1–19) — as we've seen, a story full of hope.[5] Toward the end of the story, God reaffirms the covenant:

> Because you have done this and have not withheld your son, your favored one, I will bestow My blessing upon you and make your descendants as numerous as the stars of heaven and the sands on the seashore; and your descendants shall seize the gates of their foes. All the nations of the earth shall bless themselves by your descendants, because you have obeyed My command. (Gen. 22:16–18)

When read on weekday mornings, this biblical narrative is preceded by one prayer and followed by another in which worshippers repeatedly call on God to remember in their favor Abraham's willingness to sacrifice his son.[6] The prayer following the *Akedah* concludes: "Fulfill, YHWH our God, what you have promised us through Moses Your servant: 'I will remember My covenant with Jacob; I will remember also My covenant with Isaac, and also My covenant with Abraham; and I will remember the land'" (Lev. 26:42). Here, worshippers express the hope that God's remembering the merit of the ancestors, *zekhut avot*, will arouse God's compassion for them.[7]

"Master of All Worlds": We next come to a prayer known from its opening words as "Master of All Worlds" (*Ribbon Kol Ha-olamim*), which suggests that, in contrast to the hope created by memory, forgetting life's purpose and where we fit into the scheme of things easily generates despair. In language that evokes the dour outlook of Ecclesiastes, "Master of All Worlds" initially expresses humanity's utter worthlessness: "For most of our doings are worthless, and the days of our life are vain in Your sight,

and humankind is not far above the beast, for all is vanity [or futility]."[8] Compared to God, even the wisest, most intelligent, and most famous among us don't make much of an impression.

But the prayer does not end here. It continues: "However, we are Your people, the people of Your covenant. . . . Happy are we! How good is our destiny."[9] Covenant transforms futility into purpose. We are not only heirs to God's promise for a bright future; we are covenantal partners in bringing that future into the present. From the dullness of an otherwise tedious existence, from the worthlessness of self-absorption, covenant carves a road that stretches forward to a destiny worth embracing, worth working to fulfill. Remembering the covenant orients us to the future, the target of hope.

"You Are Adonai Our God": Soon after "Master of All Worlds," the liturgy returns to the previously mentioned theme of God remembering the covenant and the Land of Israel. A prayer that begins "You Are YHWH Our God" (*Atah Hu YHWH Eloheinu*) calls on God to "gather those who hope in You under Your protecting presence" and then asks God to fulfill a divine promise recorded in the conclusion to the (late seventh-century BCE) book of Zephaniah: "At that time I will gather you, and at [that] time I will bring you [home]. For I will make you renowned and famous among all the peoples on earth, when I restore your fortunes before their very eyes—said YHWH" (Zeph. 3:20). Divine restoration of the people to the land constitutes one of Judaism's essential hopes.[10]

An Anthology of Psalms: The next section of the morning service, *Pesukei de-Zimra*, or Verses of Song, begins with a selection of verses from Psalms that includes an unusual statement about hope and covenant:

We set our hope on YHWH . . . our help and shield (33:20). . . . May we enjoy, O YHWH, Your faithful care, as we have put our hope in You (33:22).[11] Show us, O YHWH, Your faithfulness; grant us Your deliverance (85:8).

Psalms 33:22 asserts something radical: We deserve God's covenantal care not because we have observed God's commandments, but because we have hoped in God: "May we enjoy, O YHWH, Your faithful care, as we have put our hope in You" (Ps. 33:22). Here, our part of the covenantal bargain becomes maintaining hope that God will fulfill the divine half of the covenantal agreement.

Can that be true? Can we actually merit God's kindness simply on the basis of hope?

A thirteenth-century midrash answers in the affirmative: "Israel has no merit aside from hope. But they merit salvation as a reward for their hope."[12] Connecting that midrash to the aforementioned verse from Psalms (33:22), the Hasidic scholar Issakhar Solomon Teikhthal (1885–1945, Hungary and Czechoslovakia) writes that even if we have no merit for God to help us, we deserve God's faithful care as a reward because "'we have put our hope in You.' Understand this!"[13]

It may be that keeping God's commandments is the easy part. In light of Jewish history, managing to hope in God may prove more difficult and therefore merits greater reward. *Metzudat David*, an eighteenth-century commentary on Psalms, puts it this way: "According to the [extent of] hope, so will be the [extent of God's] lovingkindness."[14] Here the measure of reward hinges not on the extent of fealty to the divine commandments, as one might expect, but on the extent of Israel's hope in God.

Nehemiah's Prayer: Toward the end of Verses of Song we find two more evocations of covenant, both in a public prayer delivered by Nehemiah, a leader of the community that returned from exile in Babylonia in 538 BCE. Nehemiah recalls Israel's sacred history, beginning with God's promise to Abraham that his descendants would inherit the land of Canaan. "And You kept Your word, for You are righteous. . . . You made a name for Yourself that endures to this day" (Neh. 9:8, 10).[15] Then Nehemiah describes God's redemption of the Israelites from Egypt—setting the stage for the Song at the Sea that recounts God's salvation of the Israelites at the Red Sea.

Essentially, Nehemiah is attesting that God's covenantal promise to Abraham—that his descendants will be enslaved in Egypt but will return to the land as free people—has been kept, and not just for the Israelites who left Egypt, but again in Nehemiah's generation, with the return from Babylonia. Hope in God's trustworthiness as a covenantal partner is therefore well placed. God remembers those promises, and so do we. And when memory—God's or our own—seems to falter, the liturgy stands ready with a list of daily reminders.

The initial sections of the morning prayer service confirm what diverse observers have noted about the relationship between memory and hope. The late Shane Lopez, a particularly important researcher on the psychology of hope, observed: "We build our hopes from memories."[16] The renowned historian Yosef Yerushalmi thus explained the relation between the Jews' sense of the past and hope for the future: "The Jewish people, even so-called ordinary Jews, had access to a vast and unique reservoir of the past." They also possessed a way of interpreting historical events that gave them "the ability to endure and overcome them, to see beyond them."[17]

Yerushalmi also notes that Judaism did not use this "reservoir of the past" to inculcate a love for the study of history but to remember "above all God's acts of intervention in history and [humankind's] response to them."[18] In other words, it is the history of God and Israel's covenantal relationship that must be recalled. Remembrance of God's covenantal saving acts in the past supports the hope that the future will see them recur. Historically, that hope has sustained Israel's willingness to honor its covenantal obligations.[19]

In a theology that doesn't expect the return of God's hand to the stage of history, the burden for fulfilling covenantal hope shifts to us. As theologian Arthur Green (1941–, United States) puts it, "To stand in covenant with God is [to] accept a challenge to regard one's entire life as a channel for bringing divine presence and blessing into the world."[20]

COVENANT AS PETITION: THE *AMIDAH*

One party to a covenant has the right to ask the other to fulfill the terms of their mutual agreement. That's what we encounter in what is considered the core of Jewish prayer: the *Amidah*, "the standing" prayer, also known as the *Shemoneh Esrei*, or "Eighteen Benedictions" (though it actually includes nineteen benedictions: three opening blessings of praise, thirteen petitionary blessings, and three concluding blessings of thanksgiving).[21] When reciting the *Amidah* three times daily and in modified form on the Sabbath and all festivals, the People of Israel ask God to perform, as it were, according to their covenantal arrangement.[22]

"A cluster of approved, one might say canonical, loci of hope have endured in these basic units of [the *Amidah*] prayer for almost two millennia," says professor of Jewish philosophy Alan Mittleman.[23] The language of hope and covenant run throughout the prayer.

Opening Blessing: The opening benediction, known as *Avot*, or "Ancestors," addresses the God of Abraham, of Isaac, and of Jacob (with egalitarian prayer books adding Sarah, Rebecca, Rachel, and Leah), "who remembers the piety of our ancestors, and who brings a redeemer to their descendants for the sake of [God's] name in love."[24] Scholar of Jewish liturgy Lawrence A. Hoffman explains that *Avot* "establishes our covenantal claim on God, whom we approach knowing that we are spiritual descendants of the biblical ancestors who established the covenant in the first place."[25]

Petitionary Blessings: The *Amidah*'s thirteen petitions express a wide range of hopes, personal and collective—the hopes for wisdom, repentance, forgiveness, deliverance, healing, fertility of the land, ingathering of the exiles, restoration of just judges, punishment of slanderers and enemies of God, reward of the righteous, the rebuilding of Jerusalem, ultimate salvation, and God's hearing our prayers.

The twelfth benediction calls on the Divine to take away all hope from God's enemies: the persecutors of Israel. As such, the prayer gives voice to the vital importance of hope: Deprive God's enemies—or anyone else—of all vestiges of hope, and they will shrivel.[26]

The fifteenth blessing, coming on the heels of one calling for the rebuilding of Jerusalem and the reestablishment of the Davidic line of kingship, also stresses the theme of hope:

> Speedily cause the offspring of Your servant David to flourish, and let his glory be exalted by Your help, for we hope for Your salvation all day. Blessed are You, YHWH, who causes salvation to flourish.[27]

What precisely is the hope in the expression "we hope for Your salvation"? The phrase is the plural of one from Genesis 49:18, toward the middle of Jacob's deathbed testament. Both here and in Genesis, the Hebrew contains an ambiguity: "Your salvation" can mean salvation *by* God, as we generally read it, or the salvation *of* God.

The kabbalist Moses Alshekh (1508–93, Safed) favored the latter reading, pointing to the tradition in Jewish thought that sees both God and humanity as in need of redemption, and the two dependent on one another for it.[28]

A fifth- or sixth-century midrash put it this way: "God said to Israel, 'The time of *My* redemption is in your hand, and the time of *your* redemption is in My hand."[29] In a broken world, God and humanity suffer and redeem one another.

Blessings of Thanks: Hope returns in the eighteenth benediction, which reprises the covenantal language of the *Amidah*'s opening blessing, "our God and our ancestors' God," and thanks God for mercy without end—evening, morning, and afternoon. "You are merciful, for Your kindness never ends," the prayer concludes, "You have always been our hope."[30] Simcha Mordechai Ziskind Broide (1824–98, Lithuania), a leader of the Musar movement (which explored the realms of ethical and spiritual development), explained this passage with a twist: "Because You have always been our hope, it follows that Your kindness never ends."[31] Echoing ideas we've encountered earlier, Broide implies that receiving divine kindness is a reward not for the fulfillment of commandments but for the hope one places in God.

The conclusion of the nineteenth and final benediction expresses what might well be the Jewish people's most fervent hope—peace: "May it please You to bless Your people Israel with peace at all times and hours. Blessed are You, O [YHWH], Who blesses Your people Israel with peace."[32] In the Bible the hope for "peace" has definite covenantal overtones. A number of times the Bible refers to God establishing a covenant of peace with Israel. Moreover, the word *shalom*, "peace," makes its first biblical appearance when God enters into a covenant with Abraham, promising that he will go to his "ancestors in peace," that is, he will die in peace (Gen. 15:15).[33] This benediction also brings to mind a passage in Jeremiah: "For I surely know the plans that I have devised for you, said [YHWH], plans for peace and not for evil, to give you a future and hope. And you shall call Me and go and pray to Me, and I will listen to you" (Jer. 29:11–12).[34]

Given the travails of Jewish history, maintaining allegiance to the covenant, indeed making this theme so central to Jewish liturgy, stands as a monument to the Jewish people's unrelenting hope. It's not a stretch to say that the morning liturgy—and Jewish prayer in general—gives a hearty voice to Jewish hopes in God to *persuade* what must often have seemed like a distant or angry God to show up, as it were, to honor divine covenantal obligations and bestow a measure of faithful care on Israel.

To pray the morning liturgy is to immerse ourselves in what David Hartman called "covenantal consciousness": "We admit that darkness is present—but it is present as episodes in human history, it can never be allowed to wipe out our hope for a covenantal future."[35] We now turn to some of those episodes of darkness, ancient and modern.

Covenantal Hope and the Ancient Trials of History

We can read the Bible as an ongoing dialogue between covenantal partners, God and Israel. For example, in the book of Leviticus, God anticipates that Israel will inevitably sin and suffer punishment. But even then, the covenantal promise will endure.

> For the land shall be forsaken of them . . . while they atone for their iniquity; for the abundant reason that they rejected My rules and spurned My laws. Yet, even then, when they [Israel] are in the land of their enemies, I will not reject [*m'astim*] them or spurn them so as to destroy them, annulling My covenant with them: for I YHWH am their God. I will remember in their favor the covenant with the ancients, whom I freed from the land of Egypt. (Lev. 26:43–45)

In Psalms, the dialogue continues, with protests that the People of Israel suffer despite their faithfulness to the covenant:

> The wicked laid a snare for me, but I did not stray from Your precepts (119:110). You are my concealment and my shield, I put hope in Your word (119:114). Support me according to Your promise that I may live, disgrace me not in my hope (119:116). All this came upon us yet we have not forgotten You, and we have not been false to Your covenant (44:18). Forget not the congregation of Your poor forever (74:19). Look upon the covenant (74:20).[36]

Hope stands as the bridge between the covenantal partners. When Israel rejects its covenantal obligations, God metes out punishment but hopes for Israel's return. And when God seems to fall short, Israel confronts God and hopes for the resumption of divine favor. Hope preserves the covenantal relationship and allows the partners to remain in dialogue.

The response to the destruction of the First Temple in 586 BCE and the ensuing exile of key sectors of the populace to Babylonia provides the ancient template for how Judaism confronts the challenge of maintaining covenantal hope when catastrophe strikes. We find these responses in the books of Lamentations, Jeremiah, Zechariah, and Ezra, among others.

LAMENTATIONS

The book of Lamentations clearly describes the devastation of Jerusalem in covenantal terms: "YHWH has afflicted her for her many transgressions. . . . Has carried out the decree that [YHWH] ordained long ago" (Lam. 1:5, 2:17). But, just as clearly, Lamentations questions the severity of divine punishment. God's wrath has brought starvation: Women eat "their new-born babes" (2:20); dead bodies litter the streets. The covenant itself seems to hang in the balance: "See, O YHWH, and behold to whom You have done this! . . . And when I cry and plead, [YHWH] shuts out my prayer" (2:20, 3:8). Is covenantal hope dead? The answer emerges close to the center of the book:

> I forgot what happiness was. I thought my strength and hope had perished before YHWH (3:17–18). . . . But this I do call to mind, therefore I have hope: The kindness of YHWH has not ended, [YHWH's] mercies are not spent. They are renewed every morning—Ample is Your grace! "YHWH is my portion," I say with a full heart. Therefore I will hope in [YHWH]. YHWH is good to those who hope in [YHWH], to the one who seeks [YHWH]. It is good to hope patiently till rescue comes from YHWH (3:21–26). . . . Let [a person] put [their] mouth to the dust [an ancient gesture of submission], perhaps there is hope (3:29). . . . For YHWH does not reject forever, but first afflicts, then pardons in . . . abundant kindness (3:31–32).[37]

In the midst of such catastrophe, memories of God's goodness can easily fade. Unlike prophetic books from this period, in Lamentations God offers no consolation. In fact, God does not even speak. Lamentations' short discourse on hope ends honestly: "*Perhaps* there is hope" (3:29).[38]

That "perhaps" did not escape the early fourth-century talmudic sage Rav Ammi. When he came to this verse [and its depiction of complete submission to God] he wept and said, "All this, and only, 'perhaps?'"[39]

Lamentations ends on an admittedly disconsolate note. Even while the text alludes to God's ancient promise from Leviticus 26:44, "I [God] will not reject them [m'astim]," Lamentations concludes with these grim words: "For truly, You have rejected us [m'astanu], bitterly raged against us" (5:22). Though God may have rejected the People of Israel—and indeed, the accusation of rejection is addressed directly to God, "You have rejected us"—the author of Lamentations refuses to reject God. The covenantal relationship, including its sometimes angry dialogue, endures, despite God's seeming breach.

A midrash on this verse from Lamentations resurrects the theme of hope. "Rabbi Shimon ben Lakish said: 'If there is rejection there is no hope; but if there is anger there is hope, because whoever is angry may in the end be appeased.'"[40]

The contemporary scholar Iain William Provan notes that although the people of Jerusalem suffered greatly, they were not completely destroyed: "The covenant between God and [God's] people is still intact, and therefore hope remains that things will improve." Nonetheless, Lamentations' treatment of hope remains "a mixture of hope and despair, and it ends in a plea to God which leaves us balanced on a knife edge between the two."[41]

A later custom involving the book of Lamentations tries to nudge this balance toward hope. The reading of this book, prescribed on the Ninth of Av, the day commemorating the destruction of the First and Second Temples, does not end with the last verse and its vision of a rejecting and angry God. According to tradition, after reciting the last verse, the reader returns to the penultimate verse, which pleads for rapprochement: "Take us back, O YHWH, to Yourself, and let us come back; renew our days as of old!" (5:21). In lieu of rewriting sacred texts, at key moments in the liturgical year, Jewish custom refuses to conclude on a note of hopelessness.[42]

JEREMIAH AND ZECHARIAH

Prophesying about exile and return from Babylonia following the destruction of the First Temple, both Jeremiah and Zechariah sought to renew covenantal hope in the face of calamity, dispensing the divine consolation missing from Lamentations. Jeremiah exhorts:

> Thus said YHWH: Restrain your voice from weeping, your eyes from shedding tears; for there is a reward for your labor—declares YHWH: They shall return from the enemy's land. And there is hope for your future—declares YHWH: Your children shall return to their country. (31:16–17)... See, a time is coming—declares YHWH—when I will make a new covenant with the House of Israel and the House of Judah. It will not be like the covenant I made with their fathers, when I took them by the hand to lead them out of the land of Egypt, a covenant which they broke, though I espoused them—declares YHWH. But such is the covenant I will make with the House of Israel after these days—declares YHWH: I will put My Teaching into their inmost being and inscribe it upon their hearts. (31:31–33)

Jeremiah's hope rests not only on the exiles' return home, but on a new covenant that God will implant so deeply within the people that they will no longer desire—or perhaps even be able—to stray from it.

Zechariah's understanding of the covenant is more traditional than Jeremiah's, but he too illustrates the affirmation of covenantal hope amid the Babylonian exile. He relays that God says:

> You, too, through the blood of the covenant, I have freed your prisoners from the waterless pit. Go back to the fortress, you prisoners of hope. This very day proclaiming, double I will give back to you. (9:11–12)[43]

According to Zechariah, God remembers Israel's acceptance of the covenant at Sinai and thus intends to rescue the people from their captivity (i.e., "the waterless pit") and return them to a place of safety ("the fortress").

Most commentators understand "prisoners of hope" as the Jewish population exiled—as if imprisoned—in Babylonia, who maintained hope that God would return them to Israel. We may dispute Zechariah's notion that those who have suffered excruciating loss can be compensated by double repayment. But Zechariah's point is that, even amid the greatest pain, the covenantal relationship sustains such a compelling sense of hope that Israel is virtually imprisoned by it, powerless to relinquish it.

EZRA

As events would unfold, Israel's hope proves well founded. After some seventy years of exile, Cyrus conquers Babylonia and releases the Jews. A remnant returns to Israel, renews their commitment to the covenant, and begins construction of the Second Temple.

Upon their return, the people face a crisis: It turns out there has been extensive intermarriage among the remnant who stayed in the Land of Israel. Fearing divine retribution, Ezra, one of the community leaders, dons sackcloth and ashes. After much weeping, eventually a community member speaks up: "There is still hope for Israel, despite this. Now then, let us make a covenant with our God" to mend our ways (Ezra 10:2–3). The pledge to renew the covenant by returning to God's ways assures hope for the future.

Indeed, when times have been most bleak, hope has rested on the covenantal dialogue itself, and not on the immediate prospect of darkness lifting to light. The abiding trust that God will ultimately honor the covenant has sustained Jewish hopes over the ages. The key to maintaining the relationship has been based not only on the hope that God's anger will relent; it has been grounded in Israel's ultimate willingness to construct a narrative in which catastrophe is accepted in a covenantal framework: as divine punishment for Israel's sinful ways.

The refusal to surrender covenantal hope even in the face of exile and divine threats to wipe out the people impresses Bible scholar Walter Brueggemann as one of Israel's most remarkable qualities:

> What most strikes one about Israel in its scatteredness is its resilient refusal to accept the exile as the culmination of its destiny. . . . Hope belongs characteristically to Israel, and its most acute practice occurs in exile. . . . As a scattered community, terminated by YHWH, Israel refused to accept the scattering as its final destiny. Israel believed and insisted, in sadness and in protest but also in anticipation, that the God who scattered would also gather. If this is correct, then we may say that Israel hoped beyond the hope or intention even of YHWH,

who had no such hope or intention for Israel. That is, Israel's courage and shrillness, its defiance of its present circumstances, talked YHWH into something YHWH had not yet entertained or imagined or intended.[44]

Historically, the resilience of its covenantal hope has enabled Israel to stand before God's unfulfilled pledges and ask *when*, not *if*, they would be kept.

The Post-Holocaust Conversation

The Talmud reports that Abraham not only argues with God on behalf of the innocent residents of Sodom and Gomorrah; he also intercedes on behalf of his own descendants, who—according to God's pledge—are to inherit the land and become as numerous as the stars in the heavens:

At the time of the destruction of the Temple the Holy One found Abraham standing in the Temple. Said God, "Why is my beloved in My house?" Abraham replied, "I have come concerning the fate of my children." . . . Said God, "Your children sinned and have gone into exile." "Perhaps," said Abraham, "they only sinned in error?" God disagreed. "Perhaps only a few sinned?" God disagreed again. "Still," Abraham pleaded, "Did you remember the covenant of circumcision. . . . And perhaps if You had waited, they would have repented." God still disagreed. Then Abraham put his hands on his head, wept bitterly, and cried, "Perhaps, Heaven forbid, there is no hope for them?" Then a Heavenly Voice said, "As the olive tree produces its best only at the very end, so Israel will flourish at the end of time."[45]

Despite the tale's poignancy, its takeaway—deferring the fulfillment of Israel's hope until messianic times—fails to answer what theologians call the question of theodicy: reconciling the notions of a just, omnipotent, and omniscient God with the reality of innocent suffering.

While the problem of why the blameless should suffer was hardly new, the Holocaust forced theologians to confront it with ultimate urgency. What kind of covenantal relationship allows one partner to sit in silence while the other is annihilated? What happens when membership in a covenant with God is the warrant for the Jewish people's murder?

Here I sample the thinking of several post-Holocaust theologians on the state of the covenant after Auschwitz and whether that covenant can still remain a source of hope.[46]

RICHARD L. RUBENSTEIN (1924–, UNITED STATES)

In the early 1960s, rabbi and theologian Richard L. Rubenstein had a conversation with the seventy-year-old Heinrich Grauber, dean of the Evangelical Church of West and East Berlin. During the Holocaust, Grauber's wartime opposition to the Nazis had landed him in Dachau. A person of staunch faith, he explained that the Holocaust befell the Jews because of their covenantal relationship with God. "He spoke about the ancient covenant between God and Israel and how Israel . . . was under a very special obligation to behave in a way which was spiritually consistent with Divine ordinance," Rubenstein wrote. Grauber went on to describe the Nazis as the whip with which God punished the Jewish people, a crime for which the Nazis would endure a fate worse than their Jewish victims.

To Rubenstein, the horror of the interview was matched only by the clarity of Grauber's logic. "Can [we] really blame the Christian community for viewing us through the prism of a mythology of history when we were the first to assert this history of ourselves?" he asked.[47] Rubenstein concluded that as long as Jews believe in the notion of a special covenantal relationship between God and the Jewish people, there was no satisfactory rebuttal to the dean's argument. So Rubenstein sacrificed the covenant rather than accept Auschwitz as an instrument of punishment in God's covenantal relationship with Israel:

> We have passed beyond all illusion and hope. We have learned in the crisis that we were totally and nakedly alone, that we could expect neither succor from God or from our fellow creatures. . . . We have lost all hope and faith. . . . We accept our nothingness—nay, we even rejoice in it—for in our nothingness we have found both ourselves and the God who alone is true substance. . . . When nothing is asked for, nothing is hoped for, nothing is expected, all that we receive is truly grace.[48]

Rubenstein reluctantly accepted that his views placed him within the "God is dead" school of theology.[49] But he qualified how he understood this in various ways, pointing out, for example, that one who says God is dead reveals something about the speaker's subjective experience of God, but in actuality "reveals nothing about God."[50] To say that we live in "the time of the death of God does not mean the end of all gods. It means the demise of the God who was the ultimate actor in history. I believe in the God of Holy Nothingness known to mystics of all ages out of which we have come and to which we shall ultimately return."[51] Rubenstein gave up the belief in a God of history who acts on behalf of God's covenantal partner Israel, or anyone else. The cost of relinquishing the idea of covenant was severing any linkage to God as an external source of human hope.

None of this meant the end of Judaism: prayer, synagogue, Torah, and even God remained important in Rubenstein's thinking. He also parted company with existentialists such as Sartre and Camus over their rejection of religion. "Human hopelessness," Rubenstein said, "leads me to look to the religious community as the institution in which that condition can be shared in depth."[52]

EMIL FACKENHEIM (1916–2003, GERMANY, CANADA, AND ISRAEL)

Among the most profound writers on the Holocaust and post-Holocaust theology, Emil Fackenheim was ordained as a Reform rabbi at Berlin's Liberal seminary, the Hochschule für die Wissenschaft des Judentums (Higher Institute for Jewish Studies), before the war began. In 1939 he spent three months in a concentration camp until the Nazis released him with orders to leave Germany.

Two of his best-known essays, "The Commanding Voice of Auschwitz" and "The 614th Commandment," speak directly to the relationship between covenant and hope in the post-Holocaust era. In the first essay, Fackenheim describes four fragmentary responses to this commanding voice, the last of which commands religious Jews to wrestle with God in ever deeper ways and commands secular Jews to refrain from using Auschwitz as an "additional weapon" to deny God. In a sense, his message to religious Jews picks up where the (aforementioned) Talmud story of Abraham arguing with God in the Temple left off. Fackenheim's argument with God grows defiant:

> You have abandoned the covenant. We shall not abandon it. . . . You have destroyed all grounds for hope? We shall obey the commandment to hope which you yourself have given up! . . . The times are too late for the coming of the Messiah? We shall persist without hope and recreate hope — and as it were divine Power — by our persistence.

To allow Auschwitz to destroy "four thousand years of believing Jewish testimony" would be to do, "wittingly or unwittingly, Hitler's work."[53]

The second essay, "The 614th Commandment," famously outlines the prohibition against handing Hitler "posthumous victories" and touches on the question of despair.

> We are forbidden . . . to deny or despair of God, however much we may have to contend with him or with belief in him, lest Judaism perish. We are forbidden, finally, to despair of the world as the place which is to become the kingdom of God, lest we help make it a meaningless place in which God is dead or irrelevant and everything is permitted. To abandon any of these imperatives, in response to Hitler's victory at Auschwitz, would be to hand him yet other, posthumous victories.[54]

Notably, the titles of both essays refer to commandments. For Fackenheim, even — or perhaps especially — after Auschwitz, Jews are bound by the commandment not to forsake the heart of their ancient covenantal mission: to work with God to redeem the world. Critical to this mission, Jews are forbidden to allow hopelessness to triumph. For Jews to give up their historic covenantal hopes would violate this 614th commandment.[55]

We can sense certain tensions in Fackenheim's attitude to covenant and hope. On the one hand, Jews are prohibited from giving in to despair and forsaking ancient convictions about covenant. On the other, Jews hold onto hope and covenant as an act of defiance. In the end, Jews cling to covenantal hopes all the more strongly when others try to wrench them from their hands. Why? Because these hopes are central to the Jews as a people. "Who is a Jew?" Fackenheim asks, and answers, "One who hopes."[56]

IRVING GREENBERG (1933–, UNITED STATES)

Rabbi Irving Greenberg's struggle to articulate the impact of the Holocaust on the idea of covenant has led to a very different conclusion: The
covenantal relationship with God can no longer be commanded. The covenant's authority was broken by God's failure to protect the Jewish people
during the Holocaust; consequently, participation in the covenant is now
voluntary. At this juncture, to assume covenantal responsibility means to
shoulder the burden of making this world what God had hoped it would
be. "Hope is a dream that is committed to the discipline of becoming a
fact. . . . The covenant is the pledge to realize the dream."[57] At the same
time, Greenberg explains that

> the total assault on Judaism and on the Jewish people was an attempt
> to stamp out the covenant, the witness, and ultimately the presence
> of God, who is the ground of life and the covenantal hope. Therefore,
> the very existence of the Jewish people is a fundamental statement
> that the covenant is ongoing.[58]

Yet the balance of responsibility between the covenantal partners has
shifted radically. Before the Temple's destruction in 70 CE, God was the
active covenantal partner. After this fateful event, the Jewish people became
an active, but still junior, partner. Following the Holocaust, the Jewish
people became "the senior partner in action. In effect God was saying to
humans: You stop the Holocaust. You bring redemption . . . I will be with
you totally in whatever you do, wherever you go, whatever happens, but
you must do it."[59] God hopes we will assume these responsibilities, but
the choice to do so lies in our hands alone.

Greenberg argues that Jews remain animated by covenantal hope whether
they believe in God or not. The flourishing of postwar Jewish institutions
around the world, the growth of the world Jewish population, and, perhaps
most importantly, the outpouring of energy and support for Israel "have
given witness which shows the world that God lives and the covenantal
hope is not in vain. . . . It makes no essential difference if the Jews involved
consciously articulate the covenantal hope or express a belief in God who
is the ground of the covenant. The witness is given by their actions."[60]

The Holocaust also led Greenberg to reject the notion of Israel's exclusive covenant with God, which had led to age-old battles between Judaism and Christianity over which had been chosen as God's true covenantal partner. "There is enough love in God to choose again and again."[61] God has made multiple covenants. Replacing a covenant that isolates Jews from other peoples, covenantal pluralism becomes a force binding us together as we work to build the kind of world in which God would want to reside.

Rebbe Nachman of Breslov held that "nothing is so whole as a broken heart." By extension, Greenberg suggests that, after the Holocaust, "no covenant is as complete as a broken covenant,"[62] analogous to a relationship that undergoes a severe test and emerges with greater strength and maturity.

Greenberg's developmental approach to covenant supports a similar understanding of hope. In the first era of Jewish history, God is the active covenantal partner, fulfilling the People of Israel's hopes. From Israel's perspective, hope means waiting for God to act. After the destruction of the Second Temple, Israel becomes an active, but junior, partner. Israel waits in hope, but also acts in hope. Post-Holocaust, Israel is the sole actor. At this juncture, hope no longer includes waiting for divine intervention. Hope is about taking actions that will lead to the fulfillment of the very yearnings we had previously expected God to fulfill.

PROCESS THEOLOGY

Recent decades have witnessed the evolution of Process Theology, a theological approach based on the work of the American philosopher Alfred North Whitehead (1861–1947). In essence, Process Theology focuses on God as the creator of all possibilities who places before all human beings choices at every turn of the road. At each juncture, God provides us with a lure pointing us toward the healthiest choice. Revelation occurs when we sense a pull, a lure, to make a life-affirming choice.

God's power is limited to presenting us with choices. Gone is the God of the Exodus, who saves Israel "with a mighty hand" (e.g., Exod. 13:9). In that god's place we are left with what philosopher Hans Jonas (1903–93, Germany and United States) called "the mutely insistent appeal of [God's] unfulfilled goal."[63]

That the Holocaust targeted the very people of the covenant and that God failed to save them led Jonas to completely reject any traditional notion of covenant. It was only possible to preserve the image of a caring God by relinquishing that of an omnipotent God. God didn't act because God couldn't act. At the dawn of human history God permanently relinquished the power to affect the course of history.

How, then, does the caring God "act" in the world?

[God accompanies humanity's] doings with the bated breath of suspense, hoping, and beckoning, rejoicing, grieving, approving and frowning — and I daresay making itself felt to [humanity] even while not intervening in the dynamics of [the] worldly scene: For can it not be that by the reflection of its own state as it wavers with the record of [humanity], the transcendent casts light and shadow over the human landscape?[64]

Process Theology suggests that God's covenantal role is neither to intervene in history to save those who honor the terms of the covenant nor to punish those who violate it. In place of these divine manifestations of covenant are the divine intimations we receive about whether or not our decisions are truly life affirming. God hopes we will make the right choices, and we hope to discern God's guidance about the right ways to go. God and humanity exist in a relationship defined by hope.

Conclusion

Joseph Soloveitchik observes that when human beings address the Divine, "God joins [human beings], and at this meeting, initiated by [human beings], a new covenantal community is born — the prayer community."[65] So it is that in the daily morning liturgy, metaphors of covenant, laden with different elements of hope, frequently appear. Passages about the *Akedah*, the Exodus, and the return to the Land of Israel after the Babylonian exile keep alive the hope that God will again return to the stage of history and set things right for the Jewish people. For those who don't believe that God directly intervenes in history, these stories inspire hope that tomorrow's dreams need not be defined by today's constraints and that *our* actions can make it so.

The trials of history, ancient and modern, have put covenantal hope to the test. The array of Jewish responses to the Holocaust demonstrates that many contemporary conceptualizations of covenant still remain important sources of Jewish hope.

Consider, for example, a reading for Yom ha-Shoah by the Conservative rabbi and liturgist Jules Harlow (1931–). He quotes an ancient midrash that slightly alters the letters in one word to transform a biblical verse lauding God's power into a condemnation of God's mute silence. Instead of reading the verse, "Who is like You, YHWH, among the *celestials*?" (Exod. 15:11), the midrash reads it as "Who is like You, YHWH, among the *silent*?" That is, who remains mute despite Israel's suffering?[66]

Harlow follows this with a plea about hope and covenant:

Are you not God, Adonai, that we may hope in You? . . . Renew in Your creatures Your image which has been desecrated. Restore the covenant which Your people have maintained. Remember the hopes of the slain by sending redemption to Your shattered world. In spite of everything that strangles hope, help us to continue sustaining the song of their lives.[67]

Faithful Israel pleads with God, hoping God will finally fulfill the divine covenantal promises of old. Finally, however, after many stanzas that call on God to act, Harlow's prayer ends with the task becoming ours to fulfill. We cannot hope that God will act to send redemption to the shattered world—but we can hope that God will strengthen *our* will to redeem it.

6

The Book of Job

HOPE FOR VINDICATION

Let us remember Job who, having lost everything—his children, his friends, his possessions, and even his argument with God—still found the strength to begin again, to rebuild his life. . . . Job, our ancestor. Job, our contemporary. His ordeal concerns all humanity. . . . He demonstrated that faith is essential to rebellion, and that hope is possible beyond despair. The source of his hope was memory, as it must be ours. Because I remember, I despair. Because I remember, I have the duty to reject despair. I remember the killers, I remember the victims, even as I struggle to invent a thousand and one reasons to hope.
—Elie Wiesel, Nobel lecture, 1986

Introduction

Often thought to be the Bible's most pessimistic volume, the book of Job contains some two dozen explicit references to hope. Additionally, its frequent use of the root *kof-vav-hey*, as in *tikvah*, stands in stark contrast to the root's appearance just once in the Torah in the context of hope.[1]

The reason for Job's exceptional focus on hope may lie in its period of composition. Scholars date the book from the late sixth or early fifth centuries BCE—later than many other parts of the Bible—and classify it as Wisdom Literature, a genre in which philosophical questions about hope, and the language to discuss it, rose to a new level of prominence.

Recalling Gabriel Marcel's formulation that hope is the individual's response to a trial (see chapter 3), it's also no wonder that the book of Job has so much to say about hope.[2] The story opens with the Adversary (*ha-Satan*) asking God's permission to test Job's faith with a series of escalating blows—the loss of his property, his children, and finally, the affliction of his body with repulsive and painful sores. Job's response to his trial wavers between deep despair and defiant hope. As such, Job provides a wealth of insights about the nature of hope and the struggle to maintain it under fire. Maybe that's why a midrash says that "When they were enslaved in Egypt, Moses would bring the book of Job and show it to the elders of Israel so that they would listen and learn that there is hope for those who trust in God—that good can follow bad."[3]

This chapter reframes the book of Job from a treatise on the theological significance of human suffering to a journey about finding and maintaining hope amid catastrophe—including the hope for vindication.[4]

Reframing Job

Today, we don't all share the theological assumptions prevalent in Job's era. We don't automatically see God's punishment as the reason things go wrong or see divine reward as the reason things go well. We don't all buy into the notion that a supernatural adversary (ha-Satan) tempting the Divine—as happens in Job—would test the faithfulness of human beings by visiting calamities on them. Nor do we all find the hand of God in every chance event or natural disaster.

In his classic *When Bad Things Happen to Good People*, Harold Kushner puts it this way:

> A change of wind direction or the shifting of a tectonic plate can cause a hurricane or earthquake to move toward a populated area instead of out into an uninhabited stretch of land. Why? . . . A drunken driver steers his car over the center line of the highway and collides with the green Chevrolet instead of the red Ford fifty feet away. An engine bolt breaks on flight 205 instead of flight 209. There is no message in all of that. There is no reason for those particular people to be afflicted rather than others. These events do not reflect God's choices.[5]

If we remove God's hand from trial and tragedy, it is time that we reread Job in this light as well.

ON THE CAPACITY TO ENDURE

This reading of Job yields vital insights on the role of hope in the human capacity to endure suffering.

Job, a righteous, vigorous, powerful man, experiences one catastrophe after another: murderous criminal attacks on his livestock operations, the loss of sheep and shepherds in a lightning strike ("God's fire"), the death of his ten children in a windstorm, and, finally, illness, "a severe inflammation on Job from the sole of his foot to the crown of his head" (2:7). Understandably, Job's hope begins to run out. He doubts if life is worth continuing. He rants to his friends about the fate that has befallen him, and they only add fuel to the fire by suggesting he deserves it. Eventually, Job marshals his hope and finds his way back to life. His health returns, he has more children, and he re-creates the flourishing enterprise that spawned his wealth and influence the first time around.

Read this way, Job becomes the story of a survivor who endures terrible tragedy and wanders between hope and despair, ultimately choosing hope and managing to begin a new life. His new offspring do not erase the pain of losing his first children. Indeed, the book of Job tells us that *after* Job's fortunes are restored, his siblings and former friends "consoled and comforted him for all the misfortune that YHWH had brought upon him" (42:11). Job's second family embodies his hope for the future: the affirmation of life by a man who lost everything but refuses to give up.

FIGHTING JUSTICE DENIED

The book can also be read as Job's persistent hope and ultimate triumph over a legal system that failed to render true justice. Primo Levi (1919–87) called Job the universal "just man oppressed by injustice."[6] Legal scholar Benjamin L. Berger puts it this way:

> The fact that, in Job's suffering, the God of Justice is revealed as unjust shakes Job's world and challenges the friends in a way that other experiences of suffering cannot. It is for the same reason that wrongful convictions are such grave instances of injustice. This brand of injustice indicts the system. . . . If it inflicts suffering where none is due, the system has created senselessness instead of reason; it has become an agent of disorder.[7]

Job's decision to sue God for justice makes him a hero to all victims of injustice and their allies, to all brave enough to pick up the flag of fairness when it has fallen. His message is this: Don't give up hope on fixing the "system" that has denied you justice. Take the fight to the very top. You never know how the case will turn out. Job's friends thought his plan was sinful or crazy—until the day God announced that Job had "spoken the truth about Me" (42:7). Job won his argument, even though he never succeeded in bringing God to court. Justice may be slow in coming, but we shouldn't give up the hope of achieving it.

Verses of Despair, Verses of Hope

Many passages in Job that speak of hope and despair can deepen our understanding of how hope functions and evolves, in Job's life and in our own.

DESPAIR AS ETERNAL NIGHT

The first mention of hope in the book of Job comes from the mouth of Job after he has sat for seven days in silence with his friends who have come to comfort him:

> May those who cast spells upon the day damn it,
> The ones who are skilled to rouse Leviathan;
> May its twilight stars remain dark;
> May it hope for light and have none;
> May it not see the glimmerings of the dawn. (3:8–9)[8]

Job has just cursed the day of his birth and the night of his conception. Images of darkness, blackness, and gloom pile one upon the next as Job vents his conviction that his life is not worth the suffering he endures. Now he calls upon mighty magicians who can rouse the Leviathan, a mythological symbol of primordial chaos and disorder, to "cast spells upon the day, damn" the day of his birth.

"Given the mythological background of the stanza," the contemporary Job commentator C. L. Seow reflects,

> one wonders if there is not an allusion . . . to the sun's struggle to get through the darkness of the netherworld; let it (the sun) hope. Presumably, then, with the rousing of the chaos monster, Job means

that any hope for light would dissipate; the daily routine of the sun is broken and there will be no hope for it.[9]

Job's words illustrate the archetypal association between hope and light, despair and darkness. In rapid succession, Satan's blows knock Job from the pinnacle of happiness to the pit of misery—to the point he wishes to erase his very existence. He is overwhelmed by grief (and mental health professionals often observe expressions of hopelessness during the most acute phases of grief). Yet he is also angry and depressed (the second and third of Elisabeth Kübler-Ross's five stages of grieving).[10] Job cannot see beyond a present steeped in pain. The despair of grief is an eternal night. The losses Job has suffered lead to what Israeli philosopher Moshe Halbertal calls a "detachment from reality."[11] Job no longer knows that no night is truly without end—that "the sun also rises" as Ecclesiastes (1:5) and, later, Ernest Hemmingway put it.

And still, there is a hint of something in this passage that offers an inkling of hope. In railing against his plight, Job invokes the rhythm and imagery of nature, which convey that time *will* pass. Night will give way to morning. Darkness may give way to light, and hopelessness to hope.

GUILT IMPRISONS HOPE

Guilt may also exacerbate Job's sense of hopelessness. Perhaps guilt explains why Job cannot accept his friend Eliphaz's assurances, posed as questions, that his righteousness ought to provide him with a measure of hope:

See, you have encouraged many;
You have strengthened failing hands.
Your words have kept [one] who stumbled from falling;
You have braced knees that gave way.
But now that it overtakes you, it is too much;
It reaches you and you are unnerved. (4:3–5)
Is not your piety your confidence,
Your integrity your hope?
Think now, what innocent [person] ever perished?
Where have the upright been destroyed? (4:6–7)

As I have seen, those who plow evil
And sow mischief reap them. (4:8)

As words of comfort, Eliphaz's remarks fall short. In fact, the Talmud uses verses 4:6–7 as an example of what *not* to say to someone who is suffering, afflicted with illness, or has buried a child—all of which have befallen Job.[12] But as veiled accusations, Eliphaz's observations may well hit their mark in stirring up Job's doubts about his own goodness.

The passage begins by recalling that Job's reputation included dispensing comfort to the suffering. An early midrash recounts Job's approach: To the blind, the deaf, or the lame he would say that God had created them that way, that they had no right to protest the Creator's will, and that in time God would heal them.[13] But as Eliphaz points out, Job is not so good at taking his own advice. More than that, having now truly experienced suffering himself, perhaps Job regrets the platitudes he so readily dispensed in the name of sympathy. Perhaps now he realizes the pain he inflicted on those who sought solace. Indeed, some commentators view Eliphaz's reassurances as sarcastic, as if to say, "Your righteousness is so flawed, you *shouldn't* have hope."[14]

Pointing to another potential source of Job's guilt, Job scholar Norman C. Habel observes that "as priest of a patriarchal household, Job is responsible for the welfare of his family."[15] In the beginning of the story, when Job's sons completed their cycle of feasts, Job urged them to purify themselves, and he himself offered sacrifices on their behalf, "for Job thought, 'Perhaps my children have sinned and blasphemed God in their thoughts.' This is what Job always used to do" (1:5). Since Job felt responsible for his family's welfare, the death of his ten children had to have weighed on him as a terrible failing. Shouldn't he have done more to protect them? Further, if Job lived in fear that his children cloaked their private sinfulness in piety, from whom, if not Job, did they learn this?

Eliphaz's asking Job to reflect on his piety—and, by implication, to examine his role in his own children's deaths at the very time when his grief is still so raw—could only increase Job's sense of guilt. The grieving process often includes a measure of guilt for not having done more to preserve the duration or quality of a lost loved one's life. When excessive, guilt piled on loss makes a poor fertilizer for hope. From guilt the conviction may grow that one deserves to suffer forever in the pit. "As if

Job's suffering is not enough," Halbertal observes, "[Job's friends] would have him go to the grave with the conviction that he has sinned and thus brought evil upon his children."[16]

I once asked a friend in her nineties what she hoped for at this point in her life. She'd been an outstanding golfer, successful lawyer, and a pillar of the community. Now she was challenged by difficult but non-life-threatening health issues that compromised her quality of life. She responded with a series of veiled allusions to how she had seriously wronged her deceased husband. She felt terrible, especially because there was no way to make it up to him, no way to meaningfully apologize. She had never allowed anyone even a glimpse of her guilt. Guilt had deprived her of any right to hope for improvements in her own situation. Guilt had imprisoned her hope.

BOTH HOPE AND FOLLY?

Eliphaz, however, may mean something different than "confidence" when he asks Job:

Is not your piety your confidence,
Your integrity your hope? (4:6)

The Hebrew word for "confidence," *kislatekha*, comes from the root *kaf-samech-lamed*, which, in addition to "hope" (as in "confidence"), can mean "foolishness." Rashi and a number of commentators who followed him understood it as "foolishness."[17] Rashi thus read the verse like this: "Your fear of heaven is due to foolishness (and not to full understanding), and so are your hope and the sincerity of your ways all foolishness."[18]

Some scholars believe that the author of Job intentionally uses the ambiguous *kislatekha* (hope or foolishness) as a "double-edged word" to add another layer of meaning or irony to the passage.[19] The author may be saying that some will inevitably see a given action as hopeful, while others castigate it as foolish. The goal of a particular hope or the means to achieve it may seem foolishly unrealistic—but to abandon that hope or the path toward it prematurely may be equally imprudent. As I see it, the author of Job wants us to understand that hope lies in the eyes of the beholder. We ought to be careful when we are inclined to call someone else's hope foolish. This person may well see possibilities and paths to reach their goal that we don't. They may also have more patience than we do.

As we saw, Job's first mention of hope involved time. Job yearned to turn the clock back and erase the day of his birth. His next mention of hope connects in a different way with time: in relation to patience.

Eliphaz concludes his first speech:

> You will know that all is well in your tent;
> When you visit your wife you will never fail.
> You will see that your offspring are many,
> Your descendants like the grass of the earth.
> You will come to the grave in ripe old age,
> As shocks of grain are taken away in their season. (5:24–26)

Job responds:

> Could my anguish but be weighed, and my disaster on the scales be
>   borne,
> they would be heavier now than the sand of the sea. (6:2–3)

> If only my wish were fulfilled,
> and my hope God might grant.
> If God would deign to crush me,
> loose His hand and tear me apart. (6:8–9)

> What is my strength that I should hope?
> How long have I to live that I should be patient? (6:11)[20]

Eliphaz essentially tells Job not to reject God's reproof, as God will eventually restore Job's family and fortune—exactly what happens at the end of the story. But rather than providing comfort, Eliphaz's rosy prediction inflames Job's pain.

That Eliphaz's words of encouragement prove wanting likely comes as no surprise to those familiar with basic tenets of psychotherapy or grief counseling: Meet the client where he or she is. You can't make the client's pain magically disappear, so sit patiently with it and slowly try to understand it. The benefit to the client lies in their feeling understood and in sharing the depths of suffering with another human being who is strong enough to hear about misery without immediately trying to superimpose a happy ending. Suffice it to say, having sat with Job quietly for a week, Eliphaz's patience has worn thin, and the proverbial "patience of Job" has run out as well.[21] Job's diminished capacity to hope goes hand in hand with his feeling that life's horizon is too short to justify patience.[22]

Patience and hope: Each influences the transit from present to future. Patience reflects our equanimity during the journey. Hope embodies our vision of the destination and the sum of our efforts to reach it. Thus, "the main reason we abandon long-term hopes," explains Donald Capps, author of *Agents of Hope: A Pastoral Psychology*, "is that we cannot endure the frustration involved. Patience is the assurance that the hoped-for outcome is worth the frustration and therefore keeps us steadfast in our hope."[23] Because patience and hope are both tied to the future, each demands waiting. In fact, Hebrew verbs meaning "to hope" can also mean "to wait" and are sometimes translated as "to wait patiently."[24]

Although Job and Eliphaz share a degree of impatience, their experience of time differs. For Eliphaz, like most people in a state of reasonable mental and physical health, time stretches from the past, through the present, to the future. Hence he has no trouble forecasting a sunny future for his friend: With sufficient time, Job will rebuild his life. Job's friends "configure time as open and ample," comments Bible scholar Carole Newsom. "The future, which is always beckoning, is the space within which new things may happen, events that then confer meaning on what has come before."[25] For Job at this moment, however, time oscillates between memories of his halcyon days gone by and his present experience of suffering. Time in his psyche is warped like the clocks in Salvador Dali's painting *The Persistence of Memory*—the past and present eclipsing future possibilities.

Still, by raising the issue of patience, Job also demonstrates that he's taken a small step in his journey from ultimate despair toward hope. Doubting his ability to endure such suffering or whether he'll live long enough to get through it, Job now calls on God to strike him down, to put an end to his misery. Earlier Job wished he'd never been born because he could not imagine his pain diminishing. Now he can glimpse an end to his ordeal but doubts if he'll be able to reach it.

WATERS OF HOPE

Job uses metaphors of a journey through the desert and the inability to find water to accuse his visitors of being unreliable friends who fail to sustain his hope:[26]

> My brethren are treacherous as a wadi,
> Like a bed of wadis, they pass away— (6:15)

> The caravans from Tema look;
> The convoys from Sheba hope in them. (6:19)
> Disappointed in what they had trusted,
> They reached it and their hopes were dashed. (6:20)[27]

To Job, his friends are like a wadi, a dangerous torrent in the rainy season, or otherwise a parched riverbed, but never a secure, dependable source of life-giving water. They are like the oases of Tema and Sheba, but in this case they—the oases and the friends—have run dry.

The metaphors of journey and water are both significant with respect to hope.

Job's allusion to a journey—to movement—signifies another step beyond unremitting despair. Initially Job could only hope for death. Then he began to wonder if he'd live long enough to recover from his grief and bodily illness. Now Job is comparing himself to a parched desert traveler searching for water. We are witnessing Job's nascent understanding of recovery as a journey—albeit a tortuous one—toward hope.

The connection between hope and journey is rooted in the Hebrew language. Rashi points out that the word for hope in Job 6:19 (*kivu*) can refer to an extended line as well. Seow notes that, in ancient times, caravans followed dry wadis—like lines through the desert—"ever hopeful that they would discover" new routes.[28] In the above passage from Job, the wadi leads to dashed hopes. Even so, hope serves as a slender line or track of sorts that can guide us through hostile environments and keep us going despite inevitable disappointments.

The unavailability of water speaks to Job's friends' general incapacity to provide him with emotional support and specifically to their inability to sustain his hope. Again, the Hebrew language draws the connection between water and hope. In the Bible the word *mikveh* can refer to "hope" or to a "pool of water." Jeremiah calls God *Mikveh Yisrael*, the "Hope of Israel," and the "Fount of living waters" (Jer. 17:13). Commenting on *kivu*, Rashi also notes that this word is connected with water in the Creation story: "Let the water below the sky be gathered (*yikavu*)" (Gen. 1:9). Water sustains the body, hope the soul. When we hope we must pool our inner spiritual resources, gather our strength, so we can get through a trying situation.

HOPE IS A SLENDER THREAD

Not long after the above passage, Job reverts to the theme of time, and with it life's futility and evanescence:

> Truly [humankind] has a term of service on earth;
> [One's] days are like those of a hireling—
> Like a slave who longs for [evening's] shadows,
> Like a hireling who hopes for [the day's] . . . wage.
> So have I been allotted months of futility . . . . (7:1–3)

> My days are swifter than a weaver's shuttle;
> they end when the thread of hope gives out.
> Remember: My life is just a breath;
> my eye will never again see pleasure. (7:6–7)[29]

Hardly upbeat, the passage nonetheless reveals a development in Job's thinking. Initially Job compares himself to a day laborer, hoping, but never sure of, receiving his wages. Job depicts an arduous life, but it is no longer the life of one singled out by God for torture. The duration of his ordeal has also lost its eternal quality. Job now speaks of "months of futility," which Job translator Edward Greenstein understands as suggesting that "Job has not been suffering all that long a time."[30]

Next Job compares life and hope to a thread. Translator Raymond Scheindlin elegantly captures *tikvah*'s dual meanings: "hope" and "thread." Hope is fragile: It is no more than a slender thread of finite length and limited strength. And yet, Seow observes, "The routine activity of weaving cannot go on without *tikvah* (thread). So it is with life. When *tikvah* (hope) is gone, life for all intents and purposes is finished."[31]

Weaving requires thread; living fully demands hope. The poet Moshe Ibn Ezra (c. 1060–1135, Spain) put it this way: "Man in the world is like a weaver. He weaves his days like thread/hope. But one day it will be completed. He will run out of the hope/thread of life."[32]

Interestingly, at this point, Job compares his life to the weaver's shuttle and thread, but he is not the weaver. The thread and shuttle remain in the hand of the weaver, likely God (later, in 10:11, Job will speak of God as having woven together his body). Job has lost what psychologists call a sense of agency, the capacity that enables us to imagine ourselves making progress toward a goal. Agency constitutes a key ingredient of hope.[33] As theologian Michael Marmur explains: "Hope is a thread, however elusive, that links us to *a possible* future. It demands that we take hold of it; otherwise, it is just a loose thread."[34] Job's losses have overwhelmed his capacity to envision a brighter future. He has neither reason nor capacity to grasp the thread of hope. Indeed, he sees the thread—his life—as being solely in God's hands.

With time, Job's capacity for taking matters into his own hands—for picking up the thread of hope—will return.

HOPE NEEDS A GOAL

As Job's dialogues with his friends continue, something new begins to emerge within him: a dream of divine redress.

> He is not a man, like me, that I can answer Him,[35]
> That we can go to law together.
> No arbiter is between us
> To lay his hands on us both.
> If He would only take His rod away from me
> And not let His terror frighten me,
> Then I would speak without fear of Him;
> For that is not the way I am. (9:32–35)[36]

> Indeed, I would speak to the Almighty;
> I insist on arguing with God. (13:3)

Though He slay me, yet I will trust [or hope] in Him,
Yet I will argue my case before Him. (13:15)

Yet know that God has wronged me;
He has thrown up siege works around me.
I cry, "Violence!" but am not answered;
I shout, but can get no justice. (19:6–7)

Would that I knew how to reach Him,
How to get to His dwelling-place.
I would set out my case before Him
And fill my mouth with arguments.
I would learn what answers He had for me
And know how He would reply to me.
Would He contend with me overbearingly?
Surely He would not accuse me!
There the upright would be cleared by Him,
And I would escape forever from my judge. (23:3–7)

O that I had someone to give me a hearing;
O that Shaddai would reply to my writ,
Or my accuser draw up a true bill! (31:35)[37]

Over several chapters, Job's dream develops into a goal: to take God to court and demand justice. At first Job surfaces the idea as if it were a foolhardy fantasy doomed to fail. God showing up in court? And if God did, how could Job possibly contend directly with God when the Bible warns that no one can see God's face and live (Exod. 33:20)? Beyond this, who would serve as a neutral arbiter in court? God can't be both judge and defendant! And without an arbitrator, God's terror might strike him mute.

Eventually, Job casts these doubts aside. Slowly, the dream becomes his raison d'être, his ultimate goal. He sets his sights on bringing God to court.

The very existence of this goal represents an important step toward hope. A goal implies a desired outcome that lies in the future. Hope is another name for the positive feelings a goal inspires — and for one's ability to pursue it. "Hope is the sum of the mental willpower and waypower [capacity] that you have for your goals," writes Charles R. Snyder, a pioneering researcher in the psychology of hope.[38] Without a goal, for what can you hope? As Samuel Taylor Coleridge wrote, "Hope without an object cannot live."[39]

Still, at first blush, Job's notion seems to overflow with haughty impertinence. Who is Job, or any human being, to shake his fist and call God to court? The psychoanalytically oriented scholar C. Fred Alford concludes that this very desire reveals Job's sinful nature:

> We learn . . . that Job only appeared to be God's humble servant. In reality, Job was filled with pride—indeed, hubris—imagining that he could put God on the witness stand almost as though God were another earthly power.[40]

Yet the story of Job emerges from a tradition that not only permits, but celebrates challenging God. Job's plan to call God to account puts him in the company of biblical heroes—Abraham, Jacob, Moses, Elijah, and Jeremiah. Abraham thunders in protest to God's plan to destroy Sodom and Gomorrah: "Far be it from You! Shall not the Judge of all the earth deal justly?" (Gen. 18:25). Jacob's name becomes Israel because he has successfully striven with God (Gen. 32:29). Moses twice challenges God's angry vows to destroy the Israelites, his appeal following what has been called a "near-perfect law-court structure."[41] Elijah accuses the God of Israel of turning the hearts of the people "backward" and demands an immediate demonstration of divine power to restore their faith (1 Kings 18:37). Confronting God for making him a "constant laughingstock," the object of "constant disgrace and contempt," Jeremiah calls for divine retribution against Israel's enemies, concluding his argument with, "For I lay my case before You" (Jer. 20:12).[42] According to one study (aptly titled *Arguing with God*), the book of Job embodies the biblical apex of law-court-style arguments with God, raising the genre to a new level.[43]

Job draws hope from his spiritual antecedents, who not only chose the same strategy but model the hope inherent in doing so. Their arguments bent God's actions toward justice, and so might his.

THE AMBIGUITY OF HOPE

The development of Job's plan to take God to court is both an indication of his capacity for hope and a source of energy to bring that hope to fruition. The fact that Job builds his approach upon those of his *chutzpadik* biblical forebears adds a measure of plausibility to his hope. At the point when Job fully commits himself to the plan — telling his friends to "keep quiet" and saying "I will take my life in my hands" (13:13, 14) — he utters one of the truly immortal lines in the book:

Though He slay me, yet I will trust [or hope] in Him.
Yet I will argue my case before Him. (13:15)[44]

As translated here, the verse seems to cement the link between Job's audacious challenge to God and his hope for divine vindication. Alas, this memorable verse is also among the Bible's most enigmatic. Let's compare two Jewish Publication Society translations of the first part of the verse: the first from 1917 (Old Jewish Publication Society translation, OJPS), the second published in 1999 (New Jewish Publication Society translation, NJPS):

Though He slay me, yet I will trust [or hope] in Him.

He may well slay me; I may have no hope.

Two opposite translations. Hope versus no hope.

This is one of many places in the Bible where ancient Masoretic notes (eighth through tenth centuries and earlier) indicate a difference between how a particular word should be written and how it should be read and understood. The first, OJPS, translation follows how the verse should be read; the second, NJPS, translation reflects how it is written.

The crux of the problem revolves around the Hebrew word *lo*, which can be spelled two ways. When spelled *lamed alef*, as written in this verse, it means "not" or "no." Thus, as written, the verse means, "I will not hope." When spelled *lamed vav*, as the Masoretic note to the verse says it should be read and understood, it means "in him" or "to him." Thus the Masoretic note creates the opposite reading: "I will hope in him." To make matters more confusing, many translations render the Hebrew word for hope (in this verse, *ayacheil*) as "trust" or "wait."

Considering the history of Masoretic notes on the matter does not in itself shed additional light on the meaning. There are eighteen cases in the Bible, three in Job, where the text reads *lamed alef* (no or not), but Masoretic notes require them to be read *lamed vav* (in him or to him). In this case, it's not completely clear what motivated the Masoretes to amend the text. Possibly, versions of the text existed with different renderings: In the Dead Sea Scrolls, a combined Aramaic translation and commentary (a *targum*) reads *lamed vav*;[45] and the Mishnah, perhaps the earliest Jewish source to take up the ambiguity (c. 200 CE), quotes the verse as reading *lamed vav* (though it remained ambiguous because it could be read declaratively "in him I will hope" or sarcastically, "in *him* I will hope?").[46] Maimonides concluded that there was no way of arriving at a definitive interpretation of the verse.[47] Sometimes, he said, *lamed alef* can mean "not," and sometimes it can mean "in him"; and the same for *lamed vav*, which can sometimes mean "in him" and sometimes "not."

Modern translators, meanwhile, passionately disagree about how to render the verse. Some readers and translators conclude that Job sees God as his principal adversary, the cause of his suffering, the destroyer of his hope. Scheindlin translates the verse as "Let Him kill me! — I will not flinch," commenting:

> The familiar translation, "Though he slay me, yet will I trust in Him" . . . is based on a variant of the Hebrew text. Its moving expression of God's beneficence is completely at variance with Job's attitude in this chapter and in the rest of the poem.[48]

Others, including myself, maintain that the context of the verse — Job just having vowed to take God to court — infuses it with hope. Who initiates a suit without hope of benefit?

Seow suggests that the verse's ambiguity may well be deliberate.[49] Just when Job has chosen his path toward restoration — taking God to court and demanding justice — we're left with the conundrum: Does he hope or not? It's a universal question. We all face trials; some of us respond with hope, others do not. Or, is there a third option? Does Job—and sometimes do we—stand in a place where we feel both hope and despair? "Job," says French Bible scholar and philosopher André Neher, "pronounces two words which signify *simultaneously* hope and hopelessness."[50]

Ultimately, and perhaps most importantly, Jewish tradition has historically interpreted the verse in favor of Job's hope—and, all the more so, as a testament invoked to inspire hope in us when we face times of trial. One of many examples is the *Eleh Ezkerah*, the martyrology recited on Yom Kippur that recounts the martyrdom of ten leading rabbinic sages during Israel's revolt against Rome in 132–35 CE. Before the executions begin, the hero of the narrative ascends to Heaven to argue with God, unsuccessfully, against the decree. The Roman official conducting the executions then asks Rabbi Yishmael, about to face death, "Do you still trust [or hope] in your God?," to which, with his last breath, Rabbi Yishmael answers, "Though He may slay me, yet I will trust [or hope] in Him."[51]

We may never know the original intent of this verse. What matters is how we understand it. Over the ages, Jewish interpreters have read it as a statement—for us as individuals and as a people—of defiant hope in a god who often no longer seems to deserve it. If God is that to which we attach ultimate reality and importance, then to hope in God may mean something different to each of us. The crux of the matter is whether we are willing to invest our ultimate convictions with hope. "Job did," says Jewish tradition, "and so should we."

THE DANGER OF MAGICAL HOPE

How does the proclamation "Though He slay me, yet I will hope in Him" (13:15) square with what happens next in Job? We might expect that by now, having defined his goal, Job would proceed toward it without despair—that confronting God in the tradition of Abraham and Moses would infuse his struggle with implacable hope. But that's not what happens:

Even a tree has hope:
If you cut it, it sprouts again.
Its suckers never fail. (14:7)

But mortals languish and die . . . (14:10)

They will not rise from their sleep. (14:12)[52]

No sooner does Job embrace his plan than he falls back into doubt and misery. He may not live long enough to reach his goal. His health has diminished; he doesn't know how much time he's got left. And unlike a tree that's been felled, but then sends forth new sprouts, when Job dies, it will be the end.

Or will it? We've seen that hope demands creativity because it requires envisioning an alternative to the present. Here Job begins to think completely out of the box:

> If You would only hide me in Sheol,
> conceal me till Your anger passes,
> set me a term and then remember me
> (but if a person dies, how can he live?),
> I could endure my term in hope,
> until my time came round to sprout again.
> Then You would call, and I would answer,
> when You longed to see Your handiwork. (14:13–15)[53]

Job wonders about resurrection of the dead, a notion that would become a central pillar of Judaism, but only centuries after his story was written. In his imagination, after he dies, God will send him down to Sheol where the dead reside, but only "until my time came round to sprout again." The hypothetical resurrection allows him to pursue his challenge to God, even after death. But, his vision expresses a hope that lies even deeper than that of personal vindication. Job looks to a time when his relationship with God will be restored. Then, the Divine will no longer view Job as one who deserves torture, but will treat him once again as a piece of "Your handiwork."

And yet, however full of hope that vision may be, it lies far in the future. In the here and now, immediately after those last lines of promise, Job still experiences God as an overwhelming flood of pain:

Yes, the mountain collapses and wears away;
the cliff is dislodged from its place;
stones are scoured by water into dust,
torrents wash away earth's soil —
and You destroy man's hopes. (14:18–19)[54]

Like the mountain that collapses after unrelenting exposure to the elements, Job feels God is destroying his hope — and in the process, his life.

Perhaps Job's hope proves ephemeral because Job now doubts its realism. Drawing the distinction between magical and realistic hope, psychoanalyst Ernest G. Schachtel (1903–75, Germany and United States) explains that magical hope centers on the idea that external sources (rather than one's own hard effort) will, like magic, bring about the desired change in circumstances. "Such hope may even be relegated to an imagined world after death."[55]

Judged by this standard, Job's earlier hope that the night of his conception can somehow be stricken from the calendar has the ring of magic; indeed, Job calls upon magicians to bring this about. That his hope to be resurrected from the dead so quickly gives rise to images of hopelessness suggests that this too may strike him as a magical solution.[56] Magical hope can lift the spirit but prove flimsy, highly susceptible to disappointment, and easily replaced by despair.

Hope for Vindication

In the course of his struggles, Job concludes that he did nothing to warrant the suffering visited upon him, and his hope shifts from trying to convince his friends of this to obtaining vindication directly from God. But Job also comes to realize that he can't fulfill this hope alone. He needs someone to help him.

HOPE NEEDS A FRIEND

By the time the first of Job's visitors finishes speaking for the second time, it becomes clear that these friends don't have much empathic support to offer. Instead of standing with Job in solidarity, his friends have tried to convince him that he deserves his fate. Even Job's wife, the first to address him after tragedy strikes, has denied him any shred of sympathy. Urging him to "curse God and die," she implies that Job has no future. The empathic vacuum leads Job to seek support elsewhere:

Surely now my witness is in heaven;
He who can testify for me is on high. (16:19)

Let Him arbitrate between a man and God
As between a man and his fellow. (16:21)

My spirit is crushed . . . (17:1)

Where, then, is my hope?
Who can see hope for me?
Will it descend to Sheol?
Shall we go down together to the dust? (17:15–16)

He [God] tears down every part of me; I perish;
He uproots my hope like a tree. (19:10)

Pity me, pity me! You are my friends;
For the hand of God has struck me!
Why do you pursue me like God,
Maligning me insatiably?
O that my words were written down;
Would they were inscribed in a record,
Incised on a rock forever
With iron stylus and lead!
But I know that my Vindicator lives;
In the end He will testify on earth — (19:21–25)

Psychoanalyst Erik Erikson (1902–94, Germany and United States) argued that the capacity for hope emerges from early childhood experiences with parents and other caretakers that build basic trust. The Hebrew language likewise points to the connection between hope and trust: Many words that signify hope are often translated as "trust."[57] When life experiences undermine that foundation of basic trust, and hopelessness ensues, we turn to others to help rebuild trust—to family, to religion, to a therapist, to friends, and/or to God. Researchers refer to this relational aspect of hope as its affiliative dimension, or its social matrix.[58]

Yet Job's capacity to maintain his innocence and to envision taking God to court despite having no social support testifies to a growing inner strength. Thinking this through, Job recognizes that he can't succeed alone. *O chevruta, o mituta*, as the Talmud put it, "Either companionship or death."[59] God is simply too powerful to confront alone—and so Job casts about for an ally to testify on his behalf.

Again, the idea evolves slowly. First Job surfaces the idea of an arbiter (9:32–33), then a witness (16:19), and finally a vindicator (19:25)—a "redeemer" or "avenger," according to other translations.[60] Charting the evolution of these "imaginary companions," Job scholars William Long and Glandion Carney note how far Job has come: "Hope has become real to him through the instrument of the imaginary companion. The imaginary companion has opened Job's unknown, shaped his hope, given specificity to his longings."[61] The precise identity of these companions remains open to debate, but they seem to embody a figure (or figures, or perhaps even God) who will ultimately stick by Job and successfully advocate on his behalf—if necessary, even after he has died. Literary theorists have called such a figure a *superaddressee*, "a possible listener whose judgement would *really* count or whose advice would really help us. . . . The superaddressee embodies a principle of hope."[62]

"The foundation of all hope is and remains Job's own good conscience, with its rebellious quest for an avenger," wrote the philosopher Ernst Bloch (1885–1977, Germany).[63] Securing an avenger/advocate embodies both a source and an expression of hope. One element of that hope revolves around finding such an advocate, another around guaranteeing the advocate's access to the records of his case. Thus Job yearns for his words to be written down, "incised on a rock forever with iron stylus and lead!" This makes Job what Israeli philosopher Avishai Margalit calls a "moral witness," one who has suffered at the hands of an unfair regime and insists on bearing witness against it. Margalit credits the moral witness with a "rather sober hope: that in another place or another time there exists, or will exist, a moral community that will listen to their testimony."[64]

Job understood what the Talmud taught long ago: "A captive cannot release himself from prison."[65] Had he lived today, perhaps Job would have founded an organization like the Association in Defense of the Wrongly Convicted or the House of Renewed Hope, created by a group of exonerees dedicated to helping vindicate other wrongfully convicted prisoners. He likely would have applauded lawyer Bryan Stevenson, founder of the Equal Justice Initiative, who successfully defended Walter McMillian, a Black man framed and sentenced to death for the murder of a white woman in Alabama in 1986. Instilling hope in those whose reluctant testimony eventually exonerated McMillian proved to be a critical part of Stevenson's work. "Injustice prevails where hopelessness persists," Stevenson explained.

> I think hope is our superpower. Hope is the thing that gets you to stand up, when others say, "Sit down." It's the thing that gets you to speak, when others say, "Be quiet." . . . I get worried when I meet hopeless teachers or hopeless lawyers or hopeless politicians or hopeless advocates. Those are people who are not going to help us advance justice in the world.[66]

HOPE AND HEALING

In the end, Job does get his day in court with God. But after an overwhelming demonstration of God's creation and structuring of the cosmos, Job comes to see his complaint in a different perspective: "I knew You, but only by rumor; my eye has beheld You today. I retract. I even take comfort for dust and ashes" (42:5–6).[67] God immediately turns to Job's friends, saying, "You have not spoken the truth about Me as did My servant Job" (42:7). God instructs them to make sacrificial offerings, and Job to pray for his friends. Then, we learn, God "restored Job's fortunes after he prayed for his friends, doubling everything Job had" (42:10).[68] What is more, Job the survivor fathers ten more children. Sociologist William B. Helmreich (1945–2020, United States), who studied the successful adaptation of Holocaust survivors in America, noted that after the war, the birthrate of Jews in displaced persons camps was higher than in any other Jewish community in the world. As one survivor explained, "I have five children to fill the world with hope."[69]

Job's ability to pray for his friends embodies the last step in his journey from yearning for death as an escape from grief's bitter bite to experiencing a renewed appetite for life. That Job can pray for his cruelly unsympathetic friends attests to his capacity for re-engagement and forgiveness. In fact, his willingness to pray at all shows how far he's come. After all, earlier in the book Job rejected prayer, scornfully asking, "What do we get out of praying to Him?" (21:15).[70] "The trajectory of Job's spiritual and existential path as a mourner," Halbertal explains, "is the move from the isolated seclusion of the mourner and . . . disinterest in the world, to the caring concern and attentiveness to the needs and pains of others."[71]

Halbertal's conclusion brings to mind the words of Marcel, who defined hope as a response to a trial experienced as a "form of captivity" during which one is "deprived for an indefinite period of a certain light for which" one longs.[72]

Yemimah, the name Job gives his first daughter, supplies poetic confirmation of Marcel's observation. The name comes from *yamamah*, the Arabic word for dove,[73] a bird that makes its biblical debut near the end of the Flood, when Noah sends forth a dove from the ark. When it returns bearing an olive leaf in its beak, Noah knows the waters are receding and it will soon be safe to leave the ark.[74] The dove points both to the end of captivity within the ark and to the hope of starting life anew.[75] In Hebrew, Yemimah is connected to the word for "day," *yom*, which leads Rashi to interpret the name as "bright and white as the sun" [or day].

By the end of his journey, Job has broken through his captivity, traveling from darkness to light. He has passed through an excruciating trial, emerging healed and hopeful enough to give life another try.

Conclusion

The story of Job takes its place beside that of Abraham and Sarah and the Exodus as a third depiction of an epic trial and the response of hope it evokes. Stricken with grief over the loss of his children; pained by the sores that cover his body; angered by his "friends" who vie to ferret out the sins for which his suffering must constitute deserved divine punishment; railing against an unjust God and despairing of life to the point that he cries out for his very existence to be nullified, Job is the consummate example of a human being overwhelmed by hopelessness.

And yet, several desires ultimately fuel Job's hope. He wants his day in court to argue his case before God. He also wants his story told, and he yearns for an advocate to prove his innocence — even if it comes after his death.

It would be satisfying, but unrealistic, if Job's plan to bring God to court and his hope for an advocate permanently elevated his spirits. Paul Pruyser (1916–87, Holland and United States), one of first to write seriously about the psychology of hope, noted that when faced with adversity, people "do not make up their minds once and for all for or against hoping, but go through phases that may entail denial, anger, despair, flimsy illusions, rebelliousness, anxiousness, or hope in various sequences."[76]

Job reminds us that hope is not a piece of armor that, once donned, offers unfailing protection against despair. The imagery about hope in this tale tells a different story. Hope is a thin thread that can tear or escape our grip, but there is no weaving, or living, without it. Like a wadi, hope may run dry. Hope and despair are never far from one another and may in fact exist simultaneously.

Nonetheless, with Job's affirmation — "But I know that my Vindicator lives" (19:25) — Job, more than not, wants to live, wants to look ahead to a future in which the struggle for vindication will pay off. His unwillingness to confess to crimes he didn't commit and his stubborn hope for exoneration make him an inspiration for anyone accused or punished unjustly — and, further, for anyone who fights for worthy principles that have yet to gain respect.[77]

While the story's conclusion raises thorny theological questions, as a ray of hope to the wrongly accused, it's one of the brightest around. God says to Job's so-called friends, "I am incensed . . . for you have not spoken the truth about Me as did My servant Job. . . . [And] YHWH restored Job's fortunes" (42:7, 10).

In her autobiography, Elizabeth Keckley (1818–1907), a former slave who became the dressmaker and confidante of Mary Todd Lincoln, related an event she witnessed in the White House. It was 1863, about a year after the death of the Lincolns' son, when "the confederates were flushed with victory." The president, who had just returned from a War Department meeting, told his wife and Keckley that there was "plenty of news, but no good news. It is dark everywhere." He took a "small Bible from a stand by the head of the sofa" and read intently. After fifteen minutes Keckley noticed that "the dejected look was gone, and the countenance was lighted up with new resolution and hope." Pretending to look for something she'd misplaced, Keckley walked behind the sofa to see what the president had been reading: "I discovered that Mr. Lincoln was reading that divine comforter, Job."[78]

Two years later, Abraham Lincoln's funeral service included this verse from Job:[79]

But I know that my Vindicator lives;
In the end He will testify on earth (19:25).

7

Jewish Eschatology

HOPES FOR THE WORLD TO COME

All Israelites have a share in the world to come. . . . And these are the
ones who have no portion in the world to come. One who denies . . .
resurrection of the dead.
— *Mishnah Sanhedrin* 10:1 (Judaism's first law code, circa 200 CE)

Introduction

"Ask Jews what happens after death," *Moment* magazine commented in 2011,
"and many will respond that the Jewish tradition doesn't say or doesn't
care, that Jews believe life is for the living and that Judaism focuses on
what people can and should do in this world."[1] Woody Allen's 2016 film,
Café Society, delivered a similar message. Ben, a Jewish gangster, says he's
converting to Catholicism because "the Jewish religion doesn't believe in
an afterlife. I have to know that it all doesn't just end." His mother, Rose,
laments the decision, but can't argue. "Too bad the Jewish religion doesn't
have an afterlife," she says, "they'd get a lot more customers."[2]

The irony is that Christian hopes concerning the afterlife and resurrection grew out of Jewish sources, and these yearnings have remained
central to Judaism for almost two millennia.[3] Today, some 55 percent of
American Jews believe in Heaven and 49 percent in Hell—well below
such beliefs among Catholics and Evangelical Christians, and fairly close
to beliefs among Americans in general.[4] In younger generations, belief in
the afterlife is more widespread. Only 17 percent of Jews born between
1900 and 1970 said they believed in an afterlife, compared to 74 percent
of Jews born after 1970.[5]

This chapter follows the progression of Jewish notions of eschatology
(the end-time), including concepts about resurrection of the dead, immortality of the soul, the Messianic Era, and the world to come, from biblical
times to the present. Ideas about eschatology in the Bible, the Rabbinic

period, the work of Maimonides, and in modern times ultimately have much to teach us about hope.

The Road to Resurrection in the Bible

It's not easy to find support in the Hebrew Bible for hope that death does not have the last word. As Ecclesiastes puts it, one "who is attached to all the living still has hope (*bitachon*), for surely a live dog is better than a dead lion!" (9:4).[6] The Hebrew Bible generally speaks about death with a sense of finality. God banishes Adam and Eve from Eden with the parting words: "By the sweat of your brow shall you get bread to eat, until you return to the ground—for from it you were taken. For dust you are, and to dust you shall return" (Gen. 3:19). When Abraham reached 175 years, he "breathed his last, dying at a good ripe age, old and contented; and he was gathered to his kin" (Gen. 25:8). Job echoes death's finality: "So humankind lies down never to rise" (14:12). In Ecclesiastes, death is simply part of the life cycle: "A season is set for everything, a time for every experience under heaven: a time for being born and a time for dying" (3:1-2).

Renowned Bible scholar Geza Vermes (1924–2013, Hungary and UK) summarizes the Hebrew Bible's prime takeaways about the finality of death and the shadowy destination for the dead known as Sheol:[7]

> Absence of a second chance invested life on earth with a unique value. All good things happen to man between his birth and his death, and the practice of religion is restricted to the here and now. Since only the living thank God (Isa. 38:19), the days of this life are priceless. As reward for piety was expected before death, a kind of religious hedonism, consisting of eating, drinking, and taking pleasure, was preached by the wise men of the Old Testament (Eccl. 3:13). In lieu of mortification and asceticism, the Bible fully encourages . . . the Jew to take delight in his days.[8]

THE ROAD TO RESURRECTION

And yet, the Hebrew Bible *does* contain a few references to resurrection of the dead that evolve into a fully developed expression of this hope. As concerns the individual, the concept of resurrection implies that the state of actual death will at some point be followed by a return to life in one's fully embodied self. More broadly, Bible scholar Jon Levenson explains, resurrection is also understood to be part of a divine intervention "expected to occur in history but also to transform and redeem history and to open onto a barely imaginable world beyond any that preceded it."[9]

In charting the evolution of these ideas, we need to consider three biblical texts, from Ezekiel, Isaiah, and Daniel.

EZEKIEL

And [YHWH] said to me, "O mortal, these bones are the whole House of Israel. They say, 'Our bones are dried up, our hope is gone; we are doomed.' Prophesy, therefore, and say to them: Thus said YHWH God: I am going to open your graves and lift you out of the graves, O My people, and bring you to the land of Israel. You shall know, O My people, that I am YHWH when I have opened your graves and lifted you out of your graves. I will put My breath into you and you shall live again, and I will set you upon your own soil. Then you shall know that I YHWH have spoken and have acted." (Ezek. 37:11–14)

Ezekiel prophesied in exile in Babylonia, having lived through Babylonian king Nebuchadnezzar II's destruction of the First Temple in Jerusalem in 586 BCE. The events depicted in the book of Ezekiel fall between 593 and 571 BCE.[10]

His prophecy of resurrection here was meant to sustain hope for a devastated people. Ezekiel envisioned the restoration of the people to their homeland and the reconstruction of the Temple.

Yet, his ideas about resurrection may have been influenced by foreign concepts. Zoroastrianism, the official religion of the Persian Empire, which toppled the Babylonian kings between 546–530 BCE, possessed a well-developed concept of resurrection—although Ezekiel seems to have finished his book before Babylon's fall to Persia. Still, two features of this passage—the prominence of bones and a community-wide revivification—are both reminiscent of Persian resurrection texts.[11]

At first glance, Ezekiel's words would seem to affirm full-blown bodily resurrection. But many—from Rabbinic sages to contemporary scholars—

have read it differently: as a parable or an early, albeit important, step down the road toward resurrection.

Levenson questions whether Ezekiel provides the proof text for ultimate resurrection as Judaism and Christianity would later understand it:

> Ezekiel's vision focuses exclusively on the nation and not on the individuals who comprise it in any given generation. There is, therefore, no reason to think that Ezekiel saw the individuals who were resurrected in the valley as now endowed with mortality. What does not die is the people Israel, because God has, despite their grievous failings, honored [God's] indefensible pledge to their ancestors. *Israelite people* die, like anyone else; the *people Israel* survives and revives because of God's promise, despite the most lethal defeats. For this reason, although Ezekiel's vision in the valley does not attest to the expectation of resurrection in the later sense, it does constitute a significant step in the direction of the later doctrine.[12]

Though Ezekiel's vision does not seem to support hope for resurrection of the Israelites as individuals, it speaks powerfully to the revival of the nation. Bible scholar Michael Fishbane writes that Ezekiel's prophecy, which is read on the Sabbath during Passover, "breathes hope into the nation—announcing their rebirth from the grave of despair and their restoration to the Land of Israel."[13] Millennia later, Ezekiel's words—with a twist—would find a home in Israel's national anthem, "Hatikvah" ("The Hope"). Where the prophet says, "our hope is gone" (*avdah tikvatenu*), "Hatikvah" proclaims, "our hope is not yet gone" (*od lo avdah tikvatenu*).

ISAIAH

Two passages from the Isaiah Apocalypse (chapters 24–27, viewed as a later addition to the book, dating from between the sixth century and the third century BCE)[14] prophesy the end of days, when Israel's enemies will be called to account and the faithful will be rewarded:

> [YHWH] shall swallow up death forever, and . . . [YHWH God] shall wipe the tears from every face, and [God's] people's disgrace [God]

shall take off from all the earth, for [YHWH] has spoken. And it shall be said on that day:

> Look, this is our God in Whom we hoped, and [God] rescued us,
> This is our own God in Whom we hoped,
> Let us exult and rejoice in [God's] rescue. (Isa. 25:8–9)[15]

> Oh, let Your dead revive! Let corpses arise! Awake and shout for joy, you who dwell in the dust! For Your dew is like the dew on fresh growth; You make the land of the shades come to life. Go, my people, enter your chambers, and lock your doors behind you. Hide but a little moment, until the indignation passes. For lo! YHWH shall come forth . . . to punish the dwellers of the earth for their iniquity; and the earth shall disclose its bloodshed and shall no longer conceal its slain. (Isa. 26:19–21)[16]

Here, the image of God swallowing up "death" clearly harkens back to ancient Canaanite mythology in which one god, Mot (Death), swallows another, Baal. In the end, Baal comes back to life but nonetheless must co-exist with Mot. Isaiah reverses the roles and the outcome: God swallows Mot forever and reigns supreme.[17]

Maimonides expressed "doubt as to whether such [the verse in Isaiah] is an allegory or is really true," and indeed many modern scholars read this passage allegorically.[18] John J. Collins suggests that "Isaiah 26 can be read by analogy with Ezekiel 37: Israel was dead in the Exile, and its restoration is as miraculous as the resurrection of the dead, while the power of Babylon is gone forever."[19] Levenson notes that the reference to "[God's] people's disgrace" (Isa. 25:8, above) may speak to God's intent to resurrect just those who had suffered this particular tragedy rather than the people as a whole. Abraham Joshua Heschel reads God's swallowing up death and wiping away all tears in the context of Isaiah's prophecy of the ultimate victory of peace over war: "Nation shall not take up sword against nation; they shall never again know war" (2:4).[20]

Levenson does make a convincing case that Isaiah's words have a stronger end-time feel than Ezekiel's, which justifies treating Isaiah as a further step toward the kind of resurrection envisioned by later Jewish and Christian sources.[21] Here God will come forth to punish sinners, and the reference to dew, literally "a dew of lights," may contain "a hint of the ultimate transformation of the natural order."[22]

DANIEL

Daniel is the latest composition in the Hebrew Bible: Chapters 7 through 12 were likely written around 164 BCE, during the Maccabean revolt.[23] Set in the sixth century BCE, the book—this passage included—takes up the theme of Israel's ultimate deliverance from subjugation by foreign powers:

> At that time, the great prince, Michael, who stands beside the sons of your people, will appear. It will be a time of trouble, the like of which has never been since the nation came into being. At that time, your people will be rescued, all who are found inscribed in the book. Many of those that sleep in the dust of the earth will awake, some to eternal life, others to reproaches, to everlasting abhorrence. And the knowledgeable will be radiant like the bright expanse of sky, and those who lead the many to righteousness will be like the stars forever and ever. (Dan. 12:1–3)

Most contemporary scholars take this to be the Bible's most literal statement about resurrection. Even Maimonides, often quick to offer allegorical interpretations, concluded that "the resurrection of the dead, which is the return of the soul to the body after death, has been mentioned by Daniel in such a way that it cannot be interpreted allegorically."[24]

Note that Daniel's language also harkens back to the preceding Isaiah text. Both passages refer to the dead as asleep in the dust, and both use the same Hebrew verb, *l'hakitz*, for "awakening." C. D. Elledge, author of *Resurrection of the Dead in Early Judaism*, suggests, "By shading its language with the accents of earlier Isaianic expressions, Daniel's resurrection prophecy strikes a strong chord of continuity with earlier prophetic hopes."[25]

While Daniel couched his prophecy in language that would resonate with earlier sources, events of his own time raised theological questions that transformed what had been metaphors about resurrection into profoundly literal hopes. Ideas about resurrection of the dead had already begun to gain some currency in Jewish circles; the martyrdom of pious Jews during the Maccabean Revolt (167–164 BCE) only accelerated this process.

For some during this period, the theology that had helped Jewish exiles in Babylonia cope with their plight centuries earlier had worn thin. In Ezekiel's day God had punished the people with exile and allowed the Temple's destruction because of their sins: "Strangers have been cheated in your midst, orphans and widows have been wronged within you. You have despised My holy things and profaned My sabbaths" (Ezek. 22:7–8). For this and more, God had poured divine fury upon Israel. But in the end, Ezekiel prophesied, the covenant between the people and God would be restored. Israel would repent; God would relent and bring the people back home. Events seemed to prove Ezekiel right. After seventy years of exile, the Persian king Cyrus permitted the exiles to return home and rebuild the Temple.

But events of Daniel's time strained Ezekiel's theology to the breaking point. During the Maccabean revolt, *pious* Jews were tortured and killed because they *refused* to forsake Jewish law. The Second Book of Maccabees, composed around 100 BCE, recounts the martyrdom of seven brothers and their mother:

> [The fourth brother to the King:] One cannot but choose to die at the hands of mortals and to cherish the hope God gives of being raised again by [God]. But for you [the King] there will be no resurrection to life! (7:14). [Last to die, the mother encourages her last son's faithfulness:] Therefore the Creator of the world, who shaped the beginning of humankind and devised the origin of all things, will in . . . mercy give life and breath back to you again, since you now forget yourselves for the sake of [God's] laws (7:23). I beg you, my child, to look at the heaven and the earth and see everything that is in them, and recognize that God did not make them out of things that existed. And in the same way the human race came into being. . . . Accept death so that in God's mercy I may get you back again along with your brothers (7:28–29). [Before his death the last son tells the King,] You have not yet escaped the judgment of the almighty, all-seeing God. For our brothers after enduring a brief suffering have drunk of overflowing life, under God's covenant; but you by the judgment of God, will receive just punishment (7:35–36).[26]

Gabriel Marcel's formulation of hope as the response to the trial helps illuminate the relationship between martyrdom and the hope for resurrection. As faithful Jews endured the brutal test of martyrdom, a new hope began to emerge—bodily resurrection. This hope also provided a new solution to the old problem of theodicy. The suffering of innocents could be reconciled with an all-just and omnipotent God: God would redeem the pious martyrs from death and justly punish their persecutors. Lest the reader doubt God's power to do so, the text adds something not found in earlier Jewish texts. In Genesis, God creates by imposing order on chaos: God fashions Adam from the dust of the earth. Here, God creates *ex nihilo*, from nothing, as if to say, nothing is too difficult for God, even resurrecting bodies that have been cut to pieces.[27]

Hope for bodily resurrection was not the only way to deny death's finality. Greek philosophy had long posited immortality of the soul. In *Phaedo*, one of Plato's dialogues, Socrates says that

> the soul is most like the divine and immortal and intellectual and uniform and indissoluble and ever unchanging, and the body, on the contrary, most like the human and mortal and multiform and unintellectual and dissoluble and ever changing. (80b)[28]

In some Jewish circles, these ideas proved more attractive than resurrection of the body. Philo of Alexandria (born Yedidiah Ha-Cohen, c. 20 BCE–50 CE), clearly influenced by Plato and Greek philosophy more generally, described martyrdom "as an entrance to immortality."[29] The Essenes, known for their scrolls at Qumran, also subscribed to immortality of the soul, a hope that functioned for them during war against Rome (66–70 CE) in much the same way as hope for bodily resurrection had for the Maccabees in their rebellion against the Seleucid Greeks about two centuries earlier. The Jewish historian Josephus (37–100 CE) put it this way:

> Although they [the Essenes] were tortured and distorted, burnt and torn to pieces, and went through all kinds of instruments of torment, that they might be forced either to blaspheme their legislator, or to eat what was forbidden them, yet could they not be made to do either of them, no nor once to flatter their tormentors, or to shed a tear; but they smiled in their very pains, and laughed those to scorn who

inflicted the torments upon them, and resigned up their souls, with great alacrity, as expecting to receive them again.[30]

Again, the trials of martyrdom fueled hope for an afterlife—in the case of the Essenes, one characterized by immortality of the soul.

The Rise of the Rabbis and the Triumph of Resurrection

For reasons that are not well understood, by the end of the first century CE, the Essenes vanished from the scene.[31] This left two competing positions on the afterlife.

SADDUCEES VERSUS PHARISEES

The Sadducees, commonly thought to be associated with the priestly community, denied the existence of an afterlife, including resurrection. The Pharisees, likely composed of subordinate government "officials, bureaucrats, judges and educators," trumpeted it. It took time for their theology to achieve dominance.[32]

Josephus wrote about the Pharisees' beliefs, though scholars now believe Josephus colored them with his own brush. Heavily influenced by Hellenistic thought, Josephus likely would have been more comfortable amplifying the Pharisees' Greek-inspired belief in immortality of the soul along with their belief in resurrection of the dead:

[The Pharisees] believe that souls have an immortal vigour in them: and that under the earth there will be rewards, or punishments; according as they have lived virtuously or viciously in this life: and the latter are to be detained in an everlasting prison; but that the former shall have power to revive and live again. On account of which doctrines they are able greatly to persuade the body of the people: and whatsoever they do about divine worship, prayers, and sacrifices, they perform them according to their direction. Insomuch, that the cities give great attestations to them, on account of their entire virtuous conduct, both in the actions of their lives, and their discourses also.[33]

The New Testament's Acts (composed 89–90 CE) may come closer to telling the truth about the Pharisees' beliefs. Here, Paul, a Jew, stands before the Council of Elders in Jerusalem after his preaching about how he came to believe in Jesus has caused a public disturbance:

> When Paul noticed that some were Sadducees and others were Pharisees, he called out in the council, "Brothers, I am a Pharisee, a son of Pharisees. I am on trial concerning the hope of the resurrection of the dead." When he said this, a dissension began between the Pharisees and the Sadducees, and the assembly was divided. (The Sadducees say that there is no resurrection, or angel, or spirit; but the Pharisees acknowledge all three.) (23:6–8) . . . "But this I admit to you, that according to the [Christian] Way, which they call a sect, I worship the God of our ancestors, believing everything laid down according to the law or written in the prophets. I have a hope in God—a hope that they themselves also accept—that there will be a resurrection of both the righteous and the unrighteous" (Acts 24:14–15).

Paul suggests that, far from being guilty of anything, he's only spreading "hope for resurrection"—an idea that had already found a home within a significant segment of the Jewish community.

THE RISE OF THE RABBIS

Rabbinic Judaism succeeded the Pharisaic movement in the post-Temple period (after Jewish zealots' failed rebellion against Rome led to the Second Temple's destruction in 70 CE), though the relationship between the two remains murky.[34] As Bible scholar Claudia Setzer observes, both Pharisaic and Rabbinic Judaism shared a number of characteristics: strict adherence to Jewish law, a unique approach to scriptural interpretation, belief that God actively intervenes in human affairs, and surety that God would resurrect the dead. Both groups also needed to persuade sectors of the population who held different views.[35]

As such, the following Rabbinic text from *Mishnah Sanhedrin* was likely designed to forewarn deniers of resurrection of the punishment to come for their refusal to champion this key belief—even though in this case, enforcing the penalty was left to God:

All Israelites have a share in the world to come. . . . And these are the ones who have no portion in the world to come. One who denies that resurrection of the dead [is a teaching which derives from the Torah] and the Torah does not come from Heaven. . . . Rabbi Akiva says, "Also: One who reads heretical books."[36]

Setzer offers a compelling sociological analysis of resurrection as a symbol and a strategy at the time. First, as a symbol, "resurrection condenses a worldview." It expressed belief in an active and just God in an era when events raised questions about both. Second, "resurrection is imprecise and abstract." It was wide open to interpretation; therefore it could appeal to people who viewed resurrection in different ways. Third, "belief in resurrection as a symbol draws boundaries." Particularly in such times of change, symbols drew distinctions between groups. Fourth, "resurrection constructs community." Symbols reinforced group identity. And fifth, "resurrection confers legitimacy on those who employ it."[37] As resurrection drew adherents, the authority of its champions grew.

Setzer concludes that resurrection of the dead functioned as a not-necessarily-conscious strategy for the Rabbis to define themselves, build their popularity on the shoulders of their Pharisaic forebears, and help their followers make spiritual and political sense of their world. God's hand may have seemed remote, but the concept of resurrection promised hope for an awesome return. And after a second disastrous revolt against Rome (132–35 CE), the empire's brutal hand was easier to endure with the hope for life after death.

Like all effective strategies, this one, too, drew strength from pre-existing cultural resources: in this case, the words of Ezekiel, Isaiah, and Daniel. For example, one talmudic sage argued that the resurrection Ezekiel described was not a parable but real: "The dead that Ezekiel resurrected went up to the Land of Israel, married and fathered sons and daughters." Another sage averred that he was one of their descendants and that his tefillin (phylacteries) had been handed down to him from one of those Israelites who had been resurrected.[38]

Another talmudic debate centered around a contradiction between two prophecies by Isaiah: one that God will "swallow up death forever" (Isa. 25:8); the other that one "who dies at a hundred years shall be reckoned a youth" (Isa. 65:20), meaning that people will still die, but their lifespans will be greatly lengthened. How to resolve the conflict? The first passage refers to the Jews, the second to idolaters.[39] Another verse from Isaiah— "And it shall be said on that day: 'Look, this is our God in Whom we hoped, and [God] rescued us'" (25:9)—was interpreted as a description of the righteous joyously dancing in a circle around God in the world to come.[40]

And when it comes to finding proof texts for resurrection in the Bible, one talmudic list ends with two passages from Daniel, neither requiring the typical Rabbinic feats of interpretation to make the case. "Many of those that sleep in the dust of the earth will awake, some to eternal life, others to reproaches, to everlasting abhorrence.... As for you [Daniel], go to the end and you shall rest, and stand up for your destiny at the end of days" (Dan. 12:2, 12:13).[41]

Perhaps Rabbinic Judaism's greatest legacy concerning resurrection of the dead can be found in the *Amidah*, Judaism's central prayer, recited three times daily, four times on the Sabbath and holidays, and five times on Yom Kippur. The *Amidah*'s second blessing, known as *Gevurot* (God's Power), speaks repeatedly of God giving life to the dead in language reminiscent of the aforementioned Isaiah and Daniel passages:

You are forever mighty, Adonai: giving life to the dead, You are a mighty savior. [From *Sh'mini Atseret* to the first day of Passover, add: You cause the wind to blow and You cause the rain to fall.] [From the first day of Passover to *Sh'mini Atseret*, add: You bring down the dew.] You sustain life with kindness, giving life to the dead with great mercy, supporting the fallen, healing the sick, and freeing the captive, and keeping faith with sleepers in the dust. Who is like You, master of might, and who resembles You, a King who causes death and causes life, and causes salvation to flourish. You faithfully give life to the dead. Blessed are You, Adonai, who gives life to the dead.[42]

While the precise wording of the prayer did not become established until the medieval period, the shorthand way in which early Rabbinic texts allude to it suggests a high degree of familiarity with its ideas eighteen hundred years ago. For example, the Mishnah, compiled around 200 CE, notes, "We make mention of 'the Power of Rain' [as in 'You cause the rain to fall'] in [the Benediction known as] 'the Resurrection of the Dead.'"[43] Short of adopting something equivalent to Christianity's belief in the resurrection of Jesus, it is hard to imagine how the Rabbis and their successors over the ages could have more actively promoted resurrection than by lodging it so prominently in Judaism's most central prayer.

How Jews read this prayer is another matter. Some read it literally, fully hoping that if we are deserving, a re-embodied life awaits us at some point after death. Yet, if one reads it metaphorically, as I do, it can also serve as a fountain of hope. To be overwhelmed by despair is to be cut off from the future, to feel dead. To say God revives the dead may mean that God restores a sense of future possibility and hope where none existed before. Read this way, the prayer may speak to the parts of ourselves that we've allowed to die because we no longer view them as having any hope of fulfillment. Moreover, when we are alive we often act as if we're dead—dead to the wonders and responsibilities enveloping us every minute. God reminds us of infinite possibility. God calls us to wake up and live life more fully—prompts that come with such force, it's as if we've been revived from the dead.

This may sound very contemporary, but the roots of such a metaphoric reading go back a long time. The Talmud prescribes a blessing to be said upon seeing a friend one hasn't encountered for at least a year: "Blessed be God, who gives life to the dead."[44] Elsewhere, expounding on Ecclesiastes 9:5, "the dead know nothing," the Talmud says this refers to "the wicked who in their lifetime are called dead," and cites as illustration Ezekiel 21:30, which calls King Zedekiah a "wicked corpse," though he was fully alive at the time.[45] Later commentators would explain why the Talmud regarded the wicked as dead during their lifetimes—because they didn't help the needy, because they didn't recite blessings acknowledging their life's bounties, and so forth.[46] Read metaphorically, the *Amidah*'s benediction about resurrection of the dead inspires the hope that we, the living, can live life more fully.

The Messiah of the Rabbis

The Rabbinic sages believed that resurrection of the dead would occur. They just didn't know when. While some couldn't resist trying to calculate a specific date, more often the sages pointed to an era at the end of time: *Yemot ha-Mashiach*, the "days of the Messiah," for some, or the "world to come."

The concept evolved from humble roots. *Mashiach* comes from the Hebrew root *mem-shin-chet*, meaning to anoint with oil in a process of consecration. In the Bible, kings are anointed in the course of coronation. Kings are called "YHWH's anointed." Priests are also anointed, but so are inanimate objects—the Tent of Meeting, the altar, and unleavened bread when used for sacrificial purposes. The word "christ" comes from the Greek *chrio*, which means "anointed."

As with resurrection of the dead, the Bible supplies the hints of a messianic figure upon which later literature elaborated. A paradigmatic example is the following text from Isaiah—God gathering the People of Israel "from the four corners of the earth and returning them to Israel." Though Isaiah's prophecy doesn't mention resurrection or "an anointed one," it embodies what we now call a vision of messianic redemption:

> But a shoot shall grow out of the stump of Jesse [i.e., the house of King David], a twig shall sprout from his stock. The spirit of YHWH shall alight upon him: a spirit of wisdom and insight, a spirit of counsel and valor, a spirit of devotion and reverence for YHWH. . . . Thus he shall judge the poor with equity and decide with justice for the lowly of the land. He shall strike down a land with the rod of his mouth and slay the wicked with the breath of his lips. Justice shall be the girdle of his loins, and faithfulness the girdle of his waist. The wolf shall dwell with the lamb, the leopard lie down with the kid; the calf, the beast of prey, and the fatling together, with a little boy to herd them. . . . In all of My sacred mount nothing evil or vile shall be done; for the land shall be filled with devotion to YHWH as water covers the sea. In that day, the stock of Jesse that has remained standing shall become a standard to peoples—nations shall seek his counsel and his abode shall be honored. (Isa. 11:1, 2, 4–6, 9, 10)

It's no surprise that the Talmud (Megillah 31a) selects this passage from Isaiah as the prophetic reading for the last day of Passover. As Michael Fishbane writes, "All these hopes are recited on the eighth day of Passover, concluding the festival of freedom with hopes of the great redemption to come."[47] In the same spirit, Israel's official rabbinate ordained this as the prophetic reading for Israel's Independence Day. (The prayer for the State of Israel likewise refers to Israel as "the beginning of the flowering of our redemption.")

After the Mishnah's composition (c. 200 CE), the sages began extensive elaboration on its relatively slim comments about the Messiah.[48] Elijah was commonly identified as the herald of the Messiah, whose arrival would initiate resurrection of the dead.[49] Some Rabbis thought he would return three days before the Messiah.[50] Others imagined the Messiah sitting at the city wall, changing the bandages of lepers every day. When a sage approached him asking when he would announce himself, he replied, "Today." The sage later accused the Messiah of lying, because the momentous event had failed to occur, but Elijah explained that the Messiah was quoting the first word of a verse from Scripture: "Today—if you will listen to [God's] voice" (Ps. 95:7).[51] A medieval text avers that both the Messiah and Elijah will arrive on the night of Passover—a source for the seder ritual of opening the door for Elijah.[52]

Rabbi Akiva (d. 135 CE) also claimed to have met the Messiah—Shimon ben Kosiba—whose adopted name, Bar Kokhba (son of a star), alluded to a verse from Numbers. Rabbi Akiva often expounded, "A star rises from Jacob, a scepter comes forth from Israel" (Num. 24:17). When he beheld ben Kosiba, he exclaimed, "This is the king Messiah," a belief his colleagues sharply derided.[53] Additional Rabbinic pushback came in midrashic texts condemning Bar Kokhba, who led a disastrous rebellion against Rome (132–35 CE), for "hastening the end"—grievously interfering with God's redemptive timetable:

> God adjured Israel that they should not rebel against the Governments, that they should not seek to hasten the end [hasten God's timetable for the Messiah's arrival] . . . and that they should not attempt to go up from the diaspora by force. For if they do, why should the King Messiah come to gather the exiles of Israel?[54]

To the Rabbis, it was better to follow the advice of the prophet Habakkuk: "Even if it tarries, wait for it still. For it will surely come, without delay" (2:3).[55]

The ban on hastening the coming of the Messiah did not extend to the power of piety: "If Israel repented for a single day, immediately the son of David would come. If Israel observed a single Sabbath properly, the son of David would immediately come."[56] Disagreement arose about whether God or the Messiah would rebuild the Temple, but, in any case, sacrifices—just the thanks offering—would resume.[57]

A measure of solace also came from the notion that extreme economic, political, and social decline plaguing large swaths of the Jewish population in talmudic times represented the "birth pangs" or "footprints" of the Messiah. It was said, "The son of David will only come in a generation that is wholly innocent or wholly guilty."[58] Things would be so horrendous that several sages said, "Let him come, and let me not see him."[59] The growing darkness thus strengthened the hope that the Messiah was just over the horizon.

Comfort also came from Rabbinic predictions that the wonders of the Messianic Era would transcend nature itself. The light of the moon would be as light as the sun. Healing waters would gush from Jerusalem and cure all ailments.[60] A single grape would be so large it would fill an entire wagon, and provide one's home with at least thirty kegs of wine. Wheat would grow as tall as palm trees.[61] Grain would ripen in fifteen days, and newly planted trees would bear fruit in a month.[62]

Others held a more sober view. Rabban Yochanan ben Zakkai, the leader of the Jewish community and an opponent of the first revolt against Rome (66–70 CE), urged that practical considerations take priority over messianic fervor.[63] Shmuel, one of the most influential Babylonian sages of his era (mid-third century CE), arrived at a conclusion that has continued to influence discussion on messianic matters: "The only difference between this world and the days of the Messiah is that oppression by other nations will then cease."[64] But that too would be worth the wait.

As with resurrection of the dead, the sages inserted a statement about messianic redemption into the *Amidah* (see chapter 5), the very heart of Jewish liturgy:

Speedily cause the offspring [*tzemach*] of Your servant David to flourish, [*tatzmiach*] and let his glory be exalted by Your help, for we hope for Your salvation all day. Blessed are You, YHWH, who causes salvation to flourish [*matzmiach*].[65]

The prayer did not reach its final form until the ninth century or possibly later, although the Talmud refers to it in a discussion of the *Amidah*.[66] Its language harkens back to Jeremiah's prophecy about the coming days when God will keep God's promises to Israel: "In those days and at that time, I will raise up a true branch of David's line [*atzmiach l'david tzemach*] [who] . . . shall do what is just and right in the land" (33:15).[67] By contrast to Jeremiah, the tone in the *Amidah* is more plaintive. As renowned Judaic scholar Louis Finkelstein (1895–1991, United States) wrote, "It is as if the Deity were reminded of His promise and asked to fulfill it."[68]

As with the *Amidah*'s benediction concerning the resurrection of the dead, the question for us is how we can meaningfully interpret this prayer that depicts us hoping for divine salvation "all day" long. In our day, this blessing can serve another purpose. The Talmud tells us that when we face judgment in the world to come we will be asked six questions, the fourth being, "Did you hope for salvation?"[69] The kabbalist Isaac Luria (1534–72, Israel) linked reciting this prayer to providing evidence of an affirmative answer (thrice daily!) to the Talmud's query.[70] Some claim that when Luria prayed and the prayer leader said, "We hope for Your salvation," the congregation would respond with words that echoed those used in the Talmud: "And we hope for salvation."[71] We may not believe in a heavenly judgment that depends on whether or not we hoped for divine salvation. But the notion that we ought to judge ourselves in part by the content and strength of our hopes rings true.

Writing about this passage from the perspective of "creative hope," the contemporary commentator Shlomo Aviner stresses that it is not about passively sitting on the sidelines and hoping for salvation. He compares the *Amidah*'s promise of salvation to a bird that will hatch from an egg within a nest. No one can yet see the fledgling, yet one day it will emerge as the product of all the nurturing it has received. "All are therefore called to act" to bring about redemption.[72]

Maimonides on the Messiah and the Afterlife

Ideas about resurrection, the afterlife, and the Messiah continued to develop over the centuries. The thinking of physician, astronomer, philosopher, and codifier of Jewish law Maimonides (1137/38–1204) constitutes one particularly important step in that evolution. Though his beliefs in this regard were controversial in his day, they have exerted significant influence on modern thinking about the ideas under discussion.

THE MESSIANIC ERA

Maimonides believed that hope of attaining life in the world to come depended on two merits: the acquisition of wisdom and the performance of religious precepts. As he saw it, the problem was that "when one is troubled here on earth with diseases, war or famine," one "does not occupy" oneself "with these requirements."[73] He also thought that the Messianic Era would enable people to do what was necessary to fulfill their hopes of reaching the world to come. Therefore, he said, "all Israelites, their prophets and sages longed for the advent of Messianic times" so they could devote themselves to studying Torah, fulfilling religious obligations, "getting wisdom"; they would thereby "attain . . . life in the world to come."[74]

Thus Maimonides situated the Messianic Era within—not after—history: "The Messianic era . . . will be realized in this world; which will continue in its normal course except that independent sovereignty will be restored to Israel."[75] He characterized the Messiah as a king from the House of David who "will teach the whole of the Jewish people and instruct them in the way of God and all the nations will come to hear him."[76] While "there will still be rich and poor, strong and weak," nonetheless "it will be very easy . . . to make a living."[77] As a result, the People of Israel would be able to fully devote themselves to serving God so that "knowledge, wisdom and truth will increase" and wars shall cease.[78] The Messiah would die and be succeeded by his son and then his grandson. Because "grief and hardship" would diminish, life expectancy would increase, and "it would not be surprising if his dominion lasted for thousands of years. As our sages have put it, 'When good is gathered together it cannot be speedily dissipated.'"[79]

Following the lead of the great Babylonian sage Shmuel, Maimonides demythologized the Messiah and the Messianic Era, explaining both in completely human terms. He rejected the notion of an apocalyptic rupture in which a radically new and fully formed epoch would suddenly burst forth. Instead, the Messianic Era would unfold over time: "Knowledge, wisdom and truth will *increase*." Guided by the intellect, spiritual values would incrementally triumph over materialism:

We do not long and hope for the days of the Messiah because of an increase of productivity and wealth which may occur then, or that we may ride on horses and drink wine to the accompaniment of song, as some confused people think. The prophets and the saints looked forward to the days of the Messiah and yearned for them because then the righteous will be gathered together in fellowship, and because goodness and wisdom will prevail.[80]

To Maimonides, the Messiah is a king unlike any the world has seen. Instead of waging war, accumulating riches, and conquering territory, this king would set a powerful enough example of fairness and justice to influence leadership throughout the world to fundamentally improve society. Maimonides scholar Kenneth Seeskin explains:

[Maimonides] . . . has not set the bar for the Messiah so high that no one can cross it. On the contrary, by doing away with the miraculous dimension of messianism, he has lowered the bar to the point where the expectations we have for it could possibly be fulfilled. To be sure, they are not easy to fulfill and would require historical progress unlike anything witnessed thus far. But difficulty is one thing, possibility another. As long as there is possibility, there is ground for hope.[81]

Maimonides tethered the Messianic Era to this world and sided with those in the Rabbinic tradition who viewed it as the outcome of incremental human effort rather than a sudden miraculous event. In doing so, he expressed his profound hope in humanity—that eventually we shall complete the work of God's creation and usher in a Messianic Era.

RESURRECTION AND SPIRITUAL IMMORTALITY

Maimonides also offered hope that, after the Messianic Era, the human soul would find eternal life. He first wrote about this at length in his commentary on the tenth chapter of *Mishnah Sanhedrin*, which begins, "All Israelites have a share in the world to come." As Maimonides understood it, the world to come would follow the Messianic Era, during which human beings would achieve a measure of perfection. "When one becomes fully human, [one] acquires the nature of the perfect human being; there is no external power to deny [one's] soul eternal life. [One's] soul thus attains eternal life . . . which is the world to come."[82] Maimonides described this as a disembodied state of spiritual delight comparable to that of angels, who "have no bodily delight . . . since they have no physical senses, as we do."[83]

Note that here Maimonides made no mention of bodily resurrection of the dead. Maimonides would continue to avoid this topic for decades — one of the issues that outraged his critics. The great Spanish scholar of Talmud and religious law, Meir Abulafia (1170–1244), for example, argued that Maimonides was undermining a cornerstone of Jewish faith. "If bodies will not be resurrected how can the promise of a redeemed Israel be fulfilled. . . . If God does not resurrect, where is the hope for those who at great personal sacrifice obey [God's] law."[84]

Finally, in 1191, thirteen years before Maimonides' death, in hopes of mollifying his opponents, clarifying his position, or some combination thereof, Maimonides wrote a *Treatise on Resurrection*, where he addressed the question head-on:

> Thus, the resurrection of the dead, which is the return of the soul to the body after death, has been mentioned by Daniel in such a way that it cannot be interpreted allegorically. For he said, "Many of those that sleep in the dust of the earth will awake, some to eternal life, others to reproaches, to everlasting abhorrence." . . . It is also apparent to us from those (Talmudic) statements that those individuals whose souls return to their bodies (after death) will eat and drink and engage in sexual intercourse and sire children and die after an extremely long life like the life which will exist during the days of the Messiah. Further, the life following which there is no death, is the life in the world to come because there are no (physical) bodies there. We firmly believe — and this is the truth which every intelligent person accepts — that in the world to come souls without bodies will exist like angels.[85]

Throughout his life, Maimonides sought to demythologize Jewish thought and to demonstrate the complete compatibility of Judaism with reason, science, and the truths of Greek philosophy. His efforts to bridge the gap between Greek philosophy (or rationalism) and traditional Jewish thought regarding resurrection led him to postulate what theologian Neil Gillman (1933–2017, Canada and United States) calls a doctrine of "double dying."[86] When life ends, we die. In the Messianic Era, our bodies come back to life. When the Messianic Era ends, our bodies die again—and then our now-disembodied souls awaken forever. The disembodied souls of the meritorious awake to immortality and eternal communion with the Divine—that is, the world to come. The souls of the undeserving, too, "will awake . . . to reproaches, to everlasting abhorrence" (Dan. 12:2). Thus Maimonides could support traditional beliefs about bodily resurrection while also remaining true to Greek concepts of the immortal soul. Nonetheless, controversy swirled around Maimonides for a century after his death. Some critics argued that disembodied souls could "not receive their reward or punishment in the *Olam ha-Ba* [world to come] except conjoined with their bodies."[87] Others believed that Maimonides' penchant for reading the Bible allegorically would dangerously undermine adherence to the laws anchored in those texts.

Among his many legacies, Maimonides' hopes about the immortality of the soul and the Messiah would live on. They would find a home in Reform, Conservative, and Reconstructionist Judaism, all of which have largely demythologized the Messiah and affirmed the immortality of the soul, regardless of their different views on resurrection of the dead.[88] His conviction that human beings have the potential to bring the Messianic Era by curing the ills of this world allies him with Jews today who define their hopes in terms of *tikkun olam*. His willingness to translate hopes for an afterlife into spiritual terms speaks to many of us who share that hope and cannot quite embrace the notion of bodily resurrection. And that he had the courage to express those hopes at a time when the Jewish world largely opposed them makes him an inspiration to all whose hopes sometimes push the envelope.

Reform Judaism's Hopes for the Afterlife

In the modern era, Judaism has continued to evolve in its understandings of resurrection. The Reform movement's journey away from and then back to tradition represents one such example. Deeply colored by Maimonidean thought and the Enlightenment's commitment to rationalism and science, the evolving theology of late nineteenth-century American Reform Judaism would come to both reflect and refashion old/new Jewish hopes about the afterlife and the Messiah.

From its early days in America, Reform Judaism had taken issue with traditional hopes for bodily resurrection and a divinely anointed Messiah.[89] In 1825, when a gathering of Jews established the Reformed Society of Israelites, it articulated ten articles of faith, modeled after Maimonides' Thirteen Principles, its fifth article reading: "I believe, with a perfect faith, that the soul of man is breathed into him by God, and is therefore immortal." The society's last principle replaced the concept of a personal Messiah (taking an implicit swipe at Christianity) with this: "I believe, with a perfect faith, that the Creator . . . is the only true Redeemer of all his children and that he will spread the worship of his name over the whole earth."[90]

These sentiments found their way into Reform prayer books. For example, the 1872 version of *Minhag America: The Daily Prayers for American Israelites* eliminates the reference to the Davidic Messiah and instead expresses the hope that God's servants will walk in God's ways. Where the *Amidah* traditionally refers to God as giving life to the dead, here God is a Sovereign "who killest, revivest, and speedest salvation."[91] In his 1872 Reform prayer book, *Olat Tamid: Book of Prayers for Israelitish Congregations*, David Einhorn also omits the messianic section of the prayer. His treatment of resurrection in the Hebrew—left untranslated in the original—echoes the blessing recited after a portion of Torah has been read. It refers to God as the One "who plants within us eternal life."[92]

This was also an era, as historian Akiba Lerner puts it, when "Transcendental hopes for reward in an afterlife gave way to secular forms of utopianism and emancipation predicated on changing this world through the power of science and humanistic values."[93] The Reform movement's positions on the Messiah and resurrection in its 1885 Pittsburgh Platform— the Central Conference of American Rabbis' first official statements of principles—bear out Lerner's observations:

> We recognize, in the modern era of universal culture of heart and intellect, the approaching of the realization of Israel's great Messianic hope for the establishment of the kingdom of truth, justice, and peace. . . .

We recognize in Judaism a progressive religion, ever striving to be in accord with the postulates of reason. . . . We reassert the doctrine of Judaism that the soul is immortal, grounding the belief on the divine nature of human spirit, which forever finds bliss in righteousness and misery in wickedness. We reject as ideas not rooted in Judaism, the beliefs both in bodily resurrection and in Gehenna and Eden (Hell and Paradise) as abodes for everlasting punishment and reward.[94]

Years later, however, the 1975 prayer book *Gates of Prayer* restored—with modifications—much of the *Amidah* that had been removed in 1895. Yet in place of the traditional prayer hoping for the flowering of the Davidic kingship and messianic deliverance, it called for the flowering of justice.[95]

The Reform rabbinate's most recent platform in 1999, a response to "a new interest in the religious life of the Jewish individual,"[96] addresses questions about the Messiah and the afterlife far more extensively than its antecedents. The section titled "Torah" includes the statement: "Partners with God in *tikkun olam*, repairing the world, we are called to help bring nearer the messianic age."[97] Additionally, the movement's commentary on the platform speaks of hopes for a Messianic Age, likely far off:

Still, we renew our hope for it when we express the belief that Shabbat is *mei-ein olam haba*, a sampler of the world to come, when we sing about Elijah, herald of the messiah, when *Havdalah* brings Shabbat to a close, when we open the door for Elijah late in the Pesach Seder, and when we express the hope in the first paragraph of the *Kaddish* that God's sovereignty will be established in our days.[98]

This commentary also refers to hopes for resurrection expressed by both Ezekiel and Daniel as envisioning afterlife, albeit interpreting both in terms of spiritual immortality rather than bodily resurrection:

Regardless of what you may have heard, the promise of eternal life of the spirit is part and parcel of Reform Judaism. . . . Several generations of Reform Jews took as a matter of Reform Jewish faith the denial of any life after death beyond the naturalist concepts of living on in memory or in deeds. Clearly this was a function of the dominant philosophical and cultural climate in which Reform Jews lived and with which they identified. Some Reform Jews have tended to characterize certain areas of belief as either Christian or Orthodox Jewish. In either case, that rendered them outside the pale of Reform, though many longed for a comforting belief in a life that could transcend death. . . . The Bible promises, "I shall not die but live" (Psalms 118:17), and the Reform prayer book tells us, "There is something of us that can never die."[99]

To its credit, the Reform rabbinate has been quite frank about acknowledging the evolution of its thinking about the afterlife:

This principle, although in one sense a restatement of that which all three previous platforms affirmed, marks a great change because of the changed nature of the Reform Jewish community and its newly acknowledged needs. Most contemporary Reform Jews do not feel that their intellectual and scientific credentials are at issue. The religious issue is meaning in life and hope after life, not the need to make religion subservient to culture, science or some form of reason.[100]

In 2007, the Reform movement took still a further step in its new prayer book, *Mishkan T'filah*. It restored long-expunged words about God bringing life to the dead, though as a parenthesized alternative: "who gives life to all (revives the dead)." *Mishkan T'filah* editor Elyse Frishman explained, "For a number of people in our movement, reclaiming traditional language feels very meaningful. And when that language resonates positively, people want it." The commentary accompanying the addition elucidated: "The resurrection of the dead, which may be taken literally, is best understood as a powerful metaphor for understanding the miracle of hope. Winter gives way to spring."[101]

At the Reform movement's 1997 Biennial, as the movement began to reconsider its views about the afterlife, Rabbi Marc Gellman delivered the keynote address:

Somewhere between what we want and what we inherit, what we invent and what we are bequeathed, is what we need. And what spir-

itually enlightened Jews need now is to believe in life after death. . . .
Why have Reform Jews abandoned the most assuring of all beliefs?
. . . In the face of our finitude, only religion can offer hope—hope
that the good in us will win, and hope that we will not be separated
forever from those we love. If a religion can no longer offer hope, it
is, simply, no longer a religion. After 25 years in the rabbinate I've
learned that some things are true at the edge of the grave that do not
seem true anywhere else.[102]

This brief case study of the Reform movement demonstrates Judaism's continuing capacity to evolve—itself an enormous source of Jewish
hope. Long-banished liturgical evocations of resurrection of the dead have
returned to the prayer book in Hebrew with true English translation. The
hope for resurrection seems to enjoy eternal life.

Humans Fulfilling Hopes for Immortality?

The Isaiah Apocalypse we've explored placed its ultimate hope for fulfilling messianic yearnings and conquering death in the Divine: God "shall
prepare a banquet for all the peoples on this mountain, a banquet of rich
food, a banquet of well-aged wines. . . . [God] shall swallow up death forever, and . . . shall wipe the tears from every face" (Isa. 25:6, 8).[103] First God
treats humanity to a messianic banquet, and then God vanquishes death.

THEOLOGICAL PERSPECTIVES

Echoing Maimonides, theologians in our time have shifted the responsibility for messianic redemption from divine to human hands. Joseph B.
Soloveitchik asserts that humanity "shares the divine execution of covenant realization. The messianic hope is based on this. . . . Man acts as a
divine agent and redeems himself."[104] The title of Reform rabbi Robert N.
Levine's book captures this well: *There Is No Messiah and You're It*. The old/
new concept of *tikkun olam* now incorporates the ancient messianic idea.
When we work to repair the world, *tikkun olam*, we are acting as a messiah. So it is that messianic hope keeps us committed to the task, propels
us forward despite setbacks, times of despair, and the lure of cynicism.

This theological perspective also implies that God has handed over to us the ultimate divine intervention, swallowing up death forever, as Isaiah prophesied (25:8). In our era we might understand Isaiah as pointing to the time when we, created in God's image, will have the option first of postponing and then of conquering death. A breathtaking medieval midrash put it this way:

This is how God spoke to the righteous. "Behold, you are My equals . . . *If you produce what is noble out of the worthless, you shall be My spokesman* (Jer. 15:19). Even as I . . . resurrect the dead, so shall you."[105]

Arguably, whenever a human being successfully engages in life-saving measures without which someone would have died, we witness the still early signs of human intervention allowing life to triumph over death. In time, those signs are likely to multiply, and the quality of extended life as well.

FUTURISTS ON TRANSCENDING DEATH

Israeli philosopher and historian Yuval Noah Harari documents the current advances—and tremendous financial investments—in the human quest for immortality. He describes this "upgrading of the humans into gods" as demanding a "godlike control of their own biological substratum" to the point that "life [will] have no expiry date."[106]

Some futurist thinkers believe that rapid developments in Artificial Intelligence (AI) are giving rise to a transition from *Homo sapiens* to "techno sapiens" and the concept of posthumanism. Inventor and futurist Ray Kurzweil asserts,

As we cross the divide to instantiate ourselves into our computational technology, our identity will be based on our evolving mind file. *We will be software, not hardware.* . . . Our immortality will be a matter of being sufficiently careful to make frequent backups. If we're careless about this, we'll have to load an old backup copy and be doomed to repeat our recent past. . . . We don't always need real bodies. If we happen to be in a virtual environment, then a virtual body will do just fine.[107]

In a similar vein, professor of religious studies Robert M. Geraci writes, "Our new selves will be infinitely replicable, allowing them to escape the finality of death."[108]

We've only just begun to explore these frontiers, which one day may well extend to resurrection. Sooner or later studies like this may succeed:

> A team of Japanese researchers extracted nuclei of cells from a wooly mammoth that had died 28,000 years ago. When the nuclei were implanted in mouse egg cells "the ancient mammoth chromosomes swam into view and began to link up with the mouse egg's spindles" and the cell began to show early signs of dividing. Progress stopped at that point, possibly due to damage in the mammoth's DNA.[109]

The future of medical science may increasingly force us to develop new understandings of Deuteronomy's injunction: "I have put before you life and death, blessing and curse. Choose life" (30:19). In this context, hope will entail the struggle to assure that new technologies are applied with true justice and wisdom. In the world that lies ahead, hope will take on the enormous challenge of proving that Heschel was not correct when he said, "Humanity without death would be arrogance without end."[110]

Technological breakthroughs notwithstanding, when it comes to living forever, perhaps there won't be so many takers. A 2015 poll found that only 14 percent of Americans would choose to do so if they could.[111]

Conclusion

Many Jews identify hopes concerning the afterlife and resurrection of the dead with Christianity, but these hopes have been part and parcel of Judaism for millennia (albeit less central than in Christianity). Why these yearnings receive so little attention in the Bible in contrast to the scriptures of other ancient Near Eastern cultures remains an unsettled question. Perhaps scholar of ancient religions Alan F. Segal was right when he suggested that "presumably, any extended discussion of life after death or the realm of the dead with its pantheon of divinities would open the door for idolatry or veneration of ghosts, which the Bible, in its final and present form, has entirely forbidden."[112]

Against this biblical backdrop, how these hopes became so important to Judaism attests to the strength of human longings for some kind of immortality. Thus the sages of the Rabbinic period utilized the Bible's few texts that speak of resurrection and others that refer to the finality of death in more nuanced terms as the foundation for building an elaborate structure of eschatological hopes about the afterlife, bodily resurrection of the dead, and the Messianic Era. With a few important exceptions, the sages imagined an otherworldly Messianic Era of complete perfection and extended the hope of resurrection beyond those martyred for their faith to all who properly adhered to Judaism's religious precepts. Maimonides, however, stressed spiritual immortality rather than bodily resurrection and underscored that the Messianic Era would be the natural outcome of incremental human efforts to repair *this* world. While some attacked him for undermining dogmas of the faith, he would wield enormous influence in shaping contemporary Jewish hopes for the afterlife and the world to come across much of the denominational spectrum, especially within the Conservative, Reform, and Reconstructionist movements, as well as Modern Orthodoxy. Furthermore, the Reform movement's more recent liturgical resurrection of references to God giving life to the dead attests to the abiding power of Judaism's eschatological hopes.

At the same time, despite these diverse expressions in different ages and communities, Jewish thought about the afterlife and the Messianic Era has persisted as a mainstay of hope. Theologian Milton Steinberg (1903–50, United States) put it this way:

"And there is hope for your future" sang the prophet [Jer. 31:17]. A threefold hope is its reference. The hope . . . for the Jewish people: the expectation of its ultimate deliverance and vindication. A hope also for the individual soul: the trust that it will not be swallowed up in death. . . . A hope for society: the assurance that it will in the end be regenerated into something fairer, its evils purged away, its good perfected and made permanent. . . . [The Messiah will] not arrive all at once. It will be achieved slowly, cumulatively, "precept by precept, precept by precept, line by line, line by line; here a little, there a little" [Isa. 28:10]. . . . [And where is God] in this process . . . ? [God] is, as always, at work in [people], in their hopes and aspirations, in the skill and fortitude with which they pursue them.[113]

8

Israel

HOPE IN THE HOMELAND

As long as in the heart within
The Jewish soul yearns,
And toward the eastern edges, onward,
An eye gazes toward Zion
Our hope is not yet lost,
The hope that is two thousand years old,
To be a free nation in our land,
The Land of Zion, Jerusalem.
—"Hatikvah" ("The Hope"), Israel's national anthem

Introduction

Jewish restoration to the Land of Israel has constituted a central component of Jewish hopes for millennia. Jeremiah, who prophesied Israel's exile
to Babylonia in 586 BCE, also envisioned the people's return: "And there is
hope for your future—declares YHWH. Your children shall return to their
country" (Jer. 31:17)—and he was right; the Babylonian exile lasted just
seventy years. But in 135 CE the Bar Kokhba revolt led to the exile of the
vast majority of Jews from the Holy Land. Despite sporadic, small-scale
efforts to return over the years, this hope would not be fulfilled until the
twentieth century.

This chapter focuses on the hopes of pre-state Zionism; the challenges of fulfilling them with statehood; efforts by Israel's former
president Reuven Rivlin to build what he calls *Tikvah Yisraelit*, vari-
ously translated as "Hope for Israel" or "Israeli Hope"; and the work
of Israeli activists to sustain hope for themselves, their communities,
and their country.

Zionist Hope

Throughout the centuries, Jewish hopes and yearnings for Zion had long found expression in daily prayers and in the concluding words of the Passover seder and the Yom Kippur liturgy: "Next Year in Jerusalem!"—but that was a far cry from sustained collective action to fulfill them. Since talmudic times, Jewish teachings had held that God would see to the people's return to Zion. Therefore, human efforts in this direction were seen as dangerously misguided efforts to "push the end," by interfering with God's ordained messianic timetable.[1]

The shift from waiting for God to taking collective human action to return to Israel began in the nineteenth century. In 1897, Max Nordau, vice president of the first World Zionist Congress, held in Basel, Switzerland, described the change of mind among Jews who had waited long enough:

> They no longer hope in the advent of the Messiah, who will one day raise them to Glory. . . . [They] hope for the salvation from Zionism . . . not the fulfillment of a mystic promise of the Scripture, but the way to an existence wherein the Jew finds at last the simplest but most elementary conditions of life, that are a matter of course for every Jew of both hemispheres: viz, an assured social existence in a well-meaning community, the possibility of employing all his powers for the developments of his real being instead of abusing them for the suppression and falsification of self.[2]

Thus, at its very core, Zionism would not only re-orient the horizon of messianic hope from the world to come to this world but transfer responsibility for fulfilling it from divine to human hands.

MIKVEH YISRAEL, PETACH TIKVAH, "HATIKVAH"

In its earliest days, Zionism and hope were almost synonymous. Writing in 1862, Moses Hess (1812–75, Germany and France), the father of Labor Zionism, stressed the critical role of hope in restoring Jewish nationhood. "What we have to do at present for the regeneration of the Jewish nation is, first, to keep alive the hope of the political rebirth of our people, and next, to reawaken that hope where it slumbers."[3] In 1870, the founders of Palestine's first agricultural school named it Mikveh Yisrael, "Hope of Israel."[4] Eight years later, twenty-six observant families from Jerusalem purchased a tract of land for what would become the first Jewish agricultural settlement in the country, naming it Petach Tikvah, meaning "Gateway of Hope" or "Opening of Hope."[5] Malaria drove the settlers out, but in 1883 a different Zionist group, the Pioneers of Bilu, arrived in Israel.[6] Their manifesto concluded with the words, "The Lord is our God, the Lord is one, and our land Zion is our only hope."[7]

In 1878, possibly inspired by Petach Tikvah's founding, the Jewish poet Naftali Herz Imber (1856–1909, Galicia, Israel, New York) penned a nine-stanza poem, "Tikvatenu" (Our hope).[8] By 1888 his poem had become a song, soon renamed "Hatikvah," Hebrew for "The Hope." Samuel Cohen, a Romanian immigrant, fashioned the melody from a Moldavian folk song. The Jewish Pioneers embraced "Hatikvah" as part of the early Zionist culture of song and folk dance, and, at the Eighteenth Zionist Congress in 1933, the song was officially adopted as the movement's anthem.

Imber's original poem referenced the theme of hope in four of its nine stanzas. Several of those stanzas would be modified to create what would become Israel's national anthem:

I
Our hope is not yet lost,
The ancient hope:
Returning to the land of our ancestors,
To the city where David camped.

II
As long as in his heart within
The Jewish soul yearns
And toward the eastern edges, onward,
His eye gazes toward Zion.

VIII
As long as the feeling of love of nation
Beats in the heart of a Jew

We can still hope even today
That an indignant God will have mercy upon us.

IX
Listen my brothers in the lands of my wanderings
To the voice of one of our visionaries:
That only with the last Jew
Is the last of our hope![9]

Notably, the first line of his poem, "Our hope is not yet lost," turns the Bible upside down. In the book of Ezekiel, the Israelites say, "Our bones are dried up, and our hope is lost; we are clean cut off" (37:11).[10] And while Imber's poem mentions God, the anthem omits God entirely—an expression of secular Zionism's conviction that the task of returning and building the land lies in human rather than divine hands.

Imber died in 1909 in New York. In his eulogy, Rabbi Judah Magnes of Temple Emanu-El said, "Imber outdid greater poets than he because his poems expressed in song the joys and the hopes of the Jewish people."[11] Ten thousand people followed his coffin to the cemetery—singing "Hatikvah" as they walked.

BEN-YEHUDA'S HOPES FOR REVIVING THE HEBREW LANGUAGE

Imber wrote his poem, in Hebrew, even before the Vilna-born Eliezer Ben-Yehuda (1858–1922) arrived in Palestine in 1881. Ben-Yehuda, who would become known as "the father of modern Hebrew," was determined to revive a language that with few exceptions had not been used beyond religious contexts for more than two thousand years. In an 1880 letter he put it this way:

Today we may be moribund, but tomorrow we will surely awaken to life; today we may be in a strange land, but tomorrow we will dwell in the land of our fathers; today we may be speaking alien tongues, but tomorrow we shall speak Hebrew. This is the meaning of the hope for redemption, and I know of no other; our hope is for redemption, in its clear and literal sense not some veiled and oversubtle substitute.[12]

Ben-Yehuda's words echo the Passover Haggadah: "Now we are here. Next year in the land of Israel. Now we are slaves. Next year we will be free." But for him those were not just words to be recited year after year as Jews remained in exile. He saw his moribund people in need of resurrection and would not consign that rebirth to some far-off eschatological promise. The Jewish people's hope for redemption demanded concrete action: returning home and speaking their ancestral tongue—not next year, but tomorrow.

Vowing to speak only Hebrew to one another, Ben-Yehuda and his first wife, Devora, raised the first child ever to speak modern Hebrew. While Ben-Yehuda's early articles on the subject evoked derision—"A pious dream," said one critic[13]—this high-hope man of action persisted. He published a Hebrew-language newspaper (*Ha-Tzvi*, The Gazelle); a high-quality Hebrew-language intellectual journal (*Hashkafah*, Outlook); and the first volumes of a modern Hebrew dictionary (*Milon ha-Lashon ha-Ivrit ha-Yeshanah v'ha-Chadashah*, A Complete Dictionary of Ancient and Modern Hebrew).[14] He also assiduously pushed for Hebrew to become the language of instruction throughout Palestine's secular schools.

Opposition to reviving the Hebrew language was fierce on multiple sides. Orthodox Jews in Palestine railed against using the holy tongue for secular purposes. Secularists argued that diverting precious resources needed to develop the community in Palestine to learning Hebrew was misguided. In 1909 Ben-Yehuda took on opponents of a high school that planned to offer instruction in Hebrew:

> Not by cold judgment and the precise, factual approaches of sensible people are all the steps of human progress in the world made, all the revolutions great and small. In every new event, in every step, even the smallest in the path of progress, it is necessary that there be a Nachshon to jump into the sea without leaving any possibility of turning back! . . . I recognize well such people of good will—who talked and acted.[15]

Even the devoutly secular Ben-Yehuda drew hope from the biblical figure of Nachshon, who, after the Exodus from Egypt, is said to have plunged into the Red Sea while the rest of Israel debated.[16]

By 1916, six years before Ben-Yehuda's death, the revival of Hebrew that he championed was already well on its way to success. A census that year found that 40 percent of non-Orthodox Jews spoke Hebrew as their first language.[17]

The years 1917 and 1918 saw the publication of Ben-Yehuda's serialized autobiography, *Ha Chalom v'Shivro* (the dream and its interpretation, published in English as *A Dream Come True*). Near the conclusion, he recalled the community's terrible disappointment in 1882 when the Ottoman sultan Abdul Hamid II had closed the door to Jewish immigration to Palestine. The Sultan issued his decree on the Ninth of Av—the day Jews mourn the destruction of the First and Second Temples. This could "have put an end to the whole enterprise initiated in blind faith by a handful of dreamers."[18] But history works in strange ways, Ben-Yehuda observed. Six days after the decree, "did those dreamers respond with two deeds." First, immigrants to Palestine founded Rishon le-Tziyon, the first settlement. And on the very same day, Ben-Yehuda's first son was born, "a child in whose person the first attempt to revive the Hebrew language in spoken form would be conducted."[19]

One of those dreamers writ large, Ben-Yehuda's hopes were matched by his determination to make them come true.

THEODOR HERZL'S HOPES FOR A JEWISH STATE

Although hope had infused Zionism from its earliest days, the movement had lacked a clear political goal. Theodor Herzl (1860–1904, Hungary and Austria), who shared Ben-Yehuda's capacity to hope on a grand scale and to build an infrastructure capable of transforming dreams into reality, would change all that.

As a journalist covering the case of Alfred Dreyfus, a Jewish officer in the French army who was falsely accused in 1894 of selling military secrets to Germany, Herzl witnessed a degree of antisemitism in the public's response that convinced him Jews would never truly be integrated into European society. Obsessed with solving the "Jewish question" and convinced of the inability of European nations to deliver on their promise of equal protection before the law, Herzl concluded that the only solution was Jewish statehood.

Herzl's vision and determination embodied a level of hope extraordinary by any measure. C. R. Snyder, until his death the preeminent scholar of the psychology of hope, boiled down his definition to this: "Hope reflects a mental set in which we have the perceived willpower and the waypower [strategies] to get to our destination."[20] Herzl's will found expression in what became the Zionist mantra, "If you will it, it is no dream." And his pursuit of Jewish statehood never lacked for strategies, from soliciting political support from the German kaiser and the Ottoman sultan, to founding the Jewish Colonial Trust to purchase land in Palestine, to proposing the establishment of an interim Jewish state in Uganda to rescue Russian Jews from pogroms.

Though Herzl generally radiated confidence, he also struggled with bouts of despair. When prepublication reactions to his 1896 volume, *The Jewish State* (*Der Judenstaat*, literally, "The state of the Jews") began to trickle in, they were far from positive. A Jewish journalist compared Herzl to a "Jewish Jules Verne." A friend wondered if the manuscript was "a joke or something meant to be serious."[21] When the first printed copies arrived in Herzl's apartment of what would arguably become the preeminent work in the canon of Zionist literature, he wrote in his diary, "I was terribly shaken. This package of pamphlets constitutes the decision in tangible form. My life may now take a new turn. . . . I recalled the fisherman [at an Austrian mountain lake] who said: 'The most remarkable thing is a man's never giving up hope.'" Ridicule mounted, and those who had advised Herzl on the project withdrew support. Herzl felt alone. "At my side I feel no one but my dear old dad. He stands firm as a rock. But a man who is to carry the day in thirty years has to be considered crazy for the first two weeks."[22]

Just about a year and a half later, Herzl convened the First Zionist Congress. He planned to hold the conference in Munich, but German Jewry objected on patriotic and religious grounds, urging "all who are concerned with the welfare of Judaism to stay away from the above mentioned Zionist endeavors."[23] Herzl relocated the congress to Basel, Switzerland, where 204 delegates gathered from fifteen countries. To augment the gravitas of the moment, Herzl insisted that all participants dress in formal wear. After a few words of formalities, Herzl addressed the congress with these words: "We wish to lay the cornerstone of the house in which the Jewish nation will one day find shelter."[24]

Rather than creating a state (political Zionism), some congress participants favored slowly building up a Jewish presence in Palestine that would enliven Jewish diaspora communities around the world (cultural Zionism). But even they had to acknowledge that when it came to implementation, Herzl had more to offer. As the Russian cultural Zionist leader Menachem Ussishkin said: "[Herzl and his friends] have hope, but they have also a concrete plan; we have hope, but we don't know what to do with it."[25]

Herzl's immersion in Zionism led to changes in his personal life. In December of 1897, he lit Hanukkah candles for the first time and used the experience to publish a thinly fictionalized story about the struggle to fulfill his hopes for the fledgling movement:

The occasion became a parable for the enkindling of a whole nation. First one candle; it is still dark and the solitary light looks gloomy. Then it finds a companion, then another, and yet another. The darkness must retreat. The young and the poor are the first to see the light; then the others join in, all those who love justice, truth, liberty, progress, humanity and beauty. When all the candles are ablaze everyone must stop in amazement and rejoice at what has been wrought. And no office is more blessed than that of a servant of light.[26]

The commitment to "justice, truth, liberty, progress, humanity and beauty" reflected not only Herzl's characterization of his supporters but his hope for the Jewish state:

We are strong enough to form a state, and a model state at that. We have all the human and material resources required for it. . . . Every man will be as free and as unrestricted in his belief as he is in his nationality. And should it happen that men of other creeds and nationalities come to live among us, we shall accord them honorable protection and equality before the law.[27]

On September 3, 1897, not long after the First Zionist Congress, Herzl wrote in his diary:

Were I to sum up the Basel Congress in a word—which I will guard against pronouncing publicly—it would be this. At Basel I founded the Jewish State. If I said this out loud today, I would be answered by universal laughter. Perhaps in five years, certainly in fifty, everyone will know it.[28]

Herzl died seven years after that First Zionist Congress, but despite setbacks and conflicts on many fronts he managed to lay secure enough footings for others to build upon and found the State of Israel, not fifty years, but fifty-one years, after the First Zionist Congress.

BEN-GURION AND STATEHOOD

David Ben-Gurion (born Gruen, 1886–1973, Poland/Russia and Israel) was one of those who would carry on Herzl's work. In 1904, the already ardent eighteen-year-old Zionist would eulogize his idol, Herzl, at a memorial service in the Ben-Gurion family's Polish synagogue. The following year, as pogroms swept through Russia and his efforts to found a new Zionist organization in Warsaw hit a brick wall, Ben-Gurion fell into despair. In a letter to Shlomo Zemach, one of his close friends who had recently moved to Palestine, he expressed his need for hope:

> I ask for nothing of life, I want neither pleasures nor education, not honor and not love, I'll give it all up, all I want is one thing—hope!!! I ask for the ability to hope and believe and then I am prepared to bear the hardest labor and the heaviest yoke![29]

Arriving in Jaffa harbor at nine in the morning of September 7, 1906, Ben-Gurion, twenty, met up with Zemach, and seven hours later they headed for Petach Tikvah, an agricultural settlement Ben-Gurion had dreamed of visiting.[30] With work as a day laborer proving less than exhilarating, he returned to the city of Jaffa and joined a series of Zionist political parties associated with the labor movement, quickly rising through their ranks. During a return visit to Petach Tikvah in 1907 he wrote his father: "In Petach Tikvah we founded the first trade union." As Israeli historian Tom Segev observes, Ben-Gurion's language echoed "Herzl's famous declaration, 'At Basel I founded the Jewish state.'"[31]

Meanwhile, the Zionist movement continued to gather steam. In 1917, the British government issued the Balfour Declaration, which viewed "with favour the establishment in Palestine of a national home for the

Jewish people." In 1937, the Peel Commission recommended partitioning Palestine into two states, one Jewish and one Arab. In 1947 the United Nations' Special Commission on Palestine and the UN General Assembly did the same.

Six months later, on May 14, 1948, standing beneath a portrait of Herzl, David Ben-Gurion proclaimed Israel's independence and read the new state's Declaration of Independence, which declared that the Jewish people had "never ceased to pray and hope for their return" to their homeland. "In the year 1897," he read from the Declaration's third paragraph, "the first Zionist Congress, inspired by Theodore Herzl's vision of a Jewish state, proclaimed the right of the Jewish people to a national revival in their own country." The audience spontaneously sang "Hatikvah" before and after the reading.

Ben-Gurion and his colleagues in the Zionist movement fulfilled Herzl's vision of statehood. Understanding the necessity of combining hope with action, they also gave ample testimony to the truth of the Zionist mantra: "If you will it, it is no dream." Herzl had coined that phrase in *Altneuland* (Old/New Land), his 1902 utopian novel about the Jewish state. In the novel's epilogue, Herzl elaborated on the relationship between dream and action:

> But if you will not will it, it is and will remain a dream. . . . [Herzl now refers to the book as a child and to himself as its father.] You will have to make your way through hostility and misrepresentation, through a dark, evil forest. But if you meet kindly people, my child, greet them in the name of your father. He believes that dreaming is as good a way of spending our time on this earth as any other, and *dream and action are not so far apart as is often thought.* All the activity of mankind was once a dream.[32]

Fulfilling the Hopes of Statehood

Ben-Gurion's reading of the Declaration of the Establishment of the State of Israel signified the fruition of but one of political Zionism's yearnings: statehood. The Declaration also embodied Zionism's other hope: the creation of a just society, with peaceful relations among its constituent groups and with its neighbors:

The State of Israel will . . . foster the development of the country for the benefit of all its inhabitants; it will be based on freedom, justice and peace as envisaged by the prophets of Israel; it will ensure complete equality of social and political rights to all its inhabitants irrespective of religion, race or sex; it will guarantee freedom of religion, conscience, language, education and culture. . . . We extend our hand to all neighbouring states and their peoples in an offer of peace and good neighbourliness, and appeal to them to establish bonds of cooperation and mutual help with the sovereign Jewish people settled in its own land. The State of Israel is prepared to do its share in a common effort for the advancement of the entire Middle East.[33]

Israel's accomplishments have been impressive by any measure. Virtual miracles have abounded, from the tiny state's ability to absorb hundreds of thousands of Jews from Islamic countries in the early 1950s (though not without problems), and nearly a million from the former Soviet Union in the 1990s, to Israel's prowess as an entrepreneurial, high-tech "Start-Up Nation," with a vibrant cultural life, excellent universal health care, world-class universities, and a fully developed sector of vigorous nongovernmental organizations (NGOs). Although peace with the Palestinians remains elusive, and Hamas, Hezbollah, and Iran remain implacable enemies, Israel's military, technological prowess, economic strength, and status as a major regional exporter of natural gas have transformed the country into a regional superpower.

Nonetheless, realizing certain hopes of Israel's Declaration of Independence — to "ensure complete equality of social and political rights to all its inhabitants irrespective of religion, race or sex" — remains a work in progress, as it does for any democracy worthy of the name.

Reuven Rivlin, president of Israel from 2014 through 2021, and activists within the NGO community, have been endeavoring to realize these hopes, despite underlying trends — explained first, below — that make their work so difficult, and so important.

A CONSTITUTION?

One of the hopes expressed in Israel's Declaration of Independence involved creating a constitution that would enshrine into law the Declaration's promises of social and political equality and its guarantees of fundamental freedoms. The Declaration stipulated that a Constituent Assembly, designed to draft the constitution, was to be convened no later than October 1, 1948. Work on the constitution had begun as early as 1947, and drafts had circulated to Jewish communities around the world. Elections for the Constituent Assembly took place in January 1949, but, two days after the Assembly convened, it instead voted itself into office as the first Knesset.

Continuing to debate the issue, the Knesset decided by 1950 that a constitution would be adopted over time, chapter by chapter, in a series of basic laws. But there was a fundamental problem with this plan, which is why Israel ultimately failed to adopt a constitution, argues Israeli constitutional law scholar Gideon Sapir. "In a parliamentary democracy, coalition parties rule the legislature. A constitution limits the legislators' powers, and therefore the ruling parties have a stake in avoiding the enactment of a constitution."[34] The window for adopting a constitution had largely shut.

So far the Knesset has adopted eighteen basic laws, most remaining susceptible to amendment or revocation by a simple majority. Two basic laws adopted in 1992—Human Dignity and Liberty, and Freedom of Occupation—created an opening for the Supreme Court to strike down legislation that conflicted with the spirit of Israel's Declaration of Independence. Since 1997 the court has struck down twenty laws covering a range of issues from discrimination against an ultra-Orthodox Torah student in obtaining social security to detaining illegal immigrants for three years without a trial.[35] In late 2020, the court began hearings on a suit challenging a controversial 2018 basic law—opposed by then Israeli president Rivlin—defining Israel as the state of the Jewish people, with no reference to equality for all citizens.[36] In a society as polarized as Israel, it's no surprise that some champion the court as others vilify it. In recent years, the Likud and other political parties have championed an "override clause bill" that would strip the court's power of judicial review.

Israel's failure to adopt an entrenched constitution—the provisions of which would require more than a simple parliamentary majority to amend—both reflects and contributes to a certain weakness in its democratic fabric. Israeli political scientists Itzhak Galnoor and Dana Blander conclude: "In 1949, an opportunity was missed for building a broader base for a democratic political culture in Israel—not just the rules of the game concerning majority politics and elections — but a constitution anchoring these rules in an ethos of equality and liberty."[37]

THE SIX-DAY WAR'S LEGACY

One of Israel's most stunning accomplishments was its triumph in the 1967 Six-Day War. Yitzhak Rabin, then chief of staff of the Israel Defense Forces (IDF), recalled his experience of approaching the Western Wall a day after the IDF overtook Jordanian forces in the city:

> I was breathless. It seemed as though all the tears of centuries were striving to break out of the ... [Israeli soldiers] crowded into that narrow alley, while all the hopes of generations proclaimed: "This is no time for weeping. It is a moment of redemption, of hope." ...
> I felt truly shaken and stood there murmuring a prayer for peace.[38]

Israel's victory brought with it a host of unanticipated consequences that fundamentally transformed — and deeply divided — Israeli society. While completely vanquishing its enemies, Israel also assumed control of territories that included a major chunk of biblical Israel. The emotional pull of these lands was so enormous that by July of 1967 it gave rise to the founding of the Movement for Greater Israel, which advocated building Jewish settlements in the newly conquered territories and extending Israel to its biblical borders.

To some in the religious community, the victory seemed to be a sign from God that it was time for Israel to return to these ancestral biblical territories. To others, it was a sign to occupy the Temple Mount and rebuild the Temple. Sectors in the Orthodox community that had opposed using force to push God's messianic timetable soon argued for the imperative to settle in the West Bank (which they referred to as Judea and Samaria) even if doing so violated Israeli law. Thus, in April of 1968, masquerading as Swiss tourists, Rabbi Moshe Levinger and a group of followers rented rooms in Hebron (in the newly captured West Bank) to celebrate Passover, refusing to leave after the festival ended. The government eventually moved them to nearby Kiryat Arba. In response, a dovish group of Tel Aviv University academics founded the anti-annexationist Movement for Peace and Security. The question of Israel's boundaries, one of the bitter divides between Right and Left in the pre-state period, returned to the political agenda.

The victory and the occupation of Gaza and the West Bank that came with it also affected Israel's Arab citizens. Until 1966, this minority, then about 15 percent of the population, had full rights as citizens, while living under the rule of a sometimes harsh military administration and subject to discrimination in other spheres as well. After 1967, along with feeling like second-class citizens, Arabs in Israel began to experience a new and politically galvanizing reality: Their country, Israel, had become the occupying power over their people, the Palestinians.

POLARIZATION AND THE ASSASSINATION OF YITZHAK RABIN

Worrisome signs of polarization and extremism within Israeli society began to attract serious attention in the 1980s. In 1983, a right-wing activist threw a hand grenade at participants in a Peace Now rally, killing one and wounding nine others. A year later, Meir Kahane (1932–90) won a seat in the Knesset, running on a platform of expelling all Arabs from the country and calling the Declaration of Independence a "schizophrenic document."[39] That year Israeli security forces apprehended members of the Jewish Underground—leaders of Gush Emunim, the West Bank settler's movement—and foiled plans to blow up the mosques on the Temple Mount. The Underground's actions found full or partial support among nearly a third of Israeli Jews.[40] Soon after that, a soldier who had a religious vision during the 1967 liberation of Jerusalem founded the Temple Institute, an organization dedicated to rebuilding the Temple in Jerusalem. In his 1984 Rosh Hashanah address, Israeli president Chaim Herzog uttered a warning:

> Despite the many dangers from the outside, the greatest danger is from the inside. This danger is rooted in shaken human relations . . . in a non-civilized mode of public debate which sometimes deteriorates into violence. This danger derives from the polarization between different parts or sectors of the people, a polarization which finds its expression in incitement and physical violence. . . . And in all this cauldron which threatens our security, there have also lately devel-

oped some indications—in some opinion surveys—that it is possible to give up democracy.[41]

For many, the 1992 election of Yitzhak Rabin as prime minister represented an opportunity not only to make peace with the Palestinians but to address some of Israel's long-simmering internal conflicts. In his opening address to the Thirteenth Knesset, Rabin acknowledged that all Israelis were looking to the new government "with a prayer of great hope." His speech repeatedly evoked the hopes of the nation's Declaration of Independence, affirming its vision of freedom and equality:

> The Government will refrain from any religious or anti-religious coercion. . . . Members of the Knesset, it is proper to admit that for years we have erred in our treatment of Israel's Arab and Druze citizens. Today, almost 45 years after the establishment of the state, there are substantial gaps between the Jewish and Arab communities in a number of spheres. On behalf of the new Government, I see it as fitting to promise the Arab, Druze, and Bedouin population that we shall do everything possible to close those gaps. We shall try to make the great leap that will enhance the welfare of the minorities that have tied their fate to our own.[42]

Religious extremists feared that the Oslo Peace Process would result in ceding parts of the West Bank to the Palestinians. Some began to teach about the rabbinic "Law of the Pursuer" that sanctioned killing an individual believed to be in pursuit of another with the intent to commit murder.[43] Taking that teaching to heart, the right-wing extremist Yigal Amir assassinated Rabin at a Tel Aviv peace rally in 1995. A blood-stained song sheet found in Rabin's pocket bore the hope-filled words of the peace movement's unofficial anthem, "Shir LaShalom" ("Song for Peace").

AN EMBATTLED ANTHEM

The fractures cleaving Israeli society in the 1980s and 1990s have yet to be healed. Today, Israel's national anthem—that touchstone of hope eternal—serves as a useful prism through which to view them.[44]

In 2004 the Knesset officially designated "Hatikvah" as Israel's national anthem, but more than 40 percent of Israel's population does not sing it. Many ultra-Orthodox Israelis won't sing "Hatikvah" because it doesn't mention God and instead gives supremacy to being a "free nation in our land." (Little-known fact: In 1929 Rav Kook, Israel's first Ashkenazi Chief Rabbi, wrote an alternative anthem, "The Song of Faith," to be sung to the tune of "Hatikvah."[45]) Additionally, the country's Arab minority does not feel comfortable singing an anthem that speaks exclusively of a "Jewish soul" (that's why it was not sung at the Hebrew University's 2017 graduation ceremony).[46] Concern with the Arab minority's difficulty with "Hatikvah" led then president Rivlin to suggest that Israel consider revising its anthem.[47]

Behind these disputes about "Hatikvah" lurk deep worries. Israeli Democracy Institute surveys in 2018 and 2019 revealed that the tension between Jews and Arabs in Israel, long identified as the country's deepest rift, had slipped to second place (28 percent), behind the Right-Left split (36 percent), pointing to the growing polarization within the country's Jewish majority. That polarization shows up in surveys asking about optimism for the future of Israeli democracy: Among Jews, 7 percent of those identifying as Left are optimistic, compared to 34 percent of centrists and 65 percent of those on the Right.[48]

Reuven Rivlin's Israeli Hope

In 2015, against the background of bitter division, former president Rivlin launched an effort to create a new, more inclusive sense of hope for Israel's citizens. He calls it *Israeli* hope, implicitly broadening and distinguishing it from the Jewish hope of "Hatikvah."

Grounding the initiative in an address (now known as the "Four Tribes Speech") at the 2015 Herzliya Conference (a prestigious annual public policy conclave), Rivlin spoke about the need to "draw together all the tribes of Israel, with a shared vision of Israeli hope." He offered himself as a partner to anyone willing to help with this task. "Only in this way," he concluded, "together and in partnership, shall we be able to rekindle the Israeli hope."

Rivlin identified four groups in Israel society, each with its own state-supported school system and distinctive identity: Secular (41 percent of first-graders), Arab (23 percent), National Religious (or Modern Orthodox) (15 percent), and ultra-Orthodox (21 percent).[49] Each tribe lives separately, attends separate school systems, gets news from its own media platforms, and has its own unique relationships to the state. Only two tribes (Secular and National Religious) sing Israel's national anthem and routinely serve in the army. The other two tribes (Arabs and ultra-Orthodox) do not identify with the state's Zionist ethos and are significantly overrepresented among Israel's poor. Rivlin stressed what's at stake:

> We are dealing here with a cultural and religious identity gap and sometimes an abyss between the mainstreams of each of the camps; between four different and rich engines of identity. The "new Israeli order" ... [is] a reality with far-reaching consequences for our national strength, for the future of us all. From an economic viewpoint, the current reality is not viable. The mathematics is simple, any child can see it. If we do not reduce the current gaps in the rate of participation in the work force and in the salary levels of the Arab and Haredi [ultra-Orthodox] populations—who are soon to become one half of the work force—Israel will not be able to continue to be a developed economy.[50]

Rivlin then expressed four principles upon which a new sense of partnership must rest. First, security that one's basic identity is not being threatened. Second, the responsibility of all tribes is to actively participate in that new sense of partnership. Third, equity and equality: "that no citizen is discriminated against, nor favored, simply because they belong to a specific sector." Fourth, the development of a new sense of "shared 'Israeliness.'"

Following his "Four Tribes Speech," the former president launched Israeli Hope (Tikvah Yisraelit), an umbrella organization covering programs from the business and NGO sectors working in education, employment, advertising, sports, and academia to increase equality and forge better relations among Israel's four tribes.[51] In 2017, he called on diaspora Jewry to help Israel bridge the gaps between the four tribes by supporting Israeli Hope:

In order to meet this challenge we need the partnership with you, the fifth tribe, the Jews of the Diaspora. Ensuring "Israeli Hope" for every young man and woman in Israel is also the key to ensuring the Jewish Hope. This is the Jewish and democratic state that we all dreamed of for two thousand years.[52]

The president's support for the democratic values that suffuse Israeli Hope have not been met with universal support in Israel. When he criticized the Netanyahu government for its "continued effort to weaken the gatekeepers of Israeli democracy," graffiti calling Rivlin a "Nazi apostate from Judaism" appeared in the mostly ultra-Orthodox city of Bnei Brak.[53] Then coalition chair and Likud member David Bitan said that the president, himself a veteran politician from the same party, "has long since stopped being one of us."[54]

Snapshots of Israeli Hope: Israeli Activists Speak

Now join me for a tour of Israel, a record of my conversations with activists during a weeklong visit to Israel in the fall of 2018 about what sustains hope for them and their community. Activists from Israel's "four tribes" (identified below by their ages at the time of the interviews, and their jobs updated as of early 2021) discuss what they are doing to build Israeli Hope and address the kinds of problems former president Rivlin put on the table. Our itinerary also features several topics that the president did not single out. For example, his analysis does not make reference to gender, race, or peace; we'll add a few stops along the road to see what activists in these areas have to say as well.

Yoaz Hendel, director, Institute for Zionist Strategies; founder, Blue & White Human Rights (now a member of Knesset with the New Hope Party and minister of communications in the government)

Meeting Yoaz Hendel, forty-three, at Café ha-Ivrit in the Givat Ram campus of the Hebrew University, down the hill from the Israel Museum, I couldn't help but be impressed. Résumé: raised in the West Bank religious settlement of Elkana; former combat officer in an elite naval commando unit; one-time director of communications for Prime Minister Benjamin Netanyahu; senior military and diplomatic commentator for *Yedioth Ahronoth*, Israel's largest circulating daily newspaper; and since 2012 director of the Institute for Zionist Strategies (IZS), an NGO "dedicated to the preservation of the Jewish and democratic character of the State of Israel, according to the principles of Israel's Declaration of Independence." But there's more. Yoaz, a member of what former president Rivlin calls the National Religious (or Modern Orthodox) tribe, defines himself as a "liberal nationalist" and worries about the Left gaining a monopoly on human-rights issues. So in 2013 he founded Blue & White Human Rights (now part of IZS), called by some "Israel's first right-wing Palestinian rights watchdog."[55] Among other things, it monitors IDF abuses of Palestinians at checkpoints and works with the army to reduce them.

I'd sought Yoaz out because of his latest book: *Frank Conversations about Israeli Hope: Yoaz Hendel with President Reuven (Ruby) Rivlin.* If the title were not enough to whet my curiosity, the first sentences of Yoaz's introduction took care of that: "In the beginning was hope. Much before the birth of words and deeds. Without hope to be a free people in our own land we would not have achieved freedom."[56]

"What led you," I wondered aloud, "to initiate that dialogue with the president?"

"Debates," Yoaz replied, "have always been part of our history—Hillel and Shammai. But the debates in Israel now should not be about demonizing the other but for the sake of Heaven, *le'shem shamayim*. What we have here in Israel is a miracle. Whether you're religious or secular, it's a miracle. With all the problems, we have a way of maintaining democratic, liberal Jewish values that don't exist in any other country in our region. My greatest hope is to build on that fact, to maintain the third Jewish commonwealth, to reduce the great divisions we face and maximize the potential of the Jewish people. We do have great potential—to destroy ourselves or to create and to fulfill our dreams. When the first Zionists came here they had nothing but their hope. Now we don't face any existential threats. Now our hope is to keep this miracle alive."

"No existential threats? What about Iran?" I wondered.

"Without getting into all the details," he says, "our enemies could cause a catastrophe for us, but they can't destroy the state. The only thing that could do that is our own tribalism. So we have to keep the Israeli spirit alive, and that includes the kind of hope that built this country. It's our greatest strength."

What diminishes Yoaz's sense of hope?

"I belong to the group that is optimistic. I see hope in every corner. But there are two dimensions within the Jewish people. One is pessimistic—that we are a people that dwells alone. The other is optimistic—that we are a light unto the nations.[57] That's how I see it. I see the Jewish brains. It's not the government that created Israeli high tech, that made so many great doctors, and all the NGOs in this country. What weakens my hope? The Talmud says that the Second Temple was destroyed because of baseless hatred among ourselves.[58] It was tribalism. And today our politicians know that the difference between Right and Left is not really as great as it seems. So they need to exaggerate the differences to define themselves. And it creates an atmosphere where it's easier to hate than to debate. But we need debate, with all the issues on the table like in the Talmud, where there is more than one legitimate way of seeing things. That's the soil of our creativity. And we still have a lot of creativity. There are more books per capita published in this country than in any other."

I invite Yoaz to speak more personally about experiences that sustain his hope.

"It's happened a few times. When I've been called up to my unit because we're going into Gaza. You see people's creative spirit and mutual responsibility. You see the goodness of people. And that's the hidden dimension, the spirit that is still there, often hidden, but still there. It's a feeling of unity and love—not so common to see here. It's the same spirit that built Israel. The same hope. And then, I'm standing by the road in my uniform, and strangers are lined up giving soldiers cups of coffee. That cup of coffee is the best symbol—without words."

"So, Yoaz, is that cup of coffee filled with hope?"

He looks down for a minute, then raises his eyes with a sheepish smile. "Yes. It is!"

Eilon Schwartz, executive director, Shaharit: Creating Common Cause

I arrived at Eilon's sunny Tel Aviv office at 9:00 a.m., appropriate because Shaharit means "morning." Aged sixty and living in Israel since 1983, he apologized for the modest digs until he came to two large bookshelves, a lending library of books in Hebrew and English on community organizing and social change. "This—I'm really proud of!"

Eilon teaches graduate-level courses on cultural criticism, social-environmental politics, and education at the Hebrew University's Melton Center. He's also author of *At Home in the World: Human Nature, Ecological Thought & Education after Darwin*, published in 2010.

His founding of Shaharit—"a synergistic mix of think tank, leadership incubator, and community organizing hub"—two years later anticipated President Rivlin's Israeli Hope initiative.

Eilon talks a lot about bubbles, the communities where like-minded people congregate, feel comfortable, but shut themselves off from different communities. "Shaharit," he explained, "is about getting outside your bubble and building new relationships. But that takes time."

He beamed as he described a recent example of the fruits born of this long cultivation: a July 2018 conference for social-change activists and candidates running for local office. The 350 participants, from all four of Rivlin's tribes—nine different political parties, seventy-five towns and cities—came to reaffirm their commitment to common-good solutions, to network, and to hone their skills in developing win-win outcomes in workshops ranging from urban planning to religion in the public square.

"You need to understand that gatherings as diverse as this in Israel just don't happen," he told me. "It's all about relationships. Some of these people are entering politics, so what we're doing on this level, down here, will percolate up."

The results of the October 2018 municipal elections were promising. Council members who had participated in Shaharit programs—all having pledged to advance "common-good values"—were elected in twenty localities.

"I think hope is a choice," Eilon said. "The easiest thing is to be cynical, pessimistic. There *are* a lot of bad signs. But things could be a lot worse. So how do you want to see the glass? Half empty or half full? My hope is grounded. It's not naiveté or Pollyannaish optimism. Hope for me is a reasonable position, based on a reasoned look at the whole—the good and the bad. Take conflicts over religion. You *could* be convinced that there's a culture war here that's getting worse all the time. But if you look inside the ultra-Orthodox world you see things changing—more people going to work and to university. Our board chair is a Haredi rabbi, dean of a yeshiva in Jerusalem. He's willing to work with people from all communities for the common good. But, he pays a price. People accuse him of being a Trojan Horse for Reform Judaism and a lot worse than that.

"Or take the Arab minority. There *is* terrible rhetoric on both sides. Some Jews want Arabs to be second-class citizens. Some Arabs say that Israel is a racist state. But then you look at a city like Haifa where Jews and Arabs are well integrated. And you look at hospitals where Arab doctors serve as department chairs.[59] And you look at this right-wing government that passed an economic development plan spending three to four billion dollars over the next five years to narrow gaps between the Arab and Jewish sectors. Left-wing governments never did anything on this scale before.[60]

"None of this fits into the neat categories of what you'd expect. And that itself supports hope. Because hope is about new possibilities."

Eilon's opening words at the July 2018 conference encapsulate his understanding of hope:

If you want to leave your bubble, and build a joint life together, it can't happen without relationships based on trust between people. Relationships beat out ideologies. . . . When you look away from the spotlight, you discover that underneath almost every rock in Israeli society and especially in the socioeconomic periphery, you can find the seedlings of a future that is good for all. Realizing this hope will take persistence. It will take a belief in people, created in the image of God. It will take empathy and patience. And it demands hard work.[61]

Rabbi Ilay Ofran, Modern Orthodox rabbi, psychologist, and educator

---

We meet at Kibbutz Be'erot Yitzhak, a sprawling religious kibbutz not far from Ben-Gurion Airport. Something new under the sun is taking root here — Ruach ha-Sadeh (Spirit, or Wind, of the Field), a one-year experimental educational program for Modern Orthodox high school graduates that precedes military service. Ilay, thirty-six, the rabbi of Kibbutz Yavne, Israel's largest religious kibbutz, directs the preparatory program.

"What makes it special?"

Ilay described a scandal a few years back when antidemocratic curricular material from the Modern Orthodox pre-army preparatory programs leaked to the press. "That's a problem — for our community and for society. Kids from our community grow up in their own world. They're very comfortable but know nothing about the complexities about this country. They've never had interactions with secular Jews or Arabs. Here we want them to learn what a complicated country this is, to make connections with different kinds of people. Today the kids are at a secular kibbutz for a day of dialogue with students in a preparatory program there. Our message is *petichut u'mechuyavot*, 'openness and religious obligation.'"

This budding openness within parts of the Orthodox community in Israel is an important, but still underreported, story in the country.

Ilay's latest book, *Torah of the Soul* (at the time, no. 4 on *Ha-aretz's* best-seller list) includes a chapter about Genesis 49:18, the only verse in the Torah that contains a form of the common word for hope, *tikvah*. That chapter begins with an overview of C. R. Snyder's work on hope: stressing the importance of a goal, of determination, and of devising strategies to reach it. "For me hope is the pair of glasses that I decide to wear," Ilay told me. "It's like a Rorschach test. What you see in it says more about you than about what's in the card itself. There have always been two parties in Judaism about this. In the Talmud the House of Shammai argued that it would have been better if humanity had never been created. The House of Hillel disagreed. After two and a half years of arguing, they finally voted and this was one of the rare cases in which the House of Shammai won. And there have always been some voices saying that things were better in the past and others saying that they will be better in the future. One group always had more hope, one less.[62] But I'm an educator and a psychologist. And I couldn't do this work unless I believed that change is possible."

Ilay sees Judaism as a source of hope. "I believe God speaks to us not only through Torah but also through reality. There is a big *tikkun* taking place in the modern world, and it's part of the way that God talks with us. I worked with survivors of sexual abuse, and the whole way we relate to this issue reveals a big change in the world. It didn't start with Torah and Jewish law. It began in the world, and it's bringing the world closer to God's will. What's happening in the world—not all, but some of it—is like a prophet that speaks with us. God is speaking to us, revealing to us that the world can change, that there is hope we can reach a higher spiritual level.

"So to find God's will you can't just look in the books. You need to look at positive developments in the world. Hope is about looking forward. I believe that in these modern processes of change there is a commanding voice. It tells me what I have to do to bring the world closer to God's will."

Sigal Kanotopsky, director, Olim B'Yachad, "Rising Up Together" (now VP of resource development at Maoz)

When I arrive at Tenat, an outstanding Ethiopian restaurant in Tel Aviv, Sigal and the owner/chef are deeply engaged in conversation about the prospects of successfully integrating Israel's nearly 150,000 Ethiopian Jews.

It's a serious question. Despite progress, among Israeli-born Ethiopian Jews enrolled in the secular Israeli school system, only 22 percent continue their education after high school, compared to 47 percent of other Israeli Jews. Income levels among the Ethiopian community are about three-quarters of the national average.[63] Sigal mentioned a soon-to-be-published survey finding that 60 percent of white Israelis would oppose the marriage of their child to an Ethiopian Jew.

Sigal's family came to Israel from Ethiopia in 1983, when she was five. Rumors had begun to reach their small village that if they traveled to Sudan they would be taken to Israel. "We had no way of knowing if there was any truth to this, but my father decided we couldn't miss the chance. Even as a child in my village I remember that everything was about Jerusalem. Our dream was to be there. With twelve members of our family and our horse we walked for three months to Sudan. Israeli agents met us at the border, and six months later we flew to Israel. You wouldn't start that journey without hope and faith, and you couldn't survive it without hope and faith."

Then, she added, "Coming to Israel was just the first step. Now that we're here it's about creating equal opportunities."

Building on her master's degree in conflict resolution from Tel Aviv University, Sigal now leads Olim B'Yachad, "Rising Up Together." The organization's name puns on the fact that *olim* means "rising" or "going up" but is also the word for new immigrants to Israel, that is, those who have "ascended" to Israel. Olim B'Yachad works with a network of two thousand volunteers, including six hundred business leaders, to provide mentoring and job placement assistance to Ethiopian college graduates unable to find work in their fields. As of 2018, of the one thousand Ethiopian participants since Olim B'Yachad's inception in 2007, 88 percent had been placed in a job within their field.

"The hope is that this will change the perception of our community. These people are often the first Ethiopian employees at their company or in their department. We train them to be ambassadors for our community and role models for our younger generation.

"We have to be honest. Some of the negative perceptions about hiring Ethiopians come from the fact that people think that we've just arrived. They see us as immigrants and less capable. But there's also an element of racism." Sigal told me about the army's segregated remedial training course for Ethiopian recruits. After much protest, in 2017 the army scrapped the program, folding it into the program for all other recruits needing remedial training.[64]

"When we came here the hope was to be here. We came to *Yerushalayim shel matah*, 'the earthly Jerusalem,' and now we have to build *Yerushalayim shel malah*, 'the heavenly Jerusalem.' I'm doing *tikkun olam* every day—fixing what's broken and the wrongs toward my community in Israel. But it's *tikkun olam* in a more general way. I want Israel to be an example for the world about how to deal better with racial diversity. My parents had to be proactive about getting here, and I have to be proactive about dealing with our situation here. Their narrative was one of hope and faith, and so is mine."

Alice Shalvi, educator and founder, Israel Women's Network

In the mid-1980s, Alice and a handful of feminist colleagues created the Israel Women's Network (IWN), the first Israeli NGO dedicated to lobbying to improve the status of women—from within the courts and the Knesset to classrooms and the media.

Alice was born in Germany into a family that fled to Britain after Hitler's rise to power. She came to Israel in 1949, earned her doctorate in English literature in 1962, became involved with feminism in the 1970s, served as principal of the Pelech School (a progressive high school for Orthodox girls) from 1975 to 1990, led IWN from 1984 through 2000, and was awarded the Israel Prize in 2007 for Lifetime Achievement and Special Contribution to Society and the State of Israel.[65]

"I am hopelessly hopeful," Alice, ninety-one, told me, the quality of her voice and eloquence still rivaling that of the silver-tongued Abba Eban. "Sometimes I feel I'm being too Pollyannaish, but I don't think one can go on living a purposeful life without hope. One thinks one can make some progress in the world. And that's been very essential in my life. I tend to be sad more than I used to be, but that's because the hopes have still not yet been fulfilled. The mood of 1948—having experienced a miracle, you almost take for granted that the miracle will continue. One of the things that gives me hope is civil society, the people and the organizations. Their unfailing dedication. And the Pelech alumni who have changed the Orthodox world.

"The Israel Women's Network changed so much in this country. When we started, people didn't know there was discrimination against women. Even the women didn't know. We've come a long way, baby! But there's still far to go."

When IWN began its work, the Knesset included ten women (8 percent). By 2018, it included thirty-six (30 percent), the goal IWN had set for itself back in the 1980s.[66] Two days after Alice and I met, Haifa, Israel's third-largest city, elected its first woman mayor; and, in a truly stunning upset, Beit Shemesh, a largely ultra-Orthodox city, elected a Modern Orthodox woman to be its first woman mayor. The number of women running for local office had almost doubled from the previous municipal elections.

But Alice's life as an activist has not been a picnic. The Ministry of Education's threat to revoke the Pelech School's accreditation because of her criticism of the Chief Rabbinate's discrimination against women in matters of divorce forced her resignation, and IWN developed in some ways she wished it hadn't.[67] Still, she retains hope. "Despair," she told me, "is completely paralyzing. The basis of Judaism is the possibility, the importance, and the responsibility for human beings to create a better world. My father used to say: The great thing about the Messiah is the striving to bring the Messiah. And the belief in some greater spirit toward which we aspire. Aspiration is hope—to be better, to strive simply to be better. We don't all feel that enough, that striving as an expression of hope.

"Some people want to change 'Hatikvah.' I know the Arab population is not happy with it. But it means so much to me. There's hardly an occasion when I sing it that I don't get emotional. *Od lo avda tikvatenu!* 'We have not lost our hope.' There is always something more to achieve. And I don't say that in despair."

Rabbi Tamar Elad-Appelbaum, founder of the Zion Community in Jerusalem; co-founder of the Beit Midrash for Israeli Rabbis of the Hartman Institute and the Midrasha

---

Born in 1975 to an Orthodox Jerusalem family, Tamar attended the Pelech School when Prof. Alice Shalvi served as its principal. Now she's Alice's rabbi, ordained by both the Masorti [Conservative] movement in Israel and by the Beit Midrash for Israeli Rabbis. "Tamar gives me hope," Alice told me.

Tamar's understanding of hope grew from the tears she shed when her brother, Nadav, a paratrooper, died in Hebron in 2001. "I had an inclination toward hope from my own soul and as an Israeli, but it was innocent and vague," Tamar reflected. "When Nadav was killed it was a betrayal of everything I had hoped for. And it aroused such hard questions—'Why . . . ?' 'If . . . ?' It was then that my hope transformed into a deep hope of choice, of *af-'al-pi-khein*, 'in spite of it all.'[68] Many Jews find hope inspiring, but it doesn't stand on *af-'al-pi-khein*. Since Nadav's death it's been about choosing hope. And to do that you have to jump over an abyss. Choosing hope comes with knowing and acknowledging the full reality. A hope of adults, of holding a torch up high in shadow and darkness.

"At my brother's first yahrzeit I spoke about hope. On the third day of Creation God 'gathered the waters,' *yikavu ha-mayim*. Those waters were my tears. But *yikavu*, 'gathered,' shares the same root as 'they shall hope,' *yekavu*. My tears were brought together. There was a unification, and from that came hope—*af-'al-pi-khein*, 'in spite of it all.'"

An early Martin Buber essay identifying three central concepts in Judaism—unity, deeds, the future—has been central to Tamar's thought.[69] Tamar links each one to an element of hope. "Unity. Something is broken in people. Look at all the hateful speech we hear every day. There is no sense of hope in all this fracturing. We are talking about recovering the foundation of unity, which is the first foundation of hope. Deeds. Hope has to be experienced and expressed in deeds. Future. In the world of no hope people feel imprisoned by the past or the present. After two world wars it seemed as if humanity lost hope, each individual went into a room to mourn the broken connection with the collective and cried trying to heal privately through psychology, and now, we are coming out, seeking once again with renewed tools, for each other, for our shared dreams, wondering what can be when we come together. We need to find language for the presence of a future that we can't articulate. That's what prayer does. It helps articulate that future."

Tamar's ideas about hope suffuse the synagogue she has created. Kehillat Tzion, "The Community of Zion," embraces all—religious and secular, Jews, and often Muslims, who come to teach, offer prayers, and sometimes share holiday celebrations. Members of Tzion do the same in prayer houses of Christians and Muslims. "Prayer is the gateway to the soul, the airport for the soul. When we pray together, suddenly hope is substantial, tangible, and then more people come. They already know the world that separates people and says there is no hope. People come to Tzion to re-dream together, to build a new kind of community. It's a labor of hope. Hope needs to be experienced in community. Deeds give it real presence. Our first deed was coming together, religious and secular. Separateness is a place of despair. You have no reason to think empathy is possible. You feel alone. Coming together teaches you that you can worry together. Heal together. That is a space of hope. And that, to me, is the story of Jerusalem for all religions. A space of hope."

The Beit Midrash for Israeli Rabbis, sponsored by HaMidrasha at Oranim and the Hartman Institute, two prestigious Israeli centers of Jewish thought and education, reflects the same thinking. "Bring spiritual leaders from different communities to learn together, and you will create a new space of a shared responsibility, of hope, and a rabbinate committed to religious pluralism in Israel. So far, we've had Orthodox, secular, Haredi, Conservative, Reform, Russian, Ethiopian, Sephardic, and Ashkenazic participants. They come here because we all live in a world of broken unity. They all chose to break out, and take upon themselves one shared family name beyond all differences, the title *Rav Yisraeli*, 'Israeli Rabbi.' The mission statement of the Rabbinic Beit Midrash includes the phrase 'living hope' because we want our graduates not only to be loyal to each other, but loyal to hope."

Remaining loyal to hope is not easy, Tamar acknowledged. "You have to work on that all the time." She offers her own midrash on a verse from Psalms: "I have set YHWH always before me" (Ps. 16:8).[70] The familiar verse frequently appears in conjunction with what is known as the Menorah Psalm, the sixty-seventh Psalm, often written in the shape of a menorah and used in amulets. Moses, Tamar explains, "wants to know God's name, and God tells him: 'I will be what I will be.' God's name equals the future. God's most common name, 'Adonai,' *yud-hey-vav-hey* [here rendered YHWH], also points to the future. God is about the future, and the future is the place of hope. The psalm says, 'I have set YHWH always before me.' It means that you have to work to keep hope before you—always."

Rabbi Menachem Bombach, founder, Hasidic Academy in Beitar Illit

---

With a master's degree in public policy from the Hebrew University, Menachem, forty-two, has come a long way from where he spent his first twenty years: Jerusalem's ultra-ultra-Orthodox Meah She'arim. Believing that it is unhealthy and unrealistic for the ultra-Orthodox community to maintain its strict separation from modern Israeli society, Menachem decided his community needed a revolutionary approach to education. In 2014 he founded a Hasidic high school in Beitar Illit, a thriving settlement of more than fifty thousand Hasidic Jews in the Gush Etzion block of the West Bank, about eighteen miles south of Jerusalem. Unlike other ultra-Orthodox schools that exclude secular subjects, this one teaches math, science, history, English, and computer science along with traditional Hasidic learning.

Four years later Menachem created a service for Israel's Yom ha-Zikaron (Memorial Day) in his school. Historically, the Haredi community had studiously ignored the observance of Yom ha-Zikaron, refusing to stand in silence when a memorial siren blew throughout the country—an expression of longstanding discomfort with embracing the rituals and symbols of a secular state. Although in recent years some ultra-Orthodox religious leaders have participated in state-sponsored Memorial Day services, and some students have marked the day by reading psalms, Menachem's approach went further. He began by handing out a photograph of a child lying on his father's grave and asking pupils to talk about how it made them feel. He spoke about soldiers who died defending Israel, saying, "We can't just ignore that." Nothing like this had ever been done in a Haredi school. A video of the commemoration went viral.[71]

Menachem's office featured a typical *yeshivish* bookshelf, multivolume texts with their titles glittering gold, but the wall-sized quotation behind his desk surprised me: "Find a job you love and you will never work a day in your life. Confucius."

Menachem's opponents regularly deface his home. "I don't like that, but I'm living with it," he told me. "What I can't accept is that more than 50 percent of my Haredi community is living in poverty.[72] And with an average of 6.7 children per family, that's only going to get worse. If you don't have the right knowledge in this society you are disabled. I want my community to know that they can be God-fearing. They can study Torah. But they can also take care of themselves. People who can't take care of themselves are disabled.

"So we now have five high schools for girls and boys. Our kids will go to college and be able to find jobs. My goal is to reach 10 percent of the Hasidic community. That will be the tipping point. But the goal is not that they should be doctors. The goal is that they should be tolerant, know what empathy is, and know that you can be part of this country without losing your Haredi identity."

Menachem suggests that tolerance and empathy are catalysts for developing a sense of a shared future and therefore shared hopes with other Israelis. His hope envisions a future that moves beyond the strife and isolation that often surrounds his community.

An American opens the door and apologizes for the interruption. "Rabbi, I need just a minute of your time. I talked to the kids about what kind of business project they want to learn about. They want to make pizza. I have contacts with a lot of chefs. I'll get one to teach the kids how to make pizza. We'll make it for the whole school. Then I'll teach them the economics of running a pizza business. Two questions, rabbi. Is this idea okay with you, and can we use your kitchens?"

"Of course! *Baruch Ha-Shem!*" ("Blessed is God," literally, "Blessed is the Name.") Menachem beamed. The visitor leaves quickly. "He's a high-tech person from San Francisco spending some time in Israel," Menachem explained. "He gets it. He wants to help.

"It's not just that *Ha-Shem* didn't create us to live in poverty. We won't survive if we don't go in this new direction. Halakhah, the word for Jewish law, comes from the word 'to walk,' to move. Halakhah always changed. It wasn't about freezing things. Separation from society won't work anymore. The internet cuts through walls. A quarter of this community admits that it has access to the internet, and probably another quarter has it in secret. And Israel needs us. The army chief of staff gave a speech saying that Israel can defend itself against Iran but not against ignorance. He was talking about my community.

"When I think about hope, I think about creating a reality. It's not a naive thing. So many people said, 'It won't work.' I say, 'I'm creating something new. Who wants to go with me, good. Who not, okay.' I was born with a smile, my mother said. She taught me that there are three ways of dealing with a problem: do nothing, complain, or try to change the situation. Hope is to create something new, not to submit to what exists. That's why Haredi politicians don't like me. They want followers, and I want people to think.

"The actions we take here make hope real. We start every day in every class with kids expressing a hope for the day. 'It should be a great day.' 'It should be a happy day.' And then every day, right before *Ein Kelokeinu* [There Is None Like Our God] we say Psalm 27, which ends, 'Hope to *Ha-*

Shem [YHWH]! Let your heart be firm and bold, and hope to *Ha-Shem* [YHWH].' With children, the only way you can get them through difficult situations is to help them see that, yes, things may be tough now, but they can change. That kind of hope is such a big part of Judaism. The only way we survived through two thousand years is hope—'Hatikvah.' It's so great! Hope's not static. You reach one part of the dream, and then hope changes. It's very dynamic. Hope also has a lot to do with love. When you approach someone with love it makes hope possible."

Lina Alatawna, director general, Project Wadi Attir; and **Amran Armani**, director of training, education, and ecotourism, Project Wadi Attir (now chief compliance officer and pedagogy coordinator, High Tech High Community, Israel)

If you came to this spot in Israel's Negev desert before 2007, you would have found little more than cracked, cement-hard earth with occasional tufts of green clinging to crevices in a dried-out riverbed. Eleven years later, a welcome sign greets you with the names of Wadi Attir's partners: the Sustainability Laboratory; the ministries of Agriculture and Rural Development, Development of the Negev and Galilee, Finance, Social Equality, and Energy; Jewish National Fund USA; Ben-Gurion University of the Negev; and donors from around the world. Then a Bedouin agricultural enterprise unfolds before you. It raises goats and sheep; grows indigenous vegetables; produces honey, cheeses, yogurt, and a host of products made from medicinal plants cultivated on the farm; and runs a sustainability educational center that sponsors programs for Bedouin students and for teachers across the country. Pomegranate and olive trees, grasses, wildflowers, insects, foxes, rabbits, and birds fill the landscape. Much of the water to sustain all this comes from simple catchment areas carefully placed to retain enough of the Negev's sparse rainfall to support an array of animal and plant life year-round. Michael Ben-Eli is the sustainability expert who conceived Wadi Attir. He had intentionally designed a project with the Bedouin, Israel's most disadvantaged community, located in the Negev, the most arid and ecologically devastated region in the nation: "If we could succeed here, we could succeed anywhere."

With a master's degree in industrial engineering and management in hand, Lina, twenty-nine, came to Wadi Attir as director of operations in 2016 and two years later became director of the entire project. Honoring traditional Bedouin norms, she wears clothing that covers all but her face.

"There are so many negative stereotypes of the Bedouin," she told me. "I came here not just because of work, but to contribute to my community, to be an example so that people both from my Bedouin community and outside it could come here and learn from us. They learn about sustainable agriculture. But our principles of sustainability also apply to creating sustainable relationships. That means whoever comes here, to work or to visit—we treat them with acceptance and respect. This country is for all of us, and if we can't respect one another, the country can't be sustained. So we are an example of the kind of relationships that this country needs in order to be sustainable.

"I always explain to people that aside from the buildings and all the programs, the value added is hope. People feel the hope here. And that matters to the twenty-nine of us who work here. We were having some cash-flow issues, and the staff were willing to contribute their own money so the project wouldn't fail. It didn't come to that, but they were willing. There's always a choice between hope and despair. And it takes a lot of strength to choose hope."

Amran, thirty, an Arab citizen of Israel from the North of the country, earned his master's in environmental science and ecology. Before becoming director of Wadi Attir's educational outreach programs in 2015, he was a star biology teacher in Rahat, a Bedouin town that ranks near the bottom on most of Israel's socioeconomic measures. While raising his students' educational level, Amran also worked hard to honor the community's values and cultural authenticity. When he came to Wadi Attir, parents in the community trusted him. By 2018, 2,100 students a week were participating in Wadi Attir's educational activities, and Israel's Ministry of Education had designated their work as a model program. "Our programs are not about hugging trees," he said. "They are about taking responsibility, thinking critically, building self-confidence, increasing equity, learning how to be a role model to others, and connecting with hope."

He told me a story about Bedouin high school students who'd come to Wadi Attir to do a field-based research project: the effect of ants on arid-zone soil quality. The research was completely new to the kids, and their high school teachers thought it would be a waste of time. Turns out, the study went on to win a national competition for high school research and was later presented at a conference in Vienna. "This experience completely changed what these kids—and their teachers—thought was possible. When kids learn they have the power to make a change in their situation, that's hope. One of our sustainability principles has a lot to do with hope: 'Don't let yourself be captured by the problems. Look to the dreams.'" And Amran's dream is to build a school for sustainability education that brings different populations to learn and work together. "My hope is to make this a model for Wadi Attir and beyond."

"My father used to tell me to be the bee, not the fly. Be the bee that looks for the flowers, not the fly who goes to the dirty thing. Have the glasses of the bee."

Kher Albaz, co-executive director, AJEEC-NISPED, Arab-Jewish Center for Empowerment, Equality, and Cooperation/Negev Institute for Strategies of Peace and Economic Development

---

The oldest of twenty-one children born to his father's three wives, Kher tells me, "There are two options in life: the almost-certain future and the created future. Here's the almost-certain future. I was born in the Bedouin tribe ten kilometers east of Beer-Sheva and at the age of sixteen moved with my family to the Bedouin town of Tel Shevah, then and still one of the poorest in towns in all of Israel. I will stay there, most likely won't go to college, maybe find a simple job or maybe something illegal. I decided to go with the created future. I will take nothing as a given and will do my utmost to change the future. Hope is the belief that I can enroll enough resources to get there. To fulfill that kind of hope you need to move beyond the comfort zone. If you stay in your comfort zone you can't change the future. There's another condition. To fulfill that kind of hope you have to give up something."

I told Kher about what God tells Abraham: "Go forth from your native land and from your father's house to the land that I will show you" (Gen. 12:1). Kher smiled. "That's the created future!"

Kher, fifty-six, now has degrees in social work, social planning, and business administration—from Wilfrid Laurier University in Ontario—as well as seven children. In 2009, when he was director of social services for the Bedouin, he gave a talk on the education of Bedouin students, during which he observed that only three or four were enrolled in engineering courses. This led to the creation of the 100 Bedouin Engineers Project at the Sami Shamoon College of Engineering, for which Kher found a donor. The donor said he was sure the project would be a complete failure but agreed to fund it as long as Kher remained involved. At this point the project has produced eighty graduates. "Lina [Alatawna, of Project Wadi Attir, see previous section] was in the second cohort. It's a great story of hope!"

With AJEEC-NISPED Kher has continued to create a new future for the Bedouin and Jewish communities in the Negev and beyond. The organization employs a staff of two hundred, making it one of the largest NGOs in Israel working in the domain of shared living/shared space. Programs run the gamut, including Arab-Jewish business partnerships; the country's only Jewish-Arab gap-year training initiative, in which participants from both communities, paired for ten months, receive intensive intercultural training and work as volunteers in the Jewish and Arab schools; and Jewish/Arab encounter programs at more than fifty schools nationwide, facilitated by the organization's Volunteer Center. Also known as "the Tent," the Volunteer Center harnesses the energy of 1,300 volunteers to promote civic engagement in the Bedouin community and equality between Jewish and Arab communities throughout the country.

It hasn't always been easy. In 2011 arson destroyed the Volunteer Center. In an act of courage and hope, hundreds of Jews and Arabs representing NGOs, local municipal councils, and government ministries stood in solidarity as the rubble was cleared for rebuilding. In 2016 the Tent received then president Rivlin's award for Excellence in an Israeli Volunteer Organization for its work in fostering the goals of the president's Israeli Hope initiative.[73]

Kher pointed to the significance of the word *ajik* (which sounds exactly like AJEEC—Arab-Jewish Center for Empowerment, Equality, and Cooperation). In Arabic it means, "I will come to you."

"If that isn't building hope, what is?" he asked me. "I am coming to you!"

For Jews and Arabs in Israel, this embodies a brand-new kind of relationship. It's not built on what Jews owe Arabs because of past discrimination but on the benefits to both communities of building a healthier future "where everyone is hopeful for a better life with a sense of respect and acceptance."

Professor Eran Halperin, founder, Applied Center for the Psychology of Social Change (now head and founder of aChord: Social Psychology for Social Change, at the Hebrew University, Jerusalem); and **Shir Nosatzki**, founding partner and director, Have You Seen the Horizon Lately?

It's noisy in the small waiting room of the Applied Center for the Psychology of Social Change in Herzliya. The doors to several conference rooms open as meetings break up.

Today is the center's weekly gathering of people connected with President Rivlin's Israeli Hope initiative, Eran, forty-two, explained. "We're working with dozens of educators from all four of the country's school systems [Secular, Arab, Modern Orthodox, and ultra-Orthodox] to develop an ideal gold standard for education in a shared society. We're trying to develop a shared definition of the ideal graduate. So far these are some of the characteristics we're exploring: tolerance of other groups, sensitivity to inequality and willingness to act toward equality, ability and motivation to work with people from other groups, a sense of shared identity while respecting the particularism of one's own group." With many conflicting visions of an "ideal graduate," conversations among these diverse educators are spirited, to say the least.

Eran's left arm is mangled, with twisted bones and scars. "I was seriously injured in Lebanon, twenty-one years ago yesterday," he told me. "You're only seeing part of it. It took me five years of intensive PT to recover. That's when I decided to go in the direction of conflict resolution and hope.[74] We can't believe that doing the same thing over and over again will produce new results."

Eran began to study the impact of experiences that demonstrate that change is possible. His research engaged subjects in a workshop illustrating the malleability of groups in different business situations (e.g., a simulated negotiation between management and union representatives at the end of which both parties modified their initial positions). Two control groups each had a different workshop: the first on coping skills, the second on taking the perspective of others. None of the workshops referred to the Israeli-Palestinian conflict. Two weeks and six months later, in comparison to the control groups, participants in the malleability workshop showed greater support for Israeli concessions to the Palestinians, greater acknowledgment of the Palestinians as a nation, and greater levels of hope regarding the conflict.[75]

A related study explored the effects of a workshop on group malleability on encounters between Israeli Jewish and Palestinian adolescents. In separate workshops, Jews and Palestinians learned about group malleability while control groups learned about coping skills. When the Jews and Palestinians were brought together to work on a collective task—building a tower with straws, marshmallows, and tape—the towers of the malleability group were almost 60 percent higher than in the control group. Participants in this group also gave significantly more positive emotional ratings of the joint tower-building exercise than their peers in the control group.[76]

In short, Eran has shown that exposing people to situations that model malleability changes their views about the conflict and improves their ability to interact with their adversaries.

Despite the dissemination of his work in more than 150 academic publications to date, Eran is primarily interested in applying his research to resolving conflicts in the real world. An opportunity to move in that direction arose in 2016 when Dalia Rabin, daughter of the late prime minister, suggested a meeting with Shir Nosatzki, thirty-six, one of the main organizers of the 2011 social protest movement. During the summer of 2011 hundreds of thousands of Israelis had taken to the streets and lived in tent cities to protest against unaffordable housing; in response, the government created programs that led to a substantial increase in the building of affordable housing units. Although it didn't solve the problem, the movement pushed this and other social justice issues higher on Israel's political agenda. This led Shir and other movement leaders to wonder why one particular issue never seemed to gain much traction in the activist community—the conflict between Israel and the Palestinians.

"Millennials have plenty of political awareness, but the conflict is off the table for them," Shir told me. "There's a sense of despair, a feeling that you can't do anything about it. We're surrounded by messages of despair. 'There is no partner for peace on the other side.' 'We've tried giving back territory and look what it brought us.' You hear these messages everywhere. People see peace with the Palestinians like the weather—not something you can change, but something you have to live with. That's what we have to overcome."

To do that Shir and her colleagues founded "Have You Seen the Horizon Lately?" Launched in the spring of 2018 with a series of TED Talk–style programs across the country that focus on the themes of Eran's research, the initiative is designed to deliver messages of hope to Israeli millennials and to stimulate activism. Here are summaries of two talks; the complete program is available online with English subtitles.[77]

Israeli writer Maya Savir describes the well-known 1994 genocide in Rwanda. In one hundred days the Hutu majority systematically slaughtered nearly 800,000 people, 70 percent of the Tutsi minority. But few have heard the story she tells about the country's dramatic, and so far successful, efforts toward reconciliation. Savir concludes her talk with a question: "Is our conflict more difficult, more painful, more bleeding than the conflicts these people endured, who chose reconciliation?"[78]

Management consultant Michal Engelberg discusses a research intervention carried out in the right-leaning town of Givat Shmuel—blanketing the town with ultra-extreme, right-wing messages about the conflict. In two weeks the intervention produced the paradoxical effect of increasing support for a halt in settlement building by 78 percent and reducing perceptions of Arab hostility toward Israel by 38 percent.

The test run for Have You Seen the Horizon Lately? went well. In Tel Aviv, two thousand people attended the program of seven fourteen-minute talks. Eran has been studying their impact—complete with a control group who did not hear the talks. At two weeks and then at six months after the talks, attendees retained signs of change. Compared to the control group, more of the attendees believed that Palestinians could change and that the conflict is solvable. They also took more responsibility for the conflict, identified more as peace activists, and were more motivated to participate in events that promote peace.

Shir looks at hope and despair as contagious viruses. "Hope spread very quickly in the 1990s, and now despair has spread. To see the horizon, we have to spread hope again."

Conclusion

Since the nineteenth century, Zionism has transferred responsibility for fulfilling the Jewish people's hopes for a collective return to their home-land from divine to human hands. The lives of those who gave birth to Zionism, those who built the state, and those who are fighting to fulfill its founding promises are profiles in hope. Scholars of hope call people like this Super-Empowered Hopeful Individuals. SEHIS, as they are known in the literature, are people who "believe the future will be better than the present—for everyone—and that they can make it happen. They believe that changing the world is a realistic goal despite every obstacle imaginable."[79]

Let's read SEHI as Super-Empowered Hopeful *Israelis*. The country is full of the NGOs they have created. For many years, the website of Makom: The Jewish Agency for Israel Education Lab included a section under social justice called "The Hope—Israeli NGOs."[80]

The Super-Empowered Hopeful Israelis in this chapter and beyond recognize that trying to *predict* Israel's future is a waste of time; trying to *build* a better future is not. All they—and we—need to know is that change is possible. The willingness to act on that knowledge is called hope, *tikvah*. *Od lo avda tikvatenu!* "We have not yet lost our hope!"

9

Jewish Humor

THE CURRENCY OF HOPE

There was nothing jolly and hilarious about the destitution that lay like a curse on millions of Jews in the Yiddish-speaking world. . . . They were miserable, and knew it; but the question that haunts us historically is, why did they not disintegrate intellectually and morally? How were they able, under hideous oppression and corroding privation, under continuous starvation — the tail of a herring was a dish — to keep alive against a better day the spirit originally breathed into man? The answer lies in the self-mockery by which they rose above their condition to see afar off the hope of the future.

— Maurice Samuel, *In Praise of Yiddish*

Introduction

Judaism's central narratives, beliefs, and rituals have provided the Jewish people with deeply sustaining sources of hope. To these, one more must be added: humor, what author Steve Lipman calls "the currency of hope."[1]

If the Jewish people are distinguished by their hope, they are equally known for their humor. As Irish film critic Paul Whitington observed: "The ubiquity of Jewish people in American comedy remains staggering, so much so that you're mildly surprised when a brilliant American screen comic like Steve Martin, for instance, isn't Jewish."[2] The former chief rabbi of the UK Jonathan Sacks (1948–2020) was right when he called humor "a first cousin to hope."[3] In fact, for Jews, hope and humor may be even more closely related.

This chapter explores the nature of the relationship between hope and humor, the Bible's first instance of laughter, two key motifs of Jewish humor (the Messiah and the schlemiel), the role that humor played for Jews during the Holocaust, and Judaism's view that even God — the butt of so many jokes — has a sense of humor.

Humor and Hope

Fascinating studies point to a significant relationship between humor and hope. People's exposure to humorous videos (in one trial, excerpts from the comedy reality TV show "Just Kidding") actually increased their scores on measures of hope compared to the scores of a control group exposed to neutral videos ("The Magic Eye," featuring 3D illusions), which remained unchanged. Another study found the kind of humor that amuses or entertains others tends to be correlated with optimism, while humor that aggressively puts others down is associated with higher levels of psychological distress.[4] A journal review, "Effect of Positive Emotions on Health: Hope and Humor," concludes, "In many cases, laughter and hope—which patients can be encouraged to develop—are indeed good medicines that may be contagious in the best sense of this word."[5]

Humor and hope are also connected in that both of them require a special kind of creativity, relying on a shared sense of social context, reflecting a sense of transcendence, expressing an element of chutzpah (audacity), and depending on the perception of incongruity.

CREATIVITY

"Art is the highest form of hope," painter Gerhard Richter memorably observed, and, some would argue, that includes humor too.[6] Jokes "must be seen as individual works of art created by particular human artists," wrote the philosopher Steven Gimbel, "even if—as with the cave paintings in France—the name of the artist is lost to history."[7] Like an artist considering a landscape and choosing the proper vantage point from which to depict it, both hope and humor enable us to see a bit beyond what's staring us in the face. Both are often most palpable in times of duress because they provide the means to envision, or briefly enter, a more palatable world. Hope and humor involve taking a step back—even a small one—from our travails. This allows us to formulate a thoughtful response, rather than reacting on the basis of pure emotion, which often only exacerbates a difficult situation. C. R. Snyder, a psychologist who spent much of his life studying hope, concludes:

Higher-hope people use humor to cope with the nuisances and blemishes of life. They are able to laugh at the things happening around them, and perhaps more importantly, they are able to laugh at themselves. This is especially true when they are stuck, trying to find some way to solve a thorny problem. A good laugh is energizing and allows us to put things in perspective. After all, is our particular goal really that important? Are we really that important? To see the humor in one's predicaments places the high-hope person in the throes of the larger existential ridiculousness of much of life.[8]

Hope's creativity allows us to imagine the road from here to there; humor helps makes the trip bearable.

SOCIAL CONTEXT

Hope and humor also reinforce one another through a shared social context. Shared humor binds us to other human beings in ways that enable us to overcome existential aloneness and build relationships that nurture hope. Philosopher Ted Cohen, author of *Jokes: Philosophical Thoughts on Joking Matters*, makes this point beautifully:

> When we laugh at the same thing that is a very special occasion. It is already noteworthy that we laugh at all, at anything, and that we laugh all alone. That we do it together is the satisfaction of a deep human longing, the realization of a desperate hope. It is the hope that we are enough like one another to sense one another, to be able to live together.[9]

On a collective level, Jewish humor functions similarly. Generally drawing upon the historical status of Jews as outsiders, and highlighting the boundary between "us and them," Jewish humor reinforces a sense of belonging: being part of that Jewish in-group that "gets" the joke. By strengthening in-group solidarity, Jewish humor fortifies the social bonds that support hope. Misery loves company, and not just for the sake of company: groups sustain hope more effectively than do isolated individuals. Psychologists Anthony Scioli and Henry Biller, authors of *Hope in the Age of Anxiety*, lists supportive relationships as a primary ingredient in building hope.[10]

TRANSCENDENCE

Hope and humor also share a kindred relationship to matters of the spirit. The American Psychological Association's landmark 2004 volume on positive psychology, *Character Strengths and Virtues: A Handbook and Classification*, identifies strengths of transcendence "encompassing hope (optimism, future-mindedness, and future-orientation) and humor (playfulness), along with appreciation of beauty and excellence, gratitude, and spirituality."[11] Each of these virtues "allows individuals to forge connections to the larger universe and thereby provide meaning to their lives.... Hope connects someone directly to the dreamed-of future. Humor ... connects someone directly to troubles and contradictions in a way that produces not terror or anger but pleasure."[12]

The connections among the trio of hope, humor, and transcendence run deep. Sociologist Peter Berger traces the development of all three to that early stage in human life when basic trust develops. Building on psychologist Erik Erikson's work on basic trust, which Erikson had identified as giving rise to the character strength of hope and the social institution of religion,[13] Berger adds the capacity for humor. At around eight months children begin to laugh when their caretakers play peekaboo with them. It's generally considered among the first interactions—and it seems to be nearly universal—that produces laughter in children without actual physical contact.[14] From the child's perspective the game revolves around the pleasure of experiencing the return of an anticipated, familiar face. The child hopes the face will reappear and laughs, in relief, when it does. Berger suggests that the spiritual analogue lies in the quest for God, whose face likewise appears and disappears, and in the possibility that humor is a "signal of transcendence":

> God's dealings with mankind can be seen as a cosmic game of hide-and-seek. We catch a glimpse of [God] and then [God] promptly disappears. [God's] absence is a central feature of our existence, and the ultimate source of all our anxieties. Religious faith is the hope that [God] will eventually reappear, providing that ultimate relief, which, precisely, is redemption.... Perceived in faith, the comic becomes a great consolation and a witness to the redemption that is yet to come.[15]

Berger's insight gains acuity if we consider two things. First, in the nearly thirty times God refers to hiding the divine face in the Bible, it is always associated with inducing fear and suffering. Second, the only book in the Bible in which God does not appear is Esther, the book read on Purim—the only Jewish holiday that virtually requires celebration with humor. Indeed, a growing literature analyses the book of Esther as what Bible scholar J. William Whedbee calls a "magnificent illustration of the comic vision in ancient Israel."[16] Berger might say that the ritualized laughter on Purim points to the hopeful expectation that the absent God will reappear—maybe not on Purim, but on Passover, just one month later on the Hebrew calendar, when God fulfills the Israelites' hopes for redemption "with a strong hand and an outstretched arm."

CHUTZPAH

Hope and humor also share a measure of audacity—or *chutzpah*, a Yiddish word that has become almost as common as bagels. Hope looks at the world and audaciously denies that today will define tomorrow.[17] Humor creates a safe place for even the most *chutzpadik* confrontations. Here's an example from a medieval midrash:

> When Israel worshipped the Golden Calf, God's wrath waxed hot against the people. *But Moses implored God* (Exod. 32:11), saying, "They've only given You an assistant. You are annoyed with them? You will cause the sun to rise, and it will cause the moon to rise. You will look after the stars, and it will look after the constellations. You will cause the dew to descend, and it will cause the winds to blow."
>
> God: "Are you making the same error as they did? Surely there is nothing real in that calf."
>
> Moses: "If that's the case, why does your anger wax hot against Your people?"[18]

If Moses had no hope that God could be appeased, he would not have bothered to try. If the author of this midrash had no sense of humor, he would not have had the gall to implore God in this particular way. (For more on the relationship between Exodus 32:11 and hope, see the "Hope Fights Back" section of chapter 4.)

INCONGRUITY

Finally, both hope and humor revolve around incongruity. According to scholars who study humor—there is an International Society for Humor Studies and an *Encyclopedia of Humor Studies!*—"incongruity, unexpectedness, and playfulness ... characterize all forms of humor."[19] Given the proper context, when we expect X and get Y, we laugh. When one character hits another on the head with a frying pan and we hear the vibrating clang of metal against metal, we laugh because *that* is not the sound we anticipate. Hope addresses the sometimes jarring incongruity between the way the world is and how we expect it should be. Humor's playfulness with that difference momentarily takes the sting out of life's pains and disappointments.

Much of Jewish humor relies on incongruity of a particular kind: the great expectations flowing from God's covenant with the People of Israel versus a history that so often seems to make mockery of those divine pledges. Sholem Aleichem called it the incongruity between "the Promise and the Pale," that yawning chasm between promise and actuality.[20] God spoke of a world at peace where the lion would lie down with the lamb, but that day remains painfully distant. ("How does the zoo manage to keep the lion and the lamb in the same cage? They put in a new lamb every night.") God spoke of the Israelites as God's chosen people. ("Please God, next time choose someone else.") God will hear and answer your prayers. ("Asked what it's like to pray so fervently, the most pious Jew at the Western Wall replied, 'It's like talking to the wall.'")

Many of these themes converge in a story about the Hasidic master Rabbi Levi Yitzhak of Berditchev (1740–1809). The Berditchever reminds God that "God's *tefillin* (phylacteries) contain the words 'Who is like Your people, Israel, a unique nation on earth' (1 Chron. 17:21). But if You won't forgive the Jewish people of its sins and redeem us, then we will be just like the rest of the nations, and those words will be false. If You redeem us, all will be well. But if not, I shall feel compelled to reveal publicly to the world that Your *tefillin* are invalid!"[21]

The Beginning of Jewish Laughter

Laughter makes its biblical debut in Genesis with the story of Isaac's birth—Isaac's name in Hebrew, Yitzhak, means "he shall laugh." Laughter and hope intersect at the very heart of Judaism's founding narrative. The moment arrives with the fulfillment of an essential element of God's covenantal oath to Abraham: that he and Sarah will produce offspring.[22] God informs Abraham that his wife shall conceive a son (see chapter 3), but given their old age, hope for a child seems absurd. In these passages from Genesis, incongruity reigns supreme:

> Abraham threw himself on his face and laughed, as he said to himself, "Can a child be born to a man a hundred years old, or can Sarah bear a child at ninety?" (17:17) God said, "Nevertheless, Sarah your wife shall bear you a son, and you shall name him Isaac." (17:19) Now Abraham and Sarah were old, advanced in years; Sarah had stopped having the periods of women. And Sarah laughed to herself, saying, "Now that I am withered, am I to have enjoyment—with my husband so old?" Then YHWH said to Abraham, "Why did Sarah laugh, saying, 'Shall I in truth bear a child, old as I am?' Is anything too wondrous for YHWH?" (18:11–14) Now Abraham was a hundred years old when his son Isaac was born to him. Sarah said, "God has brought me laughter; everyone who hears will laugh with me." (21:5–6)[23]

Abraham and Sarah have great faith in God, but here they react as if God were joking. Who conceives children at such an advanced age?[24]

Picking up on God's question to Abraham. "Is anything too wondrous for YHWH?" (Gen. 18:14), the fifth- or sixth-century midrash Genesis Rabbah compares God's query to that of a man who had two parts of a lock in his hand and went to a smith. "Can you repair these?" he asked; the smith replied, "From the outset I can create them. To repair them, I can't?!" Similarly here, God said, "From the outset I can create human beings. To restore their youth, I can't?!"[25]

Another humorous element is the implied comparison between a lock that no longer functions properly and the superannuated parents-to-be. In the context of procreation, it's not hard to imagine a key and padlock that had developed a bit of rust from age and lack of regular use.[26]

Imagine the rich flow of humor and hope as this rusty couple resumes long abandoned, but newly necessary, activities. Hope and humor enable the fulfillment of God's covenantal promise to Abraham and Sarah—and to all their descendants, from Isaac to the Jewish people today.

Several scholars of Jewish humor have noted the implications of the Isaac-laughter connection for the darkest chapter of Isaac's life: the *Akedah*. Ted Cohen put it this way:

> If Isaac meant laughter when he was born, then does he not still mean that now, when God directs Abraham to sacrifice a ram but to free Isaac? Is not God . . . directing that laughter be freed and let loose in the world? Let us hope so.[27]

Elie Wiesel takes these implications further:

> Isaac survived; he had no choice. He had to make something of his memories, his experience, in order to force us to hope. . . . As the first survivor, he had to teach us, the future survivors of Jewish history, that it is possible to suffer and despair an entire lifetime and still not give up the art of laughter. Isaac, of course, never freed himself from the traumatizing scenes that violated his youth; the holocaust had marked him and continued to haunt him forever. Yet he remained capable of laughter. And in spite of everything, he did laugh.[28]

Waiting for the Messiah

The coming of the Messiah constitutes classical Judaism's most ardent hope. Whether the Messianic Era is thought to usher in supernatural changes, such as resurrection of the dead, or more modest developments, like an end to Israel's oppression by the nations, it's all about hope for a better future. The irony of comparing that messianic promise and Jewish history is what professor of comparative literature Sidra DeKoven Ezrahi calls "the comic spirit tak[ing] up residency in the elasticity of the messianic promise."[29] The comic sensibility insulates the fragile vision of that promise from outright rejection with a protective wrapping of laughter and thus helps keep its hope alive. A more down-to-earth formulation is the Yiddish expression voiced in frustration when someone is late: *Er vet kumen ven Moshiach vet kumen* — "He'll get here when the Messiah gets here!"

Humorous treatments of the Messiah go back a long time. A midrash: "Rabban Yochanan ben Zakkai used to say, 'If you are about to plant a sapling and they call you saying, 'Behold the Messiah is here,' go plant the tree and then welcome the Messiah.'"[30] Ben Zakkai had led the Jewish community in Israel during the disastrous Jewish revolt against Rome (66–70 CE). Opposing the rebellion as foolhardy, he arranged with Emperor Vespasian to take refuge with his students at Yavne; there he founded a center for learning that kept the Jewish future alive.[31]

Not everyone heeded Ben Zakkai's warning. Rabbi Akiva, for one, supported Israel's next doomed rebellion against Rome (132–35 CE), championing the revolt's leader, Bar Kokhba, as the Messiah. The Jerusalem Talmud reports his colleagues' disagreement with a line that sounds like it could have come straight from Sholem Aleichem: "Akiva, grass will grow from your cheeks [i.e., you will long be dead and buried] and still the Messiah will not come!"[32]

Fast forward to the Middle Ages. Abraham Ibn Ezra (c. 1090–1165), poet, grammarian, philosopher, biblical commentator, astronomer, and physician, wandered through Europe and North Africa, teaching, writing books, and engaging with local scholars. Generally impoverished, according to legend, "He laughed at his own poverty. . . . And many witty epigrams have been attributed to him."[33] Here is one:

> If I should undertake to sell candles,
> The sun would never set;
> If I should deal in shrouds,
> No one would ever die.[34]

Of course, we hear the complaint of a man who sees himself as a luckless schlemiel who ruins whatever he touches. But there's more. This unlucky fellow also plays with the idea that though nothing goes his way, he exerts enormous power on the universe. Ibn Ezra's epigram plays with Isaiah's prophetic visions of Messianic Times: "Your sun shall set no more . . . for YHWH shall be a light to you forever, and your days of mourning shall be ended" (60:20).

One of Freud's disciples, Theodore Reik, tells a related joke:

People are saying that the Messiah will come soon. You know, I don't relish that at all. We would have to leave all and go to Israel. Now, when we finally have a pretty little house.

Don't worry Moische, God has saved you from Pharaoh, he has protected us from Haman—he will guard us from the Messiah too.[35]

Both Ibn Ezra's epigram and Reik's joke play with the Messiah's arrival in the near term. More typically, Jews give this possibility long odds:

They tell a story of a little town in the old country. It was out of the way, in a valley, so the Jews were afraid that the Messiah would come and miss them. . . . So they built a high tower and hired one of the town beggars to sit in it all day long.

A friend of his meets this beggar and he says, "How do you like your job, Baruch?"

So he says, "It doesn't pay much, but I think it's steady work."[36]

Rabbi Levi Yitzhak of Berditchev, a man whose faith in the Messiah no one doubted, used to address his wedding invitations like this: "The wedding will take place . . . at five o'clock in Jerusalem, the holy city. But if, God forbid, the Messiah will not have come by then, it will take place in Berditchev."[37]

And then there's the twelfth of Maimonides' Thirteen Principles: "I believe with perfect faith in the coming of the Messiah. And even though he may tarry, I await his coming every day." A renowned physician, Maimonides (1138–1204), known to have had a good sense of humor, would doubtless have approved of the Berditchever's joke. To restore a sick person to health, Maimonides used to recommend "telling the patient joyful stories that dilate his soul and chest [i.e., make them expand with joy] . . . telling him tales that divert him and make him laugh."[38]

The great Jewish philosopher Martin Buber once addressed a gathering of Catholic priests. Acknowledging that the great difference between believing Christians and believing Jews was that Jews were still waiting for the Messiah, while Christians were waiting for the Messiah to come again, Buber appealed to the group: "Let us wait for him together." Then, in a genial Hasidic improvisation, Buber continued:

And, when the Messiah comes, we will ask: "Have you already been here?"
When that happens, Buber said, "I hope to be close enough so I can whisper in the Messiah's ear: for heaven's sake — don't answer!"[39]

The Schlemiel

The poor schlemiel, that icon of Jewish humor, has not only brought laughter to generations of Jews but has now become the object of serious study. Professor of Yiddish and comparative literature Ruth Wisse notes that the schlemiel, traditionally depicted as an inept male, reflects all the complexities of Jewish identity. For some, he "embodied those negative qualities of weakness that had to be ridiculed to be overcome." For others, he was "the model of endurance, his innocence a shield against corruption, his absolute defenselessness the only guaranteed defense against the brutalizing potential of might." Either way, hope plays a central role in humor involving the schlemiel, whom Wisse describes as being suspended "between despair and hope."[40]

Bible translator and professor of comparative literature Robert Alter explains schlemielian humor as a response to a fundamental contradiction: the inherent dignity of an individual created in the image of God who lives a demeaning life, full of suffering. But here too hope plays a critical role, Alter explains:

The perception of incongruity implies the perception of alternate possibilities, humor peeking out beyond the beleaguered present toward another kind of man, another kind of time; for the very aura of ridicule suggests that it is not after all fitting for a man to be this pitiful creature with a blade of anguish in his heart and both feet entangled in a clanking chain of calamities.[41]

Wisse begins her classic *The Schlemiel as Modern Hero* with a dry joke that toys with this question of fundamental human dignity:

Sometime during World War I, a Jew lost his way along the Austro-Hungarian frontier. Wandering through the woods late at night, he was suddenly arrested by the challenge of a border guard: "Halt, or I'll shoot!"

The Jew blinked into the beam of the searchlight and said: "What's the matter with you? Are you crazy? Can't you see this is a human being?"

Here we encounter the schlemiel in all his vulnerability—a Jew lost in the woods in the middle of the night, in the midst of war, near the frontier, facing an armed border guard. But our poor friend knows the way out: simply remind the border guard of his error—guns are pointed at animals, not human beings. Herein lies the hope: the recognition of shared humanity will point the way forward. Alas, the clueless schlemiel's quaint assertion of humanity hardly answers the guard's interest in checking a potential intruder from penetrating enemy lines. But in announcing that *he* is not an animal, the schlemiel implies that his adversary *is*. Only an animal would point a gun at a being created in the image of God.

A more well-known war joke makes the same point:

A Jewish soldier in the Russo-Japanese war shoots up in the air instead of at the enemy. He is brought before a Russian court martial and asked why he fired upwards.

In apparent innocence, he replies, "What do you mean? In front of me there were people; if I'd shot at them I might have killed someone!"[42]

In "Berl Debates the Jesuit Priest," my favorite story in Ted Cohen's *Jokes*, we meet a truly first-class schlemiel:

A Polish nobleman hired a brilliant Jesuit theologian to debate a Jew from a village within his vast land holdings. The first one unable to answer a question would be beheaded. The leaders of the Jewish village asked for volunteers, and Berl, a poorly educated fellow who lived off charitable donations, raised his hand. At the debate, Berl won the coin toss to decide who would ask the first question. "What does 'Ani lo yodea' [I don't know] mean?" he asked. The theologian answered: "I don't know." He was instantly beheaded. Overjoyed, the villagers asked Berl how he thought of that question. Berl explained that when he was young, the famous Rabbi Weinstein once visited his school, and he asked him a question. "Rabbi Weinstein, please, what does this mean — 'Ani lo yodea'? And he said, 'I don't know.' Today I thought, if even Rabbi Weinstein didn't know, then surely this Jesuit priest doesn't."[43]

This tale evokes the disputations of the medieval period, which never ended well for the Jews. In 1263, when Nachmanides won a debate with a Christian monk (a Jewish convert) and received a prize from the king, he was still forced to flee for his life. Here Berl, the town ignoramus, stands in for one of Europe's most brilliant Jewish scholars. Where Jews had long been completely defenseless, this story creates a separate little world where hope and faith, even when born of ignorance, can bring the mighty and arrogant low. It also touches upon a critical ambiguity surrounding the schlemiel. "[He] is the eternal innocent, and yet one is never sure if he is merely a good-natured fool or if there is a reservoir of hidden wisdom beneath his foolishness."[44]

In this case, Berl literally doesn't know what he doesn't know. His victory brings to mind Haman's downfall and with it the defeat of all who had plotted against the Jews. Have enough faith in Rabbi Weinstein, and you too might triumph! The Jewish people will finally be rescued — by an army of schlemiels!

The schlemiel Hymie, introduced by Sanford Pinsker, author of *The Schlemiel as Metaphor*, also appeals to our hopes for a prosperous future:

The employees of a large company decided to have a weekly lottery, just to liven things up. The man who picked the lucky number won the jackpot.

For three weeks running Hymie had the lucky number. His coworkers couldn't figure out how Hymie did it. Was it just plain luck, or did he have a method of figuring it out?

At lunch one of his friends said, "Hymie, how come you're the lucky one three weeks in a row?" Another said, "Do you have some kind of system?"

"It's simple," said Hymie. "I dream. The other night I saw eight sevens dancing before my eyes. Eight sevens are forty-eight, so I figured forty-eight had to be the lucky number; so I picked it."

"But Hymie, eight sevens are fifty-six, not forty-eight!"

"*Nu!*" answered Hymie, "So *you* be the mathematician!"[45]

Whatever else it may be, the dream of winning the jackpot is a metaphor for hope.

Laughing and Hoping in Hell

On Dante's journey to Hell, he reads a faint inscription over the portal: "All hope abandon, ye who enter here." Dante then goes on to describe the sounds he hears:

> Here sighs, with lamentations and loud moans . . .
> . . . Various tongues,
> Horrible languages, outcries of woe,
> Accents of anger, voices deep and hoarse,
> With hands together smote that swell'd the sounds,
> Made up a tumult, that forever whirls.[46]

There's no hope or laughter in Dante's Inferno. We might have expected the same in concentration camps and ghettos during the Holocaust. But that would be very wrong.

When the Nazis arrested Tristan Bernard (1866–1947), the French Jewish playwright quipped to his wife, "Before we had been living in anguish. Now we will live in hope."[47]

Steve Lipman, author of *Laughter in Hell: The Use of Humor during the Holocaust*, explains the relationship between hope and humor during this period:

> Humor, the currency of hope, did not flourish in the Holocaust for its own sake, but for a deeper reason. . . . Humor was both a psychological weapon and a defense mechanism. It was a social bond among trusted friends. It was a diversion, a shield, a morale booster,

an equalizer, a drop of truth in a world founded on lies. In short, a cryptic redefining of the victims' world.[48]

Indeed, the Holocaust provides a grim laboratory for probing the depth of the relationship between hope and humor. From the large and still growing literature on humor during the Holocaust, let's look at a few examples that highlight the connection between these two strengths of character.

Man's Search for Meaning, Viktor Frankl's distillation of what he learned from his years in three concentration camps, includes many discussions of humor. Along with hope, "humor was another of the soul's weapons in the fight for self-preservation. It is well known that humor, more than anything else in the human make-up, can afford an aloofness and an ability to rise above any situation, even if only for a few seconds."[49] In one case, Frankl encouraged a co-worker on an assembly line, a surgeon, to promise him that they would invent at least one amusing story every day about how their experience in the camp would intrude on their life after liberation. One story pictured his surgeon friend performing an operation and someone suddenly shouting "Action! Action!"—the words the assembly line foreman yelled when higher-ups made their inspection tours, and he wanted the workers to speed up. Another inmate imagined himself at a dinner party where he might forget himself and when soup was served urge the hostess to serve it from the bottom.[50] In the camps the soup was mostly water, the few solids sitting on the bottom of the pot.

Joking in Auschwitz about the awkwardness of unlearning the ways of the camp after liberation—what a bond between humor and hope! Humor-hope was also the bedrock of the comedic play produced by inmates of Dachau, "The Night of Blood on the Rock of Horrors or Knight Adolar's Maiden Voyage and Its Gruesome End or That Is Not the True Love," which ran for six weeks during the summer of 1943. The play's main character, a sadistic buffoon named Adolar, bore more than a passing resemblance to Hitler, but, apparently unaware of the extent to which the play parodied the Third Reich, the Dachau commandant approved the performances. A surviving member of the cast would later explain: "Many of [the inmates] who sat behind the rows of the SS each night and laughed with a full heart didn't experience the day of freedom. But most among them took from this demonstration the strength to endure their situation." The play's concluding lines offered this message: "Everything is hell, / Soon it will get well / Through this magic word: humor, humor!"[51]

God Laughs Too

The incongruity in Jewish humor, that piling up of contradictions—like the contrast between the darkness of Jewish experience and the Bible's often sunny promises—has given rise to a pithy saying: "We have a God in Heaven, thank God; but he has got a people on earth, God help Him!"[52]

What might God think of a joke like this? Does God have a sense of humor?

It would be logical to assume so. Human beings are created in God's image. We have a sense of humor; ergo, God should too. The sages of the Talmud definitely believed in God's sense of humor and tendency to laugh, sometimes precisely when humanity fulfilled God's hopes. In one story—in which the humorous dimension is often overlooked—a majority of sages reject God's attempts to influence their rulings on Jewish law. Rabbi Eliezer invokes a series of special effects to affirm his interpretation of the law. He calls for a tree to move from here to there, a stream to flow backward, and the walls of the building they are in to lean perilously inward. Still unable to sway his opponents, Rabbi Eliezer calls on Heaven for more direct support. A voice from Heaven asks: "Why do you dispute with Rabbi Eliezer? Don't you know that in all matters Jewish law agrees with him?" To which his chief opponent replies, citing a verse from Deuteronomy: "It is not in the heavens" (30:12).[53]

The responsibility for interpreting Jewish law rests upon human beings, not God—even though tradition holds that God dictated those very laws to Moses. The story ends with a report from the prophet Elijah, herald of the Messiah. When God saw what had transpired, God laughed, saying, "My sons defeated me!" God laughs with mirth (just as we do when our hopes come true). The sages had finally fulfilled one of God's great hopes—that human beings would take more responsibility for figuring out how to run the world.

Elsewhere, the Talmud mentions that part of God's daily routine involves playing with the Leviathan, a primordial sea monster associated with chaos.[54] (The Talmud's word for "play" or "sport," *misachek*, can also mean "laugh.") In a eulogy for a deceased colleague, Rabbi Joseph Soloveitchik argued that this seemingly superfluous detail about God's schedule teaches a vital lesson: Created in God's image, human beings need not "take everything so seriously." When Aryeh Kaplan, one of the greatest Modern Orthodox scholars of the twentieth century, was asked if the Talmud included any jokes, he answered, "Yes, but they're all old."[55]

Conclusion

Humor does more than make us laugh. It keeps us going, keeps us human. Theologian Harvey Cox wrote about an "irrepressible radical hope [that] remains alive and well in the comic. . . . It could conceivably disappear, and where laughter and hope have disappeared man has ceased to be man."[56]

The literature on humor and hope during the Holocaust bears out Cox's insight. The antidote to despair is laughter, unearthing the humorous not just in jokes, but wherever we can. When we do, we may experience a sense of hope that flows from an enhanced ability to imagine a world better than the one we're facing at that or any given moment—such as when life is not flowing: "What's the difference between the plumber and the Messiah? The Messiah might yet show up, but the Hebrew plumber never comes . . ."[57]

Final Thoughts

To be a Jew is to be an agent of hope. Every ritual, every command, every syllable of the Jewish story is a protest against escapism, resignation and the blind acceptance of fate. Judaism, the religion of the free God, is a religion of freedom. Jewish faith is written in the future tense. It is belief in a future that is not yet but could be, if we heed God's call . . . and act together as a covenantal community.

The name of the Jewish future is hope.

—Jonathan Sacks, *Future Tense: Jews, Judaism, and Israel in the Twenty-First Century*

A Succinct Jewish Theology of Hope

A modern Jewish theology of hope, in my view, rests on two principal ideas:

· Human beings are created in the divine image.
· God has put the responsibility for fulfilling our hopes in our hands.

Creation in God's image implies that we possess a fundamental goodness we can build on, and that because others do as well, we can form relationships and work together to realize shared hopes. In order to allow humanity to fulfill its ultimate potential of completing Creation and repairing the world, God does not interfere in human history. When we act in godly ways, God acts through us. God can help us to discern whether our hopes are worthy, and, when they are, God roots for us, inspiring us as we try to bring our hopes to fruition. Kabbalist and ethicist Moshe Chaim Luzzatto (1707–46, Italy, Holland, Israel) taught that the very start of God's Creation of the cosmos began with hope.[1] As images of God, the ultimate creator, we too can conceive of realities yet to be and breathe life into them. And because we are created in the divine image and God transmits hope, we can transmit hope too. Elie Wiesel expressed it this way:

> Created in the image of [God] who has no image, it is incumbent upon our contemporaries to invoke and create hope where there is none. For just as only human beings can push me to despair, only they can help me vanquish it and call it hope.[2]

Finding Hope in Our Ancient Texts

This theology, however, differs from more traditional Jewish approaches to hope. To appreciate the difference, consider this verse from Psalms: "I hope for Your deliverance, O YHWH; I observe Your commandments" (Ps. 119:166). Traditionally, the human hope for God's salvation hinges on our faithfulness to divine law. In other words, *we* don't fulfill our deepest hopes, *God* does, and only if we deserve it.

If you, like me, see a more active role for humans in fulfilling our hopes, how can we best relate to texts that seem to leave hope in God's hands alone?

First, it's important to remember that despite our pious ancestors' faith in God, they were human beings, neither possessing an endless source of hope nor an impenetrable shield against despair. As historian Yosef Hayim Yerushalmi observes, "To explain hope with a mere shrug of the shoulders by saying 'but of course, they believed in God' . . . is to explain nothing."[3] The truth is that faith in God has often raised as many questions about hope as it answered.

Consider an eleventh-century midrash composed by Tuvia ben Eliezer. Early on in this lengthy midrash the author explicitly describes the slaughter of pious Jews in Ashkenaz in 1096 during the early days of the First Crusade. In addition to those murdered by marauding Christians, large numbers of Jews killed their families and then themselves, lest they fall into the Crusaders' hands. These deaths, especially those wrought by Jews, were viewed as supreme acts of sanctification of God's Name.[4] Building on a verse from the Song of Songs, a biblical book often interpreted as an allegory of the love between the Divine and Israel, the midrash recounts Israel's experience of abandonment by God:

I opened the door for my beloved, but my beloved had turned and gone. I was faint because of what he said. I sought him, but found him not; I called, but he did not answer (Songs 5:6). . . . For behold, Israel hopes in every generation for God's salvation and they are slaughtered to sanctify [God]. And still we are expectant, we wait, we hope, "Perhaps there is hope" (Lam. 3:29). As scripture says, "O Israel, hope in YHWH; For with YHWH there is mercy, and with [YHWH] is plenteous redemption" (Ps. 130:7).[5] *I sought him, but found him not.* . . . This is like what the prophet Habakkuk said, "For there is yet a prophecy for a set term, a truthful witness for a time that will come. Even if it tarries, wait for it still; for it surely will come, without delay" (2:3). . . . *I called, but he did not answer.* . . . As scripture says, "I am exhausted from my calling out. My throat is hoarse. My eyes fail from hoping for my God" (Ps. 69:4).[6] "How long will You hide Your face from me?" (Ps. 13:2). And there are many references in scripture that speak to the long exile we are in.[7]

Faith puts the author's hope to the test as an ever-silent God nearly exhausts his hope. Here he adds his voice to the ancient biblical verses narrating the ongoing battle to hold on to hope amid calamities. Citing the text from Lamentations, composed in response to the Babylonians' destruction of the First Temple in 586 BCE, the author connects the horrors of the ancient past to those of the present and thus points to the ongoing challenge of retaining the covenantal hope of God's salvation (see chapter 5 of this volume).

The very fact that texts like these reveal the struggle to hold onto fundamental beliefs that sustain hope—in the trustworthiness of either God or humanity—gives us an entryway to relate to them. We can identify with this author's refusal to relinquish a particular hope against a wash of experience over the centuries that might well justify despair. Hope versus despair: It's a test we all face, regardless of our beliefs. Texts like this shine a light on how hard our ancestors fought to choose hope and can provide inspiration to us as we try to do the same.

Hope Means Work

The work of hope takes place on three interrelated planes:

- Our core selves
- The trials we face in our personal lives
- Our efforts to repair the world at large.

Judaism provides resources to help us respond with hope to all three.

OUR CORE SELVES

Teshuvah (repentance) is Judaism's methodology for doing the work that will let the divine image within shine forth more brightly (see chapter 1 of this volume). *Teshuvah* enables us to become the better selves we yearn to be—and includes a renewed willingness to choose hope over despair and an increased capacity to work toward our deepest hopes.

Although Judaism supplies Jews with a richly orchestrated season when we do *teshuvah* with our entire community, the daily prayers make it clear that *teshuvah* can be an ongoing process of personal growth. We are not fated to live with our flaws. That Judaism supplies multiple means for overcoming them itself constitutes an enormous source of hope.

Prayer can play an important part in *teshuvah*. In deep private prayer, the dialogue we may experience with the One of Being can help us assess the worthiness of our hopes, abandon those that don't measure up, and stand behind those that do with renewed energy. Prayer can help us remember that when it comes to our most noble yearnings we, created in the divine image, share common hopes with God. So too, the mode of prayer can provide a special space—not unlike a dream—where we can discover strategies for more effectively pursuing a particular hope. When we lose hope that we can create the changes we'd like to see in ourselves, or in the world, the process of prayer can remind us that we are not alone in this struggle. Steeped in the language of covenantal hope, the content of much of Jewish liturgy reinforces the conviction that on the deepest level we remain in relationship with the Divine, come what may. The bevy of prayers and biblical passages recalling God's saving hand makes the daily morning service a fine illustration of why philosopher Gabriel Marcel calls hope "a memory of the future."[8] Praying the words of this liturgy while holding in mind that we are images of God can open us to an enormously empowering sense of possibility (see chapter 5). And prayers promising that God will resurrect the dead can remind us how often we, the living, are asleep to the possibilities that lie within our grasp (see chapter 7). Despite diverse understandings in different ages and communities, Jewish thought about the afterlife persists as a mainstay of hope.

The two steps forward, one step back process of building the selves we hope to be can be a frustrating slog, better undertaken with a smile and without losing one's sense of humor (see chapter 9). Hope researcher and psychologist C. R. Snyder encouraged his clients to see the humorous or even absurd aspects of their struggles. He believed that our capacity to laugh at ourselves boosts willpower, a vital ingredient in the pursuit of challenging goals:

> The delightful paradox is that we can get a boost by acknowledging our fallibility. I would suggest placing a sign somewhere in your mind, and looking at it when things seem particularly bleak. That sign reads: If you don't laugh at yourself, you have missed the biggest joke of all.[9]

Theologian Harvey Cox calls laughter "hope's last weapon," which can help us through all of life's tough times.[10]

Ephraim Kishon (1924–2005, Hungary, Israel, and Switzerland), a Holocaust survivor and Israeli satirist whose worldwide book sales topped forty million, wrote a humorous fictional story about a brilliant professor of economics at the Hebrew University. Despite herculean efforts to save money, his fixed salary and annually rising taxes reduced him to poverty. The solution? Selling candy to the students, which ultimately led to his resignation—and becoming a wealthy candy magnate. The story ends on a wry note: "Moral: do not lose hope in the most desperate situations. You never know when the tide is going to turn."[11]

OUR TRIALS

Nothing can spare us from life's trials. The question is: How do we respond to them? Judaism's key narratives remind us how to do so with hope.

Abraham and Sarah, childless, their lives stuck at a crossroads, receive God's offer of a new homeland along with the dual promises of offspring and of becoming a great nation (see chapter 3). Abraham only has to do three *small* things—abandon his aged father, leave his native land, and head off into the arid landscape, destination unknown. God helps Abraham imagine what his fulfilled hopes will look like, but God doesn't pack up his belongings, or saddle up his mules. God leaves the work of fulfilling their hopes to Abraham and Sarah.

We can see the same thing again when God tells the aged couple that Sarah will bear a son. Both Abraham and Sarah laugh; Sarah says, "Now that I am withered, am I to have enjoyment—with my husband so old?" (Gen. 18:12). Perhaps God restored the couple's fertility, but this was no case of Virgin Birth. To fulfill their hope of children, the old-timers had to do their part, which at their advanced ages may have entailed as much work as pleasure.

And then God tests Abraham once more: telling him to take the couple's long-awaited son, Isaac, and raise him up for a sacrifice. Abraham moves through the ordeal with hope in his every utterance—assuring his servants that he and Isaac will return from the mountaintop and that God will provide the sacrificial sheep. Hope leads him through the trial.

Exodus recounts an ordeal of a different kind (see chapter 4). The enslaved Israelites hope for freedom, but they don't get it by waiting for God to give it to them. First the midwives refuse to follow Pharaoh's order to kill all the newborn Israelite males. Then Moses' mother orchestrates a defiant plan to save her newborn son from being drowned in the Nile. Then God demands that, before leaving Egypt, the Israelites must slaughter and sacrifice the very kind of animals the Egyptians worshipped as gods. Finally, after the people leave Egypt and find themselves trapped between Pharaoh's approaching army and the Red Sea, God says to Moses, "Why do you cry out to Me? Tell the Israelites to go forward. And you lift up your rod and hold out your arm over the sea and split it, so that the Israelites may march into the sea on dry ground" (Exod. 14:15,16). Only then does God act. Realizing the Israelites' hopes in Egypt and at the Red Sea requires human action.

The book of Job describes a still different kind of trial: the grief and suffering of a man who suddenly loses everything he has—his children, his health, his wealth—and hope as well (see chapter 6). Usually read as a treatise on the nature of God and the problem of innocent suffering, we can equally read Job as a journey from near-suicidal despair to "a hard-fought hope" and re-engagement with the world.[12] Job's first steps toward hope begin with his ability to conceive of allies taking his side even—or especially—when his friends refuse to support him. A succession of imagined allies—an arbiter, a witness, and finally a vindicator—enables Job to hatch an extraordinary plan: proving his innocence by calling God to court. And God shows up, acknowledging Job's innocence, condemning his foolish friends, and satisfying Job's abiding hope for vindication. Job's successful struggle for exoneration stands as a beacon of hope for those who are unjustly accused or convicted, and reminds us that it's possible to climb out of even the deepest abyss of despair.[13]

The fact that Job's hope hinges on his ability to find allies—even if he has to create them—attests to the significance of hope's social matrix, that hope "constitutes itself through a we and for a we," as Marcel maintains.[14] My interviews with activists in Israel bear that out (see chapter 8). They are not sole practitioners. They all work in organizations and/or coalitions that bring people together with a common subtext: helping participants to choose hope.

In any joint undertaking—from marriage to business to politics—our partners can help us stave off despair and go further than we could alone. One team member may be aware of a piece of progress that has escaped notice, an insight that spurs persistence when one might otherwise give up. Some partners may be better at detecting the light at the end of a particularly long tunnel, at generating new strategies to reach a goal when others have run out of ideas, or at galvanizing group action toward the goal. In his victory speech following his 2021 election as Georgia's first black senator, Raphael Warnock put it this way: "We were told that we couldn't win this election, but tonight, we proved that with hope, hard work, and the people by our side, anything is possible."[15]

OUR WORLD

The concept of *tikkun olam* fashions the above lessons about hope and action into what many thinkers take to be Judaism's ultimate hope: slowly but relentlessly pushing the world from what is to what ought to be (see chapter 2). The expression seems to be based on language appearing in the pessimistic book of Ecclesiastes (1:15): "That which is crooked cannot be made straight [*l'tkon*]." Coining the phrase *tikkun olam* almost two millennia ago, the Rabbis pointedly used it as the basis for straightening out unfair laws—even as they believed these laws to have been transmitted by Moses from Sinai—in the hope of improving society.

In so doing, they aligned themselves *against* Ecclesiastes' dour maxim and *with* the Rabbinic tenet that God created the world with imperfections so humanity could assume responsibility for fixing them. As one ancient midrash said, "Whatever was created by God during the six days of Creation needs further improvement" or work.[16] In our era, Joseph B. Soloveitchik, the guiding light of Modern Orthodoxy, championed this view, arguing that it gives "expression to [the Jewish people's] hope for the perfection of creation and the repairing of the defects in the cosmos."[17]

Working in partnership with God, in my view, means that although we cannot hope that God will act to bring redemption to the shattered world, we *can* hope that God will strengthen *our* will to redeem the world. Maimonides and many following him believed that the Messianic Era, the object of age-old Jewish hopes, "will be realized in this world" by the enlightened actions of human beings.[18] Thus the hope of repairing *this* world succeeds the earlier yearning for an otherworldly Messianic Era.

Underlying the idea of *tikkun olam* is the special part that each of us who shares a particular hope is meant to play in its fulfillment. And the joy of working with others to birth a shared hope can more than offset the pain of living with a dream yet to be fulfilled. When we work in tandem to realize a hope and the inevitable setbacks occur, we become comrades in arms who fortify one another's resolve. The view from the trenches of *tikkun olam* almost always looks more encouraging than the view of the uninvolved. From up close we can observe and "enjoy the fruit of [our] . . . labors" (Ps. 128:2), even tiny ones that reinforce the conviction that change is possible—that with enough effort, by enough people, little by little, contrary to Ecclesiastes, the crooked *can* be made straight.

Realizing the scope and difficulty of fulfilling this hope, Jewish tradition also provides a classic tonic against burnout: "The day is short and the work is much. . . . It is not your responsibility to complete the work, but neither are you free to desist from it" (*Pirkei Avot* 2:21). We need to do the work *and* have reasonable expectations. We may not realize our larger hopes in our lifetimes, but our hope-laden work to try becomes a foundation for the next generations to build upon. Moses and Martin Luther King Jr. viewed the Promised Land only from afar, but both knew their descendants would see it up close. They passed their best hopes on to the next generations; we can, as well.

Transmitting Our Heritage of Hope

One of my hopes is that, after reading this book, your commitment to choose hope will be a bit stronger — in your personal life as well as in regard to the broader issues facing society, the Jewish community, Israel, and the world. I hope you'll feel even more comfortable choosing to side with the prophetic view of human possibility and responsibility over Ecclesiastes' insistence on the futility of any efforts to improve the world. Maybe when you hear someone say that antisemitism or racism will *always* be with us or that Israel and the Palestinians will *never* make peace, you'll say, "Really?"

And then, I hope, each of us will work to strengthen our individual capacity to transmit hope to those around us, especially the next generations. Because choosing hope matters, and to do this vital work, we ourselves have to believe that choosing hope matters.

The process begins by expanding our images of ourselves. In addition to everything else we are, it's important to think of ourselves as transmitters of hope. In the poem Amanda Gorman recited at Joe Biden's 2021 Presidential Inauguration, what she said about light could well be said about hope: "For there is always light if only we're brave enough to see it, if only we're brave enough to be it."[19]

We know, for instance, that our behavior weakens or strengthens the ethical norms of our families and communities. The same applies to hope. How we respond to the trials in our lives makes us models for those around us.

Seminal research by C. R. Snyder demonstrates that holding onto hope depends on two factors: the strength of our determination to reach a goal and our capacity to develop new strategies to reach it.[20] When we persevere and keep trying to figure out new ways to get there, we teach the lessons of hope.

We can all play a role in transmitting hope. When we share the narratives of the Jewish people and interpret them through the lens of hope, we spread hope. For example, at a Passover seder we might lead a discussion about what hope means, or what examples in the Haggadah illustrate hope or hopelessness, or how the Exodus has inspired hope in people across the ages (see chapter 4), or who should take responsibility for fulfilling our hopes in the world today. Likewise, congregational rabbis might make the conscious choice to transmit hope more programmatically—to learn, teach, and talk about hope; to use prayer to explore hope; to both celebrate and model hope. Scholars of Judaism might deepen the study of hope's role in Jewish history and Judaism.[21] All in all, it means studying how Jews chose hope throughout history—hope *af-'al-pi-khein*, "in spite of it all," as Rabbi Tamar Elad-Appelbaum explains. And it means confronting the difficulties of maintaining hope in dark times and sharing experiences that affirm hope. These can be important conversations.

Taking on this task in a systematic way could help us create communities of hope in our families, communal organizations, synagogues, and society at large.

It's important to remember that transmitting hope is itself a two-way street: rabbis, teachers, and parents certainly transmit hope to their congregants, students, and children, but the reverse is also true. British psychoanalyst Charles Rycroft suggests that hope is an open system; like a river, it depends on inputs of rain, springs, and streams, but it feeds back nourishment to the surrounding environment.[22] Despite differences in our roles and generations, we can all be transmitters of hope. And when that happens, our reservoir of hope expands, because in the end, as Marcel reminds us, hope grows best in fellowship.[23]

I witnessed this during my interviews with Israeli activists. Our conversations were surprisingly emotional for everyone involved. Even though hope plays a central role in their lives, few of these people had ever been asked about it so directly. That's true of many of us. Hope lives close to the heart and feels private. But sharing hopes with an interested listener strengthens hope—in this case, both the activists' and mine. These conversations brought to mind a phrase in Deuteronomy (30:19)—*u'vacharta ba-chayim*, "choose life"—because hope too is a choice. And without choosing hope, life is not life.[24]

At the end of one of my last interviews, a thought popped into my head. When we conclude reading one of the Five Books of Moses we say, *Chazak, chazak, v'nitchazek*, "Be strong, be strong, and we will strengthen one another!" Suddenly it came to me: *Kaveh, kaveh, v'nitkaveh*, "Hope, hope, and we will build one another's hope!"[25]

The future we hope for is waiting for us to create it.

Notes

ABBREVIATIONS

Alter	Robert Alter, *The Hebrew Bible: A Translation with Commentary*
Artscroll	Nosson Scherman, *Artscroll Tanach*
BDB	*The Brown-Driver-Briggs Hebrew and English Lexicon*, Francis Brown et al.
BI	Bar Ilan Responsa Project, version 26+
BT	Babylonian Talmud
HB	Hebrewbooks.org. To find the volume, put the HB number after the forward slash at www.hebrewbooks.org/
Jastrow	Marcus Jastrow, *Dictionary of the Targumim, Talmud Babli, Yerushalmi and Midrashic Literature*
JT	Jerusalem Talmud
Koren	Harold Fisch, *The Jerusalem Bible*
Marcel	Gabriel Marcel, "Sketch of a Phenomenology and a Metaphysic of Hope"
MPPB	*My People's Prayer Book*, Lawrence A. Hoffman
MR	*A Maimonides Reader*, Moses Maimonides
MRI	*Mekhilta de-Rabbi Ishmael*, Jacob Lauterbach
NJPS	New Jewish Publication Society translation of the TANAKH
OJPS	Old Jewish Publication Society translation of the TANAKH
PRE	*Pirke de Rabbi Eliezer*, Gerald Friedlander

INTRODUCTION

1. Marcel, 30.
2. The expression appears in Moltmann, *Theology of Hope*, 20. Moltmann seems to be paraphrasing Kierkegaard's views as expressed in *Sickness unto Death*, 27–28. For Kierkegaard on hope and possibility, also see his *Works of Love*, "Love Hopes All Things—and Yet Is Never Put to Shame," 246–63.
3. Marcel, *Tragic Wisdom and Beyond*, 143.

4. For more about the relationship between faith and hope, see "What Is Hope?" under resources at choosinghope.net.

5. Solnit, *Hope in the Dark*, 3.

6. Musschenga, "Is There a Problem with False Hope?," 430.

7. Snyder et al., "'False' Hope," 1007–8.

8. Ojala, "Hope and Climate Change," 625–42.

9. Head, *Hope and Grief*, 78.

10. Gallagher and Lopez, *Oxford Handbook of Hope*. For specific findings, see the following pages: physical activity (161), resilience (163), depression (209–19), living longer (145), athletics (120), academics (119–20), work (328), well-being (287–98), old age (143–55).

11. Wiesel, "A Meditation on Hope," pages unnumbered.

12. It's not clear whether these two homonymous roots are linguistically related or independent.

13. Lopez, *Making Hope Happen*, 21, 37–38, Kindle.

14. Gallagher and Lopez, *Oxford Handbook of Hope*, 110–11.

15. Yerushalmi, "Toward a History of Jewish Hope," 6203–5, Kindle.

16. Yerushalmi, "Toward a History of Jewish Hope," 6207–17, Kindle.

17. MPPB, *Amidah*, 2363, Kindle.

18. The translation follows Birnbaum, *Daily Prayer Book*, 90.

19. Soloveitchik, *Emergence of Ethical Man*, 185.

20. Soloveitchik, *Halakhic Man*, 105, 99. See also 107.

21. Ecclesiastes Rabbah 7:13, fifth or sixth century.

22. Kushner, *God Was in This Place*, 122.

23. Cox, *Feast of Fools*, 157.

24. See Botterweck, *Theological Dictionary*, 6:362, 12:565. The second expression of hope, from the root *yud-chet-lamed*, can indeed mean "wait," as when Noah "waited [*va'yachel*] another seven days" to send the dove from the ark (Gen. 8:10). Even here, "waiting" may express a "patient expectation," something akin to hope (Botterweck, *Theological Dictionary*, 6:55). But this root, especially in the Psalms and Wisdom Literature, can also mean "hope." For instance, Alter, and many others, translate the last phrase in Psalms 31:25 (*kol ha-m'yachalim l'YHWH*) as "all who hope in YHWH." Some scholars have suggested a neat distinction between these two roots, *kof-vav-hey* and *yud-chet-lamed*, the former signifying hoping and the latter waiting. But this view has been credibly challenged in favor of understanding both Hebrew roots as largely synonymous. As one scholarly analysis concludes, "Their semantic development has so converged through centuries of analogous use that distinct translation has little more than stylistic significance" (Botterweck,

Theological Dictionary, 4:362). *The Theological Dictionary of the Old Testament* does support a preference for translating *kof-vav-hey* (as in *tikvah*) as "hope" rather than "wait" when God is "directly or indirectly the object of the verb" or "named indirectly or by extension" in passages speaking of God's name or help, as is commonly the case in the Bible (12:568–69).

25. Jonathan Sacks, "Future Tense—How the Jews Invented Hope," *Jewish Chronicle*, April 1, 2008, https://rabbisacks.org/future-tense-how-the-jews -invented-hope-published-in-the-jewish-chronicle/.

1. REPENTANCE

1. Arnow, "Seder for Rosh Hashanah," 14, https://www.bjpa.org/bjpa/search -results?Author=David+Arnow&search=.

2. Maimonides, *Mishneh Torah*, Laws of Repentance 2:9, 2:11, Simon Glazer translation, 1927, available at Sefaria, https://www.sefaria.org/Mishneh _Torah%2C_Repentance.2?lang=bi.

3. Maimonides supports this view, writing in his Laws of Repentance 7:3: "Do not say that one need only repent of sinful deeds such as fornication, robbery, and theft. Just as [one] needs to repent of these sins involving acts, so [one] needs to investigate and repent of any evil dispositions [i.e., bad character traits] that [one] may have, such as hot temper, hatred, jealousy, scoffing, eager pursuit of wealth or honors, greediness in eating, and so on. . . . They are graver than sinful acts; for when one is addicted to them it is difficult to give them up." In MR, 79. See also 7:4.

4. Maimonides, *Mishneh Torah*, Laws of Repentance 7:4, https://www.sefaria .org/Mishneh_Torah%2C_Repentance.7.4?lang=bi&with=all&lang2=en.

5. Some view hopelessness or despair as a sin against God. The French philosopher Emmanuel Levinas (1906–95) draws another important relationship between hope and *teshuvah* when he lists despair right alongside idolatry as a sin against God. This seems to relate to his view that "not to believe in the triumph of the good" would be considered an offense against God. See Levinas, *Nine Talmudic Readings*, 22. In the Christian tradition, sloth, one of the seven deadly sins, is also related to despair. Known as *accidia* in Latin, it means "listlessness" and "despondency." See Moltmann, *In the End*, 1179–85, Kindle.

6. Kook, *Orot Ha-Teshuvah*, 101.

7. Rabbi Matthew Futterman shared this story in a 2018 sermon but wasn't sure of its original source. In a 1993 Yom Kippur sermon Rabbi Edward Feinstein told the same story and attributed it to an unnamed midrash. See https://www.vbs.org/worship/meet-our-clergy/rabbi-ed-feinstein/sermons

/gods-four-questions, accessed June 14, 2021. The story seems to combine several elements that appear in Genesis Rabbah 8:11 and BT *Sanhedrin* 38b, but none of these includes the motif of the angels hiding the divine image.

8. OJPS. Rabbi Bradley Shavit Artson (1959–, United States) connects this voice with Process Theology: "Scripture speaks of a *kol d'mamah dakah*, a small, still voice. I think that's what Process thinkers mean by the lure. We sense that our intuition is God's lure when it is life-affirming, when it calls us to more empathic relating, more compassionate justice, solidarity expressed through engagement, more expansive love. If you ever find yourself summoned to be small or stingy, know that this voice is not God's, and try not to let it distract you." Artson, *God of Becoming*, 2541–52, Kindle.

9. Process Theology refers to the call for improvement as awareness of the lure that God places before you: "God is the One who offers us the best possible options for our own future and who lures us to attain the divine goals of maximal relationship, engagement, love, compassion, and justice." Artson, *God of Becoming*, 836–37, Kindle.

10. Heschel, *Insecurity of Freedom*, 96.

11. Kook, *Orot Ha-Teshuvah*, 98.

12. Kook, *Orot Ha-Teshuvah*, 106, 107, 97. See Hosea 2:17.

13. The first part of Rabbi Nachman's teaching can be found in Gordon Tucker's commentary on *Pirkei Avot*. See Cohen, Elad-Appelbaum, and Tucker, *Pirkei Avot*, 23. The second is my translation of an additional portion of Rabbi Nachman's commentary on the same Mishnah from *Pirkei Avot*. See Likutei Moharan, part 1, section 282, https://www.sefaria.org/Likutei_Moharan.282 .1?lang=bi&with=all&lang2=en, accessed July 9, 2021.

14. See Graetz, *History of the Jews*, 3:580, available at https://archive.org/details /historyofjews03grae/page/580.

15. Rabbeinu Yona of Gerona, *Mishle*, Prov. 3:26, BI, HB 39300. The translation of Ecclesiastes 9:4 follows Gordis, *Koheleth*, 188. Most translations of this verse render *bitachon*, usually "trust," as "hope" in this context. NJPS and Alter depart from this practice. Notably, this biblical verse contains a word that is written *yivchar*, "will choose," but is to be read *yichubar*, "is attached" or "is joined." Many commentaries on the verse follow the written version and emphasize the importance of *choosing* to do *teshuvah*. See, for example, Midrash *Lekach Tov* and Rashi on Ecclesiastes 9:4. The Jerusalem Talmud (JT Berakhot 9, halakhah 1, 63b) is the earliest source to focus on the difference between the written and read word in this verse. The verse from Ecclesiastes is interesting because it seems to include a superfluous word, "One who is attached to *all* the living has hope." Perhaps the message is that hope rests

on a connection to all of humanity and is not just a function of whether or not we are alive and still able to change our ways.

16. BT *Avodah Zarah* 17a.

17. *Pesikta de-Rav Kahana*, 24:4.

18. Heschel, *Moral Grandeur and Spiritual Audacity*, 258.

19. See Heschel, *Between God and Man*, 198, 199, 200, 208. The last quoted source comes from Ibn Gabirol, *Choice of Pearls*, 66, no. 43. Ibn Gabirol's statement captures Heschel's sense of the centrality of hope in prayer and also his belief that prayer utilizing words was the lowest form of prayer. See Heschel, *Man's Quest for God*, 41–42.

20. Koren. Proverbs includes a number of variations on this theme. See Prov. 11:23, 23:17–18, 26:12.

21. Kant, *Critique of Pure Reason*, Transcendental Doctrine and Method, chapter 2, section 2, https://www.gutenberg.org/files/4280/4280-h/4280-h.htm, accessed July 9, 2021. Much of Kant's answer to this question involves the moral worthiness of what one pursues to achieve happiness.

22. Snyder, *Psychology of Hope*, 232, Kindle. See "What Is Hope?" under resources at choosinghope.net.

23. Author's translation.

24. Marcel, *Being and Having*, 1112, Kindle.

25. The sources for Moses' ascent of Mount Sinai on the first of Elul are midrashic, *Pirkei de Rabbi Eliezer*, chapter 45 (ninth century) and *Tanḥuma* (tenth century), Warsaw recension, Ki Tissa 31. Other midrashic sources (e.g., *Seder Olam Rabbah*) have a slightly different chronology, but all agree that Moses returned from Sinai on the tenth of Tishrei.

26. Exodus Rabbah 46:1.

27. Maimonides, *Mishneh Torah*, Laws of Repentance 3:4, in MR, 76.

28. BT *Yoma* 86a. Brown, *Spiritual Boredom*, points out that Kook's reading of this talmudic source differs significantly from that of Maimonides. "Rabbi Kook analyzes this . . . statement and believes that when we change, the world looks different *to us*. When we repent, we look at the world with more optimism and hope. We redeem the world not because it has changed, but because *we* changed" (139).

29. The many explanations about why this psalm is recited at this time of the year indicate that the original reason probably remains uncertain. See Alan Cooper, "Psalm 27: The Days of Awe," http://www.jtsa.edu/psalm-27-the-days-of-awe, accessed June 14, 2021. Chaim Vital (1542–1620), the chief disciple of Isaac Luria (1534–72), relates his master's kabbalistic practices associated with prayer and refers to the recitation of the entire psalm on a daily

basis. See Vital, *Pri Etz Chaim*, 5:23 and 6:6, https://www.sefaria.org/Pri_Etz
_Chaim,_Gate_of_Prayer.5?lang=bi. Also see Vital, *Gate of Torah Reading*,
http://bit.ly/2zBhHRO, accessed June 14, 2021. This would suggest that, at
least in some circles, the psalm had achieved an elevated status well before
the eighteenth century.

30. BT *Berakhot* 32b, with Rashi on *kaveh*, and Deuteronomy Rabbah 2:12. Ps.
27:14 has also entered the liturgy elsewhere. Sephardim recite it with several other biblical verses daily except on Shabbat, and Ashkenazim (e.g.,
Birnbaum, *Daily Prayer Book*, 405) do so only on Shabbat prior to *Ein K'eloheinu*. Just when these customs began is difficult to ascertain.

31. BT *Berakhot* 32b.

32. A ninth-century midrash, *Pirkei Rabeinu Ha-Kodesh* 4:11, lists Psalm 27:14
among thirteen biblical verses or liturgical phrases that should be recited
every day. The midrash can be found in Eisenstein, *Otzar Midrashim*, vol.
2 510, BI, HB 2585.The same practice is recommended by Rabbi Israel ben
Rabbi Joseph Al-Nakawa (fourteenth century, Spain) in his *Sefer Menorat
ha-Ma'or*, 4:592 (not to be confused with a book of the same title by Isaac
Aboab), HB 20975, BI.

33. The translation follows NJPS except for the last verse, which combines Alter
and Artscroll's "hope to." [YHWH] substituted for masculine pronouns.

34. Benjamin Segal ("Where Liturgy and Bible Meet") uses these terms,
although he argues for the unity of the psalm. Hermann Gunkel's form-
critical analysis of the Psalms, for example, classifies the first six verses
among the psalms of trust and the remainder among those he calls psalms
of individual lament. For a handy summary of Gunkel's classification, see
Tyler Williams, "A Form-Critical Classification of the Psalms According to
Hermann Gunkel," 2006, https://studylib.net/doc/8738728/a-form-critical
-classification-of-the-psalms-according-to . . . , accessed June 14, 2021.

35. Feld, *Joy, Despair, and Hope*, 83, Kindle.

36. Albo, *Sefer Ha-Ikkarim*, vol. 4, part 2, 464, 466, 470.

37. This translation follows NJPS except for verse 5, which is my translation, in
which "hope" has been rendered consistently, as Alter does. In verse 7 my
preference is to render the verb *l'yachel* as "hope" instead of "wait." Elsewhere, but not here, Alter himself often does the same. See, for example, his
translation of Ps. 31:25, 39:8, 119:43, and 119:114.

38. *Mishnah Ta'anit* 2:3. The Midrash on Psalms (130:2) links the reference to
forgiveness in verse 4 to the period between Rosh Hashanah and Yom Kippur. The earliest written account of recitation of the psalm during this season of which the author is aware dates back to the early seventeenth century

and appears in Vital, *Pri Etz Chaim*, the Gates of Prayer for Rosh Hashanah, chap. 7. Be'er Heitev, an eighteenth-century commentary on the Shulḥan Arukh (*Oraḥ Ḥayyim*, 54) also endorsed the custom, as did the *Mishnah Berurah* in the early twentieth century.

39. The earliest description of this ritual of casting sins into the river dates back to *Sefer Maharil* (Warsaw, 1875, HB 14721, 38) by Jacob Moellin (1365–1427); see customs, the laws of Rosh Hashanah. Related customs date back much further and give voice to ancient beliefs that God or spirits of other kinds inhabited bodies of water and were therefore more accessible in these locations. See Lauterbach, "Tashlik," available at https://babel.hathitrust.org/cgi /pt?id=uc1.b3367512;view=1up;seq=317, accessed July 9, 2021.

40. David Kimchi (Radak), *Commentary on Psalms*, 130, 261–62, HB 52665, BI.

41. Bachya ben Asher, *Kad Ha-Kemach*, vol. 1, sec. 3, p. 57, HB 41684, BI.

42. Cohen, *Prayer and Penitence*, 22.

43. Nebenzahl, *Thoughts for Rosh Hashanah*, 22.

44. Luzzatto, "Drush B'inyan Ha-Kivui," 246–47.

45. Quoted in Peli, *On Repentance*, 180–81.

46. Based on Arnow, "Reflections on Jonah and Yom Kippur," 33–48. For the article and its more extensive notes, see resources at www.choosinghope.net.

47. Muffs, *Personhood of God*, 100. Muffs writes that in the Bible, God is "*sublime* but not *abstract*." Theologian Jack Miles writes: "Contradictory as this must seem [God] also enters time and is changed by experience. Were it not so, [God] could not be surprised; and [God] is endlessly and most often unpleasantly surprised. God is constant; [God] is not immutable." See Miles, *God: A Biography*, 12.

48. Rashi (Gen. 6:11) notes that the same word, *chamas*, "violence," appears in connection with the sins that preceded the Flood and those committed by the Ninevites. The eighth confession of the Yom Kippur *Vidui* is *chamasnu*, "we have committed violence." On Yom Kippur we are confessing the same sin that led to the destruction of the world and later nearly brought doom to Nineveh! In the contemporary context the message is powerful: *Our* actions will determine whether or not life on earth will endure.

49. Based on OJPS.

50. Based on OJPS.

51. The prophet Balaam says: "God is not human to be capricious, or mortal to have a change [*v'yitnecham*] of heart" (Num. 23:19). This is the reflexive form of the verb we are exploring. It bears essentially the same meaning. Balaam seems to forget that, as it were, God indeed *can* have change of heart or repent. Witness the Flood.

52. *PRE*, ch. 43, 341–42.

53. This translation follows Propp, *The Anchor Bible: Exodus 1–18* and *Exodus 19–40*. See Exodus 3:14 in *Exodus 1–18* and appendix C in *Exodus 19–40*.

54. It appears in the *Hin'ni* recited before the *musaf* on Rosh Hashanah and Yom Kippur. Here the context implies that God's ability to be what God will be caps a list of four other divine attributes—great, mighty, awesome, and exalted.

55. Teikhthal, *Mishneh Sakhir* on Nitsavim, written in 1943, vol. 1, 204, HB 53767, BI.

2. TIKKUN OLAM

1. *Sefer Ha-Shorashim* (Berlin, 1847, Impensis B. Bethge, 415, HB 43656), by Bible commentator, philosopher, and grammarian David Kimchi (1160–1235, Provence), cites all three examples from Ecclesiastes and defines the root as meaning "the opposite of crooked."

2. This part of the verse reflects the OJPS translation, which renders "crooked," as opposed to "twisted" in the NJPS.

3. Immanuel Kant (1724–1804) famously paraphrased this verse: "Nothing straight can be constructed from such warped wood as that which man is made of." Nonetheless, Kant believed in the potential for political change, which "encourages the hope that, after many revolutions, with all their transforming effects, the highest purpose of nature, a universal cosmo-politan existence, will at last be realized as the matrix within which all the original capacities of the human race may develop." See Reiss, *Kant: Political Writings*, 46, 51.

4. This phrase follows OJPS as well.

5. Seow, *Anchor Bible: Ecclesiastes*, 147–48.

6. Lichtheim, *Ancient Egyptian Literature*, 145. Both Fox (*JPS Commentary: Ecclesiastes*, 9) and Seow (*Anchor Bible: Ecclesiastes*, 147) cite this comparison. The issue of straightening the crooked appears in Greek mythology, notably at the beginning of the story of Pandora's jar in Hesiod's "Works and Days," 3, http://www.perseus.tufts.edu/hopper/text?doc=Perseus%3Atext%3A1999 .01.0132%3Acard%3D1: "And easily he [Zeus] straightens the crooked and blasts the proud," accessed July 9, 2021. The implication seems to be that for Zeus the job is easy, whereas for others it is difficult, but not impossible. The third-century BCE philosopher Hsun Ching asserts that because human nature is essentially evil, "a crooked stick must be submitted to the pressing-frame to soften and bend it, and then it becomes straight.... So the nature of [human beings] ... being evil, must be submitted to teachers and laws,

and then it becomes correct." Bracket and ellipses were added by this author to create a more gender-sensitive text. See Legge, *Chinese Classics*, 79, https://archive.org/details/chineseclassics02minggoog/page/n90, accessed July 9, 2021.

7. The root *tav-kof-nun* also appears in Ecclesiastes 12:9: "He listened to and tested the soundness [*tikein*] of many maxims." The meaning of the root is not clear in this case. Michael V. Fox (*JPS Commentary: Ecclesiastes*, 83) argues that it "implies authorship." Similarly, Alter uses "framed many maxims." OJPS renders "set in order many proverbs." BDB, 1075, suggests "put straight, arrange in order (proverbs)."

8. Fox, *JPS Commentary: Ecclesiastes*, 9–10, xxxi.

9. Mordecai Kaplan (*Future of the American Jew*, 266–67) contrasts the pessimistic view expressed in Kohelet's conclusion that the crooked cannot be made straight with "faith in the future," which "characterized the religious heritage of the Jewish people."

10. See, for example, Alter, 99815, and Sneed, *Politics of Pessimism in Ecclesiastes*, 1.

11. The Mishnah (*Yadayim* 3:5) links Ecclesiastes' canonization to the period when Rabban Gamaliel II was briefly deposed and replaced by Rabbi Elazar Ben Azariah, in the decades following the Second Temple's destruction in 70 CE. See also BT *Shabbat* 30b and Megillah 7a. The midrash Ecclesiastes Rabbah (1:3) suggests that Kohelet's futility ran so deep, it even discouraged meaningful engagement with Torah.

12. Gordis, *Koheleth*, 156.

13. Fox, *JPS Bible Commentary: Ecclesiastes*, 22.

14. See, for example, "The Greek Word: The Greek Old Testament (Septuagint)," https://www.ellopos.net/elpenor/greek-texts/septuagint/chapter.asp?book=27&page=3; the Vulgate, http://www.latinvulgate.com/verse.aspx?t=0&b=23&c=3 (both accessed July 9, 2021); OJPS; and Koren. NJPS renders "eternity."

15. Sources of the translations: Jastrow; Blackman, *Mishnayot*, vol. 3, *Gittin* 4:2–3; Kehati, *Mishnah*, vol. 11, *Gittin* 4:2–3; Neusner, *The Tosefta*, *Gittin* 3:7. The Mishnah included in the Soncino Talmud reads "to prevent abuses" (BT *Gittin* 32a) with a note: "Literally, 'for the better ordering of the world.'" Judith Hauptman (*Rereading the Rabbis*, 110) offers the translation "in order to repair the social order."

16. Rosenthal, "*Tikkun ha-Olam*," 217; Birnbaum and Cohen, *Tikkun Olam*, 20–21, Kindle. The title page reads, "Tikkun Olam: Repair/Perfect the World."

17. Hauptman, *Rereading the Rabbis*, 112.

18. Boyarin, *Intertextuality and the Reading of Midrash*, 16.

19. Samely, *Rabbinic Interpretation of Scripture in the Mishnah*, 32. This general statement supports the particular case being argued: that Mishnah *Gittin*'s phrase, *tikkun ha-olam*, uses allusions to Ecclesiastes and places them in a context that subverts their original biblical message.

20. Fox, *A Time to Tear Down*, 66.

21. Among the canonical Wisdom Books (Ecclesiastes, Job, and Proverbs) Ecclesiastes is the only one where the Bible's typical words for "hope" (*tikvah* and *tochelet*) fail to appear. Many render *bitachon* in 9:4 as "hope": "For to one who is joined among the living there is hope." Seow (*Anchor Bible: Ecclesiastes*, 300) writes: "The word *bitachon* does not mean 'hope' as most translations have it. . . . Rather the word refers to one's confidence or certitude that something will happen."

22. The translation of the bracketed sentence follows Hoffman, "Image of the Other," 2.

23. Some have claimed that the "original" of the prayer did not use the word *l'takken*, which means "repair" or "perfect," but *l'takhen*, which means "establish." There are indeed early examples of *l'takhen*, such as the prayer book of Saadia Gaon (882/892–942). But a version of the prayer from another old source reads *l'takken*. See Swartz, "'Alay Le-shabbeah," 182 (the longer recension). Whatever the "original" version of the text may have said, by the early Middle Ages *l'takken* had become the accepted spelling by the leading rabbis of Ashkenazi Europe, and, with the exception of the Yemenite community, this has long been the norm in all other communities as well.

24. The translation in the opening words of the second paragraph has been modified to more closely reflect the order of the Hebrew. See MPPB, *Tachanun*, which reads, "Adonai our God, we therefore hope," 2676, Kindle.

25. Blech, "The Biblical Source for Tikkun Olam," 908, Kindle.

26. Some traditionalists have attributed *Aleinu* to Joshua; others maintain the prayer dates back to the Second Temple period; others hold that it was composed by Rav, a third-century rabbinic sage from Babylonia. For an overview, see Nulman, *Encyclopedia of Jewish Prayer*, 24–26.

27. See Swartz, "'Alay Le-shabbeah,'" 179–90.

28. See Zev Eleff, "The Parenthetical Problem of *Alenu*," *The Lehrhaus*, https://www.thelehrhaus.com/commentary/the-parenthetical-problem-of-alenu/, accessed June 10, 2021. For elements of anti-Christian polemic, see Hoffman, "Image of the Other," 1–41; and Yuval, *Two Nations in Your Womb*, 190–96.

29. Chazan, "Blois Incident of 1171," 13–31.

30. See Hoffman, "Image of the Other," 7. These liturgical developments seem to have begun in England and in Worms, in the Rhineland. One of the ear-

liest injunctions for the daily recital of *Aleinu* appears in the *Sefer Rokeach* (sometimes called *Sefer Rokeach Hagadol*) of Eleazer ben Judah of Worms (c. 1160–1238) and includes both paragraphs of the prayer, which suggests that, at least in the eyes of tradition, this is what the Jews of Blois did as well. See *Sefer Rokeach*, 57b (bottom left col.), *The Laws of Prayer*, 324, HB 44332, BI.

31. Dorff, in MPPB, *Tachanun*, 2731, Kindle.

32. The first translation appears in the 2003 *Siddur Sim Shalom for Weekdays* (83), the second in the 1946 *Sabbath and Festival Prayer Book* (37), both published by the Rabbinical Assembly. Gilbert Rosenthal ("*Tikkun ha-Olam*," 220) alludes to the difficulties in syntax. Gerald Blidstein also acknowledges ambiguity in God's role here. See his "Tikkun Olam," note 10, Kindle. If we assume that *tikkun olam* will be carried out by "YHWH our God," who is invoked in the beginning of the second paragraph, then we are asking YHWH *l'takken olam b'malkhut Shaddai*, "to perfect the world under the Almighty's kingdom." The presence of multiple names of God in the same sentence creates a bit of confusion here as to who does what. Perhaps YHWH performs certain actions, but another — human — actor perfects the world under the Almighty's sovereignty.

33. Dorff, in MPPB, *Tachanun*, 2731, Kindle.

34. *Etz Hayim*, 89. *Etz Hayim* cites a version of the midrash that appears in the tenth-century midrash *Tanḥuma* (Lekh Lekha 25). Also note that the traditional circumcision ritual itself is laden with longings of hope for better times. These are expressed through the evocation of Elijah the prophet, herald of the Messiah, in conjunction with the recitation of Genesis 49:18 ("For Your salvation I hope, YHWH") and Psalms 119:116 ("I hope for Your deliverance [or salvation], O YHWH; I observe Your commandments"). The first phrase of the latter verse is repeated twice.

35. *Tanḥuma* (Tazria 7) on Lev. 12:3. See Townsend, *Midrash Tanḥuma: Exodus and Leviticus*, 242.

36. BT *Shabbat* 119b.

37. Lorberbaum, "'Tikkun olam,'" 81.

38. Maimonides, *Mishneh Torah*, Laws of Kings, 11:4, in *Book of Judges*, xxiii–xxiv. Beginning in the early sixteenth century, parts of this passage were suppressed by Christian censors but were preserved in earlier printed editions and manuscripts. See Kraemer, *Maimonides*, 6449, Kindle. Many contemporary editions still do not reflect the uncensored text. The verse from Zephaniah has many parallels with Zech. 14:9, with which *Aleinu* concludes.

39. Soloveitchik, *Halakhic Man*, 105, 99. See Mordecai Kaplan (1881–1983) with regard to *Aleinu*: "We cannot consider ourselves loyal servants of the Divine

King, unless we take upon ourselves the task 'to perfect the world under the Kingdom of the Almighty.'" Kaplan, *Meaning of God*, 124, 130.

40. Quoted in Idel, *Messianic Mystics*, 152.

41. See *Sifra*, Kedoshim 2:4 and Genesis Rabbah 24:7.

42. Moses Cordovero, *Tomar Devorah*, 10, HB 42018. Cordovero paraphrases *Mishnah Avot* 2:10: "Let the honor of your friend be as dear to you as your own."

43. Fine, *Physician of the Soul*, 201.

44. *Sha'ar Ha-Kavvanot* 1:2a–b, quoted in Faierstein, *Jewish Customs of Kabbalistic Origin*, 1–2.

45. See, for example, the Conservative movement's *Siddur Sim Shalom for Weekdays*, 4; or the standard Chabad Siddur, *Tehillas HaShem*, 12; or the Reconstructionist movement's *Kol HaNeshamah for Sabbath and Festivals*, 150.

46. Benyosef, *Living the Kabbalah*, 30.

47. The letters *shin* (300), *lamed* (30), *hey* (5), totaling 335, are added to 1,240, which yields 1,575. For details on converting years in the Jewish calendar to the Gregorian, see "About the Hebrew Calendar," Yale University Library, https://web.library.yale.edu/cataloging/hebraica/about-hebrew-calendar, last modified October 6, 2014. For more on these speculations, see Silver, *History of Messianic Speculation*, 132–38.

48. Scholem, *Sabbatai Ṣevi*, 271.

49. Scholem, *Major Trends in Jewish Mysticism*, 5892–95, Kindle.

50. Luzzatto, *Otzrot Ramch"al, Drush B'inyan Ha-Kivui*, 246–47, HB 51264. Author's translation of Gen. 49:18.

51. Jonathan Krasner, "The Americanization of Tikkun Olam," *eJewish Philanthropy*, February 27, 2015, http://ejewishphilanthropy.com/the -americanization-of-tikkun-olam/.

52. Peter Salovey, "Repair the World!," Baccalaureate Address, Yale College, May 16, 2015, http://president.yale.edu/speeches-writings/speeches/repair -world. For a critique of the contemporary embrace of *tikkun olam*, see Cooper, "Assimilation of Tikkun Olam."

53. Barack Obama, "Transcript of Obama's Speech in Israel," *New York Times*, March 21, 2013, http://mobile.nytimes.com/2013/03/22/world/middleeast /transcript-of-obamas-speech-in-israel.html.

54. Barack Obama, "Statement from the President on Passover," April 3, 2015, https://www.whitehouse.gov/the-press-office/2015/04/03/statement -president-passover.

55. For the presence of *tikkun olam* on Google Ngram Viewer (a search tool that charts the frequency of designated words appearing in books during spec-

ified time periods), see Krasner, "Place of Tikkun Olam," available at http://jcpa.org/article/place-tikkun-olam-american-jewish-life1/, accessed June 14, 2021.

56. See Krasner, "Place of Tikkun Olam."

57. JCCA, "Who We Are: History," https://www.jccany.org/who-we-are/history/, accessed July 9, 2021; courtesy of UJA/Federation of New York, offline archives from January 2015.

58. For example, see the 2013 AJWS annual report, sections 4 and 7, https://ajws.org/wp-content/uploads/2015/03/ajws-annual-report-2013.pdf, accessed June 14, 2021; and "Messinger of Hope: A Portrait of Ruth Messinger," AJWS, 2015, https://ajws.org/wp-content/uploads/2016/11/Ruth_book_web-reduced.pdf, accessed July 9, 2021. Despite the ubiquity of this statement—generally attributed to Grace Paley—I am unable to find its source.

59. Ruth Messinger, personal communication, June 16, 2021.

60. Salovey, "Repair the World!" Richard Rorty's conceptualization of social hope and philosophical pragmatism brought him to a conclusion close to Rabbi Tarfon's: "But though maximality cannot be aimed at, you can aim at . . . being concerned about more people. . . . You cannot aim at moral perfection, but you can aim at taking more people's needs into account than you did previously." Rorty, *Philosophy and Social Hope*, 83. Also see Robert F. Kennedy's 1966 speech, "RFK in the Land of Apartheid: A Ripple of Hope," http://www.rfksafilm.org/html/speeches/unicape.php, accessed June 14, 2021.

61. See the section on Charles R. Synder in "What Is Hope?" under "Resources" at www.choosinghope.net.

62. Between 132 and 136 CE Simon Bar Kokhba led a failed rebellion against Rome during which Hadrian's forces slaughtered hundreds of thousands of Jews and executed many of the most important Jewish sages of the period. Jews were banned from Jerusalem, renamed by Hadrian as Aelia Capitolina.

63. Scholem, *Messianic Idea in Judaism*, 1–36.

64. Max Roser and Mohamed Nagdy, "Optimism and Pessimism," OurWorldInData.org, 2014, https://ourworldindata.org/optimism-pessimism, accessed June 10, 2021.

65. John Gramlich, "5 Facts about Crime in the U.S.," Pew Research Center, October 17, 2019, https://www.pewresearch.org/fact-tank/2019/10/17/facts-about-crime-in-the-u-s/. In 2020, which saw the onset of COVID-19 and protests following the killing of George Floyd, a BBC analysis reported that in America "overall, violent crime was up by about 3% in 2020 over the previous year, but this should be seen in the context of the longer term downward trend from a peak in the early 1990s." See Jake Horton, "US Crime: Is Amer-

ica Seeing a Surge in Violence?," BBC News, July 6, 2021, https://www.bbc
.com/news/57581270.

66. Pinker, *Better Angels*, 200–202, 185, Kindle.

67. "Poverty and Shared Prosperity: 2020," World Bank Group, fig. 0.3, 5,
https://openknowledge.worldbank.org/bitstream/handle/10986/34496
/9781464816024.pdf, accessed June 10, 2021.

68. "Life Expectancy of the World Population," wordometer, https://www
.worldometers.info/demographics/life-expectancy/, accessed June 10, 2021;
Max Roser and Esteban Ortiz-Ospina, "Literacy," OurWorldInData.org, 2018,
https://ourworldindata.org/literacy, accessed June 10, 2021; UNESCO Institute for Statistics, "Literacy Rate, Adult Total," September 2020, https://data
.worldbank.org/indicator/SE.ADT.LITR.ZS.

69. Pinker, "Psychology of Pessimism," 1–5, available at https://object.cato.org
/sites/cato.org/files/pubs/pdf/catosletterv13n1.pdf.

70. Baumeister et al., "Bad Is Stronger Than Good," 361.

71. Herman, *Idea of Decline in Western History*, 220–21, Kindle.

72. Eibach, "When Change in the Self Is Mistaken for Change in the World," 927.

73. Twersky and Kahneman, "Availability," 207–32, available at https://people
.umass.edu/biep540w/pdf/Tversky%20availability.pdf, accessed July 9,
2021.

74. "The Optimists," *Time Magazine*, January 15, 2018. See also Joshua Rothman,
"Are Things Getting Better or Worse?" *New Yorker*, July 23, 2018; Figueres and
Rivett-Carnac, *The Future We Choose*, 41–54.

75. "The Optimists," 2.

76. Falk, *Book of Blessings*, 467.

77. Bornsztain, *Shem MiShmuel* on Leviticus, Shabbat Chol haMoed Pesach, 1916,
https://www.sefaria.org/Shem_MiShmuel%2C_Passover.19?lang=bi, BI. The
source for the reference to Hillel is *Mishnah Avot* 1:14, and the BT is *Sanhedrin*
37b.

3. ABRAHAM AND SARAH

1. Moltmann, *Theology of Hope*, 20. The preceding statement about the relationship between faith and hope follows the thinking of John Calvin, which
Moltmann's words echo. For more on Calvin and the relationship between
faith and hope, see "What Is Hope?" at www.choosinghope.net, under
Resources.

2. Genesis Rabbah 38:13.

3. "*Ma'aseh Avraham Avinu . . . im Nimrod*." The midrash can be found in Eisenstein, *Otzar Midrashim*, vol. 1, 3, BI, HB 2603. It's interesting that Ur of the

Chaldees and Haran, locations both heavily identified with Abraham, are believed to have been centers of moon worship. See Green, *City of the Moon God*. Jubilees (12:17), a Hebrew text from the second century BCE, likewise recounts Abraham's insight that God controlled the moon and the stars.

4. Maimonides, *Mishneh Torah*, Laws of Idolatry, 1:3, in MR, 73.

5. Marcel, 30.

6. *Pirkei Avot* does not list the trials. Midrashic sources differ on their order and details. *Avot de Rabbi Natan* A (33) begins its list with God's initial call. Avot de Rabbi Natan B (chap. 36) briefly enumerates the trials. See also PRE, ch. 26, 187. For a more recent list of the trials, see Cassuto, *Commentary on the Book of Genesis*, 2:294, 295.

7. For the fact that Abraham left Charan while his father was still alive, see Cassuto, *Commentary on the Book of Genesis*, 2:259, 282, 317.

8. See "Charan" in BDB.

9. Quoted in Zornberg, *Beginning of Desire*, 74.

10. Genesis Rabbah 49:2.

11. The Zohar maintains that the world would have been saved had Noah prayed for salvation. Zohar, Addenda (Hashmatot) to Bereshit, 254b; 3, 14b.

12. This translation follows Alter.

13. In the Bible, the word *ulai*, "perhaps" or "maybe," is often a powerful indicator of hope. For example, the word first appears when Sarah wonders if "perhaps I shall have a son through" Hagar, that is, perhaps the offspring of Hagar and Abraham will become the son of childless Sarah (Gen. 16:2). Similarly, after the Golden Calf incident, Moses tells the Israelites that "perhaps I will win forgiveness for your sin" (Exod. 32:30). According to BDB, 19, the word "perhaps" "usually expresses hope . . . but also fear and doubt."

14. See *P'nei David* on the fourth chapter in Genesis, Va-yera (Jerusalem: N.p., 1959), 19b, HB 40237, BI.

15. Midrash *Tanḥuma* (Va-yera 4) on Gen. 19:24. See Townsend, *Midrash Tanḥuma, Genesis*, 103.

16. Holy Bible: New Revised Standard Edition. Paul used his midrash to argue that God rewarded Abraham for his righteousness on the basis of his hope rather than his fulfilling a particular religious commandment; Paul contends that salvation does not depend on fulfillment of the law. To counter this, Rabbinic Judaism developed the notion that Abraham indeed fulfilled all 613 commandments even before they were revealed at Sinai. See Green, *Devotion and Commandment*, 28–30.

17. Genesis Rabbah 53:3.

18. See Frantz and Stimming, *Hope Deferred*; Cardin, *Tears of Sorrow*.

19. For Ephraim ben Jacob of Bonn's composition, see Spiegel, *Last Trial*, 139–52.
20. Our most profound mythic texts are subject to reinterpretation in light of historical circumstances. At times when Jews felt under attack physically and spiritually, they needed and found (sometimes constructed) in Abraham an icon of unflinching faith and courage; otherwise delving into the nuances of Abraham's doubts and hopes would have served little purpose. Today, when Jews generally live with a greater sense of security, those nuances are a good deal more interesting. For an overview of how history has shaped our understanding of the *Akedah*, see Sagi, "The Meaning of the 'Akedah' in Israeli Culture and Jewish Tradition." David Hartman provides a striking example of how contemporary values influenced his reading of the *Akedah*: "I do not believe in submission and surrender as the faculties that make Judaism vital; for me, personal expression and individual agency are the values that are most constitutive of Judaism." Hartman, *From Defender to Critic*, 167, Kindle.
21. BT *Sanhedrin* 89b. Translation of Gen. 22:2 follows OJPS.
22. Auerbach, "Odysseus' Scar," 12.
23. For more interpretations along this line, see Boehm, *Binding of Isaac*; Bodoff, *Binding of Isaac*; and Wiesel, *Messengers of God*. On the contrast between the Abraham of the *Akedah* and the Abraham of Sodom and Gomorrah, see Hartman, *Defender*, 171. Here Hartman maintains "that the Akedah is not constitutive of Judaism," that one must choose between Abraham's posture toward God in these two situations, and that the Abraham who argues with God over the fate of Gomorrah and Sodom "is the one I look to for relating to the Divine" (174).
24. Sarna, *Understanding Genesis*, 158.
25. By my reading, had God not intervened, Abraham would have concluded that worshipping this God was not much of an improvement over worshipping idols and would have continued his spiritual search.
26. Marcel, 60. See also Kierkegaard, *Works of Love*, 255: "No one can hope unless he is also loving; he cannot hope for himself without also being loving, because the good has an infinite connectedness; but if he is loving, he also hopes for others. In the same degree to which he hopes for others, he hopes for himself."
27. Marcel, 35.
28. See Gellman, *The Fear*, 43–44, for midrash Ha-Gadol on Genesis 22:2. For related midrashic sources, see Genesis Rabbah 56:8; and *Lekach Tov* and *Sekhel Tov* on Genesis 22:2.

29. This midrash does conclude that, in either case, Abraham would have followed God's command.

30. Boehm, *Binding*, 85. Boehm concludes that Maimonides' superficial and esoteric levels teach completely opposite lessons and the norms of conventional Judaism required him to cloak his deepest truths in more conventional garb. For Maimonides' discussions of prophecy, see *Guide of the Perplexed*, 2:45, and for the *Akedah*, see 3:24. For Abraham as a prophet, see Gen. 20:7.

31. Leiner (1802–54), *Mei ha-Shiloach*, part 2, 12, on Va-yera, HB 19936, quoted in Gellman, *The Fear*, 24–25.

32. Marcel, 38.

33. Marcel, 38–40.

34. Green, *Language of Truth*, 22–23. The *Sefat Emet's* commentary paraphrases that of Shlomo Ephraim ben Aaron Luntschitz (1550–1619), also known as K'li Yakar, on Leviticus 18:4. David Hartman (*From Defender to Critic*, 172) says something similar: "The Akedah instructs us to be quiet and to go on."

35. Marcel, 53.

36. The notion that Abraham and Isaac expressed their hope for Isaac's salvation through worship/prayer has ancient roots. During the month of Elul (and on other occasions as well), when traditional Jews recite penitential prayers called *Seliḥot*, a key element of the service includes a prayer that asks God to "answer us" as God answered other figures in the Bible. The nineteen-stanza prayer begins with these two:

> The One who answered Abraham our father on Mount Moriah: May The One answer us.
> The One who answered his son Isaac when he was bound atop the altar: May The One answer us.

The Mishnah (*Ta'anit* 2:4), the source of the prayer, affirms the above inference about hope. In describing the procedure for beseeching God to end a severe drought, the Mishnah calls for fasting and for publicly reciting a series of biblical verses. Each verse is to be followed by a refrain mentioning a biblical figure who received an answer from God. The first refrain: "May The One who answered Abraham our father on Mount Moriah answer you and hear the voice of your crying today."

37. Gersonides, Rabbi Levi ben Gershom (RaLBaG), *Commentary on the Torah*, 31b, HB 42541.

38. Herring, *Joseph Ibn Kaspi's Gevia' Kesef*, 230.

39. Marcel, 34.

40. Some translations read "concubine" instead of "wife," although as Alter (Kindle 2594) notes, "The word used, however, is not *pilegesh* but *'ishah*, the same term that identifies Sarai at the beginning of the verse" (i.e., Gen. 16:3).
41. Marcel, 36.
42. Wouk, *This Is My God*, 92.
43. Genesis Rabbah, 61:2. Genesis 17:17 tells us that Abraham was ten years older than Sarah. He was therefore 137 years old when she died at age 127.

4. THE EXODUS

1. Brueggemann, *Hope within History*, 87, 10. In the first chapter of this volume, "The Exodus Narrative as Israel's Articulation of Faith Development" (7–26), Brueggemann uses the Exodus narrative to illustrate key moments of transition in Israel's stages of faith, reminiscent of Fowler's *Stages of Faith*.
2. Brueggemann, *Hope within History*, 80–81.
3. Note that in the retrospective retelling of history in Deuteronomy (26:7) Israel cries to God: "We cried to YHWH . . . and YHWH heard our plea," but in Exodus, Israel's cry lacks any such target.
4. Brueggemann, *Hope within History*, 87, 20, 86. Joseph Soloveitchik also viewed the Israelites' cry in Egypt as the prototype of Jewish prayer: "With suffering came loud protest, the cry . . . Who prays? Only the sufferer prays . . . [Prayer] tells [humankind] the story of [its] hidden hopes and expectations. It teaches [one] how to behold the vision and how to strive in order to realize this vision, when to be satisfied with what [one] possesses, when to reach out for more" (66). Soloveitchik comments: "The slaves were gloomy, voiceless and mute. . . . Torture was taken for granted. They thought this was the way it had to be. . . . They did not rebel against reality; they lacked the tension that engenders suffering and distress. The voice was restored to them at the very instant they discovered, emotionally, their need awareness and became sensitive to pain in a human fashion" (59–60). Soloveitchik explains that before the Israelites' cry, they lived in such a state of numbness that "they were unaware of any need" (59). See Soloveitchik, "Redemption, Prayer, Talmud Torah," 55–72.
5. Brueggemann, *Hope within History*, 20, 24.
6. Brueggemann, *Hope within History*, 80.
7. Greenberg, *Jewish Way*, 36.
8. Kaplan, *Meaning of God*, 61, 270.
9. Goldberg, *Jews and Christians*, 13.
10. Greenberg, *Jewish Way*, 34.

11. Fishbane, *Text and Texture*, 121. Fishbane (121) writes: "A concord between the first and succeeding redemptions is the issue, for each generation looked to the first exodus as the archetypal expression of its own future hope."

12. Eliade, *The Sacred and the Profane*, 102.

13. I review this issue in Arnow, "The Exodus from Egypt: The Question of Archeology," in *Creating Lively Passover Seders*. See also "The Exodus Is Not Fiction: An Interview with Richard Elliott Friedman," ReformJudaism.org, Spring 2014.

14. Hammer, "Impact of the Exodus on Halakhah (Jewish Law)," 113.

15. Hartman, "Sinai and Exodus," 381–82. A similar version of this essay also appears in Hartman's *From Defender to Critic*. Hartman distinguishes between the Exodus and Sinai as models of hope and prefers the latter, which he feels is rooted in incremental progress through Jewish law rather than apocalyptic yearnings. For more on this, see David Arnow, "Reply to David Hartman's 'Sinai and Exodus,'" under Resources at choosinghope.net.

16. Hartman, *From Defender to Critic*, 150.

17. Borowski, *Agriculture in Iron Age Israel*, 88.

18. Greenberg, *Jewish Way*, 60.

19. For good reviews of the development of the Exodus motif throughout the Bible, see Fishbane, *Text and Texture*; Barmash, "Out of the Mists of History," 1–22.

20. OJPS.

21. It is generally agreed that Sukkot was the preeminent festival, at least in the period of the First and Second Temples. Solomon dedicated the First Temple on Sukkot, and the Bible refers to it as "the festival" in several places (e.g., 1 Kings 8:1–5, 2 Chron. 7:8).

22. Bokser, *Origins of the Seder*, 9.

23. The prayer books of the ninth-century *Ge'onim* (Natronai and Amram) are the earliest sources that preserve an approximation of these words from the Haggadah.

24. For the "Matzah of Hope," see the *Jewish Telegraphic Agency*, March 22, 1972, http://www.jta.org/1972/03/22/jewish-holidays/passover/matzah-of-hope -for-soviet-jewry.

25. For additional connections between the tallit and the Exodus, see Rashi on Numbers 15:41.

26. A very similar version of the phrase in Grace after Meals appears in BT *Berakhot* 14b. The earliest source that includes this language for the Sabbath *Kiddush* is the ninth-century Responsa of Natronai Gaon; for the festival

Kiddush it is the ninth-century prayer book of Amram Gaon, although the text of this book that has come down to us may contain later additions.

27. Altmann, "Saadya Gaon: Book of Doctrines and Beliefs," 169. The translation of Psalm 31:25 follows Alter.

28. Saadia makes this identification in his Torah commentary, *Tafsir Rasag*, on Exodus 1:11, https://www.sefaria.org/Tafsir_Rasag%2C_Exodus.1?lang=bi.

29. Greenberg, *Jewish Way*, 38.

30. Yerushalmi, "Toward a History of Jewish Hope," 6226–29, Kindle.

31. Aviva Zornberg comes to a similar conclusion, writing, "In this reading, things get worse before they get better. This is the pattern: suffering, hope, and worse suffering." See her *Moses*, 482, Kindle.

32. Deuteronomy Rabbah 1:23.

33. *Tanḥuma* (Be-ha'alotkha 23) on Numbers 3:16. See Townsend, *Midrash Tanḥuma: Numbers and Deuteronomy*, 92.

34. Teikhthal, *Mishneh Sakhir*, on Va-Era, Exodus 6:5, 161, HB 53714, BI. This work was written between the two world wars. See Avishai Elboim on Teikhthal, http://www.zomet.org.il/eng/?CategoryID=160&ArticleID=6828, accessed June 14, 2021.

35. BT *Sotah* 11a.

36. Midrash Ha-Gadol on Exodus 1:11.

37. Exodus Rabbah 1:10, vol. 5, 21 (Hebrew), in Mirkin, *Midrash Rabbah*.

38. Judah Loew ben Bezalel, *Gevurot Ha-Shem*, chapter 15, 21b (right col.), BI, available at Google Books, https://bit.ly/32QKFI3.

39. For example, BT *Gittin* 52a: "Rabbi Yose said: All my life I have never called my wife my wife nor my ox my ox but my wife my house and my ox my field."

40. Midrash Ha-Gadol on Exodus 1:14.

41. This midrash appears in *Tanḥuma* (Va-era 4) on Exod. 5:9. See Townsend, *Midrash Tanḥuma: Exodus*, 21, Exodus Rabbah 5:18, and Midrash on Psalms 119:38. Exodus Rabbah 1:28 explains how Moses negotiated for the Israelites one day of rest.

42. Vaclav Havel, "Never Hope against Hope," *Esquire Magazine*, October 1, 1993, https://classic.esquire.com/article/1993/10/1/5-never-hope-against-hope.

43. Exodus Rabbah 1:9.

44. Noah Ben Pesach, *Toldot Noach*, 4b, HB 45284.

45. Chaim Tirer of Chernovitz, *Be'er Mayim Chayim* on Genesis, Vayechi, 49:9, https://www.sefaria.org/Be'er_Mayim_Chaim%2C_Genesis.49.9.2?lang=bi; and Numbers, Balak, 23:10, https://www.sefaria.org/Be'er_Mayim_Chaim%2C_Numbers.23.9?lang=bi.

46. For this and the next midrash, see BT *Sotah* 12a–13b.

47. Indeed, other midrashim identify Miriam as one of the midwives, and her mother as the other. See Steinmetz, "Miriam in Rabbinic Midrash."

48. Hirsch, *Hirsch Chumash*, on Exod. 6:14, 95–96.

49. Brown, *Inspired Jewish Leadership*, 1386–91, Kindle.

50. BT *Sotah* 11b. When teaching this midrash, I am often asked if apples were grown throughout the ancient Near East. They were. Rameses II, a likely candidate for the Pharaoh of the Exodus, had apple trees planted in gardens in the Nile Delta. See Brothwell and Brothwell, *Food in Antiquity*, 132.

51. BT *Pesachim*, 116a.

52. Quoted in Ginzberg, *Legends of the Jews*, 2:254. See *Sefer Ha-Yashar* (Venice: N.p., 1635), 128b, HB 44477.

53. *Tanhuma* (Shemot 4) on 3:10. See Townsend, *Midrash Tanhuma: Exodus*, 15.

54. Leviticus Rabbah 1:3 and Midrash Lekach Tov, Exod. 2:10.

55. Rashi (BT *Berakhot* 55a) and Tosafot (BT *Rosh Hashanah* 16b). See also BT *Berakhot* 32a and the Septuagint on Exodus 32:11.

56. Albo, *Sefer Ha-Ikkarim*, vol. 4, part 2, 457.

57. Brown, *Inspired Jewish Leadership*, 1362, Kindle.

58. Boyatzis and McKee, *Resonant Leadership*, 150, Kindle.

59. Fanon, *Wretched of the Earth*, 39, 53.

60. For a close reading of biblical texts linking the memory of slavery with empathy, see Carmy, "'We Were Slaves to Pharaoh in Egypt.'"

61. BT *Shabbat* 31a.

62. Nelson, *Mekhilta de-Rabbi Shimon bar Yochai*, 46, Pischa 14:1.

63. Rorty, *Philosophy and Social Hope*, 202–3.

64. Ochs, *Passover Haggadah*, 173.

5. THE COVENANT

1. For an overview of the biblical range of relationships between God and Israel, see Norman Solomon's lecture at Oxford University, "On Covenant," September 2001, http://www.bc.edu/content/dam/files/research_sites/cjl/texts/center/conferences/solomon.htm.

2. Mintz, *Hurban*, 19.

3. For more on this topic, see "Covenant and Hope in the Morning Liturgy" under Resources at choosinghope.net.

4. Marcel, 53.

5. The custom of reciting the story of the *Akedah* in the morning service arose in the medieval period. The first source to recommend it was the Tur (*Orah Hayyim*, The Laws and Customs for the Morning, 1:13) by Jacob Ben Asher (1269–1343, Germany and Spain). The Perishah, a sixteenth-century com-

mentary on this work by Joshua Falk (1555–1614), explains that doing so will lead God to look favorably upon us by remembering the merit of Abraham and Isaac (*Orah Hayyim* 1:13). The Shulhan Arukh (1565) recommends the practice as well. The *Akedah* appears in most Ashkenazi Orthodox prayer books, though many non-Orthodox prayer books omit it. Its presence is thought to reflect the elevated status given to the story during the Crusades, when many Jewish communities in the Rhineland were attacked and chose to kill themselves rather than fall into the Crusaders' hands. See Ephraim ben Jacob of Bonn, "The Akedah," in Spiegel, *Last Trial*, 139–52. For more, see MPPB, *Birkhot Hashachar*.

6. Both prayers are drawn from the *Zikhronot*, "Remembrances," section of the Rosh Hashanah liturgy.

7. In rabbinic sources the power of ancestral merit to bestir God's saving kindness cannot be exaggerated. An early third-century midrash reports that when the Israelites entered the Red Sea, Mount Moriah, with the complete scene of the *Akedah* set in place, moved from its place to the sea. Only when God saw it did God empower Moses to split the sea. See MRI, 222, vol. 1, Va-y'hi Beshalach 3. For a profound analysis of the redemptive power of the *Akedah*, especially midrashic sources that refer to the "ashes of Isaac," see Spiegel, *Last Trial*.

8. The expression "all is vanity" appears six times in Ecclesiastes. The sentiment here calls to mind a verse from Ecclesiastes (2:20) as well: "And so I came to view with despair all the gains I had made under the sun."

9. Translation based on Birnbaum, *Daily Prayer Book*, 24–25.

10. A passage from Chronicles appearing later in the morning service underscores the point: "Be ever mindful of [God's] covenant, the promise [God] gave for a thousand generations, that promise . . . made with Abraham, swore to Isaac, and confirmed in a decree for Jacob, for Israel, as an eternal covenant, saying, 'To you, I will give the land of Canaan as your allotted heritage.' . . . You were then few in number . . . [God] allowed no one to oppress them [God] reproved kings on their account, 'Do not touch My anointed ones; do not harm My prophets'" (1 Chron. 16:15–22). The context of this biblical passage is noteworthy. David orders the levitical priests and their musicians to sing these words of praise at the Ark of the Covenant's installation in Jerusalem. By bringing us back to the moment of this ancient dedication in Jerusalem, the liturgy reminds us that we are praying to a God who indeed fulfills covenantal promises. God had promised the land to the patriarchs, and, behold, David and all the people stand before the Ark of the Covenant of God in Jerusalem.

11. The verbs in these two verses differ. In Psalm 33:20 the verb is *chiktah*, often translated as "wait." In Psalm 33:22 the verb is *yichalnu*, one of the principal verbs connected with hope, though some translators routinely render this as "wait." Somewhat uncharacteristically, here NJPS translates both verbs as "hope."

12. *Yalkut Shimoni* on Psalms, section 736. See also Midrash on Psalms 40:1–2.

13. Teikhthal, *Mishneh Sakhir*, Writings on Psalms, 40:2, 612, HB 53714, BI.

14. *Metzudat David* on Psalms 33:22, https://www.sefaria.org/Metzudat_David _on_Psalms.33.20?lang=bi, BI. Written by David and Hillel Altschuler, the commentary (not to be confused with *Mitzudat David*, by the sixteenth-century sage David ben Solomon ibn Zimra) was published in 1753.

15. Some communities recite parts of this selection from Nehemiah about God's covenant with Abraham when a circumcision takes place in a synagogue.

16. Lopez, *Making Hope Happen*, 42, Kindle. Walter Brueggemann states, "It is odd, but true, that our capacity to hope is precisely correlated with our ability to remember," in *Practice of Homefulness*, 89, Kindle.

17. Yerushalmi, "Toward a History of Jewish Hope," 6416, 6420–21, 6430, Kindle. Ralph Waldo Emerson placed memory and hope in opposition to one another when he explored the roots of the conflict between conservatives and reformers. "Such an irreconcilable antagonism, of course, must have a correspondent depth of seat in the human constitution. It is the opposition of Past and Future, of Memory and Hope." Emerson, "The Conservative," 1841, https://emersoncentral.com/ebook/The-Conservative.pdf, accessed June 14, 2021.

18. Yerushalmi, *Zakhor*, 11.

19. Also see Brueggemann's analysis of the relationship between memory, hope, and covenant in Psalm 78:7: "That they might set their hope in God, and not forget the works of God, but keep . . . [God's] commandments" (Koren). See Brueggemann, *Practice of Homefulness*, 87.

20. Green, *Radical Judaism*, 108. See also Artson, *God of Becoming*, 1480–1532, Kindle.

21. For a wonderful explanation of how eighteen became nineteen, see Lawrence A. Hoffman's "How the Amidah Began: A Jewish Detective Story," in MPPB, *Amidah*, Kindle.

22. On the Sabbath and festivals, the thirteen petitionary blessings are omitted. As Hoffman explains, the traditional explanation is that these occasions "are presumed to be so perfect that what we normally lack cannot even be felt, let alone expressed in prayer." See MPPB, *Amidah*, 627, Kindle. Hoffman also notes that, in reality, the seventeenth blessing (asking God to restore the

sacrificial services to the Temple) and nineteenth blessing (asking God to grant us peace) are also petitionary. This not only weakens the traditional rationale for eliminating the other petitionary blessings but suggests that *whenever* the *Amidah* is said—including the Sabbath and festivals—we are asking God to fulfill divine covenantal promises.

23. Mittleman, *Hope in a Democratic Age*, 144. Hoffman agrees, observing that the *Amidah* embodies "what Jews pray for. . . . The Amidah is petitionary in the grand sense of its affirming our right to aspire to a higher plane and our right to believe that our aspirations are not futile." MPPB, *Amidah*, 381, 462, Kindle.

24. The translation follows MPPB, *Amidah*, 1294, Kindle.

25. MPPB, *Amidah*, 1544–45, Kindle.

26. Violence is often attributed to the loss of hope. But in these cases violence more likely represents the hope to exact vengeance or the hope that one's own death will bring suffering to an end.

27. The translation follows Birnbaum, *Daily Prayer Book*, 90. I modified the King James English and substituted YHWH for "O Lord."

28. Alshekh, *Torat Moshe*, Bereshit, Vayechi, 81a, HB 45292.

29. *Pesikta de-Rav Kahana* 17:5.

30. Birnbaum, *Daily Prayer Book*, 92.

31. Broide, *Chokhmah u'Mussar*, siman 66, BI.

32. *Siddur Sim Shalom for Weekdays*, 43.

33. For God's "covenant of peace" with Israel, see, for example, Isaiah 54:10 and Ezekiel 37:26. Toward the beginning of the nineteenth benediction, the Conservative and Reconstructionist liturgies, and in some cases the Reform as well, ask God to grant peace to the world in addition to the People of Israel.

34. Alter.

35. Hartman, *From Defender to Critic*, 176.

36. Artscroll translation except for Psalm 74:19–20, which is Koren.

37. I have mostly followed NJPS here, but consistently translated "hope" instead of "wait" or "trust." Rashi (1040–1105, France) lost friends and relatives in the First Crusade. We can feel his battle against despair in his commentary on Lamentations 3:21: "After my heart said to me that my hope from YHWH had perished, I will say this to my heart, 'The kindness of YHWH has not ended,' [the next verse from Lamentations] and I will continue to hope. Now what is it that I will reply to my heart?"

38. My translation.

39. BT *Chagigah* 4b. The Talmud reports parallel statements about two other biblical verses (Amos 5:15 and Zeph. 2:3) in which complete bowing to God's will is followed by a "perhaps" with respect to divine reward.

40. Lamentations Rabbah 5:22, the concluding words of this midrash.

41. Provan, *Lamentations*, 94, 22. There is considerable scholarly debate about the depth and reality of hope in this section of Lamentations. For a range of views, see Bier, *"Perhaps There Is Hope,"* 113–16. For a powerful affirmation of genuine hope here, see Mintz, *Ḥurban*, 17–48.

42. The origins of the custom are difficult to determine, but they were certainly known to Rashi. See his commentary on Lamentations 5:22. A similar practice extends to the liturgical readings of Ecclesiastes on Shavuot, the conclusion of Malachi (3:4–24) on the Sabbath prior to Passover, and the conclusion of Isaiah (66:1–24) when the new month begins on the Sabbath.

43. Alter translation. According to Rashi on Zechariah 9:11, the "blood of your covenant" refers to the covenant at Sinai and specifically to Exodus 24:8, which uses the phrase *dam ha-brit,* "blood of the covenant." Alter believes this phrase likely refers to the blood of circumcision, the sign of the Abrahamic covenant.

44. Brueggemann, *An Unsettling God,* 43–44, Kindle. Brueggemann discusses the resilience of hope in the face of exile in the prophetic era. As an example of what would seem to be God's unambiguous intent to destroy Israel, Brueggemann cites Jeremiah 19:11: "So I will smash this people and this city, as one smashes a potter's vessel, which can never be mended."

45. BT *Menachot* 53b. The Hebrew word translated as "hope" is *takanah,* which literally means "repair" or "remedy." Numerous translations render this as "hope," for example, the Soncino Talmud and Ibn Chaviv's *Ein Yaakov,* translated by Abraham Yaakov Finkel. God's responses to Abraham in this passage include biblical citations that I omitted here for ease of reading.

46. This sample of responses excludes the view of the Holocaust as God's punishment of Israel for the "sin" of Zionism or assimilation. For more on this, see Hutner, "Holocaust," 557–64. These positions still have plenty of advocates. See Paul Berger, "Telling the Story of the Holocaust's Horrors through Ultra-Orthodox Eyes," *Forward,* April 9, 2014, https://forward.com/news/196232/telling-story-of-holocausts-horrors-through-ultra/.

47. Rubenstein, *After Auschwitz,* 52, 54, 58.

48. Rubenstein, *After Auschwitz,* 128–29.

49. Rubenstein was initially reluctant to identify his thought with "God is dead" theology because he felt uncomfortable associating himself with the clear Christian overtones in connection with the notion that God had died. Nietzsche had coined the expression "God is dead" in a work published in 1882. See Nietzsche, *The Gay Science,* 90.

50. Rubenstein, *After Auschwitz,* 246.

51. Rubenstein, *After Auschwitz*, 154.

52. Rubenstein, *After Auschwitz*, 154.

53. Fackenheim, "Commanding Voice," 436–37. For more, see Fackenheim, "Commandment to Hope."

54. Fackenheim, "The 614th Commandment," 434.

55. In some of his later writings, Fackenheim raised doubts about his own formulations in both of these essays. "The '614th commandment' of 'commanding voice of Auschwitz' may well be a moral and religious necessity, but also, and at the same time, an ontological impossibility." See Fackenheim, *To Mend the World*, 299–300.

56. Fackenheim, *What Is Judaism?*, 255. David R. Blumenthal, who stresses the centrality of covenant, provides an interesting counterpoint to Fackenheim: "When all is said and done, 'that is [the destiny] of every person' (Eccles. 12:13). Persistence in faith, the integrity of which can be preserved through protest. Persistence in community, in loyalty to one's people, in spite of reality. In a word, persistence in covenant. . . . Persistence, not rejection. Persistence, not hope. . . . I am not sure I hope, but I persist in the face of despair." See Blumenthal, "Despair and Hope," 18, available at http://davidblumenthal.org/DespairHope.html#fn1.

57. Greenberg, *For the Sake of Heaven*, 163.

58. Greenberg, "Voluntary Covenant," 549.

59. Greenberg, "Voluntary Covenant," 547. David Hartman has also proposed a related developmental approach to covenant. See his "A Covenant of Empowerment: Divine Withdrawal and Human Responsibility," in Hartman, *From Defender to Critic*, 177.

60. Greenberg, "Voluntary Covenant," 549, 550.

61. Greenberg, *For the Sake of Heaven*, 42.

62. Greenberg, *Jewish Way*, 322.

63. Jonas, "Concept of God," 634.

64. Jonas, "Concept of God," 631.

65. Soloveitchik, *Lonely Man of Faith*, 52.

66. MRI, vol. 2, 60–61, Shirata 8:19–25. This midrash was compiled around 200 CE.

67. Harlow, "Remember," 387.

6. THE BOOK OF JOB

1. This one appearance is in Jacob's deathbed testament: "I hope for Your salvation, O YHWH!" (Gen. 49:18). Many translations render "wait" instead of "hope." For more on the issues of translating this verse, see Arnow, "Jacob's

Hope for Salvation," available at https://zeramim.org/past-issues/spring
-summer-5780-2020/jacobs-hope-for-salvation/.

2. For more on Marcel's understanding of hope, see "What Is Hope?" at
choosinghope.net, under Resources.

3. In her essay following the April 2019 elections in Israel, Jill Jacobs, executive director of *T'ruah: The Rabbinic Call for Human Rights*, quoted this
midrash, without a definitive source. *Chevruta*, a Talmud study resource
by Yaakov Shulvitz and Yehuda Leib Garnter, also cites the midrash, in the
commentary on *Bava Batra* 15a, note 26. The earliest source I can find for
this midrash is Hottinger (1620–67, Switzerland), *Smegma Orientale: Sordibus Barbarismi, Contemtui*, 453. Hottinger was a Christian theologian and
Hebraist, and his book uses Hebrew and Arabic sources to correct Latin
misreadings of various biblical texts. Hottinger says he found the midrash
in an old notebook, available at https://play.google.com/books/reader?id=A
_IDAAAAYAAJ&pg=GBS.PA453, accessed July 9, 2021.

4. The Hebrew in the book of Job is notoriously difficult to understand and
hence to translate. Because translations differ so widely, I have relied on a
number of different translations, most often NJPS (The Jewish Publication
Society's newest translation) but also Seow, *Job 1–21*; Alter; Scheindlin, *Book
of Job*; and OJPS (Old Jewish Publication Society translation). For a complete
treatment of the linguistic difficulties in Job, see Hoffman, *Blemished Perfection*, chap. 6.

5. Kushner, *When Bad Things Happen to Good People*, 53.

6. Levi, *Search for Roots*, 11. Levi's anthology begins with a selection from Job.
His diagram of the relationship between the selections in the anthology
places Job at a point from which all the "fundamental dichotomies" in life
emerge, among them hope versus despair (8–9).

7. Berger, "On the Book of Job," 112, available at https://digitalcommons
.osgoode.yorku.ca/cgi/viewcontent.cgi?article=3423&context=
scholarly_works.

8. NJPS, except the second line, which is Seow, *Job 1–21*.

9. Seow, *Job 1–21*, 353.

10. Kübler-Ross and Kessler, *On Grief and Grieving*.

11. Halbertal, "Job, the Mourner," 37–46, available at https://www.degruyter.com
/document/doi/10.1515/9783110338799/html.

12. BT *Bava Metzi'a* 58b. Also see the *Sifra* on Leviticus 25:17 ("Do not wrong one
another . . ."), Behar 4:2.

13. *Midrash Tanḥuma* (compiled between the fifth and ninth centuries),
Va-yishlach 8, on Job 4:2–7, Townsend, *Midrash Tanḥuma: Genesis*, 210.

14. See, for example, Seow, *Job 1–21*, 396.

15. Habel, *Book of Job*, 2153–54, Kindle.

16. Halbertal, "Job, the Mourner," 38.

17. When the same root appears in Job 8:14 and 31:24, Rashi reads it as "hope."

18. Rashi was not the first to offer this understanding of the verse in question. The Septuagint, the old Greek translation of the Bible, also preferred "foolishness," rendering the verse this way: "Is not your fear [piety] founded in folly, your hope also, and the mischief [foolishness] of your way?"

19. See Meshel, "Whose Job Is This?," 58, available at https://www.degruyter .com/document/doi/10.1515/9783110338799/html.

20. Alter, except for the second part of 6:11, which is NJPS.

21. The expression entered the English language from the King James Version of a verse in the New Testament's Epistle of James (5:11): "Ye have heard of the patience of Job, and have seen the end of the Lord; that the Lord is very pitiful, and of tender mercy."

22. Later, when Job concludes that the road to redemption demands confronting God, he will find patience to await his day in court. When his hope burns brightest, he will say, "But I know that my Vindicator lives; In the end He will testify on earth" (19:25). Job will wait as long as it takes. If necessary, he'll even settle for a postmortem vindication.

23. Capps, *Agents of Hope*, 151.

24. See, for example, the Koren translation of Psalm 40:2, "I waited patiently for the Lord." Or the NJPS translation of Lamentations 3:26, "It is good to wait patiently till rescue comes from the Lord." In the first case, the root is *kof-vav-hey*, and in the second, *yud-chet-lamed*. In both verses, Alter renders "hope."

25. Newsom, *Book of Job*, 130–31.

26. In the passages quoted in this section and the next, "Hope Is a Slender Thread," the author of Job uses metaphor to give us a better feel for hope. That makes sense because, as with other abstract concepts—love or God, metaphor helps bring them into sharper focus. For a study on the use of metaphor in Job, see van Loon, *Metaphors in the Discussion on Suffering*. Unfortunately, Loon focuses more on suffering and very little on hope.

27. Verses 6:15 and 19 are Seow, *Job 1–21*; verse 6:20 is Alter.

28. Seow, *Job 1–21*, 463.

29. NJPS 7:1–3, with the exception of "hopes" in 7:2, which NJPS renders "waits." "Hopes" follows Habel, *Book of Job*, and Seow's comment, 501. Verses 7:6–7 are Scheindlin, *Book of Job*.

30. Greenstein, *Job*, note 21, 1031, Kindle.

31. Seow, *Job 1–21*, 494.

32. Ibn Ezra, *Shirei ha-Chol*, 385.

33. Snyder, *Handbook of Hope*, 10. Regarding the question of agency, Job himself says, "Truly, I cannot help myself; I have been deprived of resourcefulness" (6:13).

34. Michael Marmur, "Lifeline to the Future," 51.

35. The use of masculine pronouns in Job often communicates a sense of emotional distance between Job and God and the sense that Job is being overpowered by a warrior who is cutting Job to pieces. The imagery of combat seems to justify retaining masculine pronouns when referring to God here and subsequently.

36. NJPS, except the last line of 9:35, which is Alter.

37. NJPS, except OJPS for the first line of 13:15, though I prefer "hope" rather than "trust," as in OJPS. This follows *Metzudat David*, Malbim, BDB, and many contemporary translations, including the New International Version.

38. Snyder, *Psychology of Hope*, 155, Kindle.

39. Coleridge, "Work without Hope" (composed in 1827), in *The Works of Samuel Taylor Coleridge*, 213.

40. Alford, *After the Holocaust*, 190, Kindle.

41. Laytner, *Arguing with God*, 12. Abraham challenges God's willingness to sweep away the innocent with the guilty (Gen. 18:23), and Job accuses God of destroying both the blameless and the guilty (9:22). There has been considerable research on the parallels between Abraham and Job. See, for example, Glazer, "God of Job and the God of Abraham," 41–45; van Ruiten, "Abraham, Job and the Book of Jubilees," 58–85.

42. There are many parallels between the language in Jeremiah 20 and in Job. For example, both Jeremiah (20:7) and Job (12:4) refer to themselves as "laughingstocks" (*s'chok*) and, using slightly different language, both Jeremiah (20:14) and Job (3:1) curse the days of their birth.

43. Laytner, *Arguing with God*, 32.

44. OJPS first line, NJPS second line. As previously noted, I prefer "hope" rather than "trust," as in OJPS.

45. The Dead Sea Scrolls include a fragmentary Aramaic interpretive paraphrase (*targum*) of Job in which 13:15 has been translated as "[if he slay] me I will hope for him." The *targum* on Job does not have the same chapters and verses as the biblical book of Job, and its rendering of 13:15 appears as part of what corresponds to verse 34:31 in the biblical book. See Zuckerman, "Two Examples of Editorial Modification in 11QtgJob," 273.

46. *Mishnah Sotah* 5:5. In his commentary (Tiferet Yisrael, Yachin) on this mishnah, Israel Lifschitz (1782–1860, Germany) writes: "In him I will hope? In astonishment." HB 41119, 123b.

47. See Maimonides' commentary on *Mishnah Sotah* 5:5.

48. Scheindlin, *Book of Job*, 178.

49. Seow, *Job 1–21*, 659. He renders the verse, "If one would kill me, I will wait for him." For an example of what may be another case of intentional ambiguity in the Bible, see Tucker, *Torah for Its Intended Purpose*, 90. Hesiod's well-known Greek myth about Pandora's Box (originally a jar) is also a text about hope layered with ambiguity. Zeus gave Prometheus a jar full of evils, which fell into the hands of the curious Pandora, who opened it and let evils escape into the world. When she closed the lid, only hope remained within. (For Hesiod's version of the myth, see his *Works and Days* 2:90–105, available at http://www.perseus.tufts.edu/hopper/text?doc=Perseus%3Atext%3A1999 .01.0132%3Acard%3D1, accessed July 9, 2021.) W. J. Verdenius, "A 'Hopeless' Line in Hesiod," analyzes competing interpretations of the myth, specifically concerning whether hope is seen as something positive or negative and whether the jar that contains it is viewed as a "pantry or a prison" (225). Verdenius concludes that what really remains in the jar (*elpis* in Greek) is the expectation of difficult or painful circumstances. "This continual expectation would have made life a torture beyond bearing. Zeus therefore at the last moment altered his decision: he made Pandora release the lid of the jar so that . . . [this expectation of evil] remained enclosed in it. . . . It is true that we sometimes expect evil, but this is an exception. In general evil comes unexpected, and that is a good thing too" (229). That Hesiod's story is susceptible to so many different interpretations is perhaps not an accident. Perhaps Hesiod, like the author of Job, intended to leave us with an ambiguous text, our interpretations of which would reveal our own understanding of hope as much as or more than those of the text's author. For a far less challenging version of the Pandora myth, see Babrius, fable 58 (second century CE?), many of whose fables are now known as Aesop's Fables. In this story, Jove gives humanity a cask full of blessings, and when a curious individual opens the lid, the blessings all return to heaven. "Hope only tarried . . . and thus Hope has endured in human homes. In her sole form we see earnest of all the goods, that then did flee." See *Fables of Babrius*, 52, available at https:// archive.org/details/fablesofbabriusi00babr_0/page/52, accessed July 9, 2021. Also see Panofsky and Panofsky, *Pandora's Box*.

50. Neher, *L'Exil de la parole*, 215, quoted in Kessler, "Reasoning with Violent Scripture," available at https://jsr.shanti.virginia.edu/back-issues/vol-4-no -1-july-2004-the-wisdom-of-job/reasoning-with-violent-scripture-with-a -little-help-from-job/#t21. See Zornberg's discussion of this in *Particulars of Rapture*, 389.

51. See Roskies, *Literature of Destruction*, 64. Ibn Gabirol shares this reading of the verse as well. See his *Keter Malkhut*, 11, HB 24851. Note Heschel's reading of the verse. A few weeks after the Six-Day War, Heschel traveled to Israel for a brief but emotional trip, after which he began to write *Israel: An Echo of Eternity*, his only work focused exclusively on the Land of Israel. In a chapter on Jerusalem, "The Widow Is a Bride Again," he wrote: "In Auschwitz and Dachau, in Bergen-Belsen and Treblinka, they prayed at the end of Atonement Day, 'Next Year in Jerusalem.' The next day they were asphyxiated in gas chambers. Those of us who were not asphyxiated continue to cling to Thee. 'Though he slay me, yet I will trust in him' (Job 13:15). We come to you, Jerusalem, to build your ruins, to mend our souls and to seek comfort for God and men." Heschel, *Israel: An Echo of Eternity*, 17.

52. Scheindlin, *Book of Job*, except 14:10 is NJPS.

53. Scheindlin, *Book of Job*.

54. Scheindlin, *Book of Job*.

55. Schachtel, *Metamorphosis*, 37.

56. For contrasting views on the relationship between hope and Job's wish for an arbiter/redeemer, see Wilson, "Realistic Hope or Imaginative Exploration?," 243–52; and Kummerow, "Job Hope*ful* or Hope*less*?," 1–40, available at https://www.jhsonline.org/index.php/jhs/article/download/5749/4802.

57. For Erikson on hope and basic trust, see *Childhood and Society*, 247–51, and "What Is Hope?" under Resources at choosinghope.net. See also Jastrow, 156, under *bitachon*, and compare Job 6:20, *boshu ki vatach*, which in NJPS is "They are disappointed in their hope" and in Alter, "Disappointed in what they trusted."

58. See, for example, O'Hara, *Hope in Counselling*, 14–15.

59. BT *Ta'anit* 23a.

60. NJPS: "vindicator"; Alter and OJPS: "redeemer;" Scheindlin, *Book of Job*: "avenger."

61. Long and Carney, *A Hard-Fought Hope*, 106.

62. Morson and Saul, *Mikhail Bakhtin*, 135. Also quoted in Newsom, *Book of Job*, 3134, Kindle. Philosopher Mikhail Bakhtin (1895–1975, Russia) developed the concept of the superaddressee.

63. Bloch, *Atheism in Christianity*, 117.

64. Margalit, *Ethics of Memory*, 1280, Kindle.

65. BT *Berakhot* 5b.

66. "Bryan Stevenson: Love Is the Motive," *On Being with Krista Tippit*, December 3, 2020, https://onbeing.org/programs/bryan-stevenson-love-is-the-motive/#transcript. Stevenson's defense of Walter McMillian is the subject of the 2019 film *Just Mercy* as well as Stevenson's 2014 book of the same title.

67. Scheindlin, *Book of Job*.

68. Scheindlin, *Book of Job*.

69. Helmreich, *Against All Odds*, 128–29.

70. Scheindlin, *Book of Job*.

71. Halbertal, "Job, the Mourner," 45, 46. For a contrasting interpretation of Job's prayer for his friends, see Soloveitchik, "Kol Dodi Dofek: It Is the Voice of My Beloved That Knocketh," 58–62.

72. Marcel, 30.

73. See Pope, *Anchor Bible: Job*, 352.

74. Parallels between Noah and Job include the fact that both are referred to as "blamelessly innocent," *tzadik tamim* (Gen. 6:9 and Job 12:4). For other parallels, see Joyce, "'Even if Noah, Daniel, and Job Were in It . . .' (Ezekiel 14:14)," 118–28.

75. For the dove as a biblical symbol of hope, see Allan, *Metaphor and Metonymy*, 162.

76. Pruyser, "Maintaining Hope," 469.

77. It is important to note that Job's retraction in 42:6 is not an admission of sin or of God's innocence, but functions as a withdrawal of charges against God. As Habel, *Book of Job*, argues, "The hero has come face to face with God and therefore needs no formal declaration of innocence to win his case," 15643, Kindle.

78. Keckley, *Behind the Scenes*, 54, available at http://www.gutenberg.org/files/24968/24968-h/24968-h.htm.

79. "President Lincoln's White House Funeral," Abraham Lincoln Online, http://www.abrahamlincolnonline.org/lincoln/education/whfuneral.htm.bak, accessed June 10, 2021.

7. JEWISH ESCHATOLOGY

1. Amy E. Schwartz, "Is There Life After Death? Jewish Thinking on the Afterlife," *Moment*, July 17, 2011, https://momentmag.com/is-there-life-after-death/.

2. See Elliot B. Gertel, "Kvetching about Judaism in Café Society," *Jewish Currents*, August 11, 2016, https://archive.jewishcurrents.org/kvetching-about-judaism-in-cafe-society/.

3. Early Jewish challengers of the idea of the soul's immortality include Uriel da Costa (1585–1640) and Spinoza (1632–77). Followers of Kabbalah have also advanced the idea of transmigration of souls, or reincarnation, which this chapter does not cover. For a recent comprehensive treatment of this and other aspects of Jewish eschatology, see Starr, *Toward a History of Jewish Thought*.

4. "The Values and Beliefs of the American Public," Wave III Baylor Religion Survey, September 2011, 26, https://www.baylor.edu/content/services /document.php/153501.pdf. The 2014 Pew Religious Landscape Study, https://www.pewforum.org/religious-landscape-study/religious-tradition /jewish/belief-in-heaven/, accessed June 14, 2021, found lower levels of Jewish belief in Heaven (40%) and Hell (22%) than the Baylor study, possibly as a result of differences in the wording of the questions. While in the general population belief in the afterlife has increased slightly, among Jews it has steadily climbed over the years, now reaching 55 percent. See the analysis by Allan Mazur, "A Statistical Portrait of American Jews into the 21st Century," Syracuse University, 2007, https://citeseerx.ist.psu.edu/viewdoc/download ?doi=10.1.1.514.2587&rep=rep1&type=pdf, accessed June 14, 2021. By comparison, a 1965 survey found that only 17 percent of Jews believed in an afterlife, compared to 83 percent of Catholics and 78 percent of Protestants. See Raphael, *Jewish Views of the Afterlife,* 29.

5. Greeley and Hout, "Americans' Increasing Belief in Life after Death." Among Catholics, belief in the afterlife has increased from 67 percent for those born between 1900 and 1970 to 85 percent for those born after 1970.

6. The translation of Ecclesiastes 9:4 follows Gordis, *Koheleth,* 188. Most translations of this verse render *bitachon,* usually "trust," as "hope" in this context. NJPS and Alter depart from this practice.

7. Nor does the Bible suggest that human beings possess an immortal soul. The Bible views body and soul as a single unit. While the Bible does speak of Sheol as the shadowy destination for the dead, it often sounds suspiciously like the grave: "Your pomp is brought down to Sheol, and the strains of your lutes. Worms are to be your bed, maggots your blanket!" (Isa. 14:11). The connection between Sheol and the grave is not accidental because Sheol and "the pit" are often used interchangeably. In Sheol, all connections with God are severed: "For it is not Sheol that praises You . . . nor do they who descend into the Pit hope for Your grace. The living, only the living can give thanks to You." (Isa. 38:18–19). 1 Chronicles (29:15) likewise stresses the finality of death: "For we are sojourners with You, mere transients, like our [ancestors]; our days on earth are like a shadow, with nothing in prospect [*v'ain mikveh*]." Rashi understood the last phrase, *v'ain mikveh,* 'there is no hope,' to mean that, "No one has hope that one will not die."

Some scholars challenge the notion of Sheol as death. Neil Gillman writes: "Despite our insistence that [in the Bible] *Sheol* marks the absolute end of human destiny, the fact remains that there is some form of human continuance there, that people are not totally extinguished at death." Gillman, *Death of Death*, 68. Jon Levenson's *Resurrection and the Restoration of Israel* explores biblical views on this matter in great detail.

8. Vermes, *Resurrection*, 301.

9. Levenson, *Resurrection*, 20.

10. Greenberg, *Anchor Bible: Ezekiel, 1–20*, 12, 15.

11. Segal, *Life after Death*, 190, 256.

12. Levenson, *Resurrection*, 163.

13. Fishbane, *JPS Bible Commentary: Haftarot*, 427.

14. The dating of the rest of Isaiah is likewise complicated. With some exceptions, chapters 1–39 are often dated to the eighth century BCE, while much of chapters 40–66 is often dated to the end of the Babylonian exile and the early post-exilic period, that is, mid- to late fifth century BCE.

15. Alter. Bracketed text substituted for gendered language.

16. NJPS.

17. Collins, *Introduction to the Hebrew Bible*, 42.

18. Rosner, *Moses Maimonides' Treatise on Resurrection*, section 38, 814, Kindle.

19. Collins, *Apocalypticism in the Dead Sea Scrolls*, 111. Collins is also quoted in Levenson, *Resurrection*, 199.

20. Heschel, *Prophets*, 73.

21. Levenson, *Resurrection*, 199–200.

22. Blenkinsopp, *Anchor Yale Bible: Isaiah 1–39*, 371.

23. The precise dating of the book is based on the fact that it contains a series of prophesies (written after the actual events unfolded), which are accurate until they involve the last events in the reign of Antiochus IV Epiphanes (175–164 BCE). For example, Daniel makes no mention of the king's death.

24. Rosner, *Moses Maimonides' Treatise on Resurrection*, section 22, 617, Kindle. Of note, *El Malei Rachamim* ("God Full of Mercy," a prayer recited at funerals and anniversaries of a loved one's death) borrows language from Daniel when it refers to the deceased as inhabiting a "bright expanse of sky."

25. Elledge, *Resurrection of the Dead in Early Judaism*, 69, Kindle. Elevation of the righteous as the stars of heaven also appears in other sources from the general period of Daniel. First Enoch provides a good example: "Wait with patient hope; for formerly you have been disgraced with evil and with affliction; but now shall you shine like the luminaries of heaven" (104:2). See the Richard Laurence translation (London, 1883), available at http://www.johnpratt.com/items/docs/enoch.html#Enoch_104, accessed June 14, 2021.

26. Translation from the New Revised Standard Version: Holy Bible with Apocrypha.

27. Segal, *Life after Death*, 270.

28. Plato, *Phaedo*, available at http://www.perseus.tufts.edu/hopper/text?doc=
Perseus%3Atext%3A1999.01.0170%3Atext%3DPhaedo%3Asection%3D80a,
accessed June 14, 2021.

29. Philo likens the soul to the pupil of the eye, "the eye of the eye" ("On Creation," 21:66). For Philo on martyrdom, see *On the Embassy to Gaius*, 117:369.
For an extensive review of these and other relevant sources on the immortality of the soul in the Hellenistic period, see Segal, *Life after Death*, 351–98,
and Starr, *Toward a History of Jewish Thought*, 60–90.

30. Josephus, *War of the Jews*, 2:8:10.

31. It is often thought that Essenes were celibate, which accounts for their dis-
appearance. For a short critique of the evidence of Essene celibacy, see Her-
shel Shanks, "First Person: Was the Dead Sea Scroll Community Celibate?"
Biblical Archeological Review, May/June 2017, https://www.biblicalarchaeology
.org/daily/biblical-artifacts/dead-sea-scrolls/was-the-dead-sea-scroll
-community-celibate/.

32. Saldarini, *Pharisees, Scribes and Sadducees in Palestinian Society*, 284. For a critique of equating the Sadducees with the priesthood, see 298–398.

33. Josephus, *Jewish Antiquities*, 18:1:3.

34. For contrasting overviews of the relationship between the Pharisees and the
Rabbis, see Cohen, *From the Maccabees to the Mishnah*; Schwartz, *Ancient Jews
from Alexander to Muhammad*.

35. Setzer, "Resurrection of the Dead," 65–101.

36. *Mishnah Sanhedrin* 10:1. The translation is a modification of that found in
Neusner, *The Mishnah*. I have slightly modified the translation to accommo-
date the square brackets also added. The phrase in brackets does not appear
in what are considered the most authentic manuscripts of the Mishnah.
See, for example, the Kaufman Mishnah (tenth or eleventh century, MS A50,
https://www.hebrewbooks.org/44722, 303) and the Cambridge Mishnah
(fifteenth century, MS Add.470.1, http://cudl.lib.cam.ac.uk/mirador/MS
-ADD-00470-00001/1, 128r). Early manuscripts of the Talmud, however,
do include this phrase. See, for example, the Munich Codex Hebraicus 95
(fourteenth century, http://www.seforimonline.org/babylonian-talmud
-manuscript-munich-codex-hebraicus-95/, folio 351a). All sites accessed on
June 14, 2021. Standard printed versions of the Mishnah also include the
reference to resurrection of the dead from Torah. The addition seems to har-
monize with the many discussions in the Talmud that follow this Mishnah,
which offer midrashic readings of verses from the Pentateuch and elsewhere
in the Bible to "prove" that these sources do indeed contain references to
resurrection of the dead. When the Mishnah refers to "Torah," it can mean

the entire Hebrew Bible, not just the Pentateuch. For more on the evolution of the text and its relationship to Christianity, see Yuval, "All Israel Have a Portion in the World to Come."

37. Setzer, "Resurrection of the Dead," 87–90.

38. BT *Sanhedrin* 92b.

39. BT *Sanhedrin* 91a.

40. BT *Ta'anit* 31a. Isa. 25:9, follows Alter. A beautiful Hasidic interpretation of this talmudic passage emphasizes the symbolism of a circle dance. The righteous are all equidistant from God, no one is first or last, no one is on the top or the bottom, and so there will be no jealousy or hatred among the righteous. Perhaps the author, Tzvi Elimelech Spira of Dinov (1783–1841), was envisioning an end to disputes within or among Hasidic sects or possibly between Hasidism and its opponents. See Tzvi Elimelech Spira of Dinov, *Bnei Yissakhar*, part 1, 157a, HB 4682.

41. BT *Sanhedrin* 92a; Dan. 12:2 from NJPS; and Dan. 12:13 from Alter.

42. MPPB, *The Amidah*, 1601, Kindle.

43. The Tosefta notes that a prayer called *Techiyat ha-Meitim*, "Resurrection of the Dead," should be recited as part of the Grace after Meals in the home of a mourner (*Berakhot* 3:24). The prayer should conclude with a blessing that ends with *Techiyat ha-Meitim*, likely the same blessing with which the *Gevurot* prayer in the *Amidah* ends. The Talmud (*Berakhot* 60b) does include the complete words for *Elohai, N'shamah*, "My God, the Soul," a prayer addressing resurrection, which the Talmud says should be said upon waking. The prayer was transferred to the synagogue, where it has been part of the liturgy for more than a thousand years: "My God, the soul You placed within me is pure. You created it, You fashioned it, You breathed it into me, You safeguard it within me, and eventually You will take it from me, and restore it to me in Time to Come. As long as the soul is within me, I gratefully thank You, YHWH, my God and the God of my forefathers, Master of all works, Lord of all souls. Blessed are you YHWH, Who restores souls to dead bodies." The translation follows Artscroll, but with YHWH replacing Hashem.

44. BT *Berakhot* 58b.

45. BT *Berakhot* 18b. For this translation, see Greenberg, *Anchor Bible: Ezekiel*, 21–37.

46. Townsend, *Midrash Tanḥuma: Deuteronomy*, Ve-zot Ha-berakhah 7, 374.

47. Fishbane, *The JPS Bible Commentary: Haftarot*, 431.

48. For a graph illustrating the efflorescence of messianic themes in post-mishnaic literature and its comparatively scant presence in the Mishnah, see Neusner, *Messiah in Context*, 216–18.

49. *Mishnah Sotah* 9:15. This appears in printed versions of the Mishnah but not in the Mishnah when it is printed in the Talmud.

50. *Pesikta Rabbati* 35:4.

51. BT *Sanhedrin* 98a.

52. Exodus Rabbah 18:12.

53. Versions of the story appear in the JT *Ta'anit* 4, halakhah 5, 24a, and in two different versions of Lamentations Rabbah: Buber 2:2 and Vilna 2:4. For a skeptical reading of Akiva's endorsement of Bar Kokhba, see Schäfer, "Rabbi Aqiva and Bar Kokhba," 113–30.

54. Song of Songs Rabbah 2:20.

55. BT *Sanhedrin* 97b.

56. JT *Ta'anit* 1, halakhah 1, 3b. In 1899, Shalom Dov Baer Schneerson (1860–1920), the fifth Lubavitcher Rebbe, proclaimed that "We are not permitted to hasten the end even by reciting too many prayers." See Ravitzky, *Messianism, Zionism, and Religious Radicalism*, 15.

57. Compare Exodus Rabbah 15:1 and Shitah Chadashah 2:7. This alternative ending to Genesis Rabbah, found at the end of the Vilna edition and also in the Soncino Genesis Rabbah, notes that the Temple will be built by the King [Messiah]. See also Leviticus Rabbah 9:7.

58. BT *Sanhedrin* 98a.

59. BT *Sanhedrin* 98b.

60. Exodus Rabbah 15:21.

61. BT *Ketubot*, 111b.

62. JT *Ta'anit* 1, halakhah 2, 4a.

63. See *Avot de Rabbi Natan*, a minor tractate of the Talmud, chap. 31, version B.

64. The statement appears six times in the Babylonian Talmud: *Berakhot* 34b, *Shabbat* 63a, *Shabbat* 151b, *Pesachim* 68a, and *Sanhedrin* 91b and 99a. The wording is the same in all cases but *Shabbat* 63a and *Sanhedrin* 91b, which refer to oppression of exiles versus oppression by other nations.

65. The translation follows Birnbaum, *Daily Prayer Book*, 89. I modified the Elizabethan pronouns and substituted YHWH for "O Lord."

66. BT *Megillah*, 17b. The prayer book of Amram Gaon, who died in 875 CE in Babylonia, includes the current wording of the benediction, although the text of this book that has come down to us may contain later additions.

67. This benediction omits the explicit reference to the messianic kingship of David's descendants present in the blessings after the haftarah, the *Amidah* for festivals and the new month, and the Grace after Meals. See Kimelman, "Messiah of the *Amidah*," 313–20, https://bit.ly/3AOVriL. Kimelman argues that, as with the Passover Haggadah's effort to minimize Moses and the

human role in the redemption from Egypt, this blessing in the *Amidah* likewise keeps the focus on God, rather than on a human messianic figure.

68. Finkelstein, "Development of the Amidah," 14. Also quoted in Kimelman "Messiah of the *Amidah*," 314.

69. BT *Shabbat* 31a.

70. The verb the Talmud uses for hope, *tzadie-pey-hey*, is different than *kof-vav-hey*, which appears in the Amidah. Jastrow gives both words virtually identical definitions. In this case, both verbs are also in the past tense. See Vital, *Pri Etz Chayim*, Sha'ar Ha'Amidah, chapter 9, 58b HB 19621. For a short but very useful overview of sources on this verse in the *Amidah*, see Peretz, *Otzar Piskei Ha-Siddur*, 276, HB 48841.

71. This tradition was conveyed by the Hasidic leader Rabbi Chaim Halberstam of Sanz (1793–1876). See Wienstock, *Siddur of the Geonim*, book two, part 3, 609 (Hebrew), HB 21882. The Artscroll Sephardic Siddur includes these words in parentheses with the note: "Many authorities insist that these words are not to be recited. Rather, they were originally intended only as an instruction that one should *think* about the salvation." Scherman, *Artscroll Siddur: Nusach Sefard*, 114.

72. Shlomo Aviner, *U'mitzapim Lishuah*, September 16, 2012, www.havabooks.co .il/article_ID.asp?id=1111 [defunct].

73. Maimonides, *Mishneh Torah*, Laws of Repentance, 9:1, in MR, 82.

74. Maimonides, *Mishneh Torah*, Laws of Repentance, 9:2, in MR, 83.

75. Maimonides, *Mishneh Torah*, Laws of Repentance, 9:2, in MR, 83.

76. Maimonides, *Mishneh Torah*, Laws of Repentance, 9:2, in MR, 83.

77. Maimonides, *Perek Chelek*, in MR, 414.

78. Maimonides, *Mishneh Torah*, Laws of Repentance, 9:2, in MR, 83.

79. Maimonides, *Perek Chelek*, in MR, 415.

80. Maimonides, *Perek Chelek*, in MR, 415.

81. Seeskin, "Maimonides and the Idea of a Deflationary Messiah," 99.

82. Maimonides, *Perek Chelek*, in MR, 416.

83. Maimonides, *Perek Chelek*, in MR, 411.

84. Silver, "Resurrection Debate," 1688, Kindle.

85. Rosner, *Moses Maimonides' Treatise on Resurrection*, paragraphs 22–24.

86. Gillman, *Death of Death*, 160.

87. Silver, "Resurrection Debate," 1789, Kindle.

88. For the Conservative movement's positions on these issues, see *Emet Ve-Emunah: Statement of Principles of Conservative Judaism*. Endorsement of immortality of the soul is unequivocal. The document leaves room for both literal and figurative understanding of the resurrection of the dead. The

Messiah is understood metaphorically as an improved world that human beings are charged to create in partnership with God. For the Reconstructionist view, see Kaplan, *Judaism without Supernaturalism*.

89. The rejection of resurrection of the dead was bolder in American Reform communities than in European ones. For how the European Reform prayer books dealt with resurrection, see Ellenson, "The Israelitischer Gebetbücher of Abraham Geiger and Manuel Joel," 143–64; and Ellenson, "The Mannheimer Prayerbooks and Modern Central European Communal Liturgies," 59–78. For the comparison between the Reform movements in America and Europe on this issue, see Petuchowski, "Immortality: Yes; Resurrection: No!," 133–47.

90. Phillipson, *Reform Movement in Judaism*, 465, available at https://play.google .com/books/reader?id=1M5CAAAAIAAJ&hl=en&pg=GBS.PA465.

91. Wise, *Minhag America*, 41, 47, available at http://collections .americanjewisharchives.org/wise/attachment/5329/theDailyPrayersFinal.pdf.

92. Einhorn, *Olat Tamid*, 346, available at https://opensiddur.org/compilations /siddurim/kol-bo/olath-tamid-book-of-prayers-for-israelitish -congregations-by-david-einhorn-1872/.

93. Lerner, *Redemptive Hope*, 267–69, Kindle.

94. 1885 Pittsburgh Platform, paragraph 7, https://www.ccarnet.org/rabbinic -voice/platforms/article-declaration-principles/, this and all subsequently cited CCARNET sites accessed July 9, 2021. The Central Conference of American Rabbis' 1895 *Union Prayer-Book for Jewish Worship* reflects the platform's principles. As with earlier Reform prayer books, this one too omits the part of the *Amidah* that refers to the Davidic Messiah. In place of resurrection, it too refers to God "implanting within us eternal life." See Central Conference of American Rabbis, *The Union Prayer-Book for Jewish Worship*, Part 1, 24, available at https://archive.org/details/sedertefilotyira01cent/page/24.

95. Stern, *Gates of Prayer*, 78–79, 42. The eighth option for services on Friday night retains the Hebrew for God giving life to the dead (256). The English translates this as God "whose gift is life."

96. Michael A. Meyer, "Building a Reform Platform," ReformJudaism.org, February 15, 2015, https://reformjudaism.org/blog/2015/02/26/building-reform -platform.

97. "A Statement of Principles for Reform Judaism," 1999, https://www.ccarnet .org/rabbinic-voice/platforms/article-statement-principles-reform -judaism/. The statement also includes the Hebrew for *tikkun olam*.

98. "Commentary on the Principles of Reform Judaism, October 27, 2004," https://www.ccarnet.org/rabbinic-voice/platforms/article-commentary -principles-reform-judaism/.

99. "Commentary on the Principles of Reform Judaism, October 27, 2004."

100. "Commentary on the Principles of Reform Judaism, October 27, 2004."

101. See Frishman, *Mishkan T'filah*, 246. For further contrast in the Reform movement's evolution on this subject, see the 1999 Pittsburgh Platform, and especially the commentary on it, https://www.ccarnet.org/rabbinic -voice/platforms/article-commentary-principles-reform-judaism/. Also see Abrams, "Continuity of Change in Jewish Liturgy."

102. Gellman, "Eternal Eden," 16, 18.

103. Alter. Midrashic sources tended to view this banquet as a victory celebration, where God forces Israel's enemies to drink the cup of retribution. See, for example, the *Sifre* on Deuteronomy, chapter 33, section 324.

104. Soloveitchik, *Emergence of Ethical Man*, 185.

105. Midrash on Psalms 116:8. See also PRE, 94, where the serpent in the Garden of Eden uses similar words to tempt Eve.

106. Harari, *Homo Deus*, 43, 25. Also see Tad Fried, "Silicon Valley's Quest to Live Forever," *New Yorker*, April 3, 2017.

107. Kurzweil, *Age of Spiritual Machines*, 129, 142, quoted in Delio, *Re-Enchanting the Earth*, 1843, Kindle.

108. Geraci, "Spiritual Robots," 235, quoted in Delio, *Re-Enchanting the Earth*, 1844, Kindle.

109. Elizabeth Svododa, "Cellular Life, Death and Everything in Between," *Quanta Magazine*, July 8, 2019, https://www.quantamagazine.org/cell-death -anastasis-and-resurrection-20190708/.

110. Heschel, "Death as a Homecoming," 71.

111. "60 Minutes/Vanity Fair Poll: The Afterlife," January 4, 2016, https://www .cbsnews.com/news/60-minutesvanity-fair-poll-the-afterlife/.

112. Segal, *Life after Death*, 124.

113. Steinberg, *Basic Judaism*, 159. 170. I have changed a few of Steinberg's words to make this passage less overbearingly male gendered. The translation of Jeremiah 31:17 has been changed to NJPS, and Isaiah 28:10 follows OJPS as per Steinberg, although others render Isaiah 28:10 very differently, for example, NJPS: "That same mutter upon mutter, murmur upon murmur, now here, now there." Of note: In Isaiah 28:13, where the same expression occurs as in 28:10, Rashi links the word for "line" (as in a builder's plumb line metaphorically assessing one's straightness, i.e., righteousness), *kav*, spelled *kof-vav*, with "hope": "they will hope, *yikvu* (*yud-kof-vav*) for light" (as in Job 3:9), but because they are sinful "behold there will be darkness."

8. ISRAEL

1. See BT *Ketubot* 111a; MRI, Va-y'hi Beshalach 1, vol. 1, 1:51, 173; Song of Songs Rabbah 2:20; and Ravitzky, "The Impact of the Three Oaths in Jewish History," in *Messianism, Zionism, and Religious Radicalism*, 211–34.

2. "Texts Concerning Zionism: Address by Max Nordau at the First Zionist Congress (August 29, 1897)," Jewish Virtual Library, https://www.jewishvirtuallibrary.org/address-by-max-nordau-at-the-first-zionist-congress.

3. Hess, *Rome and Jerusalem*, 145, available at https://play.google.com/books/reader?id=hmVOLme6eyQC&hl=en&pg=GBS.PA144.

4. Jeremiah 14:8 and 17:13 refer to God as the source of Israel's hope, *Mikveh Yisrael*.

5. The phrase *petach tikvah* appears in Hosea 2:17.

6. BILU is an acronym based on Isaiah 2:5: "Beit Ya'akov Lekhu Ve-Nelkha" (House of Jacob, come let us walk).

7. Troy, *Zionist Ideas*, 1634, Kindle.

8. There are disputes about when the poem was written. Historian Cecil Bloom leans toward 1878. See Bloom, "*Hatikvah*," 318, 320, 321.

9. The translation is mine and Matthew Goldstone's. Passages that appear in "Hatikvah," the anthem, are from the Government of Israel's official translation, "Hatikva—National Anthem of the State of Israel," https://knesset.gov.il/holidays/eng/hatikva_eng.htm. For the Hebrew of "Tikvatenu" and a different translation, see Dalia Marx, "Tikvatenu: The Poem that Inspired Israel's National Anthem, Hatikva," 2016, https://thetorah.com/tikvatenu-the-poem-that-inspired-israels-national-anthem-hatikva/, both sites in this note accessed June 10, 2021.

10. OJPS.

11. Quoted in Bloom, "*Hatikvah*," 327.

12. Ben-Yehuda, "Letter to *HaShahar* 1880," 161.

13. Fellman, *Revival of a Classical Tongue*, 24.

14. Ben-Yehuda's second wife, Chemdah, and son published the seventeenth and final volume in 1959, thirty-seven years after his death.

15. *Ha-Tzvi*, January 22, 1909, "Gymnazia Ivrit," 1, 2, https://www.nli.org.il/en/newspapers/hzv/1909/01/22/01/?&e=-------en-20--1--img-txIN%7ctxTI--------------1.

16. See, for example, BT *Sotah* 37a.

17. Sachar, *History of Israel*, 84.

18. Ben-Yehuda, *Dream Come True*, 105.

19. Ben-Yehuda, *Dream Come True*, 105.

20. Snyder, *Psychology of Hope*, 230–31, Kindle.

21. Herzl, *Complete Diaries*, February 1, 17, 1896, 287, 301, available at https://archive.org/stream/TheCompleteDiariesOfTheodorHerzl_201606/TheCompleteDiariesOfTheodorHerzlEngVolume1_OCR_djvu.txt.

22. Herzl, *Complete Diaries*, February 14–15, 1896, 299, 300.

23. Sachar, *History of Israel*, 44.

24. Reimer, *First Zionist Congress*, 92, Kindle.

25. Letter from Menachem Ussishkin to Ahad Ha'am, quoted in Brenner, *In Search of Israel*, 40, Kindle.

26. Herzl, "The Menorah," 203–6, available at https://herzlinstitute.org/en/theodor-herzl/the-menorah/.

27. Herzl, *Jewish State*, 49, 100.

28. Herzl, *Complete Diaries*, September 3, 1897, 581.

29. Quoted in Segev, *A State at Any Cost*, 44, Kindle.

30. Teveth, *Ben-Gurion*, 40.

31. Segev, *A State at Any Cost*, 81, Kindle.

32. Herzl, *Altneuland*, first page without number and 218. For the epigraph, the translation has been altered from "fairy-tale" to "dream," as is often done, and is carried over to the beginning of the epilogue. Subsequent references to "dream" follow the translation and the original German word, *Traum*.

33. "The Declaration of the Establishment of the State of Israel (May 14, 1948)," Jewish Virtual Library, https://www.jewishvirtuallibrary.org/the-declaration-of-the-establishment-of-the-state-of-israel.

34. Sapir, *Israeli Constitution*, 16. There are multiple explanations as to why a constitution was not adopted, including the motivation of Ben-Gurion's opposition. For an overview, see Strum, "Road Not Taken," 83–104.

35. See Amir Fuchs, "How Many Laws Were Struck Down by the Supreme Court in Israel," June 22, 2020, Israeli Democracy Institute, https://en.idi.org.il/articles/31874. Often called an overly activist court, between 1997 and 2019 the Israeli Supreme Court declared eighteen statutes unconstitutional. Comparatively, in that period the U.S. Supreme Court did the same for thirty-nine federal laws. For U.S. data, see Constitution Annotated, https://constitution.congress.gov/resources/unconstitutional-laws/, accessed July 11, 2021.

36. See Marissa Newman, "Begin Breaks Ranks to Oppose Jewish Nation-State Bill," *Times of Israel*, July 26, 2017, https://www.timesofisrael.com/begin-breaks-ranks-to-oppose-jewish-nation-state-bill/; "Israel's President: Nation-State Law Is 'Bad for Israel and Bad for the Jews,'" *Times of Israel*,

September 6, 2017, https://www.timesofisrael.com/president-nation-state
-law-bad-for-israel-and-bad-for-the-jews/. See also Uri Cohen, "Challenge
to Controversial Nation-State Law Reaches Israel's Supreme Court," theme-
dialine, December 22, 2020, https://themedialine.org/by-region/challenge
-to-controversial-nation-state-law-reaches-israels-supreme-court/.

37. Galnoor and Blander, *Handbook of Israel's Political System*, 51.

38. Rabin, *Rabin Memoirs*, 112.

39. Meir Kahane, "For a Jewish State, Annex and Expel," *New York Times*, July
18, 1983, https://www.nytimes.com/1983/07/18/opinion/for-a-jewish-state
-annex-and-expel.html.

40. Alexander, *Jewish Idea and Its Enemies*, 178.

41. Quoted in Eisenstadt, *Transformation of Israeli Society*, 548. For analyses of
political extremism and religious messianism in Israel, see Sprinzak, *Ascendance of Israel's Radical Right*; Held, "What Zvi Yehudah Kook Wrought,"
229–54.

42. "Address to the Knesset by Prime Minister Rabin Presenting His
Government—July 13, 1992," Israel Ministry of Foreign Affairs, https://
mfa.gov.il/mfa/foreignpolicy/mfadocuments/yearbook9/pages/1%20
%20address%20to%20the%20knesset%20by%20prime%20minister
%20rabin.aspx.

43. The earliest expression of the law appears in *Mishnah Sanhedrin* 8:7, c.
200 CE.

44. The first time "Hatikvah" was sung at a Zionist Congress was in 1901 at the
Fifth Congress. In 1933 it became the official Zionist anthem. In 1948 it was
sung when Israel declared its independence, but it was not made the official anthem of the state until 2004. That year it was added to the 1949 Flag
and Emblem Law, without much controversy. In 2018 its status as Israel's
national anthem was re-affirmed in the Basic Law: Israel as the Nation-State
of the Jewish People.

45. For more on this, see Seroussi, "Hatikvah," available at https://www.jewish
-music.huji.ac.il/he/node/22482.

46. Jewish Telegraphic Agency, "Hebrew University Will Skip 'Hatikvah' at Graduation to Avoid Offending Arab Students," *Forward*, May 18, 2017, https://
forward.com/fast-forward/372358/hebrew-university-will-not-play-israel-s
-national-anthem-at-graduation/.

47. "Rivlin: Rethink National Symbols, Anthem to Be More Inclusive for Arabs,"
Times of Israel, May 30, 2016, https://bit.ly/3eq37yf. Rivlin's suggestion was
not new. In 1967 some thought "'Hatikva' should simply be replaced by 'Jerusalem of Gold.'" See Segev, *1967*, 451, Kindle. In 1998 State Comptroller Mir-

iam Ben-Porat introduced legislation to modify "Hatikvah" to make it more inclusive of Israel's non-Jewish citizens. See Faier, *Organizations, Gender and the Culture of Palestinian Activism*, 228.

48. The Israel Democracy Institute, "Over Half of Jewish Israelis Support Annexation," Tamar Hermann and Or Anabi, Israeli Voice Index, May 10, 2020, https://en.idi.org.il/articles/31539. More broadly, 46 percent of Israelis as a whole express optimism about the future of Israeli democracy, as compared to 49 percent of Jews and 26 percent of Arab citizens of Israel.

49. Israeli Hope, https://israeli-hope.gov.il/, accessed June 11, 2021. Rivlin's focus on Israel's four state-supported school systems should not be taken as a complete picture of religious identification in Israel. For example, 8 percent of Israeli Jews identify as Reform, and 5 percent as Conservative. See the Jewish People Policy Institute's 2019 Annual Assessment, http://jppi.org.il/en/article/aa2019/#.YMNrAvlKiM8, accessed June 14, 2021. Additionally, about 2 percent of Israelis are Christian and 1.5 percent are Druze.

50. For this and other quotations from Rivlin's address, see "President Reuven Rivlin Address to the 15th Annual Herzliya Conference: 'Israeli Hope: Towards a New Israeli Order,'" June 7, 2015, https://israeli-hope.gov.il/sites/default/files/Herzliya%20Conf%20President%20SPEECH%20%2810%29%20new%20.pdf.

51. For more information about Israeli Hope, see https://www.israeli-hope.gov.il/, accessed June 14, 2021.

52. "President Rivlin addresses JFNA General Assembly in Los Angeles," November 14, 2017, http://embassies.gov.il/MFA/PressRoom/2017/Pages/President-Rivlin-addresses-JFNA-General-Assembly-14-November-2017.aspx.

53. Joe Bernard, "Bnei Brak Graffiti Calls Rivlin 'Nazi Apostate from Judaism,'" *Jerusalem Post*, October 25, 2017, https://www.jpost.com/Israel-News/Politics-And-Diplomacy/Graffiti-blasts-Rivlin-calls-Israeli-president-a-Nazi-convert-508356.

54. Mark Weiss, "Netanyahu's Likud Party Hits Back at President over Criticism," *Irish Times*, October 24, 2017, https://www.irishtimes.com/news/world/middle-east/netanyahu-s-likud-party-hits-back-at-israel-s-president-over-criticism-1.3267572.

55. Barak Ravid, "New Israeli Organization Aims to Be First Right-wing Palestinian Rights Watchdog," *Haaretz*, March 14, 2013, https://www.haaretz.com/.premium-rightists-want-to-safeguard-human-rights-too-1.5233945.

56. Hendel, *Sichot al Tikvah Yisraelit*, 9.

57. "A people that dwells alone," Num. 23:9; "A light unto the nations," Isa. 42:6, 49:6.

58. BT *Yoma* 9b.

59. Here's another example of such integration. In July 2019, for the first time, Bank Leumi, Israel's oldest bank, appointed Samer Haj-Yehia, an Arab, to serve as its chairman. See Michael Rochvarger and Tali Heruti-Sover, "In First, Arab Israeli Appointed Chairman of Board at Israel's Biggest Bank," *Haaretz*, July 2, 2019, https://www.haaretz.com/israel-news/.premium-in -first-arab-israeli-appointed-chairman-of-board-at-israel-s-biggest-bank-1 .7428366. And, in June 2021, Ra'am, an Arab party, was the first such party invited to serve in the government. In the 1950s the Arab Democratic List participated in ruling coalitions, but did not actually serve in the government. See "Parliamentary Groups," Knesset, https://www.knesset.gov.il /faction/eng/FactionPage_eng.asp?PG=85, accessed June 18, 2021.

60. For more on this economic development plan, see "Government Resolution 922 (GR-922): Five-Year Economic Development Plan for Arab Society 2016–2020," published by the Inter-Agency Taskforce on Israeli Arab Issues, https://www.iataskforce.org/sites/default/files/resource/resource-1976.pdf, accessed June 14, 2021. 1976.pdf. For a parallel government plan addressing the Negev Bedouin, see "Government Resolution 2397: Socio-Economic Development Plan for Negev Bedouin: 2017–2021," published by the Inter-Agency Taskforce on Israeli Arab Issues, March 3, 2017, https://www .iataskforce.org/sites/default/files/resource/resource-1500.pdf.

61. "Dr. Eilon Schwartz's Opening Remarks from the Shaharit Local Elections Conference," Shaharit, https://www.shaharit.org.il/dr-eilon-schwartzs -opening-remarks-from-the-local-elections-conference/?lang=en, accessed June 11, 2021.

62. Ephraim Urbach, one of the last century's greatest scholars on Rabbinic literature, argues that the famous debate about whether it would have better for the world not to have been created (BT *Eruvin* 13b) really pertains to the specific case about a person who studied Torah with no intention of observing it, or to other circumscribed sins: "The expression 'it were better for him not to have been created' in the aforementioned sources does not embody a pessimistic philosophy." See Urbach, *Sages*, 254.

63. "The Population of Ethiopian Origin in Israel: Selected Data," media release by Israel's Central Bureau of Statistics, November 11, 2020, https://www.cbs .gov.il/he/mediarelease/DocLib/2020/358/11_20_358e.pdf.

64. Gili Cohen, "Israeli Military to Scrap Preparatory Course for Soldiers of Ethiopian Background," *Haaretz*, November 13, 2015, https://www.haaretz .com/israel-news/.premium-idf-scraps-course-for-ethiopian-troops-1 .5420982.

65. Tamara Traubman, "Feminist Alice Shalvi Wins Israel's Top Prize for Lifetime Achievement," *Haaretz*, March 26, 2007, https://www.haaretz.com/1.4813047.

66. In a mid-1980s meeting with all ten of Israel's female members of parliament, Geula Cohen, a far-right-wing member of the parliament, suggested that IWN aim for what then seemed like a radical goal: women should comprise 30 percent of the Knesset. See Shalvi, *Never a Native*, 4930, Kindle.

67. For more on these struggles, see the chapter entitled "Israel Defense Forces" in Shalvi's *Never a Native*.

68. Tamar linked this expression to Yosef Haim Brenner, one of the early pioneers of modern Hebrew literature. He used the expression to describe his support of Zionism, which he affirmed despite certain doubts. Not in the context of hope, the expression also appears frequently in Rabbinic literature, as early as the Mishnah, c. 200 CE.

69. Buber, "Renewal of Judaism," 34–55.

70. OJPS.

71. "Rav Menachem Bombach Commemorates IDF Remembrance Day," https://www.youtube.com/watch?v=XsaJXHKF5Cg, accessed June 14, 2021.

72. For more on this issue, see "On Culture and Poverty in Haredi Society," Haredi Institute for Public Affairs, June 2017, https://machon.org.il/wp-content/uploads/2017/10/On-Culture-and-Poverty-in-Haredi-Society-Kaliner-Kasir-and-Tsachor-Shai-June-2016.pdf.

73. Rebecca Harvey, "Arab Bedouin Volunteer Center Receives Award for Excellence," *Coop News*, July 5, 2016, https://www.thenews.coop/107007/sector/community/arab-bedouin-volunteer-center-receives-award-excellence/.

74. For a list of Eran's publications, see https://www.eranhalperin.com/publications, accessed June 14, 2021. Most of these are available to read or download on this site. For anyone interested in research on the Israeli-Palestinian conflict and the role of hope, despair, fear, and so on, this is the place to go!

75. Goldberg et al., "Testing the Impact and Durability of a Group Malleability Intervention," 696–701.

76. Goldberg et al., "Making Intergroup Contact More Fruitful," 3–10.

77. "Have You Seen the Horizon Lately?," https://israel.co.il/.

78. For an overview of the reconciliation process, see Megan Specia, "How a Nation Reconciles after Genocide Killed Nearly a Million People," *New York Times*, April 25, 2017. For a deeper look, see "Rwanda Reconciliation Barometer," Republic of Rwanda National Unity and Reconciliation Commission, https://www.nurc.gov.rw/fileadmin/Documents/Others/Rwanda_Reconciliation_Barometer_2015.pdf, accessed June 11, 2021.

79. Lopez, *Making Hope Happen*, 213, Kindle. Futurist Jamais Cascio coined the term SEHI in his March 24, 2008, blog post, "Super-Empowered Hopeful Individuals," *Open the Future*, http://www.openthefuture.com/2008/03 /superempowered_hopeful_individ.html, accessed June 11, 2021.

80. Makom: The Jewish Agency for Israel Education Lab, https://web .archive.org/web/20191026194105/http://makomisrael.org/israeli-ngos/, accessed June 11, 2021.

9. JEWISH HUMOR

1. Lipman, *Laughter in Hell*, 10.

2. Paul Whitington, "From the Marx Brother to Seinfeld—How Jewish Comedy Has Dominated Hollywood," Independent.ie, February 29, 2020, https://www.independent.ie/entertainment/movies/from-the-marx -brothers-to-seinfeld-how-jewish-comedy-has-dominated-hollywood -38997386.html. The ubiquity of American Jewish comedians both reflects and contributes to the centrality of humor in American Jewish identity. In the Pew Research Center's 2013 "Portrait of Jewish Americans," 42 percent of respondents said "having a good sense of humor" was an essential part of what it means to be Jewish to them, placing "humor" between "caring about Israel" (43 percent) and "being part of a Jewish community" (28 percent). Pew Research Center, "A Portrait of Jewish Americans," October 1, 2013, 14, https://www.pewresearch.org/wp-content/uploads/sites/7/2013/10/jewish -american-full-report-for-web.pdf. By contrast, only 9 percent of Israeli Jews say that having a good sense of humor is an essential part of being Jewish. See Michael Lipka, "A Closer Look at Jewish Identity in Israel and the U.S.," Pew Research Center, March 16, 2016, https://www.pewresearch .org/fact-tank/2016/03/16/a-closer-look-at-jewish-identity-in-israel-and -the-u-s/. A 2020 study of Jewish millennials found 58 percent describe themselves as "funny," just behind the top item, "intellectually curious" (60 percent). See Atlantic75, "Unlocking the Future of Jewish Engagement," March 2020, 18, https://www.jewishdatabank.org/content/upload/bjdb /2018_Unlocking_Future_of_Jewish_Engagement_Final_Digital_Report _Mar_2020.pdf.

3. Sacks, *To Heal a Fractured World*, 186.

4. Vilaythong, "Humor and Hope," 79–89. For the study on humor and optimism, see Ford, McCreight, and Richardson, "Affective Style, Humor Styles and Happiness," 451–63, available at http://ejop.psychopen.eu/article/view /766/html.

5. Horowitz, "Effect of Positive Emotions on Health," 201.

6. From the catalogue of exhibit *Documenta 7*, Kassel, Germany, 1982. See also Phaidon Editors, *Art Is the Highest Form of Hope*.

7. Gimbel, *Isn't That Clever*, 3.

8. Snyder, *Psychology of Hope*, 1034–39, Kindle. Philosopher and professor of religion John D. Caputo comes to a somewhat similar conclusion: "A smile is a diminutive form of laughter, laughter with discretion, without disturbing anyone else with our outburst. The smile is a silent affirmation of life, a subtle embrace of life, a weak force strong enough to sustain life and give it hope. To smile when it is impossible to smile—what greater strength is there than that? . . . The smile gives us grounds for hope, albeit groundless grounds, for hoping against hope, for smiles can turn into frowns, and laughter into tears, which means that hope, an audacious hope, knows how to smile through our tears." See Caputo, *Hoping against Hope*, 40, 41, Kindle.

9. Cohen, *Jokes*, 29, Kindle.

10. Scioli and Biller, *Hope in the Age of Anxiety*, 5333, Kindle.

11. This volume is considered a landmark because it is the first comprehensive classification of psychological strengths—that is, positive psychology—as counterpoint to the weaknesses or pathologies addressed by most diagnostic manuals. This handbook lists strengths of transcendence as the last of the six strengths.

12. Peterson and Seligman, *Character Strengths and Virtues*, 519.

13. For Erikson on hope and basic trust, see *Childhood and Society*, 247–51, and "What Is Hope?" under Resources at choosinghope.net.

14. For more on peekaboo, see Fernald and O'Neill, "Peekaboo across Cultures"; Martin, *Psychology of Humor*, 230–34.

15. Berger, *Redeeming Laughter*, 211, 215. Brackets were added by this author to create a more gender-sensitive text.

16. Whedbee, *Bible and the Comic Vision*, 1904, 1905, Kindle. Also see Adele Berlin's comments about Esther as farce in Berlin and Brettler, *Jewish Study Bible*, 1623–24.

17. Barack Obama, author of *The Audacity of Hope*, knew something about humor as well. Many called him "the Comedian in Chief." See, for example, Timothy Egan, "A Farewell to the Comedian in Chief," *New York Times*, November 25, 2016.

18. Exodus Rabbah 43:6. The midrash is based on Exodus 32:11: "But Moses implored (*va'yichal*) YHWH his God, saying, 'Let not Your anger, YHWH, blaze forth against Your people, whom You delivered from the land of Egypt with Your great power and with a mighty hand.'"

19. Martin, *Psychology of Humor*, 6.

20. William Barrett, "The Promise and the Pale," *Commentary*, September 1, 1946, https://www.commentarymagazine.com/articles/the-promise-and-the -pale/. The Pale refers to the region in western Russia in which Jews were allowed to settle between 1791 and 1917. Jewish residents lived in extreme poverty and were subject to intermittent violence and harsh persecution.

21. This version of the story is a slight paraphrase of that found in Dresner, *World of a Hasidic Master*, 79, 80. The connection between God's *tefillin* and the verse from Chronicles is found in BT *Berakhot* 6a.

22. A number of writers on Jewish humor have commented on this. See, for example, Berger, *Genius of the Jewish Joke*, 32–35; Cohen, *Jokes*, 52, Kindle.

23. Based on Onkelos's Aramaic translation of the Bible, Rashi (on Gen. 17:17) distinguishes between Abraham's laughter, which he interprets as rejoicing, and Sarah's, described as sneering. For our purposes, the point is that Abraham and Sarah use the same Hebrew words when they speak of laughter. For a good treatment on humor and hope in the stories involving Isaac, see Kaminsky, "Humor and the Theology of Hope: Isaac as a Humorous Figure," 363–75.

24. Note a subtle incongruity: Sarah first refers to her aged husband, but in the subsequent verse when God paraphrases Sarah, God has her refer to her old age alone. Genesis Rabbah 48:18 explains: Had God reported Sarah's words accurately to Abraham, it could have resulted in marital strife. God therefore shades the truth. The midrash concludes, "Even scripture spoke untruthfully to preserve peace between Abraham and Sarah." God seems to understand how fragile the male ego can sometimes be; even the centenarian Abraham may take umbrage if his ninety-year-old wife impugns his virility. Anything to keep the peace.

25. Genesis Rabbah 48:19. The Hebrew involves a play on words. When referring to their ability to fashion locks and human beings, the smith and God say, *ani yakhol*, "I can." Affirming their capacity to make repairs, they conclude with an interrogative exclamation, *aini yakhol*, "I can't?!." "This I can do! That I can't?!" It sounds like the punch line of a Yiddish joke.

26. The term for the two parts of a lock, *kuplayot*, is ambiguous. Jastrow, 1338, indicates that the term can mean a padlock, which suggests the possibility that one of the two parts the man holds in his hand is the lock, and the other the key. The simile also echoes many biblical references to God's having shut fast the wombs of women unable to bear children. One such reference occurs just two verses before Sarah gives birth to Isaac.

27. Cohen, *Jokes*, 55, Kindle.

28. Wiesel, *Messengers of God*, 96–97, Kindle. Wiesel's reference to Isaac having been marked by the Holocaust reflects the fact that God tells Abraham

to offer up Isaac as an *olah*, a fully burnt offering (Gen. 22:2), and in Greek "holocaust" refers to precisely such an offering.

29. Ezrahi, "After Such Knowledge, What Laughter?," 306. For all its skepticism about when the Messiah will come, Judaism doesn't rule out the possibility. Others have viewed the concept of the Messiah as a promise that can never be fulfilled in the present. This second view prompted the French philosopher Maurice Blanchot to tell a joke about a man who meets the Messiah at the gates of the city and asks, "When will you come?" For a discussion of this, see Currie, *The Unexpected*, 91.

30. This appears in *Avot de Rabbi Natan*, a minor tractate of the Talmud, chap. 31, version B.

31. BT *Gittin* 56a and 56b relate the story of Ben Zakkai's escape from Jerusalem and encounter with Vespasian.

32. See chapter 7, note 53, p. 259.

33. *Encyclopedia Judaica*, 8:1164.

34. The epigram appears in many secondary sources. This version comes from Pinsker, *Schlemiel as Metaphor*, 6. For a slightly different version, see Dubnow, *History of the Jews*, 743.

35. Reik, *Jewish Wit*, 93.

36. Quoted in Pinsker, *Schlemiel as Metaphor*, 2.

37. Quoted in Epstein, *Treasury of Jewish Inspirational Stories*, 128.

38. Maimonides, *On the Regime of Health*, 84. For Maimonides' sense of humor, see Kraemer, *Maimonides*, 322, Kindle.

39. Recounted by Robert P. Imbelli, in "The Coming of the Son of Man," *Commonweal*, November 17, 2012, https://www.commonwealmagazine.org/coming-son-man.

40. Wisse, *Schlemiel as Modern Hero*, 117, 5.

41. Alter, "Jewish Humor and the Domestication of Myth," 26.

42. Howe, "Nature of Jewish Laughter," 21.

43. Cohen, *Jokes*, 91–93. I've condensed Cohen's original version.

44. Howe, "Nature of Jewish Laughter," 23.

45. Pinsker, *Schlemiel as Metaphor*, 178–79. When asked how he could possibly write his doctoral dissertation on the schlemiel, Pinkser told this joke.

46. Dante Alighieri, *Dante's Divine Comedy*, Hell, Canto 3, 13.

47. Quoted in Dournon, *Dictionnaire des Citations Françaises*.

48. Lipman, *Laughter in Hell*, 10.

49. Frankl, *Man's Search for Meaning*, 43.

50. Frankl, *Man's Search for Meaning*, 42.

51. Lipman includes the story of this play in a powerful chapter called "The Humor of Optimism." Lipman, *Laughter in Hell*, 71–73.

52. Howe, "Nature of Jewish Laughter," 17.

53. BT *Bava Metzi'a*, 59b.

54. BT *Avodah Zarah*, 3b.

55. For the material on Soloveitchik and Kaplan, see Daniel Feldman, "Does God Have a Sense of Humor," *Jewish Action*, May 23, 2013, https://www.ou.org /jewish_action/05/2013/does-god-have-a-sense-of-humor/.

56. Cox, *Feast of Fools*, 157.

57. Kishon, *Funniest Man in the World*, 145.

FINAL THOUGHTS

1. Luzzatto, *Otzrot Ramch"al, Drush B'inyan Ha-Kivui*, 246–47, HB 51264.

2. Wiesel, "A Meditation on Hope," last page, pages not numbered.

3. Yerushalmi, "Toward a History of Jewish Hope," 6277, Kindle.

4. Midrash *Lekach Tov* on Song of Songs 5:6. Also see Midrash *Lekach Tov* on Leviticus 22:33.

5. This verse follows OJPS.

6. This verse follows Alter.

7. Midrash *Lekach Tov* on Song of Songs 5:6.

8. Marcel, 53.

9. Snyder, *Psychology of Hope*, 3732–34, Kindle.

10. Cox, *Feast of Fools*, 157.

11. Kishon, "The Brilliant Career of Professor Honig," in *More of the Funniest Man in the World*, 131.

12. See Long and Carney, *A Hard-Fought Hope*.

13. As a meditation on the theological conundrum of innocent suffering, Job does not promote the solution advocated by Daniel, and later by most sages of Rabbinic Judaism: that the righteous will receive their due reward through resurrection and a blissful afterlife. Job hoped for vindication in this world, even if he wondered if he'd live to see it.

14. Marcel, *Tragic Wisdom and Beyond*, 143.

15. Matthew Choi, "Warnock Pledges to Be a Senator for All," politico.com, January 6, 2021, https://www.politico.com/news/2021/01/06/warnock-ahead -georgia-455289.

16. Genesis Rabbah 11:6.

17. Soloveitchik, *Halakhic Man*, 107.

18. Maimonides, *Mishneh Torah*, Laws of Repentance, 9:2, in MR, 83.

19. Amanda Gorman, "The Hill We Climb," *New York Times*, January 21, 2021.

20. Snyder, *Psychology of Hope*, 153–269, Kindle; and see "What Is Hope?" under Resources at choosinghope.net.

21. Alas, the scholarly literature on Judaism and hope remains painfully thin. A 2020 book edited by Charles van den Heuvel, *Historical and Multidisciplinary Perspectives on Hope*, with chapters on hope in ancient Greece and early Christianity, says very little about Judaism, although it does contain a wonderful chapter by psychologists Oded Adomi Leshem and Eran Halperin on hope as it relates to the Israeli-Palestinian conflict (179–96). The book can be downloaded at https://link.springer.com/book/10.1007%2F978-3-030 -46489-9.

22. Rycroft, "Steps to an Ecology of Hope," 4.

23. Marcel, 51.

24. Yitzchak Blazer, a leader of the nineteenth-century Musar movement, which concentrated on personal ethics and piety, wrote a commentary on Deuteronomy's injunction to "choose life." It begins: "For the love of life is in your hands. For God has opened before you a 'gateway of hope,' *petach tikvah* [Hosea 2:17]." See Salanter and Blazer, *Or Yisrael*, 16, HB 14564, BI.

25. Technically, the verb *l'kavot*, "to hope," does not exist in the form used in this expression, although it does for the verb *l'hikavot*, which means "to flow," "gather," or "form a body of liquid." Both verbs have identical roots, *kof-vav-hey*. Hebrew speakers familiar with the expression *chazak, chazak, v'nitchazek* understand the meaning of *kaveh, kaveh, v'nitkaveh* perfectly well.

Bibliography

Abrams, Judith Z. "The Continuity of Change in Jewish Liturgy." In *Platforms and Prayer Books: Theological and Liturgical Perspectives on Reform Judaism*, edited by Dana E. Kaplan, 119–28. New York: Rowman & Littlefield, 2002.

Albo, Joseph. *Sefer Ha-Ikkarim*. Philadelphia: The Jewish Publication Society of America, 1946.

Alexander, Edward. *The Jewish Idea and Its Enemies*. New York: Routledge, 1988.

Alford, C. Fred. *After the Holocaust: The Book of Job, Primo Levi, and the Path to Affliction*. Cambridge: Cambridge University Press, 2009.

Alighieri, Dante. *The Divine Comedy of Dante Alighieri*. New York: P. F. Collier, 1909.

Allan, Kathryn. *Metaphor and Metonymy: A Diachronic Approach*. New York: Wiley-Blackwell, 2009.

Al-Nakawa, Joseph. *Sefer Menorat ha-Ma'or*. New York: Bloch, 1843.

Alshekh, Moses. *Torat Moshe*. Belvedere: N.p. [1595?].

Alter, Robert. *The Hebrew Bible: A Translation with Commentary*. New York: W. W. Norton, 2018.

——— . "Jewish Humor and the Domestication of Myth." In *Jewish Wry*, edited by Sarah Blacher Cohen, 25–36. Detroit MI: Wayne State University Press, 1987.

Altmann, Alexander, ed. "Saadya Gaon: Book of Doctrines and Beliefs." In *Three Jewish Philosophers — Philo, Saadya Gaon, Jehuda Halevi*, 9–190. New York: Atheneum Books, 1969.

Anderson, Ben. "Becoming and Being Hopeful: Towards a Theory of Affect." *Environment and Planning D: Society and Space* 24 (October 2006): 732–52.

Arnow, David. *Creating Lively Passover Seders*. Woodstock VT: Jewish Lights, 2011.

——— . "Jacob's Hope for Salvation: The Extraordinary Career of Genesis 49:18." *Zeramim* 4, no. 3 (Spring/Summer 2020).

——— . "Reflections on Jonah and Yom Kippur." *Conservative Judaism* 54, no. 4 (2002): 33–48.

——— . "A Seder for Rosh Hashanah." *Sh'ma: A Journal of Jewish Ideas* 36, no. 623 (September 1, 2005): 14.

Artson, Bradley Shavit. *God of Becoming and Relationship: The Dynamic Nature of Process Theology*. Woodstock VT: Jewish Lights, 2013.

Auerbach, Erich. "Odysseus' Scar." In *Mimesis: The Representation of Reality in Western Literature*, 1–23. Princeton NJ: Princeton University Press, 1953.

Averill, James R., George Catlin, and Kyum K. Chon. *Rules of Hope*. New York: Springer-Verlag, 1990.

Babrius. *The Fables of Babrius in Two Parts*. London: Lockwood and Company, 1860.

Barmash, Pamela. "Out of the Mists of History." In *Exodus in the Jewish Experience*, edited by Pamela Barmash and W. David Nelson, 1–22. New York: Lexington Books, 2015.

Baumeister, Roy F., Ellen Bratslavsky, Catrin Finkenauer, Kathleen D. Voh. "Bad Is Stronger Than Good." *Review of General Psychology* 5 (2001): 323–70.

Beardslee, William A. *A House for Hope: A Study in Process and Biblical Thought*. Philadelphia: Westminster Press, 1972.

Ben Bezalel, Judah Loew (Maharal of Prague). *Gevurot Ha-Shem*. Lemberg: R. Miller, 1859.

Ben Pesach, Noah. *Toldot Noah*. Cracow: N.p., 1634.

Ben-Yehuda, Eliezer. *A Dream Come True*. New York: Routledge, 2018.

——— . "Letter to *HaShahar* 1880." In *The Zionist Idea*, edited by Arthur Hertzberg, 160–65. New York: Atheneum, 1981.

Benyosef, Simcha H. *Living the Kabbalah*. New York: Continuum Press, 1999.

Benzein, Eva, Astrid Norberg, Britt-Inger Savemans. "The Meaning of the Lived Experience of Hope in Patients with Cancer in Palliative Home Care." *Palliative Medicine* 15, no. 2 (March 2001): 117–26.

Berger, Arthur Asa. *The Genius of the Jewish Joke*. New Brunswick NJ: Transaction Publishers, 2006.

Berger, Benjamin L. "On the Book of Job, Justice, and the Precariousness of Criminal Law." *Law, Culture and the Humanities* 4 (2008): 98–118.

Berger, Peter. *Redeeming Laughter: The Comic Dimension of Human Experience*. New York: Walter de Gruyter, 1997.

Berlin, Adele, and Marc Zvi Brettler, eds. *The Jewish Study Bible*. New York: Oxford University Press, 2004.

Bier, Miriam J. *"Perhaps There Is Hope": Reading Lamentations as a Polyphony of Pain, Penitence, and Protest*. New York: Bloomsbury Publishing, 2015.

Birnbaum, David, and Martin S. Cohen, eds. *Tikkun Olam: Judaism, Humanism, and Transcendence*. New York: New Paradigm Matrix, 2015.

Birnbaum, Philip. *Daily Prayer Book*. New York: Hebrew Publishing Company, 1992.

Blackman, P. *Mishnayot*. London: Mishna Press, 1953.

Blech, Benjamin. "The Biblical Source for *Tikkun Olam*," in *Tikkun Olam: Judaism, Humanism & Transcendence*, edited by David Birnbaum and Martin S. Cohen. New York: New Paradigm Matrix, 2015.

Blenkinsopp, Joseph. *The Anchor Yale Bible: Isaiah 1–39*. New Haven CT: Yale University Press, 2000.

Blidstein, Gerald. "Tikkun Olam." In *Tikkun Olam: Social Responsibility in Jewish Thought and Law*, edited by David Shatz, Chaim I. Waxman, and Nathan J. Diament, 17–60. Northvale NJ: Jason Aronson, 1997.

Bloch, Ernst. *Atheism in Christianity*. New York: Herder and Herder, 1972.

——— . "Can Hope Be Disappointed?" In *Literary Essays*, translated by Andrew Joron, 339–45. Stanford CA: Stanford University Press, 1998.

——— . *The Principle of Hope*. 3 vols. Cambridge MA: MIT Press, 1995.

Bloom, Cecil. "*Hatikvah*—Imber, His Poem and a National Anthem." *Jewish Historical Studies* 32 (1990–92): 317–36.

Blumenthal, David R. "Despair and Hope in Post-Shoah Jewish Life." *Bridges: An Interdisciplinary Journal of Theology, Philosophy, History, and Science* 6, nos. 3/4 (1999): 1–18.

Bodoff, Lippman. *The Binding of Isaac, Religious Murders, & Kabbalah: Seeds of Jewish Extremism and Alienation?* New York: Devorah Publishing, 2005.

Boehm, Omri. *The Binding of Isaac: A Religious Model of Disobedience*. New York: Bloomsbury T&T Clark, 2007.

Bokser, Baruch M. *The Origins of the Seder*. New York: The Jewish Theological Seminary Press, 1984.

Bornsztain, Shmuel. *Shem MiShmuel*. Piotrkow: N.p., 1927–34.

Borowitz, Eugene B. "Hope Jewish and Hope Secular." In *The Future as the Presence of Shared Hope*, edited by Maryellen Muckenhirn, 84–111. London: Sheed and Ward, 1968.

Borowski, Oded. *Agriculture in Iron Age Israel*. Winona Lake IN: Eisenbrauns, 1987.

Botterweck, G. Johannes, ed. *Theological Dictionary of the Old Testament*. 12 vols. Grand Rapids MI: Eerdmans, 1974–2006.

Bovins, Luc. "The Value of Hope." *Philosophy and Phenomenological Research* 59, no. 3 (September 1999): 667–81.

Boyarin, Daniel. *Intertextuality and the Reading of Midrash*. Bloomington: Indiana University Press, 1994.

Boyatzis, Richard, and Annie McKee. *Resonant Leadership: Renewing Yourself and Connecting with Others through Mindfulness, Hope and Compassion*. Boston: Harvard Business School Press, 2005.

Brenner, Michael. *In Search of Israel.* Princeton NJ: Princeton University Press, 2018.

Broide, Simcha Mordechai Ziskind (Zissel). *Chokhmah u-Mussar.* Jerusalem: N.p., 1964.

Brothwell, Don R., and Patricia Brothwell. *Food in Antiquity: A Survey of the Diet of Early Peoples.* Baltimore MD: Johns Hopkins University Press, 1969.

Brown, Erica. *Inspired Jewish Leadership: Practical Approaches to Building Strong Communities.* Woodstock VT: Jewish Lights, 2015.

———. *Spiritual Boredom.* Woodstock VT: Jewish Lights, 2009.

Brown, Francis, et al., eds. *The Brown-Driver-Briggs Hebrew and English Lexicon.* Peabody MA: Hendrickson Publishers, 2004.

Brueggemann, Walter. *Hopeful Imagination: Prophetic Voices in Exile.* Philadelphia: Fortress Press, 1986.

———. *Hope within History.* Atlanta GA: John Knox Press, 1987.

———. *The Practice of Homefulness.* Eugene OR: Cascade Books, 2014.

———. *An Unsettling God: The Heart of the Hebrew Bible.* Minneapolis MN: Fortress Press, 2009.

Buber, Martin. "The Renewal of Judaism." In *On Judaism,* edited by Nahum Glatzer, 34–55. New York: Schocken Books, 1967.

Camus, Albert. *The Myth of Sisyphus and Other Essays.* New York: Random House, 1955.

Capps, Donald. *Agents of Hope: A Pastoral Psychology.* Eugene OR: Wipf and Stock, 1995.

Caputo, John D. *Hoping against Hope: Confessions of a Postmodern Pilgrim.* Minneapolis MN: Fortress Press, 2015.

Cardin, Nina. *Tears of Sorrow, Seeds of Hope: A Jewish Spiritual Companion for Infertility and Pregnancy Loss.* Woodstock VT: Jewish Lights, 1999.

Carmy, Shalom. "'We Were Slaves to Pharaoh in Egypt': Literary-Theological Notes on Slavery and Empathy." *Hebraic Political Studies* 4, no. 4 (Fall 2009): 367–80.

Cassuto, U. *Commentary on the Book of Genesis.* Vol. 2, *From Noah to Abraham.* Jerusalem: Magnes Press, 1992.

Central Conference of American Rabbis, ed. *The Union Prayer-Book for Jewish Worship.* Cincinnati OH: Central Conference of American Rabbis, 1895.

Chazan, Robert. "The Blois Incident of 1171: A Study in Jewish Intercommunal Organization." *Proceedings of the American Academy for Jewish Research* 36 (1968): 13–31.

Cohen, Jeffrey M. *Prayer and Penitence: A Commentary to the High Holy Day Machzor.* Northvale NJ: Jason Aronson, 1994.

Cohen, Martin, Tamar Elad-Appelbaum, and Gordon Tucker. *Pirkei Avot Lev Shalem: The Wisdom of Our Sages*. New York: The Rabbinical Assembly, 2018.

Cohen, Sarah Blacher. *Jewish Wry: Essays on Jewish Humor*. Detroit MI: Wayne State University Press, 1987.

Cohen, Shaye J. D. *From the Maccabees to the Mishnah*. 3rd ed. Louisville KY: Westminster John Knox Press, 2014.

Cohen, Ted. *Jokes: Philosophical Thoughts on Joking Matters*. Chicago: University of Chicago Press, 1999.

Coleridge, Samuel Taylor. *The Works of Samuel Taylor Coleridge: Prose and Verse*. Philadelphia: Crissy & Markley, 1853.

Collins, John J. *Apocalypticism in the Dead Sea Scrolls*. London: Routledge, 2004.

———. *Introduction to the Hebrew Bible*. Minneapolis MN: Fortress Press, 2014.

Cooper, Levi. "The Assimilation of Tikkun Olam." *Jewish Political Studies Review* 25, nos. 3–4 (November 2013): 10–42.

Cordovero, Moses. *Tomar Devorah*. New York: Shoshanim, 1960.

Cox, Harvey. *The Feast of Fools*. Cambridge MA: Harvard University Press, 1969.

Currie, Mark. *The Unexpected: Narrative Temporality and the Philosophy of Surprise*. Edinburgh: Edinburgh University Press, 2013.

Day, J. P. "The Anatomy of Hope and Fear." *Mind* 79 (July 1970): 369–84.

———. "Hope." *American Philosophical Quarterly* 6, no. 2 (April 1969): 89–102.

———. "More about Hope and Fear." *Ethical Theory and Moral Practice* 1, no. 1 (March 1998): 121–23.

Delio, Ilia. *Re-Enchanting the Earth: Why AI Needs Religion*. Maryknoll NY: Orbis Books, 2020.

Dorff, Elliot N. "'Heal Us, Lord, and We Shall Be Healed': The Role of Hope and Destiny in Jewish Bioethics." *Judaism* 48, no. 2 (1999): 149–65.

Dournon, Jean-Yves, ed. *Dictionnaire des Citations Françaises*. Paris: Archipoche, 2011.

Dresner, Samuel H. *The World of a Hasidic Master*. New York: Shapolsky Publishers, 1986.

Dubnow, Simon. *History of the Jews: From the Roman Empire to the Early Medieval Period*. Translated by Moshe Spiegel. Plainsboro Township NJ: Thomas Yoseloff, 1968.

Eibach, Richard P., Lisa K. Libby, Thomas D. Gilovich. "When Change in the Self Is Mistaken for Change in the World." *Journal of Personality and Social Psychology* 84, no. 5 (2003): 917–31.

Einhorn, David. *Olat Tamid: Book of Prayers for Israelitish Congregation*. Baltimore MD: Deutsch Golderman, 1872.

Eisenstadt, S. N. *The Transformation of Israeli Society*. London: Weidenfeld & Nicolson, 1985.

Eisenstein, Judah David. *Otzar Midrashim: A Library of Two Hundred Minor Midrashim*. 2 vols. (Hebrew) New York: J. D. Eisenstein, 1915.

Eliade, Mircea. *The Sacred and the Profane*. New York: Harcourt, Brace, Jovanovich, 1959.

Eliott, Jaklin A., ed. *Interdisciplinary Perspectives on Hope*. Hauppauge NY: Nova Science Publishers, 2005.

Elledge, C. D. *Resurrection of the Dead in Early Judaism: 200 BCE–CE 200*. New York: Oxford University Press, 2017.

Ellenson, David. "The Israelitischer Gebetbücher of Abraham Geiger and Manuel Joel: A Study in Nineteenth-Century German-Jewish Communal Liturgy." *Leo Baeck Institute Yearbook* 44 (1999): 143–64.

———. "The Mannheimer Prayerbooks and Modern Central European Communal Liturgies: A Representative Comparison of Mid-Nineteenth Century Works." In *Between Tradition and Culture: The Dialectics of Modern Jewish Religion and Identity*. Atlanta GA: Scholar's Press, 1994.

Emet Ve-Emunah: Statement of Principles of Conservative Judaism. New York: The Rabbinical Assembly and United Synagogue of Conservative Judaism, 1988.

Encyclopaedia Judaica. Jerusalem: Keter Publishing, 1972.

Epstein, Lawrence Jeffrey. *A Treasury of Jewish Inspirational Stories*. Northvale NJ: Jason Aronson, 1993.

Erikson, Eric H. *Childhood and Society*. 2nd ed. New York: W. W. Norton, 1963.

Erikson, Eric H., and Joan M. Erikson. *The Life Cycle Completed*. Extended Version. New York: W. W. Norton, 1998.

Etz Hayim: Torah and Commentary. New York: The Rabbinical Assembly and the United Synagogue of Conservative Judaism, 1999.

Ezrahi, Sidra DeKoven. "After Such Knowledge, What Laughter?" *Yale Journal of Criticism* 14, no. 1 (2001): 287–313.

Fackenheim, Emil L. "The 614th Commandment" and "The Commanding Voice of Auschwitz." In *Wrestling with God: Jewish Theological Responses during and after the Holocaust*, edited by Steven T. Katz, Shlomo Biderman, and Gershon Greenberg, 432–38. New York: Oxford University Press, 2007.

———. "The Commandment to Hope: A Response to Contemporary Jewish Experience." In *The Future of Hope: Essays by Bloch, Fackenheim, Moltmann, Metz, and Capps*, edited by Walter H. Capps, 68–91. Philadelphia: Fortress Press, 1970.

———. *To Mend the World*. Bloomington: Indiana University Press, 1982.

———. *What Is Judaism?* Syracuse NY: Syracuse University Press, 1987.

Faier, Elizabeth. *Organizations, Gender and the Culture of Palestinian Activism in Haifa, Israel.* Abingdon, England: Routledge, 2012.

Faierstein, Morris M. *Jewish Customs of Kabbalistic Origin.* Boston: Academic Studies Press, 2013.

Falk, Marcia. *The Book of Blessings.* New York: CCAR Press, 2017.

Fanon, Frantz. *The Wretched of the Earth.* New York: Grove Press, 1968.

Feld, Edward. *Joy, Despair, and Hope: Reading Psalms.* Eugene OR: Cascade Books, 2013.

Fellman, Jack. *The Revival of a Classical Tongue: Eliezer Ben Yehuda and the Modern Hebrew Language.* Berlin: Walter de Gruyter, 2011.

Fernald, Anne, and Daniela K. O'Neill. "Peekaboo across Cultures: How Mothers and Infants Play with Voices, Faces, and Expectations." In *Parent-Child Play: Descriptions and Implications,* edited by Kevin MacDonald, 259–85. Albany: State University of New York Press, 1993.

Figueres, Christiana, and Tom Rivett-Carnac. *The Future We Choose.* New York: Knopf, 2020.

Fine, Lawrence. *Physician of the Soul, Healer of the Cosmos: Isaac Luria and His Kabbalistic Fellowship.* Stanford CA: Stanford University Press, 2003.

Finkelstein, Louis. "The Development of the Amidah." *Jewish Quarterly Review* 16, no. 1 (July 1925): 1–43.

Fisch, Harold, ed. *The Jerusalem Bible.* Jerusalem: Koren Publishers, 1986.

Fishbane, Michael. *The JPS Bible Commentary: Haftarot.* Philadelphia: The Jewish Publication Society, 2002.

———. *Text and Texture: Close Readings of Selected Biblical Texts.* New York: Schocken Books, 1979.

Ford, Thomas E., Katelyn A. McCreight, and Kyle Richardson. "Affective Style, Humor Styles and Happiness." *Europe's Journal of Psychology* 10, no. 3, (2014): 451–63.

Fowler, James W. *Stages of Faith.* New York: HarperCollins, 1981.

Fox, Michael V. *The JPS Commentary: Ecclesiastes.* Philadelphia: The Jewish Publication Society, 2004.

———. *A Time to Tear Down and a Time to Build Up: A Rereading of Ecclesiastes.* Eugene OR: Wipf and Stock, 2010.

Frankl, Viktor E. *Man's Search for Meaning.* Boston: Beacon Press, 2014. Originally published 1946.

Frantz, Nadine Pence, and Mary T. Stimming. *Hope Deferred: Heart-Healing Reflections on Reproductive Loss.* Eugene OR: Wipf and Stock, 2010.

Friedlander, Gerald. *Pirke de Rabbi Eliezer.* New York: Sepher-Hermon Press, 1981.

Frishman, Elyse D., ed. *Mishkan T'filah: A Reform Siddur.* New York: Central Conference of American Rabbis, 2007.

Fromm, Erich. *The Revolution of Hope: Toward a Humanized Technology*. New York: Harper and Row, 1968.

Gallagher, Matthew W., and Shane J. Lopez, eds. *The Oxford Handbook of Hope*. New York: Oxford University Press, 2018.

Galnoor, Itzhak, and Dana Blander. *The Handbook of Israel's Political System*. Cambridge: Cambridge University Press, 2018.

Gellman, Jerome I. *The Fear, the Trembling and the Fire: Kierkegaard and Hasidic Masters on the Binding of Isaac*. Lanham MD: University Press of America, 1994.

Gellman, Marc. "The Eternal Eden." *Reform Judaism* (Summer 1998): 16, 18.

Geraci, Robert M. "Spiritual Robots: Religion and Our Scientific View of the Natural World." *Theology and Science* 4, no. 3 (2006): 229–46.

Gersonides (Levi ben Gershom) *Commentary on the Torah*. Venice: N.p., 1547.

Gillham, Jane E. *The Science of Optimism & Hope: Research Essays in Honor of Martin P. Seligman*. Philadelphia: Templeton Foundation Press, 2000.

Gillman, Neil. *The Death of Death: Resurrection and Immortality in Jewish Thought*. Woodstock VT: Jewish Lights, 1997.

Gimbel, Steven. *Isn't That Clever: A Philosophical Account of Humor and Comedy*. Abingdon, England: Taylor & Francis, 2017.

Ginzberg, Louis. *Legends of the Jews*. 7 vols. Philadelphia: The Jewish Publication Society of America, 1969.

Glazer, Nahum N. "The God of Job and the God of Abraham: Some Talmudic-Midrashic Interpretations of the Book of Job." *Bulletin of the Institute for Jewish Studies* 2 (1974): 41–45.

Godfrey, Joseph J. *A Philosophy of Human Hope*. Leiden: Martinus Nijhoff Publishers, 1987.

Goldberg, Michael. *Jews and Christians: Getting Our Stories Straight*. Philadelphia: Trinity International Press, 1991.

Goldenberg, Amit, Smadar Cohen-Chen, J. Parker Goyer, Carol S. Dweck, James J. Gross, and Eran Halperin. "Testing the Impact and Durability of a Group Malleability Intervention in the Context of the Israeli-Palestinian Conflict." *Proceedings of the National Academy of Sciences of the United States of America* 115, no. 4. (January 23, 2018): 696–701.

Goldenberg, Amit, Kinneret Endevelt, Shira Ran, Carol S. Dweck, James J. Gross, and Eran Halperin. "Making Intergroup Contact More Fruitful: Enhancing Cooperation between Palestinian and Jewish-Israeli Adolescents by Fostering Beliefs about Group Malleability." *Social Psychology and Personality Science* 8, no. 1 (2017): 3–10.

Gordis, Robert. *Koheleth — The Man and His World*. New York: Schocken Books, 1968.

Graetz, Heinrich. *History of the Jews*. 6 vols. Philadelphia: The Jewish Publication Society of America, 1902.

Greeley, Andrew M., and Michael Hout. "Americans' Increasing Belief in Life after Death: Religious Competition and Acculturation." *American Sociological Review* 64 (1999): 813–35.

Green, Arthur. *Devotion and Commandment: The Faith of Abraham in the Hasidic Imagination*. Cincinnati OH: Hebrew Union College Press, 1989.

——— , ed. *The Language of Truth: The Torah Commentary of the Sefat Emet, Rabbi Yehudah Leib Alter of Ger*. Philadelphia: The Jewish Publication Society, 1998.

——— . *Radical Judaism: Rethinking God and Tradition*. New Haven CT: Yale University Press, 2010.

Green, Tamara M. *The City of the Moon God: Religious Traditions of Harran*. Leiden: Brill, 1997.

Greenberg, Irving. *For the Sake of Heaven and Earth: The New Encounter between Judaism and Christianity*. Philadelphia: The Jewish Publication Society, 2004.

——— . *The Jewish Way: Living the Holidays*. New York: Summit Books, 1988.

——— . "Voluntary Covenant." In *Wrestling with God: Jewish Theological Responses during and after the Holocaust*, edited by Steven T. Katz, Shlomo Biderman, and Gershon Greenberg, 543–55. New York: Oxford University Press, 2007.

Greenberg, Moshe. *The Anchor Bible: Ezekiel, 1–20*. New York: Doubleday, 1983.

——— . *The Anchor Bible: Ezekiel, 21–37*. New York: Doubleday, 1997.

Greenstein, Edward L. *Job: A New Translation*. New Haven CT: Yale University Press, 2019.

Groopman, Jerome. *The Anatomy of Hope*. New York: Random House, 2003.

Habel, Norman C. *The Book of Job: A Commentary*. Philadelphia: Westminster Press, 1985.

Halbertal, Moshe. "Job, the Mourner." In *The Book of Job: Aesthetics, Ethics, Hermeneutics*, edited by Leora Batnitzky and Ilana Pardes, 37–46. Berlin: Walter de Gruyter, 2015.

Hammer, Reuven. "The Impact of the Exodus on Halakhah (Jewish Law)." In *Exodus in the Jewish Experience*, edited by Pamela Barmash and W. David Nelson, 111–46. Lanham MD: Lexington Books, 2015.

Harari, Yuval Noah. *Homo Deus: A Brief History of Tomorrow*. New York: Harper Perennial, 2017.

Harlow, Jules. "Remember." In *Siddur Shalem for Shabbat and Festivals*, 387. New York: The Rabbinical Assembly and United Synagogue of Conservative Judaism, 1998.

Hartman, David. *From Defender to Critic: The Search for a New Jewish Self*. Woodstock VT: Jewish Lights Publishing, 2012.

———. "Sinai and Exodus: Two Grounds for Hope in Jewish Tradition." *Journal of Religious Studies* 14, no. 3 (September 1978): 373–87.

Hauptman, Judith. *Rereading the Rabbis: A Woman's Voice*. Boulder CO: Westview Press, 1998.

Head, Lesley. *Hope and Grief in the Anthropocene: Re-Conceptualising Human-Nature Relations*. New York: Routledge, 2016.

Held, Shai. "What Zvi Yehudah Kook Wrought: The Theopolitical Radicalization of Religious Zionism." In *Rethinking the Messianic Idea in Judaism*, edited by Michael L. Morgan, 229–54. South Bend: Indiana University Press, 2014.

Helmreich, William B. *Against All Odds: Holocaust Survivors and the Successful Lives They Made in America*. New York: Simon & Schuster, 1992.

Hendel, Ronald. *Remembering Abraham: Culture, Memory, and History in the Hebrew Bible*. New York: Oxford University Press, 2005.

Hendel, Yoaz, and Reuven Rivlin. *Sichot al Tikvah Yisraelit* (Frank conversations about Israeli hope). Rishon LeZion, Israel: Miskal—Yedioth Books and Chemed Books, 2018.

Herman, Arthur. *The Idea of Decline in Western History*. New York: Free Press, 1997.

Herring, Basil. *Joseph Ibn Kaspi's Gevia' Kesef: A Study in Medieval Jewish Philosophic Commentary*. New York: KTAV, 1982.

Herth, Kaye A., and John R. Cutcliffe. "The Concept of Hope in Nursing 3: Hope and Palliative Care Nursing." *British Journal of Nursing* 11, no. 14 (July–Aug. 2002): 977–83.

Herzl, Theodor. *Altneuland*. Haifa: Haifa Publishing Company, 1960.

———. *The Complete Diaries*. New York: Herzl Press, 1960.

———. *The Jewish State*. New York: Herzl Press, 1970.

———. "The Menorah." Translated by Harry Zohn. In *Zionist Writings: Essays and Addresses*, 1:203–6. New York: Herzl Press, 1973.

Heschel, Abraham Joshua. *Between God and Man*, edited by Fritz A. Rothschild. New York: Free Press, 1959.

———. "Death as a Homecoming." In *Jewish Reflections on Death*, edited by Jack Reimer, 58–74. New York: Schocken Books, 1974.

———. *The Insecurity of Freedom*. Philadelphia: The Jewish Publication Society of America, 1966.

———. *Israel: An Echo of Eternity*. Woodstock VT: Jewish Lights, 2003.

———. *Man's Quest for God*. Santa Fe NM: Aurora Press, 1998.

———. *Moral Grandeur and Spiritual Audacity*. Edited by Susannah Heschel. New York: Farrar, Straus, and Giroux, 1996.

———. *The Prophets*. Philadelphia: The Jewish Publication Society of America, 1962.

Hesiod. "Works and Days." In *The Homeric Hymns and Homerica*, translated by Hugh G. Evelyn-White, 2–63. New York: Macmillan, 1914.

Hess, Moses. *Rome and Jerusalem: A Study in Jewish Nationalism*. New York: Bloch Publishing Company, 1918.

Hirsch, Samson Raphael. *The Hirsch Chumash*. New York: Judaica Press, 1989.

Hoffman, Jeffrey. "The Image of the Other in Jewish Interpretations of *Alenu*." *Studies in Jewish-Christian Relations* 10, no. 1 (2015): 1–41.

Hoffman, Lawrence A., ed. *My People's Prayer Book: The Amidah*. Woodstock VT: Jewish Lights, 2013.

———, ed. *My People's Prayer Book: Birkhot Hashachar*. Woodstock VT: Jewish Lights, 2001.

———, ed. *My People's Prayer Book: Tachanun and Concluding Prayers*. Woodstock VT: Jewish Lights Publishing, 1997.

Hoffman, Yair. *A Blemished Perfection: The Book of Job in Context*. Sheffield, England: Sheffield Academic Press, 1996.

Horowitz, Sala. "Effect of Positive Emotions on Health: Hope and Humor." *Alternative and Complementary Therapies* 15, no. 4 (August 2009): 196–202.

Hottinger, Johann Heinrich. *Smegma Orientale: Sordibus Barbarismi, Contemtui*. Heidelberg: Adriani Wyngaerden, 1658.

Howe, Irving. "The Nature of Jewish Laughter." In *Jewish Wry*, edited by Sarah Blacher Cohen, 16–24. Detroit MI: Wayne State University Press, 1987.

Hutner, Isaac. "Holocaust." In *Wrestling with God: Jewish Theological Responses during and after the Holocaust*, edited by Steven T. Katz, Shlomo Biderman, and Gershon Greenberg, 557–64. New York: Oxford University Press, 2007.

Ibn Chaviv, Yaakov. *Ein Yaakov: The Ethical and Inspirational Teachings of the Talmud*. Translated by Abraham Yaakov Finkel. Northvale NJ: Jason Aronson, 1999.

Ibn Ezra, Moshe. *Shirei ha-Chol*. Edited by Chaim Brody. Berlin: Schocken Books, 1935.

Ibn Gabirol, Solomon. *Choice of Pearls*. London: Trubner & Co., 1859.

———. *Keter Malkhut*. Shkloŭ: N.p., 1785.

Idel, Moshe. *Messianic Mystics*. New Haven CT: Yale University Press, 1998.

Janzen, Gerald J. *At the Scent of Water: The Ground of Hope in the Book of Job*. Grand Rapids MI: Eerdmans, 2009.

Jastrow, Marcus. *Dictionary of the Targumim, Talmud Babli, Yerushalmi and Midrashic Literature*. New York: Judaica Press, 1996.

Jenson, Robert W., and Eugene B. Korn. *Covenant and Hope: Christian and Jewish Reflections*. Grand Rapids MI: Eerdmans, 2012.

Jonas, Hans. "The Concept of God after Auschwitz: A Jewish Voice." In *Wrestling with God: Jewish Theological Responses during and after the Holocaust*, edited by

Steven T. Katz, Shlomo Biderman, and Gershon Greenberg, 628–36. New York: Oxford University Press, 2007.

Josephus, Flavius. *Jewish Antiquities* and *War of the Jews* in *The Complete Works of Josephus*. Nashville TN: Thomas Nelson, 1998.

Joyce, Paul M. "'Even if Noah, Daniel, and Job Were in It . . .' (Ezekiel 14:14): The Case of Job and Ezekiel." In *Reading Job Intertextually*, edited by Katharine Dell and Will Kynes, 118–28. New York: Bloomsbury, 2013.

Kaminsky, Joel S. "Humor and the Theology of Hope: Isaac as a Humorous Figure." *Interpretation* 54, no. 4 (October 2000): 363–75.

Kant, Immanuel. *The Critique of Pure Reason*. Digireads.com Publishing, 2018. Originally published 1781.

Kaplan, Kalman J., and Matthew B. Schwartz. *A Psychology of Hope: A Biblical Response to Tragedy and Suicide*. Grand Rapids MI: Eerdmans, 1993.

Kaplan, Mordecai M. *The Future of the American Jew*. New York: The Reconstructionist Press, 1981.

——— . *Judaism without Supernaturalism*. New York: The Reconstructionist Press, 1967.

——— . *The Meaning of God in Modern Jewish Religion*. Detroit MI: Wayne State University Press, 1994.

Keckley, Elizabeth. *Behind the Scenes*. New York: G. W. Carleton, 1868.

Kehati, Pinhas. *Mishnah*. Jerusalem: Eliner Library, 1994.

Kessler, Edward. "Reasoning with Violent Scripture: With a Little Help From Job." *Journal of Scriptural Reasoning* 4, no. 1 (2004).

Kierkegaard, Søren. *The Sickness unto Death: A Christian Psychological Exposition for Upbuilding and Awakening*. Princeton NJ: Princeton University Press, 1980.

——— . *Works of Love*. Princeton NJ: Princeton University Press, 1995.

Kimelman, Reuven. "The Messiah of the *Amidah*: A Study in Comparative Messianism." *Journal of Biblical Literature* 116, no. 2 (Summer 1997): 313–20.

Kishon, Ephraim. *The Funniest Man in the World*. New York: Shapolsky Publishers, 1989.

——— . *More of the Funniest Man in the World*. New York: Shapolsky Publishers, 1989.

Kol HaNeshamah for Sabbath and Festivals. Elkins Park PA: The Reconstructionist Press, 2002.

Kook, Abraham Isaac. "Orot Ha-Teshuvah." In *Rabbi Kook's Philosophy of Repentance: A Translation of Orot Ha-Teshuvah*, by Alter B. Z. Metzger, 25–113. New York: Yeshiva University Press, 1968.

Kraemer, Joel L. *Maimonides: The Life and World of One of Civilization's Greatest Minds*. New York: Doubleday, 2008.

Krasner, Jonathan. "The Place of Tikkun Olam in American Jewish Life." *Jewish Political Studies Review* 40, nos. 3–4 (November 2014): 1–34.

Kübler-Ross, Elisabeth, and David Kessler. *On Grief and Grieving: Finding the Meaning of Grief through the Five Stages of Loss*. New York: Simon & Schuster, 2005.

Kummerow, David. "Job Hopeful or Hopeless? The Significance of *Gam* in Job 16:19 and Job's Changing Conception of Death." *Journal of Hebrew Scriptures* 5 (December 2005): 1–40.

Kurzweil, Ray. *The Age of Spiritual Machines: When Computers Exceed Human Intelligence*. New York: Penguin Books, 2000.

Kushner, Harold. *When Bad Things Happen to Good People*. New York: Avon Books, 1983.

Kushner, Lawrence. *God Was in This Place and I, I Did Not Know: Finding Self, Spirituality and Ultimate Meaning*. Woodstock VT: Jewish Lights, 1991.

Kwan, Simon S. M. "'Hope'—The Pastoral Theology of Hope and Positive Psychology." *International Journal of Practical Theology* 14, no. 1 (2010): 47–67.

Lamm, Maurice. *The Power of Hope*. New York: Rawson Associates, 1995.

Lauterbach, Jacob Z. *Mekilta de-Rabbi Ishmael*. Philadelphia: Jewish Publication Society of America, 1949.

——— . "Tashlik." In *Rabbinic Essays*, 299–436. Cincinnati OH: Hebrew Union College Press, 1951.

Laytner, Anson. *Arguing with God: A Jewish Tradition*. Northvale NJ: Jason Aronson, 1990.

Lear, Jonathan. *Radical Hope: Ethics in the Face of Cultural Devastation*. Cambridge MA: Harvard University Press, 2006.

Legge, James. *The Chinese Classics: The Works of Mencius*. Oxford: Clarendon Press, 1895.

Leiner, Mordechai Joseph. *Mei ha-Shiloach*. New York: Sentry Press, 1984.

Lerner, Akiba J. *Redemptive Hope: From the Age of Enlightenment to the Age of Obama*. New York: Fordham University Press, 2015.

Levenson, Jon D. *Resurrection and the Restoration of Israel: The Ultimate Victory of the God of Life*. New Haven CT: Yale University Press, 2006.

Levi, Primo. *The Search for Roots: A Personal Anthology*. Chicago: Ivan R. Dee, 2002.

Levinas, Emmanuel. *Nine Talmudic Readings*. Bloomington: Indiana University Press, 1990.

Levine, Robert N. *There Is No Messiah and You're It*. Woodstock VT: Jewish Lights, 2005.

Lichtheim, Miriam. *Ancient Egyptian Literature: The New Kingdom*. Berkeley: University of California Press, 2006.

Lipman, Steve. *Laughter in Hell: The Use of Humor during the Holocaust*. Northvale NJ: Jason Aronson, 1991.

Long, William R., and Glandion W. Carney. *A Hard-Fought Hope: Journeying with Job through Mystery*. Nashville TN: Upper Room Books, 2004.

Lopez, Shane J. *Making Hope Happen: Create the Future You Want for Yourself and Others*. New York: Atria Books, 2013.

Lorberbaum, Menachem. "'Tikkun olam' al pi ha-rambam: Iyun be-takhliyot ha-halakhah." *Tarbitz* 64 (Tishrei-Kislev 1995): 65–82.

Lubarsky, Sandra B., and David Ray Griffin. *Jewish Theology and Process Thought*. Albany: State University of New York Press, 1996.

Luzzatto, Chaim Moshe (Ramch"al). *"Drush B'inyan Ha-Kivui."* In *Otzrot Ramch"al*, 246–47. B'nei B'rak: Chaim Friedlander, 1986.

Lynch, William F. *Images of Hope: Imagination as Healer of the Hopeless*. Notre Dame IN: University of Notre Dame Press, 1974.

Maimonides, Moses. *Book of Judges*. Translated by Abraham Hershman. New Haven CT: Yale University Press, 1949.

——— . *The Guide of the Perplexed*. Translated by Shlomo Pines. Chicago: University of Chicago Press, 1963.

——— . *A Maimonides Reader*. Edited by Isadore Twersky. New York: Behrman House, 1972.

——— . *On the Regime of Health*. Leiden: Brill, 2019.

Marcel, Gabriel. *Being and Having*. Westminster, England: Dacre Press, 1949.

——— . "Sketch of a Phenomenology and a Metaphysic of Hope." In *Homo Viator: Introduction to a Metaphysics of Hope*, 29–67. New York: Harper and Brothers, 1962.

——— . *Tragic Wisdom and Beyond*. Evanston IL: Northwestern University Press, 1973.

Margalit, Avishai. *The Ethics of Memory*. Cambridge MA: Harvard University Press, 2002.

Marmur, Michael. "Lifeline to the Future." *Reform Judaism* (Summer 2009): 51–52.

Martin, Adrienne. *How We Hope: A Moral Psychology*. Princeton NJ: Princeton University Press.

Martin, Rod A. *The Psychology of Humor: An Integrative Approach*. Burlington MA: Elsevier, 2007.

McDonald, Janette, and Andrea M. Stephenson. *The Resilience of Hope*. New York: Brill, 2010.

McGreer, Victoria. "The Art of Good Hope." *Annals of the American Academy of Political and Social Science* 592, no. 1 (March 2004): 100–127.

——— . "Trust, Hope and Empowerment." *Australasian Journal of Philosophy* 876, no. 2 (June 2008): 237–54.

Meirav, Ariel. "The Nature of Hope." *Ratio* n.s., 22, no. 2 (June 2009): 216–33.

Menninger, Karl. "Hope." *American Journal of Psychiatry* 116, no. 6 (December 1959): 481–91.

Meshel, Naphtali. "Whose Job Is This? Dramatic Irony and *Double Entendre* in the Book of Job." In *The Book of Job: Aesthetics, Ethics, Hermeneutics*, edited by Leora Batnitzky and Ilana Pardes, 47–76. Berlin: Walter de Gruyter, 2015.

Miles, Jack. *God: A Biography*. New York: Vintage Books, 1995.

Mintz, Alan. *Ḥurban: Responses to Catastrophe in Hebrew Literature*. Syracuse NY: Syracuse University Press, 1996.

Mirkin, Moshe A. *Midrash Rabbah*. Tel Aviv: Yavne, 1986.

Mittleman, Alan. *Hope in a Democratic Age*. New York: Oxford University Press, 2009.

Moellin, Jacob. *Sefer Maharil*. Warsaw: N.p., 1875.

Moltmann, Jürgen. *In the End—The Beginning: The Life of Hope*. Translated by Margaret Kohl. Minneapolis MN: Fortress Press, 2004.

——— . *Theology of Hope*. Minneapolis MN: Fortress Press, 1993.

Morson, Caryl, and Gary Saul. *Mikhail Bakhtin: Creation of a Prosaics*. Palo Alto CA: Stanford University Press, 1990.

Muffs, Yochanan. *The Personhood of God: Biblical Theology, Human Faith and the Divine Image*. Woodstock VT: Jewish Lights, 2005.

Musschenga, Bert. "Is There a Problem with False Hope?" *Journal of Medical Philosophy* 44, no. 4 (July 2019): 423–41.

Muyskens, James L. *The Sufficiency of Hope: The Conceptual Foundations of Religion*. Philadelphia: Temple University Press, 1979.

Nebenzahl, Avigdor. *Thoughts for Rosh Hashanah*. Jerusalem: Feldheim Publishers, 1997.

Neher, André. *L'Exil de la parole: Du silence biblique au silence d'Auschwitz*. Paris: Editions du Seuil, 1970.

Nelson, W. David. *Mekhilta de-Rabbi Shimon bar Yochai*. Philadelphia: The Jewish Publication Society, 2006.

Nesse, Randolph M. "The Evolution of Hope and Despair." *Social Science Research* 66, no. 2 (Summer 1999): 429–49.

Neusner, Jacob. *Messiah in Context: Israel's History and Destiny in Formative Judaism*. Lanham MD: University Press of America, 1984.

——— . *The Mishnah: A New Translation*. New Haven CT: Yale University Press, 1988.

——— . *The Tosefta*. Peabody MA: Hendrickson Publishers, 2002.

Newsom, Carole A. *The Book of Job: A Contest of Moral Imaginations*. New York: Oxford University Press, 2003.

Nietzsche, Friedrich. *The Gay Science*. Mineola NY: Dover Publications, 2006.

NJPS. *TANAKH: The Holy Scriptures*. 2nd ed. Philadelphia: The Jewish Publication Society, 1999.

Nulman, Macy. *The Encyclopedia of Jewish Prayer*. Northvale NJ: Jason Aronson, 1993.

OJPS. *The Holy Scriptures, Tanakh: 1917 Edition*. Philadelphia: The Jewish Publication Society of America, 1917.

O'Hara, Dennis. *Hope in Counselling and Psychotherapy*. Los Angeles: Sage, 2013.

Ochs, Vanessa L. *The Passover Haggadah: A Biography*. Princeton NJ: Princeton University Press, 2020.

Ojala, Maria. "Hope and Climate Change: The Importance of Hope for Environmental Engagement among Young People." *Environmental Education Research* 18, no. 5 (October 2012): 625–42.

Oppenheim, Michael. "Irving Greenberg and Jewish Dialectic of Hope." *Judaism* 49, no. 2 (Spring 2000): 189–203.

Panofsky, Dora, and Erwin Panofsky. *Pandora's Box: The Changing Aspects of a Mythical Symbol*. New York: Pantheon Books, 1956.

Parker-Oliver, Debra. "Redefining Hope for the Terminally Ill." *American Journal of Hospice and Palliative Care* 19, no. 2 (March/April 2002): 115–20.

Pattison, Natalie A. "Hope against Hope in Cancer at the End of Life." *Journal of Religious Health* 50, no. 3 (2011): 731–42.

Peli, Pinchas H. *On Repentance in the Thought and Oral Discourses of Rabbi Joseph B. Soloveitchik*. Jerusalem: Orot Press, 1980.

Peretz, Michael Ben Yosef. *Otzar Piskei Ha-Siddur*. Jerusalem: Mekhon Ben Yisachar, 1997.

Peterson, Christopher, and Martin E. P. Seligman, eds. *Character Strengths and Virtues: A Handbook and Classification*. New York: American Psychological Association and Oxford University Press, 2004.

Pettit, Phillip. "Hope and Its Place in Mind." *Annals of the American Academy of Political and Social Science* 592 (March 2004): 152–65.

Petuchowski, Jakob J. "'Immortality: Yes; Resurrection: No!' Nineteenth-Century Judaism Struggles with a Traditional Belief." *Proceedings of the American Academy for Jewish Research* 50 (1983): 133–47.

Phaidon Editors. *Art Is the Highest Form of Hope & Other Quotes by Artists*. New York: Phaidon, 2016.

Phillipson, David. *The Reform Movement in Judaism*. New York: Macmillan, 1907.

Philo. *On the Embassy to Gaius*, in *The Works of Philo: Complete and Unabridged*. Peabody MA: Hendrikson Publishers, 1993.

Pinker, Steven. *The Better Angels of Our Nature: Why Violence Has Declined*. New York: Penguin Press, 2012.

——— . "The Psychology of Pessimism." *Cato's Letter* 13, no. 1 (Winter 2015): 1–5.

Pinsker, Sanford. *The Schlemiel as Metaphor*. Carbondale: Southern Illinois University Press, 1991.

Pope, Marvin H. *The Anchor Bible: Job*. Garden City NY: Doubleday, 1965.

Propp, William H. C. *The Anchor Bible: Exodus 1–18* and *Exodus 19–40*. New York: Doubleday, 1999 and 2006.

Provan, Iain William. *Lamentations*. Grand Rapids MI: Eerdmans, 1991.

Pruyser, Paul. "Maintaining Hope in Adversity." *Bulletin of the Menninger Clinic* 51, no. 5 (September 1987): 463–74.

——— . "Phenomenology and Dynamics of Hoping." *Journal for the Scientific Study of Religion* 3 (Autumn 1963): 86–96.

Rabin, Yitzhak. *The Rabin Memoirs*. Boston: Little Brown, 1979.

Raphael, Simcha Paull. *Jewish Views of the Afterlife*. Northvale NJ: Jason Aronson, 1996.

Ravitzky, Aviezer. *Messianism, Zionism, and Religious Radicalism*. Chicago: University of Chicago Press, 1996.

Reik, Theodore. *Jewish Wit*. New York: Gamut Press, 1962.

Reimer, Michael J., ed. *The First Zionist Congress*. Albany: State University of New York Press, 2019.

Reiss, H. S., ed. *Kant: Political Writings*. Cambridge: Cambridge University Press, 1991.

Ridley, Matt. *The Rational Optimist: How Prosperity Evolves*. New York: Harper Perennial, 2010.

Rittner, Carol, ed. *Elie Wiesel: Between Memory and Hope*. New York: New York University Press, 1991.

Rorty, Richard. *Philosophy and Social Hope*. New York: Penguin Books, 1999.

Rosenthal, Gilbert. "*Tikkun ha-Olam*: The Metamorphosis of a Concept." *Journal of Religion* 85, no. 2 (April 2005): 214–40.

Roskies, David G. *The Literature of Destruction*. Philadelphia: The Jewish Publication Society, 1989.

Rosner, Fred. *Moses Maimonides' Treatise on Resurrection*. Northvale NJ: Jason Aronson 1997.

Rubenstein, Richard L. *After Auschwitz: Radical Theology and Contemporary Judaism*. New York: Bobbs-Merrill, 1966.

Rudavsky, Joseph. *To Live with Hope, to Die with Dignity: Spiritual Resistance in the Ghettos and Camps*. Northvale NJ: Jason Aronson, 1997.

Rycroft, Charles. "Steps to an Ecology of Hope." In *The Sources of Hope*, edited by Ross Fitzgerald, 3–23. Ruschcutters Bay, Australia: Pergamon Press, 1979.

Sabbath and Festival Prayer Book. New York: The Rabbinical Assembly and The United Synagogue of Conservative Judaism, 1946.

Sachar, Howard M. *A History of Israel: From the Rise of Zionism to Our Time*. New York: Knopf, 1982.

Sacks, Jonathan. *Future Tense: Jews, Judaism, and Israel in the Twenty-first Century*. New York: Knopf Doubleday, 2009.

———. *The Politics of Hope*. New York: Vintage Books, 2000.

———. *To Heal a Fractured World: The Ethics of Responsibility*. New York: Knopf Doubleday, 2007.

Sagi, Avi. "The Meaning of the 'Akedah' in Israeli Culture and Jewish Tradition." *Israel Studies* 3, no. 1 (Spring 1998): 45–60.

Salanter, Israel (Israel ben Ze'ev Wolf Lipkin), and Yitzchak Blazer. *Or Yisrael*. Jerusalem: N.p. 1971.

Saldarini, Anthony J. *Pharisees, Scribes and Sadducees in Palestinian Society*. Grand Rapids MI: Eerdmans, 2001.

Samely, Alexander. *Rabbinic Interpretation of Scripture in the Mishnah*. New York: Oxford University Press, 2002.

Samuel, Maurice. *In Praise of Yiddish*. Spokane WA: Cowles Publishing, 1971.

Sapir, Gideon. *The Israeli Constitution: From Evolution to Revolution*. New York: Oxford University Press, 2018.

Sarna, Nahum M. *Understanding Genesis: The World of the Bible in Light of History*. New York: Schocken Books, 1970.

Schachtel, Ernest G. *Metamorphosis: New Light on the Conflict of Human Development and the Psychology of Creativity*. New York: Basic Books, 1959.

Scheindlin, Raymond P. *The Book of Job*. New York: W. W. Norton, 1998.

Scherman, Nosson, ed. *Artscroll Tanach*. New York: Mesorah Publications, 1996.

———, ed. *The Complete Artscroll Siddur: Nusach Sefard*. New York: Mesorah Publications, 1985.

Schnall, Eliezer, Mark Schiffman, and Aaron Cherniak. "Virtues That Transcend: Positive Psychology in Jewish Texts and Tradition." In *Religion and Spirituality across Cultures*, edited by Chu Kim-Prieto, 21–45. New York: Springer, 2014.

Scholem, Gershom. *Major Trends in Jewish Mysticism*. New York: Schocken Books, 1946.

———. *The Messianic Idea in Judaism*. New York: Schocken Books, 1971.

———. *Sabbatai Ṣevi: The Mystical Messiah*. Princeton NJ: Princeton University Press, 1973.

Schwartz, Seth. *The Ancient Jews from Alexander to Muhammad*. Cambridge: Cambridge University Press, 2014.

Scioli, Anthony, and Henry B. Biller. *Hope in the Age of Anxiety*. New York: Oxford University Press, 2009.

Seeskin, Kenneth. "Maimonides and the Idea of a Deflationary Messiah." In *Rethinking the Messianic Idea in Judaism*, edited by Michael L. Morgan, 27–50. South Bend: Indiana University Press, 2014.

Segal, Alan F. *Life after Death: A History of the Afterlife in Western Religion*. New York: Doubleday, 2004.

Segal, Benjamin F. "Where Liturgy and Bible Meet: Psalm 27, for the Time of Repentance." *Conservative Judaism* 54, no. 4 (Summer 2002): 58–62.

Segev, Tom. *1967: Israel, the War, and the Year That Transformed the Middle East*. New York: Henry Holt, 2007.

——— . *A State at Any Cost: The Life of David Ben-Gurion*. New York: Farrar, Straus and Giroux, 2019.

Seow, C. L. *The Anchor Yale Bible: Ecclesiastes*. New Haven CT: Yale University Press, 1997.

——— . *Job 1–21: Interpretation and Commentary*. Grand Rapids MI: Eerdmans, 2013.

Seroussi, Edwin. "Hatikvah: Conceptions, Receptions and Reflections." *Yuval Online* 9 (2015).

Setzer, Claudia. "Resurrection of the Dead as Symbol and Strategy." *Journal of the Academy of Religion* 69, no. 1 (March 2001): 65–101.

Shade, Patrick. *Habits of Hope: A Pragmatic Theory*. Nashville TN: Vanderbilt University Press, 2001.

Schäfer, Peter. "Rabbi Aqiva and Bar Kokhba." In *Approaches to Ancient Judaism*, vol. 2 (Brown Judaic Studies 9), edited by William Scott Green, 113–30. Chico CA: Scholars Press, 1978.

Shalvi, Alice. *Never a Native*. London: Halban, 2018.

"Sh'ma: Inside Hope." *Sh'ma: A Journal of Jewish Responsibility* 34, no. 612 (June 2004/Tammuz 5764): 1–16.

"Sh'ma on Health, Healing, Suffering, and Hope." *Sh'ma: A Journal of Jewish Responsibility* 41, no. 681 (June 2011/Sivan 5771): 1–51.

Siddur Sim Shalom for Weekdays. New York: The Rabbinical Assembly and The United Synagogue of Conservative Judaism, 2002.

Silver, Abba Hillel. *The History of Messianic Speculation in Israel*. Whitefish MT: Kessinger Publishing, 1927.

Silver, Daniel Jeremy. "The Resurrection Debate." In *Moses Maimonides' Treatise On Resurrection*, edited by Fred Rosner, 71–102. Northvale NJ: Jason Aronson 1997.

Sneed, Mark R. *The Politics of Pessimism in Ecclesiastes*. Atlanta GA: Society of Biblical Literature, 2012.

Snyder, C. R. *Handbook of Hope: Theory, Measures, & Applications*. San Diego: Academic Press, 2000.

———. "Hope Theory: Rainbows in the Mind." *Psychological Inquiry* 13, no.4 (2002): 249–75.

———. *The Psychology of Hope: You Can Get There from Here*. New York: Free Press, 1994.

Snyder, C. R., C. Harris, J. R. Anderson, S. A Holleran, L. M. Irving, and S. T. Sigmon. "Adult Hope Scale (AHS)." *Journal of Personality and Social Psychology*, 60 (1991): 570–85.

Snyder, C. R., Kevin L. Rand, Elisa A. King, David B. Feldman, and Julia T. Woodward. "'False' Hope." *Journal of Clinical Psychology* 58, no. 9 (September 2002): 1007–8.

Snyder, C. R., David R. Sigmon, and David B. Feldman. "Hope for the Sacred and Vice Versa: Positive Goal-Directed Thinking and Religion." *Psychological Inquiry* 13 no. 3 (2002): 234–38.

Solnit, Rebecca. *Hope in the Dark*. Chicago: Haymarket Books, 2004.

Soloveitchik, Joseph B. *The Emergence of Ethical Man*. New York: KTAV Publishing, 2005.

———. *Halakhic Man*. Philadelphia: The Jewish Publication Society of America, 1983.

———. "Kol Dodi Dofek: It Is the Voice of My Beloved That Knocketh." In *Theological and Halakhic Reflections on the Holocaust*, edited by Bernhard H. Rosenberg, 51–117. Hoboken NJ: KTAV, 1992.

———. *The Lonely Man of Faith*. New York: Three Leaves Press, 2006.

———. "Redemption, Prayer, Talmud Torah." *Tradition* 17, no. 2 (Spring 1978): 55–72.

Soncino Talmud. New York: Judaica Press, 1973. CD-ROM.

Spiegel, Shalom. *The Last Trial*. Woodstock VT: Jewish Lights Publishing, 1993.

Spira, Tzvi Elimelech of Dinov. *Bnei Yissakhar*. Jerusalem: N.p., 1983.

Sprinzak, Ehud. *The Ascendance of Israel's Radical Right*. New York: Oxford University Press, 1991.

Starr, Zachary Alan. *Toward a History of Jewish Thought: The Soul, Resurrection, and the Afterlife*. Eugene OR: Wipf and Stock, 2020.

Stein, David E. S., ed. *The Contemporary Torah: A Gender-Sensitive Adaptation of the JPS Translation*. Philadelphia: The Jewish Publication Society, 2006.

Steinberg, Milton. *Basic Judaism*. New York: Harcourt Brace, 1947.

Steinmetz, Devora. "Miriam in Rabbinic Midrash." *Prooftexts* 8, no. 1 (January 1988): 35–65.

Stern, Chaim, ed. *Gates of Prayer: The New Union Prayer Book*. New York: Central Conference of American Rabbis, 1975.

Stotland, Ezra. *The Psychology of Hope*. San Francisco: Jossey-Bass, 1969.

Strum, Philippa. "The Road Not Taken: Constitutional Non-Decision Making in 1948–1950 and Its Impact on Civil Liberties in the Israeli Political Culture." In *Israel: The First Decade of Independence*, edited by S. Ilan Troen and Noah Lucas, 83–104. Albany: State University of New York Press, 1995.

Sullivan, Mark D. "Hope and Hopelessness at the End of Life." *American Journal of Geriatric Psychiatry* 11, no. 4 (July–August 2003): 393–405.

Swartz, Michael D. "'Alay Le-shabbeah: A Liturgical Prayer in Ma'aseh Merkabah." *Jewish Quarterly Review* 87, nos. 2–3 (October 1986–January 1987): 179–90.

Tehillas HaShem: Nusach Ha'Ari z"l. Brooklyn NY: Kehot Publication Society, 1993.

Teikhthal, Issakhar Solomon. *Mishneh Sakhir*. Jerusalem: Keren R"am, 2009.

Tennen, Howard, Glenn Affleck, and Ruth Tennen. "Clipped Feathers: The Theory and Measurement of Hope." *Psychological Inquiry* 13, no. 4 (2002): 311–17.

Teveth, Shabtai. *Ben-Gurion: The Burning Ground 1886–1948*. Boston: Houghton Mifflin, 1987.

Tirer, Chaim. *Baer Mayim Chayim*. Jerusalem: N.p., 1991.

Townsend, John T. *Midrash Tanḥuma*. Vols. 1–3. Jersey City NJ: KTAV, 1989, 1997, 2003.

Troy, Gil. *The Zionist Ideas: Visions for the Jewish Homeland — Then, Now, Tomorrow*. Philadelphia: The Jewish Publication Society, 2018.

Tucker, Ericka. "Hope, Hate and Indignation: Spinoza on Political Emotion in the Trump Era." In *Trump and Political Philosophy*, edited by M. A. Sable and A. J. Torres, 131–58. New York: Springer, 2018.

Tucker, Gordon. *Torah for Its Intended Purpose*. New York: KTAV Publishing, 2014.

Twersky, Amos, and Daniel Kahneman. "Availability: A Heuristic for Judging Frequency and Probability." *Cognitive Psychology* 5, no. 2 (September 1973): 207–32.

Urbach, Ephriam E. *The Sages*. Cambridge MA: Harvard University Press, 1995.

van den Heuvel, Steven C., ed. *Historical and Multidisciplinary Perspectives on Hope*. Cham, Switzerland: Springer, 2020.

van Hooft, Stan. *Hope*. London: Routledge, 2011.

van Loon, Hanneke. *Metaphors in the Discussion on Suffering in Job 3-31: Visions of Hope and Consolation*. Boston: Brill, 2018.

Van Praag, Herman M. "The Downfall of King Saul: The Neurobiological Consequences of Losing Hope." *Judaism* 35 no. 4 (1986): 414–28.

van Ruiten, Jacques. "Abraham, Job and the Book of Jubilees: The Intertextual Relationship of Genesis 22:1–19, Job 1:1–2:13 and Jubilees 17:15–18:19." In *The Sacrifice of Isaac: The Aqedah and Its Interpreters*, edited by Ed Noort and Eibert Tigchelaar, 58–85. Leiden: Brill, 2002.

Verdenius, W. J. "A 'Hopeless' Line in Hesiod: 'Works and Days' 96." *Mnemosyne*, 4th Series, 24, fasc. 3 (1971): 225–31.

Vermes, Geza. *The Resurrection: History and Myth*. New York: Random House, 2008.

Vilaythong, Alexander P., Randolph C. Arnau, David H. Rosen, and Nathan Mascaro. "Humor and Hope: Can Humor Increase Hope?" *Humor* 16, no. 1 (2003): 79–89.

Vital, Chayim. *Pri Etz Chayim*. Dubrovnow: N.p., 1804.

Wear, Andrew. *Solved: How Other Countries Cracked the World's Biggest Problems (and We Can Too)*. London: Oneworld Publications, 2020.

Whedbee, J. William. *The Bible and the Comic Vision*. Cambridge: Cambridge University Press, 1998.

Wienstock, Moshe Yair. *The Siddur of the Geonim, the Kabbalists, and the Hasidim*. Jerusalem: Shraga Weinfeld, 1971.

Wiesel, Elie. "A Meditation on Hope: The Inaugural May Smith Lecture on Post-Holocaust Christian/Jewish Dialogue." Florida Atlantic University, March 10, 2003.

——— . *Messengers of God: A True Story of Angelic Presence and the Return*. New York: Simon & Schuster, 1985.

——— . "Nobel Lecture: Hope, Despair and Memory." December 11, 1986. https://www.nobelprize.org/prizes/peace/1986/wiesel/lecture/.

Wilson, Lindsay. "Realistic Hope or Imaginative Exploration? The Identity of Job's Arbiter." *Pacifica* 9 (October 1996): 243–52.

Wise, Isaac Mayer, ed. *Minhag America: The Daily Prayers for American Israelites*. Cincinnati OH: Bloch and Co., 1872.

Wisse, Ruth. *The Schlemiel as a Modern Hero*. Chicago: University of Chicago Press, 1971.

Wouk, Herman. *This Is My God*. New York: Doubleday, 1959.

Yerushalmi, Yosef Hayim. *Haggadah and History: A Panorama in Facsimile of Five Centuries of the Printed Haggadah*. Philadelphia: The Jewish Publication Society of America, 1975.

——— . "Toward a History of Jewish Hope." In *The Faith of Fallen Jews: Yosef Hayim Yerushalmi and the Writing of Jewish History*, edited by David N. Myers and Alexander Kaye, 299–317. Waltham MA: Brandeis University Press, 2014.

——— . *Zakhor: Jewish History and Jewish Memory*. Seattle: University of Washington Press, 1982.

Yuval, Israel J. "All Israel Have a Portion in the World to Come." In *Redefining First-Century Jewish and Christian Identities: Essay in Honor of Ed Parish Sanders*, edited by Fabian E. Udoh, 114–38. Notre Dame IN: University of Notre Dame Press, 2008.

——— . *Two Nations in Your Womb: Perceptions of Jews and Christians in Late Antiquity and the Middle Ages*. Berkeley: University of California Press, 2006.

Zimmerli, Walter. *Man and His Hope in the Old Testament*. London: SCM Press, 1971.

Zommers, Zinta, and Keith Alverson, eds. *Resilience: The Science of Adaptation to Climate Change*. Amsterdam: Elsevier, 2018.

Zornberg, Aviva. *The Beginning of Desire: Reflections on Genesis*. New York: Doubleday, 1995.

——— . *Moses: A Human Life*. New Haven CT: Yale University Press, 2016.

——— . *The Particulars of Rapture: Reflections on the Exodus*. New York: Doubleday, 2001.

Zuckerman, Bruce. "Two Examples of Editorial Modification in 11QtgJob." In *Biblical and Near Eastern Studies: Essays in Honor of William Sanford LaSor*, edited by Gary A. Tuttle, 269–75. Grand Rapids MI: Eerdmans, 1978.

Subject Index

Abraham, 47–60; and the *Akedah*, 53–60, 84, 238n23; and children, 52–53; and circumcision, 32–33; constancy of, 56–57; and faith, 47; and Hagar, 58–60; and hope, 47–49, 77; and humor, 201–2, 271n23; and Job, 116, 241n41; and movement, 57–58; and Nehemiah's prayer, 86; and prayer, 239n36; and Sarah, 47, 49–60, 271n24; and *shalom*, 89; and Sodom and Gomorrah, 17, 50–52, 77, 95, 238n23; and *teshuvah* (repentance), 17; and theodicy, 95; and trials, 49–50, 217; and uncertainty, 55–56

Abulafia, Meir, 147

activism, 192–93

Acts (book of), 137

adulterous unions, 25–28

afterlife, 128, 136–37, 144–55, 216, 255nn4–5, 273n13

agency in Job, 114

Agents of Hope (Capps), 111

agricultural settlements. *See* Petach Tikvah

AI (Artificial Intelligence), 153

AJEEC-NISPED (Arab-Jewish Center for Empowerment, Equality, and Cooperation/Negev Institute for Strategies of Peace and Economic Development), 190

AJWS (American Jewish World Service), 40–41

Akedah (Binding of Isaac), 53–60, 84, 202, 238n23, 243–44n5

"The Akedah" (ben Jacob of Bonn), 53

Akiva, Rabbi, 30, 33, 76, 142, 203

Alatawna, Lina, 187–89

Albaz, Kher, 189–91

Albo, Joseph, 13, 77

Aleichem, Sholem, 200

Aleinu prayer, 29–34, 45

al-Fayumi, Saadia ben Yosef. *See* Gaon, Saadia

Alford, C. Fred, 116

Alighieri, Dante, 208

Allen, Woody, 128

Alshekh, Moses, 88–89

Alter, Robert, 205

Alter, Yehudah Leib, 57

ambiguity of hope, 117–19

American Jewish World Service (AJWS), 40–41

American Judaism, 39–41, 128

Amidah (standing prayer), xx, 6, 87–90, 139–40, 143–44, 246n23

Amir, Yigal, 170

Ammi, Rav, 92

antisemitism, 6, 15, 30, 161, 244n5

anti-supernaturalism, 63–64

Arab citizens of Israel, 169, 171, 177, 190–91

Arab-Jewish Center for Empower-
　ment, Equality, and Cooperation/
　Negev Institute for Strategies of
　Peace and Economic Development
　(AJEEC-NISPED), 190
Armani, Amran, 187–89
articles of faith (Reform, nineteenth
　century), 149
Artificial Intelligence (AI), 153
Artson, Bradley Shavit, xxi, 226nn8–9
Ashkenazic Jewry and customs, 30,
　213, 228n30, 232n23, 244n5
Atah Hu YHWH Eloheinu ("You Are
　YHWH Our God"), 85
Auerbach, Erich, 54
availability heuristic, 43–44
avenger/advocate in Job, 123–24
Aviner, Shlomo, 144
Avot (*Amidah*, opening blessing), 88
Azulai, Chaim Yosef David, 51

Babylonian exile, 15, 67, 86, 91, 92, 93,
　101, 130, 134, 156, 245n14
Babylonian Talmud, 6, 11, 33, 36, 71–73,
　74–75, 95, 108, 124, 141, 144, 210–11
Bachya ben Asher, 15
Bakhtin, Mikhail, 253n62
Balaam, 229n51
Balfour Declaration, 164–65
Bar Kokhba, 41–42, 142, 156, 203,
　235n62
Basel, Switzerland, 162
basic trust, 71, 122–23, 198
Bedouin communities (Israel), 187–90
Beitar Illit, 184–87
Beit Midrash for Israeli Rabbis, 184
Ben-Eli, Michael, 187
ben Eliezer, Tuvia, 213–14
ben Gershom, Levi (Gersonides), 58

Ben-Gurion, David, 164–66
ben Jacob of Bonn, Ephraim, 53
ben Kosiba, Shimon. *See* Bar Kokhba
Ben-Porat, Miriam, 265–66n47
Ben-Yehuda, Eliezer, 159–61
Benyosef, Simcha H., 38
ben Zakkai, Yochanan, 143, 203
Berditchever. *See* Yitzchak, Levi
Berger, Benjamin L., 105
Berger, Peter, 198–99
Bergson, Henri, 50
"Berl Debates the Jesuit Priest"
　(Cohen), 206–7
Bernard, Tristan, 208
best self, 2–3, 7–8
The Better Angels of Our Nature (Pinker),
　42–43
bias, 42–44
Biennial, Reform movement, 151–52
Biller, Henry, 197
Binding of Isaac (*Akedah*), 53–60, 84,
　202, 238n23, 243–44n5
Bitan, David, 173
bitterness, 73
Blanchot, Maurice, 272n29
Blander, Dana, 167–68
Blazer, Yitzchak, 274n24
Blech, Benjamin, 29, 32
Bloch, Ernst, 123
Blois, France, 15, 30, 34, 233n30
Blood libel (Blois), 15, 30
Bloom, Cecil, 263n8
Blumenethal, David R., 248n56
bodily resurrection, 130–31, 135, 147–
　50, 155
Boehm, Omri, 55–56, 239n30
Bokser, Baruch, 68
Bombach, Menachem, 184–87
Bornsztain, Shmuel, 45

Boyarin, Daniel, 26
Brenner, Yosef Haim, 268n68
Broide, Simcha Mordechai Ziskind, 89
Brown, Erica, 76, 78
Brueggemann, Walter, 61–63, 94–95,
    240n1, 247n44
Buber, Martin, 183, 204–5
burnout, 219–20

Café Society (film), 128
Calvin, John, 236n1
capacity to endure suffering, 104–5
Capps, Donald, 111
Caputo, John D., 270n8
Carney, Glandion, 123
Cascio, Jamais, 269n79
character (strengths or weaknesses),
    56–57, 198, 209, 225n3
Character Strengths and Virtues (Peter-
    son and Seligman), 198, 270n11
childlessness, 52–53
Chmielnitski massacres, 38
Christianity, xviii–xix, 30, 100, 128, 140, 151,
    154, 204–5, 213, 225n5. See also Paul
chutzpah, 199
circumcision, 32–33, 233n34, 245n15,
    247n43
Cohen, Geula, 268n66
Cohen, Jeffrey M., 15
Cohen, Samuel, 158
Cohen, Ted, 197, 202, 206–7
Coleridge, Samuel Taylor, 116
collective action, 157
Collins, John J., 132
"The Commanding Voice of
    Auschwitz" (Fackenheim), 97–98
commandments, xx, 9, 36–37, 49–50,
    53, 55–56, 65–67, 78–79, 82–83, 85–
    86, 97–98, 237n16, 239n29, 248n55

"The Community of Zion" (Kehillat
    Tzion), 183–84
Constituent Assembly (Israel), 167
constitution (Israel), 166–69
Cordovero, Moses, 36, 234n42
covenant: and Abraham, 54–55; concept
    of, 82–83; and covenantal pluralism,
    100; and covenantal relationship
    (with God), 82–101; in morning lit-
    urgy, 83–90; as petition: the Amidah,
    87–90; and tikkun olam, 40
covenantal hope, 82–102, 215
COVID-19 pandemic, xvi, 43
Cox, Harvey, 211, 216
creativity (humor and hope), 196–97
Crusades, 15, 53, 213, 244n5, 246n37
cultural Zionism, 163

Daniel, 133–34, 139, 150–51, 273n13
Dead Sea Scrolls, 118, 251n45
death, 152–54, 255n7. See also afterlife;
    resurrection
Declaration of Independence (Israel),
    165–67, 169–70
declinism, 43
De Profundis (From the Depths), 14
Der Judenstaat (The Jewish State)
    (Herzl), 162
despair, 59–60, 70–77, 98, 106–7, 119–
    21, 193–94, 213–14, 218, 225n5
destruction of the First Temple, 91–92, 214
destruction of the Second Temple, 92,
    130, 134, 137
diaspora Jewry, 163, 172–73
disembodied souls, 148
Divine Attributes, 9
divine image (image of God), xxi, xxii,
    2–5, 18, 19, 62, 66, 153, 177, 205,
    210–11, 212–13, 215

divine intervention, xx, 63, 100, 130, 153

divine punishment and reward, 91, 94, 96, 104. *See also* Job

divorce (in Mishnah), 24–28

Dorff, Elliot, 31–32

double dying, 148

doubt (*Akedah* and hope), 55–56

A Dream Come True (Ben-Yehuda), 161

Dreyfus, Alfred, 161

Ecclesiastes (Kohelet), xxi, 22–24, 26–28, 42, 44, 45, 129, 219, 220, 231n11, 232n19, 244n8, 247n42

"Effect of Positive Emotions on Health" (Horowitz), 196

Egypt, 74–75

Eighteen Benedictions (*Shemoneh Esrei*). See *Amidah* (standing prayer)

Eighteenth Zionist Congress, 158

Elad-Appelbaum, Tamar, 182–84, 221, 268n68

Eleh Ezkerah (martyrology), 119

Eliade, Mircea, 64

Eliezer, Rabbi, 210

Elijah, 4, 116, 142

Eliphaz, 107–11

Elledge, C. D., 133

El Shaddai, 32–33

Elul, 1, 8–9, 10, 11, 239n36

empathy, 78–81, 121–22, 226n8

Engelberg, Michal, 193

Erikson, Erik, 122, 198, 253n57

Essenes, 135–36, 257n31

Esther, 199

Ethiopian Jews, 179–80

exile, 15, 35, 47, 68–69, 94, 134

Exodus, xviii, xix–xx, 36, 61–81, 217

Ezekiel, 130–31, 134, 138, 150–51, 159

Ezra, 94–95

Ezrahi, Sidra DeKoven, 202

Fackenheim, Emil, 97–98, 248n55

faith, xiv–xv, 12–13, 47, 213–14

Falk, Joshua, 244n5

Falk, Marcia, 45

false hope, xv–xvi

Fanon, Frantz, 78

Feinstein, Edward, 225–26n7

Feld, Edward, 12–13

Figueres, Christiana, 44

Finkelstein, Louis, 144

First Zionist Congress, 162–64

Fishbane, Michael, 64, 131, 141–42

foolishness (*kislatekha*) and hope in Job, 109–10

forgiveness (human and divine), 2, 5, 8, 14, 16, 20, 77, 125, 200, 228n38, 237n13

"Four Tribes Speech" (Rivlin), 171–73

Fox, Michael V., 23, 28, 231n7

Frank Conversations about Israeli Hope (Hendel), 174

Frankl, Viktor, 209

Freedom of Occupation (Israeli Basic Law), 167

Frishman, Elyse, 151

From Defender to Critic (Hartman), 82, 241n15

Futterman, Matthew, 225n7

Future Tense (Sacks), 212

The Future We Choose (Figueres and Rivett-Carnac), 44

Gabirol, Ibn, 227n19, 253n51

Galnoor, Itzhak, 167–68

Gamaliel, Rabban, 25, 28, 231n11

Gaon, Amram, 242n26, 259n66

Gaon, Saadia, 69–70, 232n23

Gates, Bill, 44

Gates of Prayer (Stern), 150

Gellman, Marc, 151–52

gender and God language, xxiv–xxv, 251n35, 262n113

Geonic Period, 30, 241n26. *See also* Gaon, Amram; Gaon, Saadia

Geraci, Robert M., 154

Gersonides (Levi ben Gershom), 58

Gevurot (God's Power, *Amidah*), 139–40

Gillman, Neil, 148, 255–56n7

Gimbel, Steven, 196

goals and hope in Job, 114–16

God: and Abraham, 47–57; character of, 16–19; covenantal relationship with, 82–87, 90–100; and divine image, xxi, xxii, 2–5, 18, 19, 62, 66, 153, 177, 205, 210–11, 212–13, 215; and divine intervention, 153; and the Exodus, xix, 17–18, 63–66, 79–80; and faith, 47, 213–14; and humor, 201, 210–11; and incongruity, 201; and Israel's national anthem, 159; as Israel's pool of hope, 7; and Job, 103–25; and law, 65–67; and martyrdom, 135; and Messianic Era, 145–46; as *Mikveh Yisrael* (Hope of Israel), xvii, 7, 113, 263n4; and modern Jewish theology of hope, 212–13; and Moses, xvii, 8–9, 18, 19, 75–77, 104, 116, 184, 199, 217, 227n25, 237n13, 242n41, 244n7; and prayer, 6–8, 11–14; and Process Theology, xxi, 100–101, 226nn8–9; and redemption, 15–16, 39, 63, 86, 88–89, 199, 219, 250n22; and responsibility for hope, xx–xxii; sovereignty of, 31; and *tikkun*

olam, 32–33; and transcendence, 198, 199; and trials, 217–18. *See also* resurrection

God is dead school of theology, 97

"God Only Forgives Those Who Hope for God's Forgiveness" (Teikhthal), 20

God's Power (*Amidah*, *Gevurot*), 139–40

Goldberg, Michael, 64

Golden Calf, 9

Google Ngram Viewer, 234n55

Grauber, Heinrich, 96

Greek philosophy, 135, 147–48, 230n6, 252n49

Green, Arthur, 87

Greenberg, Irving, xxi, 21, 63, 64, 67–68, 70, 99–100

Greenstein, Edward, 113

group malleability (research study), 191–92

The Guide of the Perplexed (Maimonides), 56

guilt, 107–9

Gunkel, Hermann, 228n34

Habel, Norman C., 108

Ha Chalom v'Shivro (the dream and its interpretation) (Ben-Yehuda), 161

Hagar, 58–60, 237n13

Haggadah. *See* Passover Haggadah

Haggadah and History (Yerushalmi), 61

Haiti Relief Fund, 40

halakhah. *See* Jewish law (halakhah)

Halbertal, Moshe, 107, 109, 125

Halperin, Eran, 191–93

HaMidrasha at Oranim, 184

Hammer, Reuven, 66

Harari, Yuval Noah, 153

Haredi community, 185–87

Harlow, Jules, 102

Hartman, David, 66–67, 82, 90, 238n20, 238n23, 239n34, 241n15, 248n59

Hartman Institute, 184

"Hatikvah," "The Hope" (Israeli national anthem), 131, 156, 158–59, 170–71, 182, 263n9, 265–66n47, 265n44

Hauptman, Judith, 26, 231n15

Havel, Vaclav, 73–74

Have You Seen the Horizon Lately?, 193

healing, 124–25

Hebrew language, revival of, 112–13, 159–61

Hebron, 168

Helmreich, William B., 124

Hendel, Ronald, 47

Hendel, Yoaz, 173–75

Herzl, Theodor, 161–65

Herzliya Conference, 171

Herzog, Chaim, 169–70

Heschel, Abraham Joshua, 4, 7, 132, 154, 227n19, 253n51

Hess, Moses, 157–58

higher levels of hope, benefits of, xvi

High Holy Days, 6, 9, 14. See also Rosh Hashanah; Yom Kippur

high-hope individuals, xviii, 77

Hillel, 79, 174, 178–79

Hirsch, Samson Raphael, 76

Historical and Multidisciplinary Perspectives on Hope (van den Heuvel), 274n21

Hoffman, Lawrence A., 88, 245–46nn22–23

Holocaust, 95–101, 208–10, 271–72n28

hope: and Abraham and Sarah, 47–60; and action, xv, xvi, 76, 165; and afterlife, 128, 136–37, 148–55, 216; and agency, 35, 114; and the Akedah, 53–60, 84, 202; and Aleinu prayer, 29–34, 45; and Alice Shalvi, 181–82; ambiguity of, 117–19; in ancient texts, 213–14; biblical models of, xvii–xviii; book of Jonah, 16–19; and capacity to endure suffering, 104–5; and character consistency, 56–57; Charles R. Snyder on, xv–xvi, 116, 161–62, 178–79, 196–97, 220; and chutzpah, 199; classical sources on, xix–xx; and covenant, 82–102, 215; and creativity, 196–97; as defined by author, xiv–xv; and despair, 60, 70–77, 98, 106–7, 119–21, 193–94, 213–14, 218, 225n5; and doubt, 55–56; and Eilon Schwartz, 176–77; and Emil Fackenheim, 97–98; emulation of, xviii; and Eran Halperin, 191–94; etymology of, 224–25n24; and the Exodus, 61–81; and faith, xiv–xv, 12–13, 47, 213–14; and foolishness (kislatekha), 109–10; and Gabriel Marcel, xiii–xiv, 49, 55, 56, 57–58, 59, 84, 125, 134–35, 216, 218, 221; and goals, 114–16; and guilt, 107–9; and Hagar, 58–60; and healing, 124–25; and Holocaust, 95–101, 208–10; and humor, 195–211, 216; and Ilay Ofran, 178–79; and immortality, 136, 146–55; and incongruity, 200–201; and Irving Greenberg, 99–100; and Job, 103–27, 217–18; and journey metaphors, 112–13; Judaism as reservoir of, xvii, xix;

and justice, 105–6; and *kav* (line), 15–16, 39, 262n113; and Kher Albaz, 189–91; and Lamentations, 91–92; and laughter, 200–202; and leadership, 77–78; and Lina Alatawna, 187–89; as magical, 119–21; and martyrdom, 134–36; and memory, 84–87; and Menachem Bombach, 184–87; as messianic, 38, 152, 157; and Messianic Era, 202–5; modern Jewish theology of, xx–xxii, 212–13; as movement, 57–58; and optimism, xv, 42–44, 58; and patience, 111–12; paucity of scholarly literature on, xix, 274n21; and prayer, xiv–xv, 6–8, 11–14, 19, 183–84, 215–16, 227n19; and Process Theology, 100–101, 226nn8–9; and progress, 42–44; and Psalm 27, 11–14; and Psalm 130, 14–19; and Rafael Moshe Luria, 38–39; real vs. false, xv–xvi; responsibility for, xx–xxii; and resurrection, 129–55; role of, in influencing positive outcomes, xvi; role of, in Jewish history, 74, 82–83, 99–100, 221; and salvation, 39; and schlemielian humor, 205–8; and Sigal Kanotopsky, 179–80; social context of, 121–23, 197, 218; and Sodom and Gomorrah, 50–52; and statehood, 157–59, 161–66; and supportive relationships, 59–60, 197; and Tamar Elad-Appelbaum, 182–84; and *teshuvah* (repentance), 1–10, 16, 17–19, 82, 215–16, 225n5; and thread, 113–14; and *tikkun olam*, 21–46, 218–20; and time, 110–11, 113–14; as topic of Jewish study,

xvi, xviii–xix; and transcendence, 198–99; transmission of, 220–22; and trials, xvii–xviii, 49–50, 216–18; and trust, 122–23; and Vaclav Havel, 73–74; for vindication, 121–24; and Wadi Attir, 187–89; and Walter Brueggemann, 61–63, 94–95, 247n44; and water, 112–13; and willingness to choose, xvi; work of, 215–20; and Yoaz Hendel, 173–75; and Zionism, 157–65, 194

Hope in the Age of Anxiety (Scioli and Biller), 197

Hope of Israel (*Mikveh Yisrael*), xvii, 7, 113, 263n4

human agency, 28, 35, 114, 238n20, 251n33

Human Dignity and Liberty, 167

human intervention, 80, 153

humor, 195–211, 216

Ibn Ezra, Abraham, 203–4

Ibn Ezra, Moshe, 114

Idel, Moshe, 35

IDF (Israel Defense Forces), 168

idol worship, 9, 48–49

illegitimate offspring (*mamzer*), 25, 27

imaginary companions, 123

Imber, Naftali Herz, 158–59

immortality, 136, 146–55, 254n3

incongruity (humor and hope), 200–201

incrementalism, 41–42

innocent suffering, 95–96, 273n13

In Praise of Yiddish (Samuel), 195

Inquisition, 6

Isaac, 53–60, 200–202, 217

Isaiah, 8, 131–33, 138–39, 141, 152–53

Ishmael, 59–60

Israel: activist snapshots from, 173–94; Arab citizens of, 169, 171, 177, 190–91; boundaries of, 168–69; and covenant, 82–87, 90–100; in Daniel, 133–34; and Israeli Hope (*Tikvah Yisraelit*) initiative, 171–73; Jewish settlements in, 168; and labor movement, 164; and messianic redemption, 141–44; national anthem of, 131, 158–59, 170–71, 182, 263n9, 265–66n47, 265n44; polarization and extremism in, 169–70; restoration to, 156; and Six-Day War, 168–69; and statehood, 157–59, 161–66; and Zionism, 157–65
Israel Defense Forces (IDF), 168
Israeli Democracy Institute, 171
Israeli Hope (Tikvah Yisraelit) initiative, 171–73, 191–94
Israel's Ministry of Education, 188–89
Israel Women's Network (IWN), 181–82, 268n66

Jacobs, Jill, 249n3
Jastrow, Marcus, 24, 260n70, 271n26
Jeremiah, xvii, 89, 92–94, 116, 144, 156
Jerusalem, 68, 88, 91–92, 157–58, 169, 180, 235n62, 244n10, 253n51, 272n31
Jerusalem Talmud, 203, 226–27n15
Jewish calendar, 67–68
Jewish Child Care Association, 40
Jewish humor, 195–211
Jewish identity, 205–8
Jewish law (halakhah), 9, 25, 45, 65–67, 81, 134, 137, 186, 210, 241n15
Jewish leadership and hope, 78
Jewish Pioneers (Palestine), 158
Jewish Publication Society, 117

The Jewish State (Der Judenstaat) (Herzl), 162
Jewish thought, 83, 88–89, 147–48
Jewish Underground (Israel), 169
The Jewish Way (Greenberg), 21
Jews and Arabs in Israel, 171, 177, 190–91
Jews in Palestine, 159–65
Job, xvii, 103–27, 217–18, 273n13
Jokes (Cohen), 197, 206–7
Jonah, book of, 16–19
Jonas, Hans, 100–101
Josephus, 135–36
Josiah (King), 68
journey metaphors, 112–13
Joy, Despair, and Hope: Reading Psalms (Feld), 12–13
Judah ha-Nasi, 6
Judaism as reservoir of hope, xvii, xix
justice, 105–6, 115–16, 124

Kabbalah, 16, 34–39, 254n3
Kahane, Meir, 169
Kahneman, Daniel, 43–44
Kanotopsky, Sigal, 179–80
Kant, Immanuel, 8, 227n21, 230n3
Kaplan, Aryeh, 211, 233n38
Kaplan, Mordecai, xxi, 63–64, 231n9, 233n38
Kaspi, Joseph ibn, 58
kav (line), 15–16, 39, 262n113
Keckley, Elizabeth, 126–27
Kehillat Tzion ("The Community of Zion"), 183–84
Kiddush (blessing over wine), 69
Kierkegaard, Søren, 223n2, 238n26
Kimchi, David, 14–15, 230n1
Kiryat Arba, 168
Kishon, Ephraim, 216

kislatekha (hope or foolishness), 109–10

Knesset, 167, 169, 171, 181, 268n66

kof-vav-hey, xvii, xxiv, 103, 224n24, 225n24, 260n70, 274n25

Kook, Rav (Abraham Isaac), 1, 2–5, 227n28

Kurzweil, Ray, 153

Kushner, Harold, 104

Kushner, Lawrence, xxi

Lamentations, 91–92

language, Hebrew, 159–61

laughter, 200–202, 210–11, 271n23

Laughter in Hell (Lipman), 208–9

Law of the Pursuer, 170

Leiner, Mordechai Joseph, 56

lekh lekha (go forth), 50, 53, 57–58

Lerner, Akiba, 149–50

level path, 12–13

Levenson, Jon, 130, 131–32

Levi, Primo, 105, 249n6

Levinas, Emmanuel, 225n5

Levine, Robert N., 152

Levinger, Moshe, 168

liberation from Egypt, 63, 67–68, 69

life expectancy, 43

Lifschitz, Israel, 251n46

The Lights of Repentance (Kook), 1

Lincoln, Abraham, 126–27

Lipman, Steve, 195, 208–9

liturgy, 6–7, 30, 68–70, 83–90, 215–16

Long, William, 123

Lopez, Shayne, xviii, 87

Lorberbaum, Menachem, 33

Luria, Isaac, 34–39, 45, 144, 227–28n29

Luria, Rafael Moshe, 38–39

Lurianic Kabbalah, 34–37

Luzzatto, Moshe Chaim, 39, 212

Maccabean Revolt, 133–34

magical hope, 119–21

Magnes, Judah, 159

Maharal of Prague, 72–73

Maimonides: and Abraham, 48; and afterlife, 144–48; and the *Akedah*, 55–56, 239n30; and ambiguity, 118; and Isaiah, 132; and Messianic Era, 145–46, 155, 204, 219; and Rabbeinu Yona of Gerona, 6; on repentance, 225n3; and resurrection, 133, 144–48; and shofar, 10–11; and *teshuvah* (repentance), 2–3; and *tikkun olam*, 33–34

Man's Search for Meaning (Frankl), 209

Marcel, Gabriel, xiii–xiv, 8, 49, 55, 56, 57–58, 59, 84, 125, 134–35, 216, 218, 221

Margalit, Avishai, 123

Marmur, Michael, 114

martyrdom, 30, 119, 134–36, 155, 257n29

Masoretic notes, 117–18

"Master of All Worlds" (*Ribbon Kol Ha-olamim*), 84–85

master story, 64–65. *See also* Exodus

McMillian, Walter, 124, 253n66

Meah She'arim, 184

meditation, 37

Memorial Day (Israel, Yom ha-Zikaron), 185

memories of the Exodus, 78–81

memory (covenant and hope), 84–87

Menorah Psalm (Psalm 67), 184

Messiah/Messianic Era, 140–46, 148–50, 155, 202–5, 219, 261n88, 272n29

messianic hope, 38, 41, 149, 152, 157

Messianic Idea in Judaism (Scholem), 41–42

messianic redemption, 141–44, 152–53

messianism, 42, 146, 265n41
Messinger, Ruth, 41
"Messinger of Hope" (Messinger), 41
Metzudat David, 86
midrashic process, 26
Mikveh Yisrael (agricultural school), 158
Mikveh Yisrael (Hope of Israel, in Jeremiah), xvii, 7, 113, 263n4
Miles, Jack, 229n47
Mintz, Alan, 82–83
minyan, 7, 83
Miriam, 75–77
Mirkin, M. A., 72
Mishkan T'filah (Frishman), 151
Mishnah, 14, 23, 24–28, 29, 49, 118, 139–40, 142, 239n36
Mittleman, Alan, 88
modern Jewish theology of hope, xx–xxii, 212–13
Modern Orthodox (National Religious) tribe (Israel), 172, 174
Moltmann, Jürgen, 47, 223n2
Moment magazine, 128
moral witness, 123
Morning Blessings, 84–87
morning liturgy, 83–90
Moses, xvii, 8–9, 18, 19, 75–77, 104, 116, 119, 184, 199, 217, 227n25, 237n13, 242n41, 244n7, 259n67, 270n18
movement and hope, 57–58
Movement for Greater Israel, 168
Movement for Peace and Security, 168
Muffs, Yochanan, 16, 229n47
myths, 64–65, 238n20, 252n49

Nachmanides, 60, 207
Nachman of Breslov, Rebbe, 5, 100, 226n13

names of God, 55–56
Nathan of Gaza, 38
National Religious (Modern Orthodox) tribe (Israel), 172, 174
Nebenzahl, Avigdor, 15–16
Negev, 187–90
Nehemiah's Prayer, 86
Neher, André, 119
Netanyahu government, 173
Newsom, Carole, 111
New Testament, 52, 137
"The Night of Blood on the Rock of Horrors or Knight Adolar's Maiden Voyage and Its Gruesome End or That Is Not the True Love" (play), 209–10
Ninth of Av, 92, 161
Nobel lecture, 1986 (Wiesel), 103
Nordau, Max, 157
Nosatzki, Shir, 192–94

Obama, Barack, 40
obedience and *Akedah*, 53–54, 55
occupation of Gaza and the West Bank, 169
Ochs, Vanessa, 81
Ofran, Ilay, 178–79
Olim B'Yachad (Rising Up Together), 179–80
100 Bedouin Engineers Project, 190
optimism, xiii, xv, 42–44, 58, 73, 171, 196, 198, 227n28
Orthodox community (Israel), 160, 168, 178–79
Oslo Peace Process, 170

The Pale, 271n20
Palestine, 159–65, 169–70, 192–93
Paris Climate Accord, 44

Passover, 67, 141–42

Passover Haggadah, 61, 68, 70, 81, 160, 221

The Passover Haggadah (Ochs), 81

patience and hope in Job, 111–12

Paul, 52–53, 137, 237n16

peace (*Amidah*, blessing for), 89

Peel Commission, 165

Pelech School, 181–82

Perishah (Falk), 243–44n5

The Personhood of God (Muffs), 16, 229n47

pessimism, 42–44, 231n10, 235n64, 236n69

Pesukei de-Zimra (Verses of Song), 84–87

Petach Tikvah, 158, 164

petitionary blessings, 88–89

Phaedo (Plato), 135

Pharaoh, 71–77

Pharisees, 136–37

Philo of Alexandria, 135

Pinker, Steven, 42–43

Pinsker, Sanford, 207–8

Pioneers of Bilu, 158

Pittsburgh Platform (Reform movement), 149–50

Plato, 135

political Zionism, 162–63

positive psychology, 198, 270n11

post-Holocaust theology, 40, 96–101

posthumanism, 153–54

poverty, 42–43

prayer, xiv–xv, 2, 6–8, 11–14, 19, 36–39, 183–84, 215–16, 227n19

prayer books, xix–xx, xxii, 30, 37, 149–52, 241n23, 244n5

Process Theology, xxi, 100–101, 226nn8–9

progress and *tikkun olam*, 42–44

Provan, Iain William, 92

Proverbs, 8, 33, 70, 74, 78

Pruyser, Paul, 126

Psalm 27, 11–14, 227–28n29

Psalm 130, 14–19

Rabbinic Judaism and Jewish eschatology, 137–44, 273n13

Rabin, Dalia, 192

Rabin, Yitzhak, 168, 170

radical messianic hope, 41–42

Rashi, 4, 11, 24, 50, 77, 109, 112–13, 125, 229n48, 246n37, 247nn42–43, 250n18, 255n7, 262n113, 271n23

realistic hope, xv–xvi, 42–44, 121

redemption, 15, 39, 63, 75–76, 82, 88–89, 141–44, 152–53, 160, 199, 219, 250n22, 260n67. *See also* covenant

Reformed Society of Israelites, 149

Reform Judaism, 148–52

Reik, Theodore, 204

release of new social imagination, 62–63

Remembering Abraham (Hendel), 47

"Repair the World!" (Salovey), 39

repentance (*teshuvah* and hope), 1–19, 82, 215–16

responsibility for hope, xx–xxii

resurrection, 129–55; belief in, 128; as bodily, 130–31, 135, 147–50, 155; in Daniel, 133–36; in Ezekiel, 130–31; and immortality, 152–54; in Isaiah, 131–33; in Job, 120–21, 273n13; and Maimonides, 133, 144–48; in Rabbinic Judaism, 137–44; references to, 129–30; and Reform movement, 148–52; and Sadducees vs. Pharisees, 136–37

Resurrection of the Dead in Early Judaism (Elledge), 133

Ribbon Kol Ha-olamim ("Master of All Worlds"), 84–85

Richter, Gerhard, 196

Rishon le-Tziyon, 161

Rising Up Together (Olim B'Yachad), 179–80

Rivett-Carnac, Tom, 44

Rivlin, Reuven, 166, 171–73

Rorty, Richard, 81, 235n60

Rosh Hashanah, xxv, 1, 9, 11, 14, 19, 30, 60, 169, 225n1

Ruach ha-Sadeh (Spirit, or Wind, of the Field), 178

Rubenstein, Richard L., 96–97, 247n49

Rufus, Turnus, 33

Ruskay, John, 40

Rwandan genocide, 193

Rycroft, Charles, 221

Sabbath, 33, 36, 69, 73, 87, 131, 139, 143, 241n26, 245–46n22, 247n42

Sacks, Jonathan, xxv, 195, 212

Sadducees, 136–37

Salovey, Peter, 39–40, 41

salvation. *See* redemption

Sami Shamoon College of Engineering, 190

Samuel, Maurice, 195

Sapir, Gideon, 167

Sarah, 47–60, 201, 217, 271n24. *See also* Abraham

Savir, Maya, 193

Schachtel, Ernest G., 121

Scheindlin, Raymond, 113, 118

The Schlemiel as Metaphor (Pinsker), 207–8

The Schlemiel as Modern Hero (Wisse), 205–6

schlemielian humor, 205–8

Schneerson, Shalom Dov Baer, 259n56

Scholem, Gershom, 35, 41–42

Schulweis, Harold M., xxi

Schwartz, Eilon, 176–77

Scioli, Anthony, 197

Second Book of Maccabees, 134

second chance, hope for, 9

Seder, 61, 68–69, 76, 80, 142, 150, 221

Seeskin, Kenneth, 146

Segal, Alan F., 154

Segal, Benjamin, 228n34

Segev, Tom, 164

SEHIS (Super-Empowered Hopeful Individuals), 194

Seow, C. L., 22, 106–7, 113, 114, 118

Sephardic Jewry and customs, 228n30, 260n71

Setzer, Claudia, 137–38

sex and prayer (Lurianic Kabbalah), 36

Shaharit, 176–77

Shalvi, Alice, 181–82

shame, 2, 5

Shammai, 23, 174, 178

shared humor, 197

Shema, 69

Shemoneh Esrei (Eighteen Benedictions), 87. See also *Amidah* (standing prayer)

Sheol, 129, 255n7

Shmuel, 143

shofar, 9–11

shortcomings, 4–5. See also *teshuvah* (repentance)

Shulḥan Arukh, 244n5

Sickness unto Death (Kierkegaard), 223n2

Six-Day War, 168–69

"The 614th Commandment" (Fackenheim), 97–98, 248n55

smile, 270n8

Snyder, Charles R., xv–xvi, 8, 116, 161–62, 178–79, 196–97, 216, 220

social context of hope, 121–23, 197, 218

social hope, 81, 235n60

social justice, 23, 26, 40, 192, 194

Sodom and Gomorrah, 17, 50–52, 77, 95, 238n23

Solnit, Rebecca, xv

Soloveitchik, Joseph B., xx–xxi, 16, 34, 101, 152, 210–11, 219, 240n4

Soviet Jewry, 69

Spain, expulsion from, 35

Spirit, or Wind, of the Field (Ruach ha-Sadeh), 178

spiritual immortality, 146–55

Steinberg, Milton, 155

Stevenson, Bryan, 124, 253n66

Sukkot, 241n21

superaddressee, 123, 253n62

Super-Empowered Hopeful Individuals (SEHIS), 194

supportive relationships, 59–60, 197. See also social context of hope

Tarfon, Rabbi, 41, 235n60

Tashlikh (ceremony), 14

Teikhthal, Issakhar Solomon, 20, 71–72, 86

Temple Mount, 168–69

teshuvah (repentance), 1–10, 16, 17–19, 82, 215–16, 225n5

theodicy, 95, 135

There Is No Messiah and You're It (Levine), 152

theurgy, 35

Thirteen Principles (Maimonides), 149, 204

Thirteenth Knesset, 170

tikkun ha-olam, 24–28

tikkun olam, 21–46; and Aleinu prayer, 29–34; and American Judaism, 39–41; in Ecclesiastes, 22–24, 219; on the Google Ngram Viewer, 234n55; and hope, 21–46; and incrementalism, 41–42; and Isaac Luria, 34–37; and Messianic Era, 148; and messianic redemption, 152–53; origins of, in the Mishnah (tikkun ha-olam), 24–28; and problems and progress, 42–44; and Rafael Moshe Luria, 38–39; and the work of hope, 218–20

Tikvah Yisraelit (Israeli Hope) initiative, 171–73, 191–94

"Tikvatenu," "Our Hope" (Imber), 158–59. See also "Hatikvah," "The Hope" (Israeli national anthem)

time, 67–68, 110–11, 113–14

Time magazine, xvi

Tirer, Chaim, 74

Torah of the Soul (Ofran), 178

transcendence and hope, 198–99

translations of hope, xxiv, 77, 111, 228n37

transmitting hope, 220–22

Treatise on Resurrection (Maimonides), 147

trials, xvii–xviii, 49–50, 216–18

trust, 122–23. See also basic trust

Tucker, Gordon, 226n13

Twersky, Amos, 43–44

Tzvi, Shabbatai, 38–39

UJA/Federation of New York, 40

ultra-Orthodox community (Israel),
    184–87
uncertainty and hope, 55–56
U'Netaneh Tokef, 9–10
UN General Assembly, 165
Union Prayer-Book for Jewish Worship,
    261n94
United Nations' Special Commission
    on Palestine (1947), 165
Urbach, Ephraim, 267n62
Ussishkin, Menachem, 163

van den Heuvel, Charles, 274n21
vengeance, 79, 81, 246n26
Vermes, Geza, 129
Verses of Song (*Pesukei de-Zimra*),
    84–87
vindication and hope in Job, 121–24
violence and loss of hope, 42, 229n48,
    246n26
Vital, Chaim, 37, 227–28n29, 229n38

Wadi Attir, 187–89
water in Job, 112–13
West Bank, 168, 169–70
Whedbee, J. William, 199
When Bad Things Happen to Good People
    (Kushner), 104

Whitehead, Alfred North, 100
Whitington, Paul, 195
Wiesel, Elie, xvi, 103, 202, 213,
    271–72n28
Wisdom Literature and hope, 103
Wisse, Ruth, 205
women's movement (Israel), xviii, 181–
    82, 268n66
work of hope, 215–20
worthlessness, 84–85

Yemimah (daughter of Job), 125
Yerushalmi, Yosef Hayim, xix, xxii, 61
Yitzchak, Levi, 200, 204
Yocheved, 76–77
Yom ha-Zikaron (Israeli Memorial
    Day), 185
Yom Kippur, 2, 16–20, 119, 139, 157,
    229n48, 230n54
Yona of Gerona, Rabbeinu, 5–6
"You Are YHWH Our God" (*Atah Hu
    YHWH Eloheinu*), 85

Zechariah, 92–94
Zephaniah, 85
Zionism, 157–65, 172, 194, 268n68
Zohar, 35–36, 51, 56, 237n11
Zoroastrianism, 130

Index of Texts

Hebrew Bible

Genesis
1:9, 113
2:1, 33
3:19, 129
6:6–7, 17
6:9, 125, 254n74
6:11, 17, 229n48
8:10, xxiv, 224n24
12:1, 49, 189
12:4, 49
15:2–3, 52
15:6, 52
15:15, 89
16:2, 51, 237n13
16:3, 58, 240n40
16:6, 60
17:1–14, 32
17:17, 60, 201, 240n43, 271n23
17:19, 201
18:11–14, 201
18:12, 217
18:14, 201
18:17–20, 51
18:19, 48
18:23, 116, 251n41
18:23–25, 51
18:25, 17, 116
18:27–28, 51
19:24, 15, 237n15

20:7, 239n30
21:1–2, 53
21:5–6, 201
21:14–16, 59
21:17–20, 59
22:1, 55
22:1–19, 84
22:2, 53–54, 55, 202, 238n28, 272n28
22:4, 56
22:5, 58
22:7–8, 58
22:11, 55
22:12, 54
22:16–18, 84
25:8, 129
32:29, 116
38:5, 38
49:9, 74, 242n45
49:18, 32, 39, 88, 103, 178, 233n34, 234n50, 248n1
Exodus
1:10, 71, 74
1:11, 70–72, 242n28, 242n36
1:13–14, 72
1:14, 73, 242n40
2:2, 76
2:4, 75
2:10, 77, 243n54
2:23, 62

3:8, xix
3:14, xvii, 19, 230n53
6:5, 71, 242n34
6:14, 76, 243n48
12:13, 80
12:22, 79
12:37, 65
13:9, 100
13:10, 67
13:16, 69
14:15, 217
14:16, 217
15:11, 102
19:4–5, 66
19:6, 63
20:2–3, 66
22:20–22, 63
23:9, 78
24:8, 93, 247n43
26:5–10, 68
31:12, 36
31:17, 36
32:11, 77, 199, 243n55, 270n18
32:30, 51, 77, 237n13
33:20, 115
34:6–7, 17

Leviticus
12:3, 33, 233n35
19:18, 36–37, 79
19:33–34, 66
25:17, 249n12
26:42, 84
26:43–45, 90
26:44, 92

Numbers
3:16, 71, 242n33
15:41, 69, 241n25
23:9, 175, 266n57

23:19, 18, 229n51
24:17, 142

Deuteronomy
5:12–15, 79
5:13–15, 79
23:8, 79
26:7, 240n3
30:12, 210
30:19, 154, 221, 274n24

Joshua
2:18, xxiv
2:21, xxiv

1 Kings
8:1–5, 241n21
18:37, 116
19:11–13, 4

2 Kings
23:21–23, 68

Isaiah
1–39, 256n14
2:4, 132
2:5, 263n6
6:2, 57
11:1, 141
11:2, 141
11:4–6, 141
11:9, 141
11:10, 141
14:11, 255n7
25:6, 152
25:8, 132, 138–39, 152, 153
25:8–9, 132
25:9, 139, 258n40
26:19–21, 132, 256n16
28:10, 155, 262n113
28:13, 262n113
38:18–19, 255n7
38:19, 129

40–66, 256n14
40:31, 8
42:6, 175, 266n57
49:6, 175, 266n57
54:10, 246n33
58:6–7, 23
60:20, 203
65:20, 139
66:1–24, 92, 247n42

Jeremiah
14:8, xvii, 158, 263n4
15:19, 153
17:13, 113, 158, 263n4
19:11, 247n44
20:7, 251n42
20:12, 116
20:14, 251n42
29:11–12, 89
31:16–17, 93
31:17, 155, 156, 262n113
31:31–33, 93
33:15, 144

Ezekiel
14:14, 254n74
21:30, 140
22:7–8, 134
37:11, 159
37:11–14, 130, 132
37:26, 246n33

Amos
5:15, 246n39

Hosea
2:17, 158, 226n12, 263n5, 274n24

Jonah
3:10, 18
4:2, 17

Micah
7:15, 70

Habakkuk
142, 214

Zephaniah
2:3, 246n39
3:9, 33
3:20, 85

Zechariah
9:11, 247n43
9:11–12, 93
14:9, 233n38

Malachi
3:4–24, 247n42

Psalms
13:2, 214
16:8, 184
27, 9, 11–14, 186–87, 227–28n29
27:1–14, 11–12
27:14, 11, 13, 228n30, 228n32
31:25, 70, 224n24, 228n37, 242n27
33:20, 85, 245n11
33:22, 85–86, 245n11, 245n14
39:8, 228n37
40:2, xxiv, 245n13, 250n24
44:18, 90
67, 184
69:4, 214
74:19, 90
74:20, 90
74:19–20, 246n36
78:7, 245n19
85:8, 85
95:7, 142
116:8, 153, 262n105
118:17, 151
119:38, 242n41
119:43, 228n37
119:110, 90
119:114, 90, 228n37

119:116, 90, 233n34
119:166, 213
128:2, 219
130:5, 15
130:7, 15
130:1–8, 14–16
130:2, 14, 228n38
130:7, 15, 214

Proverbs
3:26, 6, 226n15
10:28, 8, 227n20
11:23, 8, 227n20
13:12, 4, 70, 77
23:17–18, 8, 227n20
24:16, 74
26:12, 8, 227n20
30:21–22, 78

Job
1:5, 108
2:7, 105
3:1, 251n42
3:8–9, 106
3:9, 155, 262n113
4:2–7, 108, 249n13
4:3–5, 107
4:6, 109
4:6–7, 107–8
4:8, 108
5:24–26, 110
6:2–3, 110
6:8–9, 110
6:11, 110, 250n20
6:13, 251n33
6:15, 112, 250n27
6:19, 112, 250n27
6:20, 112, 250n27, 253n57
7:1–3, 113, 250n29
7:2, 113, 250n29

7:6–7, 113, 250n29
8:14, 250n17
9:22, 251n41
9:32–33, 123
9:32–35, 114
9:35, 114, 251n36
10:11, 114
12:4, 251n42, 254n74
13:3, 114
13:13, 117
13:14, 117
13:15, 115, 117, 119, 251n37, 251n45, 253n51
14:7, 60, 119
14:10, 120
14:12, 120, 129
14:13–15, 120
14:18–19, 121
16:19, 122, 123
16:21, 122
17:1, 122
17:15–16, 122
19:6–7, 115
19:10, 122
19:21–25, 122
19:25, 123, 126, 127, 250n22
21:15, 125
23:3–7, 115
31:24, 250n17
31:35, 115
34:31, 251n45
42:5–6, 124
42:6, 254n77
42:7, 106, 124, 126
42:10, 124, 126
42:11, 105

Song of Songs
5:6, 214

8:5, 76
Lamentations
  1:5, 91
  2:17, 91
  2:20, 91
  3:8, 91
  3:17–18, 91
  3:21, 246n37
  3:21–26, 91
  3:26, 250n24
  3:29, 91, 214
  3:31–32, 91
  5:21, 92
  5:22, 92, 247n42
Ecclesiastes
  1:5, 107
  1:9, 27
  1:12–15, 22
  1:14, 23
  1:15, 22, 219
  2:17, 23
  2:20, 23, 244n8
  3:1–2, 129
  3:11, 23
  3:13, 129
  4:1, 27
  7:13–14, 22
  9:4, 6, 129, 226n15, 232n21, 255n6
  9:5, 140
  9:7–10, 24
  12:9, 231n7
  12:13, 248n56
Esther, 199, 270n16
Daniel
  12:1–3, 133
  12:2, 139, 148, 258n41
  12:13, 133, 139, 258n41
Ezra
  10:2–3, 94

Nehemiah
  9:8, 86
  9:10, 86
1 Chronicles
  16:15–22, 244n10
  17:21, 200
  29:15, 255n7
2 Chronicles
  7:8, 241n21

Christian Bible
Acts
  23:6–8, 137
  24:14–15, 137
Romans
  4:18–19, 52
  11:1, 52
James
  5:11, 111, 250n21

Apocrypha and Pseudepigrapha
First Enoch
  104:2, 256n25
Jubilees
  12:12–15, 50
  12:17, 237n3
Second Maccabees
  7:14–36, 134

Rabbinic Literature
Mishnah
  Ta'anit
    2:3, 228n38
    2:4, 239n36
  Chagigah
    1:7, 27
  Sotah
    5:5, 251n46, 252n47
    9:15, 259n49

Gittin
   3:7, 231n15
   4:1–2, 25, 28
   4:2, 25, 27, 231n15
   4:2–3, 231n15
   4:3, 231n15
Sanhedrin
   8:7, 265n43
   10:1, 128, 257n36
Eduyot
   5:3, 23
(Pirkei) Avot
   1:6, 5
   1:14, 236n77
   2:10, 234n42
   2:21, 41, 219
   5:3, 49
Yadayim
   3:5, 231n11
Tosefta
  Berakhot
   3:24, 258n43
  Gittin
   3:7, 231n15
Jerusalem Talmud
  Berakhot
   9:1, 63b, 226n15
  Ta'anit
   1:1, 3b, 259n56
   1:2, 4a, 259n62
   4:5, 24a, 259n53
Babylonian Talmud
  Berakhot
   5b, 253n65
   6a, 271n21
   14b, 241n26
   18b, 258n45
   32a, 243n55
   32b, 228nn30–31
   34b, 259n64

   55a, 243n55
   58b, 258n44
   60b, 258n43
  Shabbat
   30b, 231n11
   31a, 243n61, 260n69
   63a, 259n64
   119b, 233n36
   151b, 259n64
  Eruvin
   13b, 267n62
  Pesachim
   68a, 259n64
   116a, 243n51
  Yoma
   9b, 267n58
   86a, 227n28
  Rosh Hashanah
   16b, 243n55
  Ta'anit
   23a, 253n59
   31a, 258n40
  Megillah
   7a, 231n11
   17b, 259n66
   31a, 141
  Chagigah
   4b, 246n39
  Ketubot
   111a, 263n1
   111b, 259n61
  Sotah
   11a, 242n35
   11b, 243n50
   12a–13b, 242n46
   37a, 263n16
  Gittin
   32a, 231n15
   52a, 242n39
   56a, 272n31

56b, 272n31

Bava Metzi'a

58b, 249n12

59b, 273n53

Bava Batra

15a, 249n3

Sanhedrin

37b, 236n77

38b, 226n7

89b, 238n21

91a, 258n39

91b, 259n64

92a, 258n41

92b, 258n38

97b, 259n55

98a, 259n51, 259n58

98b, 259n59

99a, 259n64

Avodah Zarah

3b, 273n54

17a, 227n16

Menachot

53b, 247n45

Avot de Rabbi Natan

A (33), 237n6

B (31), 259n63, 272n30

B (36), 237n6

Midrash

Mekhilta de-Rabbi Ishmael

Va-y'hi Beshalach 1, 263n1

Va-y'hi Beshalach 3, 244n7

Shirata 8:19–25, 248n66

Mekhilta de-Rabbi Shimon bar Yochai

Pischa 14:1, 243n62

Sifra

Kedoshim 2:4, 234n41

Behar 4:2, 249n12

Sifre Deuteronomy

324, 262n103

Genesis Rabbah

8:11, 226n7

11:6, 273n16

24:7, 234n41

38:13, 236n2

48:18, 271n24

48:19, 271n25

49:2, 51, 237n10

53:3, 237n17

56:8, 238n28

61:2, 240n43

98:14, xiii

Shitah Chadashah to Genesis Rabbah

2:7, 259n57

Exodus Rabbah

1:9, 242n43

1:10, 242n37

1:28, 242n41

5:18, 242n41

15:1, 259n57

15:21, 259n60

18:12, 80, 259n52

43:6, 270n18

46:1, 227n26

Leviticus Rabbah

1:3, 243n54

9:7, 259n57

Deuteronomy Rabbah

1:23, 242n32

2:12, 228n30

Song of Songs Rabbah

2:20, 259n54, 263n1

Lamentations Rabbah

2:2, 259n53

2:4, 259n53

5:22, 247n40

Ecclesiastes Rabbah

1:3, 231n11

7:13, xxi, 224n21

Tanḥuma (Buber)

Lekh Lekha 25, 233n34

Va-yera 4, 237n15
Va-yishlach 8, 249n13
Shemot 4, 243n53
Va-era 4, 242n41
Tazria 7, 233n35
Be-ha'alotkha 23, 242n33
Ve-zot Ha-berakhah 7, 258n46
Tanḥuma (Warsaw)
Ki Tissa 31, 227n25
Pesikta de-Rav Kahana
17:5, 246n29
24:4, 227n17
Pesikta Rabbati
35:4, 259n50
Pirkei de Rabbi Eliezer
26, 237n6
43, 230n52
45, 227n25
94, 262n105
Midrash of Psalms
40:1–2, 245n12
116:8, 153, 262n105
119:38, 242n41
130:2, 228n38
Yalkut Shimoni
Psalms, 736, 245n12
Lekach Tov
Genesis 22:2, 238n28
Exodus 2:10, 243n54
Leviticus 22:33, 273n4
Song of Songs 5:6, 214, 273n4, 7
Ecclesiastes 9:4, 226n15

Sekhel Tov
Genesis 22:2, 238n28
Midrash Ha-Gadol
Genesis 22:2, 55, 238n28
Exodus 1:11, 242n36
Exodus 1:14, 242n40
Otzar Midrashim
Pirkei Rabeinu HaKodesh,
228n32
Ma'aseh Avraham Avinu . . . im
Nimrod, 236n3

Dead Sea Scrolls
11QtgJob, 251n45

Greco-Roman Literature
Aesop's Fables, 252n49
Babrius, "Fables of Babrius," 52, 58,
252n49
Hesiod's Pandora's Box, 252n49
Hesiod's "Works and Days," 230n6,
252n49
Plato, *Phaedo*, 135, 257n28

Ancient Jewish Writers
Philo of Alexandria, 135
On Creation, 21:66, 257n29
On the Embassy to Gaius, 117:369,
257n29
Josephus, 135–36, 257n30, 257n33
Jewish Antiquities 18:1:3, 257n33
War of the Jews 2:8:10, 257n30

In the JPS Essential Judaism Series

Thinking about Good and Evil: Jewish Views from Antiquity to Modernity
Rabbi Wayne Allen

Choosing Hope: The Heritage of Judaism
David Arnow

The Jewish Family Ethics Textbook
Rabbi Neal Scheindlin

Thinking about the Prophets: A Philosopher Reads the Bible
Kenneth Seeskin

Thinking about the Torah: A Philosopher Reads the Bible
Kenneth Seeskin

Thinking about God: Jewish Views
Rabbi Kari H. Tuling

Justice for All: How the Jewish Bible Revolutionized Ethics
Jeremiah Unterman

To order or obtain more information on these or other Jewish Publication Society titles, visit jps.org.

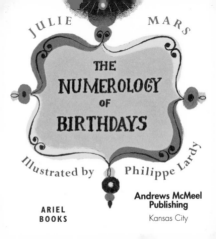

JULIE MARS

THE
NUMEROLOGY
OF
BIRTHDAYS

Illustrated by Philippe Lardy

**ARIEL
BOOKS**

**Andrews McMeel
Publishing**

Kansas City

www.andrewsmcmeel.com

Art copyright © Philippe Lardy

ISBN: 0-7407-0100-2
Library of Congress Catalog
Card Number: 99-60611

CONTENTS

Numerology:
What It Is   7

A Brief
History   13

Numerology How-To   25

Other Significant
Numbers   103

The Alphabet's
Hidden Meaning   247

person's name (which are easily converted to numbers). Learning to interpret this language of numbers can reveal basic personality patterns and hidden talents. It can enhance the quality of life and lead to better decision-making skills.

5 6 7 8 9